The Un
Coast G
National Defense

ALSO BY THOMAS P. OSTROM

The United States Coast Guard in World War II:
A History of Domestic and Overseas Actions
(McFarland, 2009)

The United States Coast Guard and National Defense

A History from World War I to the Present

THOMAS P. OSTROM

Foreword by
COMMANDER GARY M. THOMAS, USCG

McFarland & Company, Inc., Publishers
Jefferson, North Carolina, and London

Photographs courtesy the United States Coast Guard Historian's Office.

LIBRARY OF CONGRESS CATALOGUING-IN-PUBLICATION DATA

Ostrom, Thomas P.
   The United States Coast Guard and national defense : a history from World War I to the present / Thomas P. Ostrom ; foreword by Commander Gary M. Thomas.
       p.   cm.
   Includes bibliographical references and index.

   ISBN 978-0-7864-6480-7
   softcover : 50# alkaline paper ∞

   1. United States. Coast Guard — History.
   2. Coastal surveillance — United States — History.   I. Title.
VG53.O873 2012
359.9′70973 — dc23   2011036924

BRITISH LIBRARY CATALOGUING DATA ARE AVAILABLE

Front cover design by David K. Landis (Shake It Loose Graphics)

Manufactured in the United States of America

McFarland & Company, Inc., Publishers
   Box 611, Jefferson, North Carolina 28640
   www.mcfarlandpub.com

To the men and women
of the U.S. Coast Guard
who have served and defended America
at home and overseas
from 1790 to the present

Table of Contents

Table of Contents

Acknowledgments

Authors are in debt to the many people who have encouraged and contributed to their journey to publication. My gratitude and appreciation are expressed to the friends, acquaintances, and professionals who offered inspiration and guidance.

I am indebted to Elderberry Press editor David St. John who guided me through the writing and publication of my first two books, *The U.S. Coast Guard, 1790 to the Present* and *The U.S. Coast Guard on the Great Lakes.* The magnificent Soldiers Field Veterans Memorial in Rochester, Minnesota, has been an inspiration. The SFVM was constructed through the efforts and generosity of community groups and the leadership of Wayne Stillman and his dedicated committee colleagues. Stillman, a U.S. Army veteran, and Bonnie Kottschade, a publications editor and administrative member of the Daughters of the American Revolution (DAR), encouraged me to write military and Coast Guard articles for the Rochester *Post Bulletin*'s Veteran's Day magazine.

Pianist Jane Belau has performed at SFVM. When she discovered I had been in the U.S. Coast Guard Reserve and authored Coast Guard books, Belau acquired and mastered *Semper Paratus*, the U.S. Coast Guard marching song. Belau and Les Fields, a U.S. Air Force veteran and "Turkey River All Stars" band director, subsequently performed *Semper Paratus*.

Interest in my books and the facilitation of speaking and writing opportunities were stimulated by interviews and publicity from KROC-AM radio's Andy Brownell and Rich Peterson; Rochester *Post Bulletin* writer Tom Weber, a USN Vietnam veteran; *Post Bulletin* publisher Randy Chapman; and managing editor Jay Furst, whose son Petty Officer Nik Furst (USN) has served on the USS *Harry S Truman* (CVN-75).

President Don Supalla, of Rochester Community College where I taught for more than 30 years, encouraged my writing and placed my books on display and in the library. And my colleague and history buff Jim Kehoe, a

Vietnam-era U.S. Army lieutenant, encouraged my writing and inspired me with stories of his leadership experiences and service to veterans.

Rear Admiral Scott Burhoe, retired superintendent of the U.S. Coast Guard Academy, placed my books in the Academy Library and encouraged me to keep writing.

Leaders and members of the Scott Hosier World War II Round Table in Rochester, including Tom Hosier, Tom Brinkman, David Allen, Mike Pruitt, and U.S. Army veteran John Kruesel, encouraged, supported, and publicized my books, presentations, and signings.

As has Col. Don Patton (USA, Ret.) and Howard Flen (USA, Korea) of the Harold C. Deutsch World War II Round Table at Fort Snelling in St. Paul, Minnesota. Ken Wiley (USCG, Ret.), a World War II landing craft coxswain, chronicled his combat missions in his book, *Lucky Thirteen: D-Days in the Pacific*. Wiley and I shared the stage and panel at Ft. Snelling in March 2011 as guests of Col. Patton and his exemplary staff. In attendance were history enthusiasts and members of the USCG, USCG Auxiliary, and veterans of all the U.S. Armed Forces. Also in attendance was investment entrepreneur William B. Frels, former USCGR petty officer and friend who got me through recruit training at Government (now Coast Guard) Island, Alameda, California.

Ken Kauffman's invitation for me to speak at the U.S. Submarine Veterans Association in Bloomington, Minnesota, was enriching and appreciated. We crossed paths again when the USSVA held their annual dinner in Rochester in 2011, and planned to return for the 2013 convention.

I have appreciated the positive book reviews in the distinguished U.S. Naval Institute periodicals *Proceedings* and *Naval History*.

The Society of Manufacturing Engineers (SME) in Southeast Minnesota, and members Scott Brandt, Mike Rasmussen, and eclectic engineer and friend Bill Brooks, extended a speaking invitation. The SME provided technical support and insight. Sale Sedarous, a Ph.D. physicist and business professor, enriched my knowledge, as did space technology engineer Early Kyle who discussed the merits and regretted the replacement of Coast Guard LORAN stations by the technologically vulnerable Global Positioning Satellite System of location reckoning. It was suggested that LORAN remain as a backup system.

Mike Hodge and Kelly Kolb, systems engineers at BCS Computer Support in Rochester, designed my presentations, photograph and manuscript operations, computer instruction, and technological upgrades.

Several U.S. Armed Forces veterans contributed their military experiences, encouragement, and respect for the Coast Guard to my endeavors.

Captain Joe Connell (USAF rescue helicopter pilot, Vietnam); Jerry Weltzin (P01, USN, Vietnam); Ken Thamert (USA, Korea veteran); and Dr. James Graham (USAF, Mayo Clinic doctor, retired) enriched my knowledge on many fronts. Joe Connell visited Coast Guard bases, was aware of USCG SAR operations in Vietnam, and contributed Coast Guard information for my files. Dr. Graham and his spouse, Patricia, who also served in the USAF, updated me on their submariner son, Chief Petty Officer Brendan Graham (USN). CPO Graham informed me about the Coast Guard cutter escorts that accompany U.S. submarines into strategic harbor bases.

Al Miller (marketing, public relations, and communications at the University of Wisconsin–Superior), featured my books and presentations in the alumni newspaper and on the UW–S website. Miller, a former news reporter, is an author of Great Lakes maritime history. UW–S maritime archivist Laura Jacobs guided me through the magnificent Great Lakes maritime collection.

Dr. Anthony Lund was a University of Minnesota–Minneapolis dental professor and Rochester pediatric dentist. Lt. Lund (USN) served in dental and surgical capacities at Great Lakes Naval Training Center in Illinois from 1954 to 1956. Dr. Lund motivated me with stories of his USN responsibilities, and appreciation and encouragement of my writing.

As did Lt. Cmdr. Ken Fischer (MD), an Indiana ophthalmologist and former USN medical officer on the USS *Sarsfield* (DD-837) and USS *Stickell* (DD-888), and Lt. Del Thurber (USN), who served as a medical officer in the Pacific Northwest in the 1950s, and subsequently as a Mayo Clinic physician.

Cmdr. Marc Carpenter (USNR, Ret.) flew PBYs in the World War II Pacific and enhanced my understanding of those missions and the USN and USCG aviators who flew the amphibious patrol bombers. Captain John Patrick O'Grady (USN, Ret.) enlisted in the U.S. Navy in 1941 and retired in 1965. O'Grady served as a PT boat quarter master in the Pacific, deck officer on surface combat ships, USN instructor, and commander of USN submarines. Capt. O'Grady appreciated and encouraged my writing and speaking.

The Foundation for Coast Guard History inspired my work, and informed and encouraged my writing. As has John Galluzzo, a prolific writer, researcher, and author, and editor of the Coast Guard history journal, *Wreck and Rescue*. Mr. Galluzzo wrote the scholarly foreword for *The USCG in World War II*. I have had the privilege of writing articles in *Wreck and Rescue*, a publication of the U.S. Life-Saving Heritage Association.

Dr. Robert M. Browning, Jr., chief U.S. Coast Guard historian, and his associate historians at USCG headquarters in Washington, D.C., have been encouraging, have listed my books, and their sources and photographs have been invaluable. Dr. Browning also enriched a presentation I gave at the U.S. Navy Memorial Foundation (USNMF) in August 2010.

Mark Weber, the USNMF and Naval Heritage Center curator, extended an invitation for me to come to Washington, D.C., and speak about my book, *The U.S. Coast Guard in World War II*. Mr. Weber and his colleagues were extraordinarily helpful and hospitable. In attendance and speaking during the Q&A session were Dr. Robert Browning and Long Range Aid to Navigation (LORAN) Cmdr. Gary M. Thomas, a support base commander and executive board member of the Foundation for Coast Guard History.

General Michael W. Hagee (USMC, Ret.), president and CEO of the Adm. Nimitz Foundation and National Museum of the Pacific War, and his staff invited me for a book signing in May 2011. Gen. Hagee, a former U.S. Marine Corps commandant, said he visited "the Guadalcanal location where USCG SM1 Douglas Munro's actions earned him the Medal of Honor in World War II. The Marines have always enjoyed working with the Coast Guard."

USN Petty Officer First Class Frank L. Kinney (MM1, World War II) shared his files and Pacific war experiences. Kinney survived two aircraft carrier combat sinkings: on the USS *Wasp* (CV-7) and USS *Prince* (CVL-23), one by a Japanese I-boat, the other by an enemy bomber. U.S. destroyers rescued Kinney after his exposures to fuel-saturated waters and depth-charge concussions from submarine hunting U.S. destroyers. Kinney's father served in World War I, his brother in the World War II USAAF, his son in the USN and USA, and two grandsons in the USA and USMC.

I have appreciated the support and inspiration of SSgt. Robert A. Knutson (USA, LRRP, Vietnam); Cpl. Nick Carter (USMC, Vietnam); Cpl. Glenn Miller (USMC, World War II Pacific), and his spouse SN1 June Miller (World War II WAVES, USNR, Washington, D.C.); Lt. Roy Watson (USN, World War II Pacific); Col. Walter Halloran (USA, World War II Europe; Korea; Vietnam); Cpl. Russ Gunvalson (USA, World War II POW); and his son, Cmdr. Todd Gunvalson (USCG, Ret.).

Captain Fred Nobrega (USNR, Ret.) provided me with inspirational interviews about his experiences in U.S Navy aerospace medicine, survival training, the Apollo Space Program, and as a naval flight surgeon. Dr. Nobrega subsequently served as a Mayo Clinic physician, epidemiologist, professor of medicine, and director of a regional medical society.

I am indebted to my wife Mary Lamal Ostrom, a former elementary school teacher, and her brother James C. Lamal, a retired public school administrator and eclectic advanced studies facilitator. Mary and James supported and encouraged my writing and attended the USNMF presentation. As has and did my cousin, Lt. Col. George R. Ostrom (USAF, Ret.), a history buff with nautical interests. Lt. Col. Ostrom served in missile defense, intelligence, at the Pentagon, and in the defense industry. Col. Ostrom taught me about military service, command presence, leadership responsibilities, and humor.

The dedicated professionals at McFarland encouraged me to write this book, *The United States Coast Guard and National Defense*, and guided me through the process, as they did with my previous book, *The U.S. Coast Guard in World War II*. This book chronicles the role of the U.S. Coast Guard in national security and defense in war and peace at home and overseas. Those missions have included port security, drug and immigration interdiction, and the War on Terror. The Coast Guard has carried out these missions in articulation with federal law enforcement and public safety agencies, the other U.S. Armed Forces, and, since 2003, the Department of Homeland Security.

Foreword
by Commander Gary M. Thomas, USCG

From Aztec shore to Arctic zone,
To Europe and Far East,
The Flag is carried by our ships
In times of war and peace.

You need to look no further than the first verse of the Coast Guard motto, *Semper Paratus* (Always Ready), to realize that the United States Coast Guard (USCG) has been a vital component of the national defense system of the United States.

Public knowledge of the USCG's 11 statutory missions is often confined to newspaper articles of daring and dangerous rescues along coastal waters, rivers, and on the high seas; the distinctively painted helicopters and airplanes flying along the coasts; video of oil cleanup operations; and rescue boats.

And while those images of the USCG protecting people on and from the sea are defining elements of one of the world's premier maritime organizations, there is yet another mission the USCG is tasked with that is not as well known.

Since U.S. Treasury Secretary Alexander Hamilton first established a "system of cutters" in 1790 to enforce the tariff laws of the young nation, the protection of people from threats delivered on or from the sea is a mission less well known by the American public.

In fact, from 1790 to 1798, these "cutters" of the Revenue Marine, later called the U.S. Revenue Cutter Service, were the predecessors of today's U.S. Coast Guard. The Revenue Marine was the first armed seagoing service the United States had to protect its maritime interests before the emergence of the U.S. Navy in 1798.

During this early time frame, Hamilton's "few armed vessels judiciously

1

stationed at the entrances of our ports" were thrown into the front lines of national defense in the quasi-war with France (1799–1800) in partnership with the U.S. Navy.

For more than 220 years since then, the USCG has been part of America's National Defense organization and has participated in every major war and engagement. The men and women of the Coast Guard and its predecessors have earned 43 campaign and battle streamers.

From the early days of sailing cutters to the newest contemporary addition to the fleet, the National Security Cutter, the USCG has played an important role in protecting our nation. Whether landing U.S. Army and U.S. Marine personnel in Europe and the Pacific in World War II, manning the worldwide LORAN navigation system during the Cold War, serving in Iraq and Afghanistan today, or, for the second time in U.S. history, patrolling for pirates off the African coasts, the USCG continues to be an integral part of our nation's defense.

In this book, Tom Ostrom neatly lays out the history of the U.S. Coast Guard's contributions to national defense. Tom, who I first met while he was working on his previous book, *The U.S. Coast Guard in World War II*, has an easy writing style that not only conveys facts and details, but also the personal stories of those who stood the watch, helped turned the tide, and sometimes gave the ultimate sacrifice for America.

You will finish this book with a better understanding and deeper appreciation of the United States Coast Guard and the men and women who have served and are serving in the multimission sea service.

Cmdr. Gary M. Thomas (USCG) is the executive director of the Foundation for Coast Guard History, and former commanding officer of the USCG LORAN Support Unit in Wildwood, New Jersey. He is a former commanding officer of USCG Padre, homeported in Key West, Florida.

Preface

The United States Coast Guard was created on 4 August 1790 by an act of Congress in the administration of President George Washington in the first national capital, New York City. The service was originally called the U.S. Revenue Marine (USRM), later the U.S. Revenue Cutter Service. The Revenue Marine was placed under the jurisdiction of U.S. Treasury Department Secretary Alexander Hamilton.

The Revenue Marine was tasked with coastal surveillance, mapping, maritime rescue, protection of life and property at sea, and tariff and customs duties enforcement. The Revenue cutter sailing vessels and uniformed crews were armed.

Although the Continental Congress had created a colonial American Navy in 1775, the federal government banned standing military units in favor of armed citizen militias. The United States Navy was not created until 1794, ships launched in 1797, and Navy Department established in 1798. The Revenue Marine was the first federal navy charged with maritime national defense.

The U.S. Navy and Revenue Marine teamed up in 1799 to fight the undeclared (quasi) naval war against France, and the British Royal Navy in the War of 1812–1814.

In 1915 Congress merged the U.S. Revenue Cutter Service and U.S. Life-Saving Service into the new United States Coast Guard (USCG). The term "Coast" is deceptive, bringing to mind limited geographic missions confined to U.S. coastal and inland waterways.

Throughout American history to the present, the U.S. Navy and U.S. Coast Guard have partnered in national defense missions at home and overseas in the nation's wars.

As this book emphasizes, in addition to domestic maritime ship inspection and safety; law enforcement; port security; aids to navigation; environmental protection; scientific expeditions; and search and rescue missions, the

Coast Guard has been tasked with national defense missions at home and overseas. The Coast Guard maritime domain has extended from the Great Lakes to the Atlantic, Pacific, Gulf of Mexico, Mediterranean, Persian Gulf, and polar regions. The USCG has carried out those missions with the other U.S. Armed Forces: the U.S. Army, Navy, Marines, and Air Force. The Coast Guard has also articulated with the U.S. Merchant Marine, and the armed forces of allied nations.

The USCG has had liaison connections with the U.S. Navy and Department of Defense in its consecutive roles in the Departments of Treasury, Transportation, and, since 2003, Homeland Security.

In its long history, the U.S. Coast Guard has carried out national defense missions since 1799. The service participated in the pirate, slave, Seminole, Mexican, and Civil Wars of the 19th century, and the Spanish-American War (1898).

In the 20th and 21st centuries the Coast Guard fought in the Great War (World War I), Prohibition, World War II, Korea, Vietnam, the Persian Gulf Wars, the War on Terror, regional wars in the Caribbean, and drug and immigrant interdiction conflicts.

It is the purpose of this book to chronicle the national defense missions and contributions of the Coast Guard in the 20th and 21st centuries, and the commitment of the service to its heritage and motto: *Semper Paratus* (Always Ready).

Introduction

The contributions of the United States Coast Guard to national defense can be traced to the origin of the sea service in 1790. In that year an act of Congress during the administration of President George Washington established the predecessor of the Coast Guard, the U.S. Revenue Marine (USRM).

The USRM was under the jurisdiction of the federal Treasury Department and U.S. Treasury Secretary Alexander Hamilton. The Revenue Marine began its service with 10 sailing ships called revenue cutters. The mission of what was then the federal government's first navy was to enforce customs and tariff laws, secure the coasts, do geographic exploration, and protect the nation's forest resources and life and property at sea.

The Revenue Marine partnered with the fledgling U.S. Navy after 1795 in national defense missions, the wars against France (1800) and Britain (1812), and enforcing anti-slave trade laws, eighteenth-century conflicts that involved the USRM included the slave trade, piracy, Seminole wars, (1830s), Mexican War (1848), Civil War (1861–1865), and Spanish-America War (1898).

With the Spanish-American War and the U.S. purchase of Alaska from Russia (1867), U.S. naval forces expanded the American domain to the Bering Strait and Pacific Ocean. The oceanic reach gradually included the Atlantic Ocean, Gulf of Mexico, Caribbean, and Mediterranean Sea, and the polar seas of the Arctic and Antarctic.

The U.S. Revenue Marine gradually became known in the later 19th century as the U.S. Revenue Cutter Service (USRCS). The USRCS was combined by Congress with the U.S. Life-Saving Service to form the U.S. Coast Guard in 1915.

This book, *The United States Coast Guard and National Defense*, will chronicle the 20th- and 21st-century national defense missions of the U.S. Coast Guard in World War I, World War II, Korea, Vietnam, the Gulf Wars and the War on Terror, and the national security aspects of port and border security and immigration and narcotics interdiction enforcement.

The traditional missions of the U.S. Coast Guard in aids to navigation, search and rescue, law enforcement, port security, and natural resource and environmental protection will be considered as those operations relate to U.S. national defense at home and overseas. The training and contributions of Coast Guard personnel, command leadership, and the application of USCG land, air, and sea assets will also be considered.

The Coast Guard defense missions in the 20th and 21st centuries commenced with joint U.S. Navy operations in the Great War (World War I) on convoy escort and antisubmarine warfare (ASW) against German U-boats. Combat missions extended from U.S. shores and across the Atlantic Ocean. Coast Guard responsibilities included port security operations at major U.S. ports. United States Coast Guard wartime casualties were significant and included the torpedo sinking of the 190-foot USCG cutter *Tampa* off the coast of the United Kingdom in September 1918. More than 100 crew members were lost. Captain-Commandant Ellsworth Bertholf (USRCS/USCG) skillfully administered the transition from the U.S. Revenue Cutter Service to the U.S. Coast Guard in 1915, and the wartime missions of the service.

Joint-USCG/USN training and combat operations in World War II (1941–1945) were well coordinated by President Franklin Roosevelt, his top U.S. Navy, Marine and Army commanders, and the exemplary leadership of the U.S. Coast Guard commandant, Admiral Russell R. Waesche. The theaters of operation included the Atlantic, Mediterranean, Pacific, and Arctic polar regions.

Coast Guard personnel served on U.S. Navy, U.S. Army, and Coast Guard boats and cutters in every combat zone in ASW, transportation, aids to navigation (ATN), and search and rescue (SAR) missions. Coast Guard landing craft coxswains performed their combat and transportation missions heroically in the Atlantic, Mediterranean, and Pacific theaters. USCG personnel suffered significant casualties in their coordinated missions with the other U.S. Armed Forces on land, sea, and in the air. Coast Guard personnel flew USN patrol bombers, crewed Navy and U.S. Army seacraft, and manned destroyer escorts and bi-wing floatplanes. Coast Guard–manned vessels, ships, and cutters served as command and flag headquarters ships for U.S. Armed Forces commanders.

The Coast Guard was heavily tasked with fighting the Axis nations (Japan, Germany, and Italy) from Pearl Harbor (Hawaii) to the Alaska Aleutians; from U-boats off America's shores and across the Atlantic, to the Imperial Japanese Navy, kamikaze suicide aircraft, boats, and swimmers; and the typhoons of the Pacific. The hundreds of award-earning Coast Guard heroes included Medal of Honor winner SM1 Douglas Munro, and Cmdr. Edward "Iceberg" Smith, the commander of the hazardous Greenland Patrol. The Coast Guard Women's Reserve (SPARS), civilian Coast Guard Auxiliary, domestic and overseas USCG port security personnel, and civilian laborers at Great Lakes and other shipyards performed their essential tasks well, as did the brave sailors of the U.S. Merchant Marine.

David Hendrickson (Petty Officer, USCG), author of *The Patrol Frigate Story* (Fortis Publishing, 2011) sailed on the USS *Albuquerque* (PF-7) for 14 months during World War II in the Bering Sea/Aleutians maritime domain. Petty Officer Hendrickson did escort, antisubmarine warfare, and emergency service duty in hazardous seas on the well-armed 303-foot combat vessel. Hendrickson chronicled the 75 Coast Guard–manned USN frigates and their missions in every theater of war in all climate and sea conditions from the Bering Sea to the South Pacific, the icy North Atlantic, and the Korean War. Hendrickson also instructed Russian naval personnel in the top-secret Operation Hula program in Alaskan waters. The acclaimed frigate historian later taught history and geography at Fresno (California) City College.

Petty Officer Ken Wiley served as a combat landing craft coxswain in the World War II Pacific. Wiley chronicled his adventures on and off the attack transport USS *Arthur Middleton* (APA-25) in his book, *Lucky Thirteen: D-Days in the Pacific with the U.S. Coast Guard in World War II* (Casemate Publishers, 2007). Wiley's coxswain missions took his landing craft into beach assaults and behind-enemy-lines reconnaissance missions with U.S. Army, Navy, Marine and Coast Guard personnel in spellbinding combat missions. Wiley was a hydraulics engineer, and worked in sales and management after the war. I have corresponded with Mr. Wiley and shared a speaking engagement with him at the Harold Deutsch World War II Roundtable in March 2011, courtesy of Col. Don Patton (USA, Ret.) and his staff at Ft. Snelling in Minnesota. Wiley's landing craft exploits are mentioned in my previous book, *The U.S. Coast Guard in World War II* (McFarland, 2009).

The role of the U.S. Coast Guard in the Korean War (1950) was more limited. Coast Guard personnel trained the South Korean Navy between 1946 and 1950. During the war, Coast Guard cutters and personnel performed escort, patrol, transport, SAR, and weather station duties in Korean waters and ran a USCG LORAN (long-range aid to navigation) station out of Pusan, South Korea.

The Vietnam War involved U.S. Armed Forces advisors and combat military personnel from the 1950s to 1973, during the Eisenhower, Johnson, and Nixon administrations. U.S. Coast Guard cutters and craft did ocean station, port security, explosives loading, and river patrol missions in coordination with the U.S. Navy, Army, Marine Corps, and Air Force. Coast Guard aviators flew hazardous air rescue missions in USAF HH3E "Jolly Green Giant" helicopters.

Coast Guard oceangoing cutters challenged armed Viet Cong transports. Coast Guard crews, cutters, and boats performed military and naval logistical support operations, SAR and other humanitarian functions, offensive and defense river patrol missions, merchant ship inspection and safety, and ATN duties. Patrol boat crews inserted, extracted, and defended special operations units. Coast Guard petty officers and commissioned officers trained South Vietnamese Navy personnel, suffered casualties, earned military awards, and contributed innovative methods and technologies to the war effort.

After the Vietnam War, the Coast Guard returned to domestic missions and emphasized ATN, SAR, ship inspection and safety, marine environmental protection, port security, saving of life and property at sea, icebreaking, maritime fisheries enforcement and other law enforcement tasks, and immigration and narcotics interdiction. Several Caribbean Sea and Gulf of Mexico national security operations involving the U.S. Navy, Coast Guard, and the other U.S. Armed Forces were carried out in the name of national defense and hemispheric stability.

Domestic port security and contraband interdiction have national defense ramifications because national sovereignty, public safety, border security, crime, commerce, and socioeconomic disruptions are associated with and can be exacerbated by port disruptions, illegal cross-border activities, and potential sabotage, espionage, and terrorism.

The expansion of these interrelated mission responsibilities came to fruition after the 11 September 2001 (9/11) terrorist attacks on the Twin Towers in New York City; the Pentagon in Washington, D.C.; and the downed hijacked airliner in Pennsylvania. In 2003, the U.S. Coast Guard was transferred to the new Department of Homeland Security; Coast Guard defense missions overseas in the War on Terror, and the expansion of Coast Guard complements, assets, and budgets had enormous impact on the service.

Within hours of the 9/11 attacks, Coast Guard cutters, boats, aircraft, and port security teams were responding to commands from district offices and the Washington, D.C., national headquarters and office of the commandant. Coast Guard escort vessels were boarding and guarding commercial vessels and ports from the East Coast to the Gulf, from the West Coast to the Great Lakes, and on major inland waterways and strategic infrastructures. New York City Harbor and hundreds of other major U.S. ports were secured from the maritime side. Coast Guard vessels transported apprehensive New

York City residents out of the smoke, dust, and debris of 9/11 and onto ships, boats, and ferries to safer locales. Coast Guard teams provided chaplain, medical, evacuation, first responder, fire protection, and environmental purification services. Huge C-130 Coast Guard cargo planes brought medical supplies and personnel into critical zones also served by regional and national air, land, and sea assets.

And when the national response led U.S. military forces into the Middle East and Persian Gulf, Coast Guard personnel and USCG sea, land and air assets responded. Port Security Units (PSUs) operated combat patrols and guarded shoreside port and oil infrastructures in coordination with other U.S. and allied armed forces.

This book, *The U.S. Coast Guard and National Defense*, chronicles the historic and contemporary missions of the USCG and surveys air, land, and sea assets, bases and training centers, commandants, and commissioned and enlisted leadership. We will consider and explore the professionalism exemplified by the active duty, reserve, auxiliary and civilian men and women of Team Coast Guard.

1

The Coast Guard: 1790 to World War I

The United States Coast Guard is a branch of the United States Armed Forces with unique missions involving national defense, military responsibilities, law enforcement, life-saving, search and rescue, the enforcement of maritime law, management of aids to navigation, and immigration and narcotics interdiction. Unique in its outreach, the Coast Guard is the only military organization which serves and has legal authority over civilians.

The Coast Guard coordinates its peace and national defense missions with civilian public safety agencies, local state and federal law enforcement agencies, national security agencies, and the U.S. Army, Air Force, Navy, and Marines through the Pentagon.

Coast Guard stations, cutters, boats, assorted smaller watercraft, and aircraft serve on U.S. inland and coastal waters and on the high seas. The Coast Guard has a fleet of aircraft (fixed-wing propeller and jet aircraft, and rotor-wing helicopters), life-saving and patrol boats, and cutters. Coast Guard "cutters" are defined as watercraft more than 65 feet in length. The oceangoing cutters range from approximately 200 to 420 feet in length. Cutters get their name from the days of the British sailing (sail-powered) vessels that enforced revenue laws and interdicted smugglers. The U.S. Coast Guard still maintains a sailing barque, the U.S. Coast Guard Cutter (USCGC) *Eagle*, a training ship for the cadets at the U.S. Coast Guard Academy in New London, Connecticut.

In 1790 President George Washington and Congress initiated an early maritime naval force initially called the Revenue Marine, and, later, the U.S. Revenue Cutter Service (USRCS). The Revenue Marine, under Treasury Secretary Alexander Hamilton, collected customs duties, enforced maritime laws, protected life at sea, inspected seafaring vessels, charted inland and coastal waterways, and carried out national defense missions with the U.S. Navy and U.S. Army. The USRCS was involved in every American war from 1790 to World War I.

In 1915, under Captain-Commandant Ellsworth Bertholf, the USRCS Service was combined with the U.S. Life-Saving Service (USLSS) to form the United States Coast Guard (USCG). Commandant Bertholf prepared the Coast Guard to enter the Great War in 1917. Following World War I (1914–1918), Bertholf's forceful congressional testimony thwarted the attempt of federal officials to transfer the USCG permanently into the U.S. Navy (USN). The Coast Guard had been temporarily transferred by presidential order into the wartime USN. In 1919 the Coast Guard was returned to the Treasury Department.

The World War II Coast Guard Commandant, Adm. Russell Waesche, would also testify to Congress about the importance of keeping the multi-mission Coast Guard in the Treasury Department, instead of permanently transferring the sea service to the Navy.

Nonetheless, over time, the USCG migrated from the Department of Treasury to the Transportation Department (1967), and later, after the terrorist attacks by Islamic extremists upon the United States (11 September 2001), to the newly established Department of Homeland Security (2003).

Captain-Commandant Bertholf's skillful preparation of the Coast Guard for its involvement in World War I followed previous wartime experience. The Revenue Marine had coordinated with the U.S. Navy in military conflicts against the French, British, pirates and slave traders, Seminole Indians, Mexico, the Confederacy in the Civil War, in the Spanish-American War, and as the U.S. Coast Guard in the Great War (World War I).[1]

World War I ravaged Europe from 1914 to 1918. The United States belatedly entered the war in 1917 in response to German submarine (U-boat) attacks on American and British vessels, and the pro–British bias of most of the public, members of Congress, the State Department, and President Woodrow Wilson.

In 1915 the Coast Guard consisted of approximately 2,000 sailors, 2,300 lifeboat station surfmen, and a fledgling aviation arm. Orville and Wilber Wright changed transportation, search and rescue, and warfare with their mechanical skills and courage. The two bicycle mechanics experimented with gliders and motor powered aircraft. In 1903 the Wright brothers launched a heavier-than-air motor-powered aircraft at Kitty Hawk, North Carolina, with the assistance of surfmen from the Kill Devil Hills Life-Boat Station.

In 1909 the U.S. Army purchased an airplane from the brothers. Glenn Curtis Company made a floatplane in 1912, and the U.S. Navy purchased a few flying boats and initiated Coast Guard and Navy pilot training at Pensacola, Florida. In 1915 Coast Guard aviators Lt. Norman B. Hall and Lt. Elmer F. Stone were stationed on the Norfolk (Virginia) based CGC *Onondaga*. They convinced their skipper, Capt. Benjamin M. Chiswell, to let them fly borrowed aircraft on search and rescue and reconnaissance missions. Coast Guard air and sea rescue tactics evolved from that experience.[2]

On 27 May 1919 senior pilot Lt. Elmer Stone (USCG) completed the first transatlantic flight in a U.S. Navy NC-4 flying boat. U.S. Navy Secretary Franklin D. Roosevelt sent Stone a letter of commendation crediting the Coast Guard aviator for bringing "honor to the American Navy and the entire American nation."[3]

Coast Guard ship and aircraft construction was temporarily suspended on 6 April 1917 when the United States government issued a declaration of war against Germany. "PLAN ONE ACKNOWLEDGE" was official notice to the U.S. Coast Guard, Army, and Marines that American involvement in the Great War was imminent. The USCG was now assigned to the U.S. Navy for an extended, dangerous, transoceanic mission.[4]

The sacrifice of USCG personnel in World War I is memorialized at Arlington National Cemetery in Virginia with a monument on Coast Guard Hill that commemorates the sailors lost on the cutters *Seneca* and *Tampa*.[5] On 26 September 1918 the CGC *Tampa* (formerly the RC/CGC *Miami*) was torpedoed by German submarine *U-91* in the English Channel, with the loss of 131 personnel, most of whom were Coast Guard crew (111), the others U.S. Navy officers and enlisted personnel, and British military personnel and civilians.[6] Captain Charles Satterlee, the USS *Tampa* commander, went down with his ship and crew.[7]

Even in combat, the Coast Guard performed its historic search and rescue and life-saving missions that could be costly in U-boat infested waters. On 16 September 1918 a volunteer crew from the 204-foot CGC *Seneca* (Capt. William J. Wheeler, USCG) boarded the torpedoed British merchant convoy vessel *Wellington* in the Bay of Biscay off the southwest coast of Europe. The *Seneca* approached the *Wellington* while firing shells from its 4-inch deck gun and dropping depth charges to keep the spotted U-boat submerged so its deck guns could not be utilized. The Coast Guard crew was determined to sail the *Wellington* to the French port of Brest, 350 miles distant, as the civilian crewmen abandoned the ship.

Despite the valiant efforts of the skilled *Seneca* crew, on 17 September the heavily laden coal-carrying merchant vessel, as maritime historian Alex Larzelere described it, "sank in a raging storm. Of the twenty *Seneca* volunteers, eleven (ten Coast Guard and one U.S. Navy) perished in the cold waters."[8]

The Coast Guard contributed 15 cruising cutters, 5,000 enlisted men, and 200 officers to the U.S. Navy in World War I. U.S. Navy and U.S. Coast Guard warships carried out successful Atlantic antisubmarine missions. The Coast Guard oceangoing cutters included the 205-foot *Algonquin*, 205-foot *Manning*, 165-foot *Ossipee*, 204-foot *Seneca*, 190-foot *Tampa* (later lost with all 111 Coastguardsmen in a U-boat attack), and the 192-foot *Yamacraw*. The peacetime crew complements of officers and enlisted personnel on those vessels generally ranged from 73 to 75, but the wartime complement was increased as had been done on the ill-fated CGC *Tampa*.[9]

Coast Guard cutters and crews performed search and rescue (SAR) missions when ships were damaged or sunk, rescued mariners from flaming infernos in petroleum-saturated waters, and dropped depth charges on U-boat positions. Revenue cutters and Coast Guard cutters were built to support a plethora of peace- and then wartime missions. The 204-foot RC *Seneca*, launched in 1908 at Newport News (VA) Shipbuilding, cruised the New England states and removed or sunk derelict vessels that were hazards in sealanes. The *Seneca* was one of the first revenue cutters assigned to the International Ice Patrol that was initiated in 1913 after the sinking of the British passenger liner SS/RMS *Titanic* the previous year. During the Great War, the then CGC *Seneca* sailed on convoy duty off the west coast of Europe.

The RC *Miami* was launched at Newport News Shipbuilding in 1912, began ice patrol missions the following year, was renamed the *Tampa* in 1916, and was transferred to the U.S. Navy and convoy duty in European waters in 1917. Armed with four 3-inch guns, the *Tampa* escorted 18 convoys before being torpedoed and sunk by *U-91*. The German submarines, identified as "U-boats" in World War II (so designated here as *U-91*), was identified initially in World War I as *UB-91*.[10]

Within U.S. territorial waters, the USCG managed port security through Coast Guard officers designated as captains of the port (COTPs), guarded against espionage and sabotage, and supervised explosives loading in strategic ports. The USCG cooperated with civilian firefighting teams in port security and shipboard fires and explosions. Members of the U.S. Lighthouse Service (USLHS) cooperated with the Coast Guard in administering Aids to Navigation (ATN). The USCG would absorb the USLHS in 1939 shortly before the U.S. entered World War II. USLH personnel and the brave surfmen of the USLSS patrolled beaches in search of mariners in distress, spies, and saboteurs, and responded to vessels and crews torpedoed by German U-boats close to Atlantic shores.

Coast Guard cutters were damaged in collisions, and lives were lost at home and on the high seas carrying out assigned missions while adhering to the service motto, *Semper Paratus* (Always Ready). The disastrous explosions at Black Tom Island Terminal in New Jersey, across the Hudson River from New York City, caused Congress to pass the Espionage Act of 1917 which gave the USCG the responsibility of protecting waterfront and harbor areas and infrastructure. Strategic harbors were placed under COTP control in the ongoing mission of port security.[11]

With the wartime transfer of the USCG to the USN, the commanding officers of Coast Guard cutters reported to U.S. Navy district commanders. Oceangoing cutter crews slept in hammocks. The deep-sea cutters were not much over 200 feet in length,[12] small for ocean storms and equivalent to what the Coast Guard would later identify as WMECs, or medium endurance cutters, as compared to the World War II WHEC (high endurance) 327-foot cutters.

Winter ocean convoy duty challenged cutters and crews. Storms and turbulent seas could wash deck crews overboard. High seas could submerge cutter bows, deck guns, and passageways. Two- and four-hour watches were common, lookouts stood antisubmarine watch, and guns were constantly manned.[13]

Coast Guard crew duties at home and abroad, ashore and at sea, varied significantly, but each mission supported the war effort. For example, the CGC *Comanche* provided armed landing parties to accompany U.S. marshals in the seizure of Central Power vessels, usually German, in American ports. The 110-foot Great Lakes icebreaker *Mackinac* (lst Lt. Edward S. Addison) was assigned by U.S. Navy commanders to patrol the St. Mary's River and strategic Soo Locks, and then ordered to New York City and the Third U.S. Navy District. Atlantic Coast cutters were assigned search and rescue, antisubmarine patrol, minesweeping and mine planting, towing, escort and other support duties.[14]

The CGC *Androscoggin*, homeported at Portland, Maine, patrolled the North Atlantic from Boston to Newfoundland (Canada) on search, wreck and rescue, and towing missions. Captain Frank C. Billard sailed the CGC *Onondaga* along the often foggy Atlantic coast training Coast Guard cadets and enlisted personnel, aiding mariners and stranded (grounded) ships in distress, and using skilled lifeboat crews in the varied weather and seas that confronted Atlantic sailors. Coast Guard officers and enlisted personnel were assigned by the U.S. Navy to run vessels obtained from government agencies and private boat and yacht owners.[15]

Lt. Henry G. Hemmingway (USCG) was assigned to the USS *San Diego*, a four-stack U.S. Navy armored cruiser which struck a German mine on 19 July 1918 enroute between Portsmouth, New Hampshire and New York City.

The huge 504-foot, 13,680-ton warship armed with 38 3-inch to 8-inch guns sank in just 30 minutes with the loss of 6 officers and enlisted personnel out of a 1,114-crew complement. Lt. Hemmingway survived and was assigned to another ship. Navy minesweepers later found six German mines in the area of the stricken vessel.

Three USCG officers were in the 477-man complement of the 413-foot USS *Minneapolis* assigned to escort and patrol duty in the Atlantic. The gigantic U.S. Navy warship carried eight 4-inch, two 6-inch, one 8-inch, and four 8-inch guns in its arsenal.[16] Coast Guard historian and author Capt. Alex Larzelere (USCG, Ret.) published a memo from Josephus Daniels, President Wilson's navy secretary, which expressed confidence in USCG officers:

> The professional ability of the Coast Guard officers is evidenced by the fact that twenty-four commanded combatant ships operating in European waters, five vessels of the patrol force in the Caribbean, and twenty-three combatant craft attached to naval districts.... The Navy Department, naturally enough, assigned to the command of combatant ships only officers whose experience and ability warranted such detail and only those officers in whom the Department had implicit confidence.[17]

U.S. Coast Guard officers were assigned to five U.S. Navy ships that "planted" mines and patrolled the Northern Mine Barrage that stretched from Norway to Scotland across the North Sea. The huge minefield terrorized German U-boat sailors and impeded U-boat access to the Atlantic Ocean. The 250-mile string of more than 70,000 mines ranged from the sea surface to 240-foot depths. Among the Navy vessels crewed by Coast Guard officers was the 380-foot *Canandaigua*.[18]

The U.S. Lighthouse Service, an independent agency that would be absorbed by the Coast Guard in 1939, two years before the U.S. entered the Second World War, was transferred to the U.S. Navy on 6 April 1917 by the executive order of President Woodrow Wilson. The USLHS had 46 ships (lighthouse tenders), 4 lightships (floating lighthouses), 21 standing lighthouses, and more than 1,100 lighthouse keepers and assistants. USLHS watercraft conducted surveillance, planted and monitored mines, maintained aids to navigation, and placed buoys in strategic and dangerous shipping lanes, and marked shipwreck and torpedoed vessel zones.

On 6 August 1918 the large, heavily armed German submarine *U-140* surfaced off Cape Hatteras, North Carolina, within sight of the 124-foot USLHS Lightship No. *71*, which immediately radioed warnings to area ships and gave them the position of the U-boat then about two miles from the lightship. *U-140* closed in and fired its deck guns, disabling the wireless communications system. The crew of Lightship *71* took to the ship's lifeboat and was several miles from the vessel when *U-140* finally sank the ship with deck gunfire. It was estimated that the radio warnings from Lightship *71* allowed 25 vulnerable ships to find shelter away from the submarine. The crew of *LS-71* under the leadership of First Mate Walter L. Barnett was safely ashore by nightfall and transmitted the action report to naval authorities from the Cape Hatteras wireless station.[19]

Alex Larzelere cited the annual report of the secretary of the Navy that reviewed the provisions of the Espionage Act of 1917. The act created the captain of the port authority under Coast Guard jurisdiction "in the ports of New York, Philadelphia, Norfolk (Virginia) and Sault Ste. Marie and the St. Mary's River (Michigan)." The port and Sault Ste. Marie ("Soo") Locks infrastructure were essential to the shipping of natural resources, agricultural goods, and manufactured materials to U.S. and European ports. The Great Lakes–St. Lawrence maritime corridor was vulnerable to espionage and sabotage. Captain Edward S. Addison, commander of the icebreaker USCGC *Mackinac*, was also the COTP of the Sault Ste. Marie port and maritime domain. The *Mackinac* later sailed out of Sault Ste. Marie to assume port security duty out of the port of New York.

The U.S. Army Corps of Engineers administered the locks that were guarded by U.S. Army troops. Capt. F.A. de Otte was the commander of the USCGC *Morrill* out of Detroit, Michigan, and would be assigned to port security duty in Europe.

Captain Godfrey L. Carden (USCG) was appointed COTP in New York City and reported to the Treasury Department and Secretary William G. McAdoo, as well as the U.S. Navy. Carden's controversial control of the harbor, anchorages, explosives loading, and general port security was strict and successful. Overseas, Capt. F. A. de Otte (USCG) was ordered by the commander of U.S. military forces in France to assume COTP responsibilities in the port of Brest and the supervision of the maritime transportation of American troops.[20]

Alex Larzelere described the sinking of the CGC *Tampa* in the English Channel by *U-91* on 26 September 1918 as the highest naval casualty count in a single combat incident during World War I. The *Tampa*, sailing from British Gibraltar in the Mediterranean to Wales in the United Kingdom, lost 111 Coastguardsmen and 20 other passengers including U.S. Navy personnel and British civilian and military passengers.

The knowledge gained from the American naval experience in World War I influenced President Roosevelt's tactics and strategies in World War II, as did Roosevelt's experience as assistant secretary of the U.S. Navy in the Wilson administration.[21]

The Coast Guard's World War I convoy and antisubmarine warfare experience influenced World War II naval strategies. After the Japanese attack on Pearl Harbor, Hawaii, on 7 December 1941, the U.S. Navy understandably concentrated its war effort in the Pacific, leaving the American Atlantic coast vulnerable to German U-boat attacks against commercial and naval vessels.

Immediately after Pearl Harbor, Adm. Ernest Joseph King (USN) was named commander of the United States Fleet and chief of naval operations. Adm. King appointed Rear Adm. Adolphus Andrews (USN) commander of the Eastern Sea Frontier (ESF), which extended from the Canadian border to southern Florida.

Despite his requests for more force protection, Adm. Andrews had insufficient U.S. Coast Guard, Army, and Navy air, land, and sea assets to meet the U-boat threat in the Atlantic. Then a U.S. Navy staff officer presented Andrews with a naval study that illustrated the success of Navy and Coast Guard convoy escort and antisubmarine missions in World War I. The report was forwarded to Adm. King. U.S. Navy leaders reassessed the maritime situation and increased the number of patrol craft in the ESF.[22]

The Coast Guard suffered significant losses at sea, proportionately more casualties than the other U.S. Armed Forces in World War I.[23] Of the 8,835 Coast Guard personnel who served in World War I, there were 111 deaths in combat action, and 81 deaths from accidents, disease, or drowning.[24]

The U.S. Navy in World War I was the beneficiary of 5,000 Coast Guard enlisted personnel, 200 officers, 15 cruising cutters, USLHS personnel, and the experienced surfmen of the former USLSS.[25]

In the immediate postwar period (1919–1923) the U.S. Coast Guard was restored to peacetime status as it maneuvered to preserve its autonomy and avoid the proposed merger into the USN. Coast Guard commandant, Commodore Bertholf, his successor Commandant William Edward Reynolds, and Treasury Secretaries Carter Glass and David Houston fought off politicians, Navy officials, and even some Coast Guard officers to maintain the independent status of the service.

Democratic President Wilson resolved the issue with an executive order on 28 August 1919 directing the Coast Guard to resume operations under the Treasury Department. Wilson's Republican successor, Warren G. Harding, signed into law (January 1923) a measure which made Coast Guard and Navy ranks, rates, and pay more equivalent, appointed more Coast Guard officers to the rank of captain, promoted the Coast Guard commandant rank to rear admiral, and mandated more frequent and timely promotion for commissioned and enlisted personnel. Plans were made to upgrade the Coast Guard fleet. Appointments to the U.S. Coast Guard Academy were increased from 23 to 72.[26]

The Paris Peace Conference and the Treaty of Versailles (1919) ended World War I. On a return trip from Paris, President Wilson and the rest of the American delegation aboard the USS *George Washington*, a U.S. Navy transport ship, were anchored in the inner harbor outside the port of Boston, Massachusetts. The committee organized to greet the President boarded the cutter *Ossipee* under the command of Capt. William H. Munter (USCG). The *Ossipee* disembarked from the Port of Boston carrying prominent political and military officials who greeted Wilson as he boarded the cutter for the return to the Boston pier.[27]

2

World War II on Land, Sea and Air

The Coast Guard was involved in World War II (1939–1945) before the United States entered the war in 1941. The USCG waged that war for national defense at home and overseas, from the Great Lakes and domestic ports to combat missions in the Atlantic, Pacific, and Mediterranean.

Coast Guard auxiliary, reservists, and active duty men and women (SPARS) teamed up to support the war effort. The combat theaters ranged from Pearl Harbor and the Pacific islands to the Alaskan Aleutians, Greenland, the Mediterranean Sea and southern Europe and North Africa, and the Atlantic and Gulf from American shores to the furthest reaches of those maritime realms.

The logistical and tactical challenges of the Coast Guard missions, in coordination with the U.S. Army, Navy, and Marines; the nations of the British Commonwealth (Canada, the United Kingdom, Australia, and New Zealand); and other Allied nations and resistance movements, were enormous.

The heterogeneous physical geography of the wartime maritime domain posed significant problems and dangers. Seas ranged from calm to heavy, in the heat of the tropics to the frigid cold and ice floes of the Arctic and subarctic, rain, snow, hurricanes and typhoons and waves of 20 to 30 feet in height and more.

The port security mission of the Coast Guard was carried out in domestic and overseas port areas. Captains of the port (COTP) controlled harbor protection, firefighting, surveillance on land and sea, antisubmarine warfare, convoy escorts, beach patrols, explosives loading, aids to navigation (ATN), and search and rescue (SAR). The Coast Guard air and sea arms were coordinated with the other U.S. Armed Forces, and with civilian and local, state, and federal law enforcement and public safety agencies.

The security and infrastructure of the Great Lakes and internal river systems were essential elements of national defense with its civilian worker components, ship and boat building sites, and the maritime transportation of agricultural and mineral resources and manufactured goods from the Great Lakes, down the St. Lawrence River, and into the Atlantic to ports the world over. Military and civilian ships and sailors, especially the U.S. Merchant Marine, carried out the shipping to peaceful and combat zones, in calm and stormy seas, often under enemy air and sea attack, and suffered significant casualties. U.S. Navy Armed Guard gunners protected the commercial cargo and transport vessels. Coast Guard–armed buoy tenders (called "180s" because of their length in feet) built in the Lake Superior Ports of Duluth, Minnesota and Superior, Wisconsin served in transportation, ATN, and combat missions in the Pacific.

Lakes, rivers, canals, and oceans connected an essential maritime infrastructure and marine transportation routes, with international connections at the Panama Canal in the Western Hemisphere and the Suez Canal in Egypt between the Mediterranean and Red Seas.

The United States Coast Guard refined and expanded the wartime missions it had pioneered in World War I.[1]

Military casualty figures are difficult to research and assess. The casualty figures may include killed in combat action (KIA), wounded in action (WIA), missing in action (MIA), and accidental or natural on-duty accidents, from a variety of sources not all in agreement. The office of the Coast Guard historian at Coast Guard headquarters in Washington, D.C., cites the number of Coast Guard personnel who served in World War II as 242,093. Deaths in action are listed as 574, with 1,343 USCG deaths from "other causes" (crashes, accidents, drowning or disease). The "total casualties" calculation is 1,917.[2]

The significance of the home-front Coast Guard beach patrol mission as an element of national security in World War II was illustrated on a foggy night along the sandy shores of Long Island, New York, on 13 June 1942. Seaman John C. Cullen (USCG) confronted four German saboteurs just put ashore from a German submarine. SN Cullen pretended to cooperate and accept a bribe from the German agents, hastily returned to his Coast Guard station, informed his colleagues and contacted the Federal Bureau of Investigation (FBI). Within days the Long Island saboteurs and four other enemy agents reported by Florida fishermen were apprehended.[3]

Small Coast Guard boats and a variety of Coast Guard cutters served in combat just off the Atlantic coast, in the Aleutian Islands of Alaska, and in the other maritime theaters of the war. Oceangoing cutters made in lake, river and coastal ports in America performed valiantly in combat. On 13 June 1943 the Great Lakes icebreaker CGC *Escanaba* (WPG-77) was sunk by a U-boat in the frigid, rolling seas of the North Atlantic after performing SAR missions. Of the *Escanaba* crew complement, 101 Coastguardsmen were lost, and only two survived. The CGC *Hamilton* (WPG-34) was torpedoed off Iceland on 19 January 1942. The 165-foot CGC *Icarus* (WPC-110) out of Staten Island, New York, sank *U-352* in the Eastern Sea Frontier on 9 May 1942 and rescued the surviving German sailors, who became prisoners of war (POWs).[4]

The 327-foot Treasury-class oceangoing cutters (sometimes referred to as the "Secretary" class) served in antisubmarine and convoy escort patrols as flagships in the Atlantic, Mediterranean and Pacific for U.S. Navy, Army, and Marine commanders. The CGC *Taney* (WHEC-37) shot at Japanese aircraft in the Pearl Harbor (Hawaii) attack on 7 December 1941, and later patrolled the Atlantic and Pacific. The CGC *Ingham* (WPG/WAGC-35) sank the German submarine *U-626* in the North Atlantic and served as a USN flagship in the Philippines. The CGC *Duane* (WPG-33) teamed with the CGC *Spencer* (WPG/WAGC-36) in the Atlantic sinking of *U-175* on 17 April 1943. The *Spencer* also served as a USN flagship in the Philippine campaign. The 327-foot CGC *Campbell* (WPG/WAGC-32) rammed and sank *U-606* in the Atlantic in February 1943.

Numerous other cutters, rescue boats, and Coast Guard–manned U.S. Navy and U.S. Army transport, cargo, and combat ships, and the landing craft attached to the large transports and LSTs (landing ship tanks), participated in the Mediterranean invasions of North Africa, southern France, Sicily and Italy from 1942 to 1944, and in the June 1944 Normandy (France) invasion with the other U.S. Armed Forces and British Commonwealth naval and troop contingents. Coast Guard–manned and joint USN-USCG crews landed U.S. Army and Marine forces on numerous Pacific islands against Japanese foes, shot down ("splashed") Japanese suicide planes, and battled Japanese submarines (I-boats) and suicide watercraft.

In the Atlantic and Pacific campaigns Coast Guard crews carried out their traditional SAR to downed aviators and seafarers, ATN missions, and the maritime and port security duties of explosives loading and firefighting. Coast Guard sailors and aviators dodged North Atlantic ice floes and icebergs on the Greenland Patrol in SAR and combat missions against German forces on land and sea. Cutters weighed down by ice could and did capsize during their high-sea searches for U-boats. Coast Guard personnel captured German vessels and enemy forces at isolated bases and weather stations under the command of "ice captains" like Charles W. Thomas (USCG), commander of the 216-foot CGC *Northland* (WPG-49), and the tactical leadership of Cmdr. Edward "Iceberg" Smith (USCG).[5]

USS *LCI(L)-89*, Coast Guard–manned vessel at Normandy, France (1944). The 160-ft. landing craft infantry–large ferried troops and escorted landing craft from Britain to France. LCIs carried troops and equipment.

U.S. Coast Guard, U.S. Public Health Service, and Navy personnel mingled with U.S. Army and Marine ground troops on ships and smaller craft, and on Pacific shores as beach masters, cargo handlers, combat photographers, medical officers, corpsmen and pharmacist's mates, and chaplains. Not only on Pacific shores, but USCG personnel also waged war on land and sea on and adjacent to the Greenland Ice Cap, foggy Aleutians, stormy Atlantic, Gulf of Mexico, Caribbean, and Mediterranean. At home and abroad, under the exemplary leadership of Coast Guard commandant, Adm. Russell R. Waesche, active duty Coast Guard officers, enlisted personnel, reservists, auxiliaries, civilian employees, and the U.S. Coast Guard Women's Reserve (SPARS) under Capt. Dorothy Stratton, added to the service legacy and its motto, *Semper Paratus* (Always Ready).[6]

The Japanese naval carrier fleet launched the 7 December 1941 air attack on the U.S. military base at Pearl Harbor, Hawaii, that brought the United States officially into World War II. Prior to the "Day of Infamy," as President Franklin D. Roosevelt termed it, Congress had imposed an economic embargo on the expansionist Japanese government which some observers say actually stimulated Nippon's Asian imperialism and the attack on Pearl Harbor. FDR and a marginally neutral Congress also pursued policies which German dictator Adolf Hitler used to launch U-boat attacks on U.S. merchant and naval vessels. By mid–December the United States was at war with the Axis nations of Japan, Germany, and Italy.[7]

Prior to 7 December 1941, American military cryptologists had sufficiently decoded Japanese electronic transmissions to surmise that a Japanese attack was coming against allied colonies in the Western Pacific, or perhaps in the American Philippines. Pearl Harbor commanders Adm. Husband E. Kimmel (USN) and Gen. Walter C. Short (USA) were given war warnings, but nothing specific. When Pearl Harbor occurred, the two commanders were relieved of their commands.[8] The Philippines were hit by the Japanese several hours later, but the on-scene U.S. Army commander, Gen. Douglas MacArthur, was not held responsible.

The Office of Naval Intelligence (ONI) provided strategic and national security information to the federal government and other military service before, during, and after Pearl Harbor, and throughout World War II. The staff of Adm. Chester W. Nimitz (USN), commander of the U.S. Pacific Fleet, expanded to nearly 2,000 personnel in the Joint Intelligence Command Pacific Ocean Area (JICPOA). JICPOA was comprised of U.S. Army, Navy, Marine and Coast Guard personnel. Coast Guard Intelligence operatives assisted the American military at Pearl Harbor, and in the Pacific and Atlantic theaters of maritime operations.

The Coast Guard also contributed personnel to the Office of Strategic Services (OSS), the predecessor of the postwar Central Intelligence Agency (CIA). The OSS protected national security and enhanced national defense by conducting espionage missions. Coast Guard signals and information intercepts were utilized by the OSS. Coast Guard regulars, reservists, and the civilian Coast Guard auxiliary were used in port security operations. Specialized Coast Guard personnel contributed signaling, boat handling, swimming, and diving skills to OSS missions.

Lt. John Babb (USNR), chief of the OSS Maritime Unit in Asia, reported that Coast Guard operatives "were engaged in the infiltration of agents, (worked) their way into enemy lines through mangrove swamps under enemy outposts" and evaded enemy patrols. Fifty-six USCG members worked for the OSS, and several were in Operational Swimmer Group 2 (OSG 2). Lt. John P. Booth (USCGR), the field officer in Burma, earned the Bronze Star. Lt. Cmdr. Michael Bennett (USCG) has done exemplary primary source research and writing on the OSS-USCG World War II connection.[9]

Diplomatic tensions in the year prior to the Pearl Harbor attack, and concern about potential espionage and sabotage by Japanese aliens and even citizens, led to the initiation of Coast Guard patrols to keep fishing boats out of the strategic waters off Diamond Head Cape near Honolulu on Oahu Island.[10] The patrols were sensible but of course did not prevent the attack by the Imperial Japanese Navy (IJN), which was intended to weaken the U.S. Navy, prevent American intervention into Japanese East Asian conquests, and force U.S. recognition of the status quo and the necessity of diplomatic settlements. The attack proved to have the opposite effect, uniting American public opinion and leading to the eventual defeat of Japan and the loss of the Japanese Empire.[11]

The U.S. Navy, Marine, Army and Coast Guard installations in Hawaii included ten battleships; three aircraft carriers carrying 250 aircraft; 500 land-based aircraft; dozens of warships, submarines, support ships, cutters and boats; and two infantry divisions. The military infrastructure included maintenance facilities, warehouses, and fuel depots that the Japanese Strike Force (JSF) failed to completely destroy.[12]

The JSF struck from a location 250 miles north of Hawaii. The carrier air force struck Pearl Harbor at 7:55 Sunday morning in a wave of more than 140 torpedo planes and dive-bombers, and 42 fighter escorts. U.S. Fleet anti-aircraft guns and several military aircraft struck back at the invaders, but within the first hour of the attack, eight battleships and ten other types of warships were either sunk or damaged. Two hundred U.S. aircraft were destroyed, most while parked on airstrips. The American military and civilian casualties totaled 2,388 killed and 1,178 wounded. Three U.S. aircraft carriers were out to sea and survived to fight future battles. JSF losses were minimal and included 9 midget submarines and their crews, 55 aviators, and 29 war-planes.[13]

U.S. naval patrols had made contacts with suspicious unauthorized vessels prior to the Japanese attack. The USS *Ward* under the command of Lt. William W. Outerbridge (USN) on patrol outside the harbor entrance had picked up sonar evidence of a possible Imperial Japanese Navy (IJN) submarine at 7:03 A.M. The *Ward*, crewed by U.S. Navy reservists from Minnesota, depth charged the intruder and later put a shell through a Japanese submarine and sunk it. Lt. Outerbridge sent naval authorities a radio message describing the incidents but received no immediate response; and successfully requested that a U.S. Coast Guard cutter escort a suspicious sampan craft out of the unauthorized area of the harbor. Before the Pearl Harbor attack, an IJN submarine was sighted by harbor tug *YT-153* (USN) and USCGC *Tiger* (WPC-152) and narrowly escaped a ramming attempt.[14]

In April 1942 a new naval base was being built adjacent to the U.S. Marine Corps (USMC) base at Ewa on Oahu. The Barbers Point Naval Air

Station accommodated several military units including a Coast Guard station. Among the Coast Guard personnel on Oahu to spring into action during the attack was Lt. Frank Erickson. Erickson had been assigned to the USN since August 1941 when the USCG was shifted from the Treasury Department to the Navy in the Hawaiian area of operations. All USCG units were transferred on 1 November. Prior to the transfer, Lt. Erickson was an aviator assigned to the CGC *Taney* (W-37). Erickson's Navy assignment was at the aircraft control tower, from which he witnessed the JSF attacks, vessel destruction, brave responses, casualties, and flaming Pearl Harbor waters into which sailors, airmen and marines leaped.[15]

Later, Erickson became a helicopter aviator and enthusiastic supporter of and participant in rotor-wing SAR missions and the use of the Sikorsky helicopter as a tactical and reconnaissance reality. In that mission Lt. Erickson had the support of other intrepid Coast Guard, Navy, Army and Marine aviators, but he had to battle cynics and obstructionists along the way. Erickson could only imagine the lives that could have been saved at Pearl Harbor had the helicopter been available then, as it was later in World War II.

For the next 10 days following 7 December 1941, Lt. Erickson flew naval patrols in search of remnants of the Japanese fleet that some analysts predicted would return for another air attack and subsequent ground invasion. Erickson and his airborne U.S. Armed Forces colleagues flew Grumman J2F and Sikorsky JRS seaplanes (flying boats) initially armed only with shotguns and rifles. More lethal machine guns would later be added to the floatplanes.[16]

The CGC *Kukui* (WAGL-225) extinguished aids to navigation lights in the Kauai Island area to thwart enemy activities, marked shipping hazards in the devastated Pearl Harbor area, and picked up a squad of U.S. Army troops and four armed Coastguardsmen to check out an island where a Japanese aviator had reportedly crashed. Upon going ashore, the squad discovered that the enemy aviator had been subdued and killed by a Hawaiian male who was injured in the incident; he was subsequently taken on the *Kukui* to Port Allen for hospitalization and recovery.

Coast Guard boats and cutters approached suspicious vessels, gave fishing crews flags to display, escorted some fishing boats to shore, and subjected suspect individuals to internment. Wounded mariners were given medical treatment. Observation posts were manned throughout the islands, staffed by police, civilians and military personnel.[17]

In coordination with the U.S. Army, Navy, and Marines, the Coast Guard assumed the responsibility of waterfront port security, firefighting, supervision of loading and unloading dangerous military cargoes, SAR, and ATN duties. Coastguard personnel built, modified, and crewed fireboats and land-based firefighting vehicles and equipment. Male and female civilians and military personnel joined in the port security missions. The Coast Guard COTP at Pearl Harbor supervised a force of approximately 600 military personnel, including SPARS, headed by Capt. Dorothy Stratton. The SPARS (13,000 members) joined their female counterparts in the U.S. Navy WAVES (100,000), Marine Corps Women's Reserve (23,000), Army Air Force WASPS (1,100), and Women's Army Corps (WACS 150,000). [18]

The significance and contributions of the USCG to national defense in World War II at home and abroad is well illustrated by historian Malcolm F. Willoughby's magnificent classic, *The U.S. Coast Guard in World War II* (1957). Lt. Willoughby (USCGR) surveyed Coast Guard–manned ships in every overseas combat theater; SAR, antisubmarine, convoy, and weather station patrols; and port security and aids to navigation missions at home and abroad.

Willoughby described how thousands of ships and cutters had to be built to sustain the war effort. Great Lakes shipyards and civilian workers contributed to this mission, and the critical Great Lakes ports, infrastructure and waterways had to be protected from espionage and sabotage. The Great Lakes and St. Lawrence River were the maritime highways for the essential supplies, food, manufactured products, and ships sent to Allies and the global combat theaters. In the early winter and spring season, Coast Guard icebreakers kept the commercial waterways open to extend the shipping season. The protection of those routes, infrastructure, and overall port security were the responsibility of the USCG which coordinated its missions with local, state, federal and private public safety, law enforcement, intelligence and security agencies, and the other military services. The Coast Guard also assisted in the development of and manned long-range aid to navigation (LORAN) stations at isolated posts around the world. LORAN tracked and monitored the locations of U.S. Armed Forces air and sea craft around the world.

Overseas, Coast Guard personnel served with U.S. Navy crews on some vessels and operated cutters; U.S. Navy destroyers; cargo, tanker, and troop transport ships; landing craft; and U.S. Army vessels. During World War II, the Coast Guard manned hundreds of cutters (ships of 65 feet to over 300 feet in length), landing ship tanks (LSTs), patrol frigates, gunboats, submarine chasers, launches, tugboats, ferries, tenders, and other miscellaneous vessels. Coast Guard boats and cutters were armed with sonar, radar, depth charges, deck guns, and small arms.

Soldiers, sailors, and marines were transported by Coast Guard ships and landing craft to the Atlantic, Mediterranean, and Pacific maritime regions in calm and heavy seas, with temperatures and weather ranging from tropical to polar. Coast Guard coxswains maneuvered landing craft from ships far out to sea into the surf and enemy gunfire on distant beaches. Coast Guard vessels were used to transport the wounded to hospital ships and medical care. Beach masters directed boat and vehicular traffic, and combat photographers recorded battle action for intelligence purposes and the historic record. Coast Guard teams brought German and Japanese prisoners of war (POWs) back to ship and shore stations for incarceration and debriefing by U.S. Armed Forces specialists.[19]

Among the rewards of writing articles and books about Coast Guard history are the communications with Coast Guard enlisted personnel, officers, veterans, reservists and auxiliarists.

This author's book, *The United States Coast Guard in World War II: A History of Domestic and Foreign Actions* (McFarland, 2009) was reviewed in interviews with the Rochester, Minnesota *Post Bulletin* and KROC-AM radio. The publicity prompted Barbara Heins, a retired Mayo Clinic-St. Marys Hospital nurse, to contact and inform me about her uncle, Paul Inden. Mr. Inden served in the World War II Coast Guard in the extreme climate zones of Alaska and Greenland, described at length in my book.

Barbara, and her equally hospitable husband, Marvin, a retired insurance executive, purchased copies of the book and invited me to meet Uncle Paul, a Marshall, Minnesota, resident. During the interview with Paul, Barbara and Marvin contributed insightful questions and observations.

In the Korean War era, Marvin Heins served at a secret U.S. Army communications base in California where international code messages were monitored. Heins, an E-4 specialist, typed out Morse code intercepts of Chinese, Russian, and North Korean messages and forwarded them to cryptographers and intelligence specialists. Heins informed us that his former Army base subsequently became U.S. Coast Guard Training Center Petaluma.

Paul Inden came to our interview equipped with notes, documents, newspaper articles and photographs. Inden enthusiastically described his USCG service in Greenland and Alaska during World War II. Petty Officer Inden enlisted in the Coast Guard in Minneapolis, Minnesota, and served from 1942 to 1946. After his military discharge, Inden used his GI Bill money to acquire an aircraft pilot license.

Inden had worked as a motion picture projectionist and in the newspaper business before enlisting in the Coast Guard. He had basic training at Manhattan Beach Coast Guard Station, New York City. He then sailed out of Boston on the 216-foot Coast Guard cutter *Northland* (WPG-49) to join the hazardous Greenland Patrol.

President Franklin Roosevelt had fortuitously assigned the Coast Guard to Danish Greenland for search and rescue, antisubmarine warfare (ASW), and convoy protection missions. The USCG helped to secure strategic cryolite mines and prevent German troops from establishing weather and radio stations. Before the United States entered World War II, Coastguardsmen captured German military personnel and a radio station. Later, the CGC *Northland* made the first naval capture of a German warship in World War II.

Inden made trips between Boston and Greenland through heavy, icy North Atlantic seas and German submarine (U-boat) infested waters. While on his transatlantic voyages, Inden slept on hammocks and stood deck watch. On one crossing, Inden was ordered to stand watch in the perilous crow's nest high up on the mast of the 225-ft CGC *North Star* (WPG-59) because, he explained, "I had good night vision." Inden also participated in battle station and depth charge drills.

While in service, Inden learned of the torpedoing of the warship he had sailed on, the 165-foot Great Lakes cutter *Escanaba*. The CGC *Escanaba* (WPG-77) was sunk off Greenland in 1943 with the loss of over 100 crewmen. Inden was later informed of the foundering of the ice-covered 116-foot CGC *Natsek* (WYP-170) in a snowstorm. The patrol boat sank with the loss of all hands in Belle Isle Straits between Newfoundland (Canada) and Greenland.

Also part of Greenland Patrol lore were the heroic 1942 rescues of downed aviators from the ice cap by CGC *Northland* floatplane aviator Lt. John Pritchard (USCG) and radioman Benjamin Bottoms (USCG). In one mission, three Royal Canadian Air Force (RCAF) airmen were rescued. A repeat mission by Lt. Pritchard occurred a few days later when he landed the Grumman J2F amphibious plane on the ice cap to rescue the downed crewmen of a U.S. Army Air Force B-17 bomber.

The return flight encountered a snowstorm and resulted in the loss of the Grumman floatplane. The aircraft wreckage was later found, but not the bodies of Lt. Pritchard (USCG), RM1 Bottoms (USCG), and Cpl. Loren H. Howarth (USAAF) of La Crosse, Wisconsin. A Navy PBY floatplane and a U.S. Army aircraft later rescued the remaining crewmen.

On the Greenland Patrol, Inden crewed a 38-foot CG picket boat that operated out of U.S. military base Bluie West One at the southern tip of Greenland. The picket boat patrolled fjords and performed transportation missions.

Inden worked in the engine compartment and on the exposed deck of the boat, while never having learned to swim. Did that worry him? "Not really," Inden responded. "If you fell into the freezing waters you wouldn't last long" if not quickly rescued. Inden did witness a Coastguardsman's body on the icy Greenland shore, the likely victim of being washed overboard in heavy seas.

Among Petty Officer Inden's memories was taking Greenland Patrol fleet commander Edward "Iceberg" Smith (USCG) on a fishing trip on the picket boat. Rear Adm. Smith, the famed "ice captain" and oceanographer, had convinced U.S. Navy and Coast Guard superiors to requisition 10 trawlers and enlist rugged mariners from New England fishing fleets for Greenland Patrol duty. On the patrol, Inden traded goods with Eskimos (Inuit) for artifacts. Inden also paid tribute to the skilled Coast Guard artists who recorded mission histories, one of whom went down on the ill-fated CGC *Natsek*.

Inden met several famous Coastguardsmen, including Hollywood actor Victor Mature (CPO, USCGR) and heavyweight boxing champion Jack Dempsey. Cmdr. Dempsey (USCGR), a physical training director, later joined a Coast Guard team in the Pacific and disembarked from a landing craft onto a hostile Pacific island beach.

While stationed in Greenland, and then Ketchikan, Alaska, Inden experienced formidable snowstorms and gale force winds up to 150 mph. In one respite, Inden was sent to Alameda (California) Coast Guard Station on Government (now Coast Guard) Island near San Francisco and Oakland. The author trained at Alameda in the 1960s, and Inden and I both had additional training at the nearby U.S. Navy Base on Treasure Island. I had firefighting training, and Inden trained in landing craft operation. Inden's eclectic skills allowed him to eventually earn ratings as seaman second class (SN2), engineman (EM3), motor machinist mate (MMM2) and radio technician (RT3).

Inden received radio training at the Capitol Radio Engineering Institute in Silver Springs, Maryland, and then went to Ketchikan, Alaska, were he was assigned to a "radio shack." Also on Alaskan duty were members of the Coast Guard Women's Reserves, called SPARS from the Coast Guard motto, *Semper Paratus* (Always Ready). The SPARS were organized and trained by Capt. Dorothy Stratton (USN/USCG).

Returning from Greenland to the United States, Inden went by train to Seattle, Washington; by passenger ship to Ketchikan, Alaska; and then on the 200-foot CGC *Cedar* from Dutch Harbor to the Aleutians and isolated Unimak Island for assignment to a Coast Guard construction detachment. Inden ran the Scotch Cap Lighthouse generator. Scotch Cap Lighthouse was later destroyed and its five-man crew lost in an earthquake-driven tsunami on 1 April 1946, one month after Inden left the island.

Paul Inden, an ebullient and articulate 89-year-old veteran at the time of our interview, is among the many creative and courageous Coast Guard men and women who have lived up to the service motto, *Semper Paratus*.[20]

In the last months of World War II the U.S. Coast Guard and U.S. Navy secretly trained 12,000 Soviet enlisted personnel and officers to operate naval warships and landing craft scheduled for transfer to the USSR under the Lend-Lease program. The training mission, called "Project Hula," was intended to prepare the Soviet Union for the expected Allied invasion of the Japanese home islands. The August 1945 surrender of Japan ended the project as the hoped-for postwar cooperation with the USSR ended with the onset of the Cold War.[21]

SN1 David Hendrickson served out of Kodiak, Alaska, during World War II on USS *Albuquerque* (PF-7) in the Bering Sea-Aleutian Islands theater of operations in the Northwestern Sea Frontier (NSF). Hendrickson, a postwar professor of geography and history at Fresno (California) City College, has written articles and books about the PF fleet and its valiant and challenging World War II missions. The 304-foot Tacoma-class cutters did weather station, ASW and SAR missions in every combat theater of World War II and in the Korean War.[22]

Commander Kenneth E. Wilson (USCG, Ret.), future CO on the CGC *Dexter* (WAVP-385), served in the Philippines and Southwest Pacific on the USS *San Pedro* (PF-37) The author acquired information on Wilson's service in correspondence with CMDR. Wilson and his daughter, Patricia Wilson Sadd.

3

Korea: The Forgotten Cold War Conflict

The Korean War (1950–1953) has been called "the Forgotten War" by historians who believe that the initial Cold War conflict between the Communist and non–Communist nations has not been appreciated, celebrated or emphasized enough in academic and political circles. It has also been described as a war that was lost by the military forces of the United States and its United Nations allies.

The numbers of U.S. soldiers lost approximates the casualties of the subsequent War in Vietnam. The war began in 1950 when Communist North Korea crossed the 38th parallel and invaded pro–Western South Korea. President Harry S Truman acted before the UN passed a war resolution and sent allied troops to the Korean peninsula; he dispatched U.S. troops under the command of World War II hero General Douglas A. MacArthur, who later led the entire UN command. United States and other UN forces, with Republic of Korea (ROK) troops, fought their way from southern South Korea, across the 38th parallel, and up to the Yalu River border which threatened the Communist nation of the People's Republic of China (PRC). Encouraged and equipped by the Soviet Union (led by Communist dictator Joseph Stalin), the Democratic People's Republic of (North) Korea (DPRK) and PRC troops pushed UN forces across the 38th parallel back into South Korea.

UN troops eventually forced DPRK and PRC troops back into North Korea, and after several years of continued military battles and truce talks, the war was terminated in 1953 without a treaty of peace signed by the belligerents. Because the Korean peninsula was not united, some historians say that stated (but varied) UN objectives were not achieved. Therefore the U.S. and UN lost the war. Other historians claim a US/UN/ROK victory because

DPRK troops were expelled from South Korea, which remained autonomous and non–Communist.

The post–World War II demobilization of the U.S. Coast Guard occurred so rapidly and extensively that the service had to recruit more members to cope with the domestic and overseas duties assigned to it during the evolving Cold War. Former Coast Guard and Navy enlisted personnel and Reserve officers were invited to enlist or reenlist and sign on for active duty at their previous ranks. Several Coast Guard vessels were acquired from the U.S. Navy and U.S. Army.

The expanded Cold War mission of the USCG necessitated the acquisition of aircraft for domestic and overseas air stations. Helicopters, seaplanes, and land-based aircraft were added to the Coast Guard search and rescue (SAR) and defense arsenal. The national security threats posed by potential pro–Communist spies and saboteurs in American ports caused the expansion of Coast Guard duties into the granting and suspension of licenses and certificates for merchant seamen and longshoremen.

Coast Guard law enforcement operations in this Red Scare period of the Cold War led to the suspension of licenses and the arrests of individuals suspected of subversive or disloyal activities, which in turn led to challenges and court decisions involving the USCG and appeals challenges by labor unions, civil liberties, and other special interest groups. More than 3,000 longshoremen and merchant seamen suspected of radical sympathies were suspended.

Coast Guard missions were expanded in port security, safety, firefighting, vessel inspection, cargo handling, labor strikes, and antiespionage and antisabotage activities. The USCG was especially diligent in policing the ports from which military and supply ships sailed to Korea during the Korean War.[1]

Cold War surveillance missions were dangerous. In January 1953 Chinese gunners shot down a U.S. Navy (USN) Neptune patrol bomber and fired on a USN destroyer that attempted to rescue the survivors in the Formosa Strait. A USCG PBM Mariner floatplane landed on the water to rescue 11 of the 13 crewmen, but high seas and wave action struck the aircraft which crashed and burned on takeoff. U.S. and British air and surface craft, including a second Coast Guard amphibious plane, converged to rescue the USN and USCG survivors. Ten of the 21 downed military personnel were eventually rescued from the waters, and 10 were missing in action (MIA) and assumed dead or captured.[2]

The U.S. Coast Guard was not transferred from the U.S. Treasury Department to the U.S. Navy in the Korean Conflict as it had been in World War I and World War II because Congress had not made a declaration of war, and the UN termed the war a "police action" in part to prevent international treaty and alliance systems, perhaps between the USSR and the PRC, from being activated, and to prevent the geographic expansion of the war and the use of nuclear weapons.

A detachment of United States Coast Guard personnel under the command of Capt. George E. McCabe (USCG) had been sent to South Korea before the outbreak of war to train that nation's coast guard and prepare it to become the South Korean Navy. The U.S. Navy preferred that the U.S. Coast Guard train the ROK navy and, once the undeclared war erupted, carry out port security, ocean station weather, transportation, and SAR missions.[3]

The Cold War increased the need for specialized Coast Guard port security duties and gave the USCG a new mission in 1952. The U.S. State Department assigned the Coast Guard, with Treasury Department approval, the responsibility of relaying Voice of America (VOA) propaganda broadcasts to Soviet-controlled Eastern Europe. The USCG acquired a 339-foot cargo ship, transformed it into a radio station, named the vessel the CGC *Courier*, and anchored off the Greek island of Rhodes. The *Courier* maintained a crew complement of 10 officers, 80 enlisted personnel, and 3 U.S. Information Agency (USIA) radio engineers. A shore station replaced the *Courier* in 1964.[4]

The famed Bering Sea Patrol and International Ice Patrol missions of the USCG contributed to the national defense and security of the United States during the Cold War. The Kodiak (Alaska) and Seattle (Washington) based Coast Guard cutters *Storis*, *Winona*, *Klamath*, and *Wachusett* brought medical, legal, and dental services to Alaska, and supplies to military and other government installations. Royal Canadian Navy (RCN) and U.S. Navy icebreakers (later transferred to the USCG), and the CGC *Eastwind* and the CGC *Northwind*, supported Distant Early Warning (DEW) Line Defense radar and military bases. Supplies were also brought to military and civilian stations by the Military Sea Transportation Service,[5] later called the Military Sealift Command.

The number of Coast Guard personnel who served in the Korean theater was about 8,500, a figure based on the approximate number of service personnel considered eligible for the Korean Service Medal. The USCG suffered no casualties (deaths in action or wounded) in the Korean Conflict.

In the Vietnam War, 8,000 Coastguardsmen served in the combat theater of operations and suffered 67 casualties, with 7 killed in action (KIA) and 60 wounded (WIA).[6] In the Korean Conflict, the U.S. military sustained 196,000 casualties (WIA and KIA), including 54,000 KIA,[7] carrying out the Truman Doctrine policy of the "containment" of Communist territorial expansion.

The Korean War was an international struggle between the Communist and non–Communist nations over the sovereignty of North and South Korea or peninsular unification, and the geopolitical balance of power in Asia between the United Nations Command (UNC), led by the United States, and the ROK (President Syngman Rhee) versus the DPRK (Kim Il Sung), PRC (Mao Tse Tung), and the Soviet Union (USSR) under dictator Josef Stalin.

The war took place on land, sea, and air, and aviation innovations included the use of the helicopter and jet aircraft, the latter flown by North Korean, Russian, and American and UN aviators. In the initial phases of the conflict, the North Koreans pushed U.S. and UN forces back into South Korea where the UN made a final stand and finally broke out of the Pusan Perimeter. General MacArthur (USA), the USN, and the USMC launched a courageous amphibious assault close to the North Korean border at Inchon, splitting and scattering the repositioned North Korean army.

The push of UNC troops into North Korea up to the Chinese border at the Yalu River brought the PRC into the war. The massive Chinese armies drove the UNC back into South Korea, but continued military support and superior technology gradually drove the Communist forces back into North Korea and to the negotiating table at Kaesong, and then to the 38th-parallel border city of Panmunjom (1951–1953). Truce talks continued while bloody battles ravaged the peninsula, and an armistice was signed in 1953. A peace treaty was never signed, and a contentious border situation and volatile demilitarized zone (DMZ) prevailed in subsequent years down to the present day.

President Truman made his controversial decision to replace Gen. MacArthur (1951) after the general publically challenged U.S./UN war strategies and objectives and threatened to invade China to offset PRC military aggression on the Korean Peninsula. General Matthew Ridgeway (USA) replaced MacArthur, stabilized the military situation, and was subsequently replaced as UNC commander by Gen. Mark Clark (USA).

World War II military hero Dwight D. Eisenhower was elected president of the United States in November 1952. The Republican president replaced the unpopular Democratic president Harry Truman who suffered from gradual American dissatisfaction with the war, its nebulous mission, and the costs in blood and treasure.[8] President Eisenhower had visited the Korean front in 1952 and promised to end the war. As president his forceful statements of military options were thought by some historians to have motivated the DPRK PRC, and USSR to end the conflict. Historians later credited Truman with influencing Cold War belligerents to avoid direct military confrontations and not resort to the use of nuclear weapons.[9]

The first military response to the North Korean invasion of South Korea came, at President Truman's orders, from aircraft off of U.S. Navy carriers and from land-based fighters and bombers of the U.S. Air Force. The warplanes and warships came to the Korean peninsula from the Philippine-based Seventh Fleet, a destroyer-cruiser fleet from Japan including submarines. The British contributed a carrier and other warships. With the quickly established UNC command of the seas and Korean airspace, enemy forces and supply lines could be bombarded and UN forces supplied and supported.

The Inchon invasion commanded by Gen. Douglas MacArthur, commander in chief of the Far East, and naval operations chief Adm. Forrest Sherman (USN), and an international fleet of more than 200 ships, carried 70,000 U.S. Marines and soldiers to the beachhead which allowed the capture of the South Korean capital of Seoul and then the thrust into North Korea.

After the Chinese intervention, the USN evacuated more than 100,000 U.S. Army and U.S. Marine combat personnel from the northeast coast of the Korean peninsula. Airstrikes on roads, bridges and supply lines slowed down and dispersed the enemy onslaught.[10]

Scott T. Price, an associate historian in the Coast Guard Historian's office at the Washington, D.C., headquarters of the U.S. Coast Guard, has researched the contributions of the Coast Guard in the Korean War. In his *The Forgotten Service in the Forgotten War: The U.S. Coast Guard's Role in the Korean Conflict*, Price traced the history of the USCG involvement and missions in South Korea and at sea from 1946 through 1953. The following synthesis of the role of the USCG in the Korean Conflict is based on Price's research.

Famed World War II fleet admiral, Adm. Chester W. Nimitz (USN), was chief of naval operations (CNO) from December 1945 until replaced by Adm. Louis E. Denfeld in December 1947, the year the CNO suggested what the Coast Guard role would be in post–World War II conflicts.

In World Wars I and II, as in previous American wars, the U.S. Revenue Cutter Service, and since 1915, the Coast Guard, had been transferred to the U.S. Navy for the duration of the conflicts, and subsequently transferred back to the jurisdiction of the U.S. Treasury Department. In those wars, and since, the USCG performed peacetime domestic and overseas combat and combat support missions. In 1947 the CNO suggested that in future "conflicts" the Coast Guard's wartime missions and assigned "duties should be an extension of normal peace time tasks." In addition, stated the CNO proposal, the United States Coast Guard assets (personnel, facilities, ships and aircraft) "should be utilized as organized Coast Guard units rather than by (as done in World War II) indiscriminately integrating them into the naval establishment."[11]

The traditional Coast Guard duties enumerated by the CNO report included search and rescue (SAR), deepwater ocean patrol, port security, and maritime inspection and safety, the essential missions performed by the USCG in the Korean Conflict.[12] In subsequent wars (Vietnam, the Persian Gulf, the War on Terror after 11 September 2001, and in illegal drug and immigration interdiction), the Coast Guard was not transferred to the U.S. Navy but did articulate its missions and crews on separate platforms and also as integrated crews on USN and USCG ships, which illustrated the difficulty in defining and carrying out the domestic and national defense responsibilities of the multimission service in changing times.

In the year preceding the USN CNO mission suggestions for the post–World War II Coast Guard, the U.S. Army, in its own mission of supporting South Korea, requested that a unit of active-duty Coast Guard officers create and train an ROK coast guard. In August 1946 a World War II hero, Captain George McCabe, arrived to train a South Korean coast guard unit. On 17 December 1942, then Cmdr. McCabe, the skipper of the 327-foot Treasury-class USCGC *Ingham* (WPG-35), sank U-626 in the North Atlantic.

Captain McCabe commanded the fledgling South Korean Coast Guard until Lt. Cmdr. Sohn Won Yi assumed command of his nation's navy in coordination with the U.S. Coast Guard officer. The Korean officer training academy and naval base was established at Chinae. Enlisted personnel were also recruited and trained at the naval facility. Former Japanese naval vessels and discarded equipment were used in the training program. Coast Guard advisors assisted with the training. In 1948 Cmdr. William C. Achurch (USCG) was appointed chief advisor to the Korean Coast Guard commander, and headed the U.S. Coast Guard unit in Chinae.

When the South Korean government proceeded to expand its coast guard into a navy, the U.S. Coast Guard contingent terminated its mission. The U.S. Army continued its command responsibilities in South Korea and interest in establishing a native naval force. The USA recruited retired and reserve USCG enlisted men and commissioned officers to administer and train the South Korean Navy.

The Coast Guard trainers surmounted cultural and funding challenges and continued their service to the ROK. Cmdr. Clarence M. Speight (USCG, Ret.) assumed the post of chief advisor to the South Korean Navy in 1949, and Cmdr. Achurch commanded the USCG unit at Chinae.

The North Korean infantry, supported with advanced Soviet equipment, armament, vehicles and tanks, invaded South Korea on 25 June 1950. The U.S. Coast Guard contingent was then ordered back to the United States the following months, but not without some close calls while withdrawing from the advancing enemy.[13]

Oceangoing (deepwater) Coast Guard cutters patrolled "ocean weather stations" before World War II and after, until satellite global positioning systems and weather-tracking technology in the 1970s ended the need for that cutter mission. The cutters remained at sea patrolling given quadrangle areas to transmit weather information and be in position for SAR missions for air and sea craft. The missions were dangerous in World War II given the threat of German U-boats, and hazardous given the foul-weather patterns and treacherous seas that could emerge in the vast realm of Atlantic and Pacific waters.

U.S. Weather Bureau and specially trained Coast Guard, and sometimes U.S. Navy, personnel manned the vessels and utilized technology that acquired and analyzed weather data that was then communicated to other stations. The ocean station cutters also served as radio communication checkpoints for civilian air and sea craft. The cutter platforms also facilitated communications and missions for SAR and aid to injured merchant seafarers. In 1947 the crew of the USCGC *Bibb* rescued the crew and passengers from the downed Pan American airliner *Bermuda Sky Queen* in a timely and highly skilled and coordinated SAR mission.[14]

Coast Guard cutters were stationed in Pacific waters prior to and during the Korean War and were available for ocean station, communication, and transportation missions, as wartime logistical and military air and sea traffic increased to serve the war effort. The U.S. Navy transferred World War II period active and mothballed (stored) destroyers to the USCG to supplement the fleet. The naval warships were modified to accommodate weather station platforms and equipped with additional deck guns, small arms, and depth charge armament. Air, sea, and island station rescue stations were increased to meet the needs of the Korean Conflict. Periodic gale force winds and 20 to 40-foot Pacific seas challenged cutters, technology, and crews.

The 24 Coast Guard cutters and crews that served in the Korean theater of operations facilitated the safe and significant transportation of United Nations supplies and troops to the Korean Peninsula and earned the Korean Service Medal for the missions. Coast Guard cutters docked at such Japanese ports as Yokosuka and established or expanded SAR, port, and air station detachments on the Pacific islands of the Philippines, Midway, Guam, and Wake.[15]

In addition to carrying out overseas support missions in the Korean Conflict, the Coast Guard continued its SAR, ATN, and port security missions on the coasts, lakes and inland rivers of the United States. In the Korean Conflict stage of the Cold War, port security, ship inspection, and protection against sabotage and espionage were primary national security duties.

At the Chesapeake Bay entrance, the gateway to the Potomac River and the nation's capital, and the maritime highway in proximity to invaluable infrastructure and numerous population centers, the 165-foot USCGC *Tahoma* (WPG/WAGE 10) patrolled its station. The brightly colored yellow cutter with the word "Guard" emblazoned in black letters on the hull monitored incoming ships which were required to transmit by radio the name of the vessel, nation of origin, home port and last port of call, next port or destination, and ETA (estimated time of arrival) at Chesapeake Bay.

As national security and military agencies would subsequently be concerned in the 21st-century War on Terror, during the 1950s and the Cold War, the defense establishment was on watch for suspect Communist Bloc ships that might try to detonate a nuclear device in an American port. From 1951 forward, any ship entering the maritime domain of the United States was required to notify U.S. Customs of its next port of call and cargo one day in advance. Coast Guard captains of the port (COPTs) were notified of the names of the vessels and other appropriate information, and Coast Guard patrol boats monitored suspect ships and boarded and inspected suspicious vessels.

The port of New York City was thoroughly patrolled in the area of the anchored 135-foot *Ambrose Lightship* (WLV-87) station. Lightships were floating lighthouses crewed by Coast Guard personnel. Coast Guard personnel armed with Geiger counters and chemical detectors conducted periodic and random ship inspections that could last for four hours in a rigorous search for explosives, nuclear devices, and biochemical weapons.

Explosives-loading detachment teams supervised the loading and unloading of armament from and onto military ships and commercial cargo vessels and barges. Patrol boats accompanied river ammunition barges on the Pacific coast loaded with ammunition destined for Korea, with armed Coastguardsmen stationed on board cargo vessels.[16]

Clear and accurate radio communications and transmissions were an essential technological element of successful transcontinental and transoceanic SAR and warfare in World War II and Korea. LORAN (long-range navigation) was the electronic system that achieved the communications objective and was the means during war and peacetime by which air and sea craft positions were verified and tracked. The reception and triangulation of radio waves between stations and over distances from 800 to 1,400 miles accomplished the objectives. LORAN was used for domestic transportation until the system was displaced by space satellite technology decades later.

In 1941 during World War II, the British developed a pulse transmitting navigational aid that exceeded radar's 50–100 mile radius. Bell Laboratory scientists visited the United Kingdom and then developed a high-frequency shortwave system. LORAN was developed with the cooperation of Bell Laboratories, Massachusetts Institute of Technology, and, with U.S. Navy encouragement, the efforts of Adm. Julius A. Furer (USN) and radio and electronics expert Cmdr. (later Captain) Lawrence M. Harding (USCG).

Test units and stations were constructed or modified and used along the Atlantic coasts of Canada and the United States, including two inactive Coast Guard Life-Saving Station sites. The initial tests involved the Royal (British) Navy (RN), Royal Canadian Navy (RCN), a USN blimp, and a weather ship, the USCGC *Manasquan*, along other coastal and North Atlantic sites. With the work of several civilian scientists, USN, USCG, and RCN officials the tests and systems proved successful.[17] The LORAN stations were a strategic addition to the ATN arm of the USN and USCG, were served and supplied by Coast Guard buoy tenders, proved to be of inestimable value, and played a significant role in the Allied victory over the Axis powers of Germany, Italy and Japan.[18]

LORAN navigation was a significant element in the Korean War, and later in Vietnam. The LORAN station at Pusan, South Korea, was the only place Coast Guard personnel served on the Korean peninsula during the war. ELMO-4 was the classified name for the Pusan LORAN site.

Lt. John D. McCann (USCG), the commanding officer of the LORAN site, designated and constructed the station 20 miles outside of Pusan in 1952. The 12-man crew had a one-year tour of duty. The U.S. Army helped construct the station, and the U.S. Air Force supported the station with security and supplies.

The Pusan LORAN signals commenced in 1953 along with three other sites in Japan. Coast Guard assistant historian Scott T. Price described the regional LORAN stations as "lonely Coast Guard outposts (that) provided around the clock navigation assistance to United Nations maritime and air forces. Every UN vessel and aircraft utilized the new technology that permitted navigation under any weather conditions during the day or night ... courtesy of the United States Coast Guard."[19]

More than 20 U.S. Coast Guard cutters in total carried out missions in the Korean Conflict theater. The missions included ATN and LORAN, SAR, transport and troop escort, and ocean station weather information duty. A Coast Guard air detachment stationed in the Philippines served SAR and reconnaissance missions. A civilian U.S. Merchant Marine detachment and USCG Far Eastern section was stationed in Japan to serve UN forces.

The Coast Guard cutters and crews that served in the Korean War maritime realm, and were therefore eligible for the acquisition of the Korean Service Medal, included the CGCs *Bering Strait* (WAVP-382), *Chautauqua* (WPG-41), *Durant* (WDE-489), *Escanaba* (WPG-64), *Falgout* (WDE-424),

Finch (WDE-428), *Forster* (WDE-434), *Gresham* (WAVP-387), *Ironwood* (WAGL-297), *Iroquois* (WPG-43), *Klamath* (WPG-66), *Koiner* (WDE-431), *Kukui* (WAK-186), *Lowe* (WDE-425), *Minnetonka* (WPG-67), *Newell* (WDE-442), *Planetree* (WAGL-307), *Ponchartrain* (WPG-70), *Ramsden* (WDE-482), *Richey* (WDE-485), *Taney* (WPG-37), *Wachusett* (WPG-44), *Winnebago* (WPG-40), and the *Winona* (WPG-64).[20]

United States Coast Guard shore units and LORAN stations and crews that were eligible for the Korean Service Medal included LORSTA Bataan (Philippines); LORSTA Elmo No. 4 Pusan (South Korea); and the following LORSTA units in Japan: Ichi Banare, Okinawa; Iwo Jima; Matsumae, Hokkaido; Niigata, Honshu; Oshima, Honshu; Riyako Jima; and Tokyo, Honshu.

The Korean Service Medal eligibility was also extended to the Commander (USCG) Far East Section, Tokyo, Japan; and the U.S. Merchant Marine Detachment, Tokyo.[21]

On 26 July 1953 the Korean War belligerents signed a cease-fire agreement, but not a treaty to end the war. The Coast Guard responded with demobilization and the decommissioning of destroyer escorts and overseas air and SAR detachments in the Korean theater of operations.

The return to peacetime operations did not mean the end of Cold War port security missions. In fact those duties were maintained and expanded. Between 1947 and 1953 the USCG expanded from 18,000 enlisted and commissioned men and women to 35,082 personnel, including more than 1,500 members of the USCG Reserve. By the end of 1952 more than 30 female Coast Guard personnel (still referred to by the World War II name of SPARS) served on active duty and 323 in the USCGR. Post–Korean War Coast Guard commandants would assign USCG personnel to overseas combat roles in Vietnam and in the Global War on Terror.[22]

4

The Cold War from America to Vietnam

The Cold War conflict between the Communist and non–Communist nations continued after the Korean War until the end of the twentieth century. The Cold War continued in pacific and belligerent stages as the Communist powers continued the expansion of its economic and geopolitical spheres of influence and the Western nations tried to stop the expansion through a "containment" deterrent phase.

The Cold War was psychological, political, economic, military, covert and overt. The global struggle was covert and overt, and involved propaganda, espionage, sabotage, military alliances, and the formation and utilization of treaties and international organizations like the North Atlantic Treaty Organization (NATO), United Nations (UN), Southeast Asia Treaty Organization (SEATO), and other regional economic, political, and defense agreements.

The international conflict was waged in the Middle East, Western Hemisphere, Europe, Africa, Asia, and sometimes in the oceanic insular realm. The chronological span encompassed the period from the end of World War II into the 21st century (ca. 1945-2000) and beyond. After the fall of the premier Communist nation, the Soviet Union, the contest continued between the West and vestiges of Marxist-Leninism in Cuba, the People's Republic of China, and autocratic regimes of would-be Stalinists in Latin America and Africa in conventional and guerilla warfare and terrorism. "Wars of liberation" erupted across the world as geopolitical analysts quarreled over which factions were "freedom fighters" or "terrorists."

The Cold War would become hot in Vietnam and be fueled by insurgent factions — some with Marxist roots or support — in the Third World of developing nations and have repercussions in developed countries. Western intelligence agencies would become involved with their national security responsibilities, as would the law enforcement and public safety agencies, and the U.S. Armed Forces. The U.S. Coast Guard, as an agency responsible for public safety and national defense, would contribute its mission skills as well, as it has done throughout its history.

Between 1945 and 1965 the Coast Guard performed a variety of national defense missions in addition to its traditional peacetime domestic duties. The emergence of Fidel Castro as the Communist dictator of Cuba, heavily supported by the Soviet Union, challenged the United States and Latin America. The migration of Cuban dissidents and illegal immigrants from Cuba to the United States challenged the Coast Guard in its drug and migrant immigration responsibilities. The Coast Guard enforced complex and sometimes contradictory federal immigration laws and either denied entry to Caribbean migrants or allowed them access to America depending on the strategic, legal, and political circumstances in the indigenous homelands and the United States, saving the lives of hundreds of endangered migrants on the high seas in the process.

The Red Scare was heating up and the Cold War containment policy was threatened in Eastern Europe and Latin America as Marxist leaders aided by Castro attempted political takeovers, the Korea War erupted, and Vietnam was an emerging problem for the Truman, Kennedy, Eisenhower, Johnson and Nixon administrations.

The USCG was increasingly occupied with domestic port security concerns, especially at major shipping ports, and had to expand the building and acquisition of maritime and aviation assets and personnel to compensate for the precipitous demobilization that occurred immediately after World War II and Korea. Coast Guard Reserve training units were established to meet the needs of port security missions. By the end of June 1951 the USCGR numbered more than 8,000 commissioned officers and enlisted personnel. Petty officers were trained at Coast Guard, Navy and Army schools in explosives loading, law enforcement, firefighting, and other aspects of port security. Coast Guard schools were located at Groton, Connecticut; Alameda, California; and Cape May, New Jersey. The officer corps was supplemented with veteran petty and warrant officers, the awarding of officer commissions to qualified college and Merchant Marine academy graduates, and the commissioning of carefully selected and well-schooled U.S. Coast Guard Academy cadets at New London, Connecticut.

Coast Guard Yard at Curtis Bay, Maryland, constructed a variety of diesel-powered, steel-hulled patrol boats and oceangoing deepwater cutters.

Some academic social scientists, journalists, lawyers and judges, and civil libertarians were critical of alleged Coast Guard excesses in voiding the licenses and certificates of merchant mariners suspected as national security and loyalty risks. Court cases ensued that both vindicated and overruled Coast Guard national security operations and procedures as the service sought to protect vessels, cargoes, ports, and personnel from espionage, sabotage, and labor strikes.

The administration of John F. Kennedy brought more attention and funding to the Coast Guard. President Kennedy, a U.S. Navy officer in World War II, followed maritime issues and supported the requests and policies of U.S. Treasury Secretary C. Douglas Dillon, the civilian head of the Coast Guard, and Assistant Secretary James A. Reed, a veteran USN torpedo boat officer.

The Coast Guard commandants between 1946 and 1974 were, respectively, Admirals Joseph F. Farley, Merlin O'Neil, Alfred C. Richmond, Edwin J. Roland, Willard J. Smith, and Chester Bender. These worthy successors of World War II commandant, Adm. Russell R. Waesche, brought their own war and peacetime experiences to the fore and contributed the visionary leadership that facilitated the growth and effectiveness of the USCG in meeting its Cold War–era domestic and overseas missions.

By 1965 the Coast Guard air arm consisted of 156 aircraft including 56 helicopters; a fleet augmented with several donated U.S. Navy vessels, buoy tenders, patrol boats, and motor lifeboats; and modern firefighting, sonar, radar, radio direction finders, small arms, and armament and ordnance on the oceangoing cutters.[1]

From that background of mission responsibilities, training, personnel complement, air and sea craft, technology and armament, the U.S. Coast Guard prepared for its next national defense operations in Vietnam.

Admiral Edwin John Roland, U.S. Coast Guard commandant from 1962 to 1966, was an accomplished cadet athlete and later athletic coach and instructor at the U.S. Coast Guard Academy. Adm. Roland commanded a destroyer escort division in World War II, attended the National War College, and served as assistant commandant. With that background, Adm. Roland was ideally suited to prepare the Coast Guard for its maritime responsibilities in law enforcement, SAR, ATN, and national defense in Vietnam, a mission Roland thought essential to Coast Guard military credibility in the Cold War era.[2]

The Coast Guard sea fleet included sixteen 210-foot WMEC (Medium Endurance) oceangoing cutters in the mid–1960s and several sleek new 378-foot WHEC (High Endurance) cutters built at Avondale Shipyards in Louisiana. The WHECs had aluminum superstructures, side-by-side parallel (as opposed to linear positioned) stacks, diesel engines, gas turbines and helicopter decks. The cutters were armed with sonar, torpedoes, 40 mm mounts and a 5-inch deck gun.[3] Coast Guard commissioned and enlisted personnel would be running those and other cutters, buoy tenders and patrol boats in Vietnam. Coastguardsmen would experience plenty of battle action ashore and afloat in what some historians called a civil war within the country of Vietnam, and others called a war of aggression by North Vietnam (and North Vietnam Army or NVA troops) and sympathetic Viet Cong (VC) forces in South Vietnam. The Soviet Union (USSR) and the People's Republic of China (PRC) aided NVA and VC forces overtly and covertly.

The troops and sailors of South Vietnam, referred to as ARVN (Army and Navy of Vietnam), were assisted by U.S. advisors and later U.S. combat soldiers, sailors, and airmen, and several UN nations.

U.S. aid to former French Indochina (North and South Vietnam, Cambodia and Laos) began with President Harry S Truman during and following World War II as part of his Cold War "containment" policy. President Eisenhower sent U.S. combat advisors in the 1950s. President John F. Kennedy sent advisors who increasingly participated in combat missions, but the involvement and escalation of U.S. combat forces is generally attributed to President Lyndon B. Johnson (LBJ) in 1964-1965, and his ordering of U.S. military forces to Da Nang (South Vietnam) and the bombing of North Vietnam after a controversial attack by NV naval boats on U.S. Navy vessels.

Domestic discontent with the Vietnam War and its cost in treasure and blood caused Johnson to refuse to run again for office in 1968. Johnson's successor, Richard M. Nixon, alternately continued LBJ's escalation of the war and forced the NVA/VC to the negotiating table for the signing of the Treaty of Paris (France) in 1973. U.S. troops were withdrawn from Vietnam, and prisoners of war (POWs) on all sides were exchanged. By the end of 1975, the government of South Vietnam (GSV) had fallen to NVA/VC invaders. The United States had won the war on the battlefield and rivers and high seas, but with the loss of congressional support and the discontinuation of military aid, South Vietnam was doomed.[4]

By the end of 1967 the United States had 500,000 troops in South Vietnam. The number of Coast Guard personnel who would serve in Vietnam totaled 8,000, with 7 KIA and 60 WIA.[5] The contributions of the Coast Guard to the Vietnam War, the other U.S. Armed Forces, and the government of South Vietnam far exceeded those numbers.

President Johnson ordered the Coast Guard deployment to Vietnam to help the U.S. Navy interdict enemy military weapons, ordnance, and supplies being sent to the Viet Cong by sea and river systems. Coast Guard Squadron One initiated the mission with 17 82-foot USCG patrol boats (WPBs) and 250 personnel. Each patrol boat had a crew complement of nine enlisted men and two officers. Each WPB carried an 81 mm mortar gun and five .50 machine guns. The squadron patrolled the Gulf of Thailand and the gulf coast of Vietnam to the border of Cambodia. A Coast Guard division patrolled the demilitarized zone (DMZ) just south of the border between North and South Vietnam. Another flotilla of nine cutters arrived in Vietnam in 1966 to patrol the strategic and enemy-saturated environs of the Mekong Delta.[6]

A total of 26 Coast Guard WPB 82-foot cutters were deployed to Vietnam. The fast boats searched for enemy vessels. U.S. Navy, Navy SEAL commando, Coast Guard, Army, and ARVN units searched for enemy forces in the complex riverine and forest labyrinths of the Mekong Delta.

The U.S. Navy constructed a mobile pontoon base called Operation Sea Float in the middle of the Cua Lon River in the Ca Mau region. It was assumed that this military presence deep within Viet Cong–held territory would increase civilian support for the South Vietnam government. Cmdr. Paul A. Yost, who would become a Coast Guard commandant, led a military unit from Sea Float. The patrol region posed nefarious dangers because of powerful river currents, the distance from supply lines, and a strong Viet Cong presence, but Operation Sea Float deprived the enemy of a secure sanctuary and intercepted Viet Cong supply chains. Float units provided medical services to indigenous populations; destroyed tons of enemy food, weapons, and ammunition; and killed 3,000 and captured 300 Communist forces at a cost to U.S. and ARVN forces of more than 1,400 WIA and 186 KIA.[7]

The 82-foot WPBs were steel-hulled, air-conditioned boats with power steering, a 5.8-foot draft, and 17.2-foot beam that allowed mobility in shallow inland (brown) waters. The newer WPBs carried two diesel engines, was armed with one to four mounted machine guns, and cruised at about 23 knots. Fifteen WHEC cutters supplemented what was called the Market Time fleet with heavy firepower and radar. The 327-foot, 15-foot-draft ocean going cutters carried one five-inch deck gun, Two 81-mm mortars, six .50 caliber machine guns, and two torpedo launchers. Two 6,200-horsepower engines, two boilers, powered the WHECs and two engine shafts that achieved speeds up to 20 knots. The crew complement consisted of 13 officers and 130 enlisted personnel.[8]

Proficient at helicopter air and sea rescues, the Coast Guard was asked by the Pentagon to perform that function in Vietnam. Lt. Cmdr. Lonnie L. Mixon (USCG) and Lt. Lance A. Eagan (USCG) distinguished themselves as combat SAR pilots in Vietnam. The helicopter aviators and their crews earned well-deserved awards. Lt. Eagan received the Silver Star Medal, and his crew partner, para-rescue expert Airman First Class Joel Talley (USAF), earned the Air Force Cross for the rescue of a downed and injured USAF pilot under enemy fire.

Lt. Jack C. Rittichier (USCG) was among the early Coast Guard casualties in Vietnam. The Detroit (Michigan) Air Station aviator volunteered for helicopter SAR service with the U.S. Air Force. Attached to Da Nang Air Base, Rittichier was killed when his Jolly Green Giant Huey helicopter was shot down behind enemy lines during a rescue attempt. At the time of his death, Lt. Rittichier had been recommended for two Air Medals, an Air Force Cross, and three Distinguished Flying Crosses for harrowing combat rescues.[9]

Lt. Rittichier described his harrowing Vietnam rescue missions in April and May 1968 on audiotape one month before he and his three-person crew were killed in action. Rittichier flew the giant Sikorsky HH-3E "Jolly Green Giant" rescue helicopters in the USAF Aerospace Rescue and Recovery Squadron (ARRS) out of Da Nang. Rittichier graphically, methodically, and articulately described missions above and beneath the trees of Vietnam's tropical forests; rotors sometime touching branches and leaves; the sudden rain

USAF "Jolly Green Giant" combat rescue helicopter used to recover downed pilots in Vietnam. Air Force and Coast Guard pilots and crews flew the Sikorsky helicopters.

and mists which clouded the vision of crew members as they dodged mountains and enemy gunners and dropped rescue chairs, ladders, and themselves into landing zones (LZs) to rescue downed and injured U.S. Army, Navy, Marine, and Air Force crews before VC or NVA troops got to them.

Lt. Rittichier described the brave crew members, firefights with VC and NVA troops, skilled backup flying and radio communications, fixed-wing propeller plane air cover, and the flights to bases and hospitals on low fuel with wounded and sometimes deceased military personnel.[10]

In his last combat rescue mission, Lt. Jack Rittichier glided through concentrated enemy fire and hovered over a downed U.S. Marine jet fighter pilot. The injured pilot waved off the helicopter as USAF propeller fighter planes strafed the vicinity. Rittichier and his crew returned, hovered over the pilot, dropped the cable and attached forest-penetrator seat through the jungle trees, and endured concentrated enemy gunfire. Warned by a circling pilot that his chopper was on fire, Rittichier rose out of the LZ, ignited into flames, exploded, and crashed. Listed as MIA until 2003, the remains of Rittichier and his crewmates were found in 2003 by a joint POW/MIA accounting team military agency. Lt. Rittichier and his crew posthumously received the Silver Star.[11] Lieutenant Jack C. Rittichier was interred at Arlington National Cemetery (Virginia) on Coast Guard Hill in October 2003.[12]

The U.S. Navy requested Coast Guard assistance in Vietnam because of the service's previous wartime combat experience, skill at riverine piloting and small boat handling, and the oceangoing experience of Coast Guard cutters and crews. The 81-mm mortar used on patrol boats had been used for peacetime illumination in SAR missions. The manually fired mortars on patrol boat decks proved so effective that U.S. Special Forces units began to use them on flatbed trucks for fire support in their dangerous missions. The Coast Guard provided fire support from its boats and cutters in more than 6,000 instances and boarded an estimated 250,000 Vietnamese[13] watercraft in the ongoing search for weapons, supplies, enemy solders and agents.

Cutter crews searched junks and sampans and stopped arms and ammunition smugglers. WPBs operated heavy patrol schedules in varied seas and tropical weather. Coast Guard patrol boats with transportation, illumination lights, and gun and mortar fire support joined U.S. Marine, Army and Special Forces units.[14]

Squadron Three was composed of five 311-foot WHECs that patrolled in offshore Market Time missions designed by the U.S. Navy to intercept NVA and VC units. More than 8,000 Coastguardsmen and 50 cutters destroyed 2,000 enemy vessels in the "Brown Water War" (inshore waters and rivers) and suffered 60 casualties.[15]

USCG cutters destroyed enemy supply ships, provided gunfire support in naval missions, and assisted in providing medical services to the Vietnamese civilian population and U.S. military personnel. The cutters served as berthing and off-duty stations for military personnel as well. WHECs replaced USN destroyers at sea on Market Time missions after 1969. Thirty Coast Guard cutters and 4,500 officers and men were deployed in Squadron Three between 1967 and 1973.

In 1966 the U.S. Military Assistance Command (USMAC) requested the Coast Guard to supervise explosive loading detachments (ELDs) to oversee explosive loading from ships in dangerous ports where untrained Vietnamese workers posed a threat. The ELDs were initially assigned to the U.S. Army Logistical Command. During the Vietnam War, no explosive accidents or enemy action occurred in any USCG ELD supervised port.

In 1966 Gen. William Westmoreland (USA), commander of U.S. forces in Vietnam, requested the participation of a U.S. Coast Guard port security and waterways detail (PS&WD) to assist and train U.S. Army boat crews and inspect and secure port facilities. A Coast Guard marine inspector was assigned to the U.S. Navy's Military Sea Transportation Service (MSTS) to police and protect the hundreds of merchant ships supporting U.S. operations in Vietnam.

A U.S. Coast Guard aids to navigation detail stationed in Saigon manned and supervised buoy tenders, maintained navigation buoys, and established navigation aids along the Vietnamese coasts and in key ports to support merchant and combat vessel safety, transportation, and combat missions.

On 14 December 1965, at the request of the U.S. Department of Defense, the USCG began the construction, operation, and maintenance of the long-range electronic navigation system (LORAN) in Vietnam that guided military aircraft to and from their targets and bases. The transmitting station was located 40 miles south of the demilitarized zone (DMZ) between North and South Vietnam.[16]

The U.S. Navy utilized Coast Guard mission skills throughout the war. The two naval services were symbiotic in their reciprocal skills and contributions. With the formation of Naval Task Force 115 on 30 July 1965 Coast Guard personal joined Navy coastal surveillance units at An Thoi, Vung Tau, Qui Nhon, Nha Trang and Da Nang.

U.S. support of the South Vietnam Government continued as U.S. forces were gradually being withdrawn under President Nixon's Vietnamization plan of gradually turning combat duties over to South Vietnam while continuing aid and ending direct American combat missions. Between 1969 and 1970, 26 USCG patrol boats were transferred to Coast Guard–trained South Vietnamese naval crews.[17] In 1971-1972 four large Coast Guard cutters were transferred to South Vietnamese crews.[18]

Adm. Elmo Zumwalt (USN), commander of U.S. Navy forces in Vietnam, directed the Coastal Surveillance Force, Riverine Assault Force, River Patrol Force, and related Coast Guard missions and coordinated U.S. and South Vietnamese naval operations.[19] Zumwalt commanded the "Brown Water Navy" river patrol boats along the Vietnam coast in the Mekong Delta. Operation Sealord intercepted Viet Cong supply lines from Cambodia. Adm. Zumwalt initiated the spraying of the controversial vegetation defoliant Agent Orange into the Mekong Delta, a policy that ironically and regrettably may have exposed his son, swift boat commander Lt. (jg) Elmo R. Zumwalt III (USN) to the herbicide. The young U.S. Navy officer died of cancer in 1981.[20]

Getting U.S.-based Coast Guard cutters to Vietnam posed a significant logistical challenge. Coast Guard Squadron One, composed of three divisions, was commissioned at Alameda, California, on 26 May 1965 under Cmdr. James A. Hodgman (USCG). The original 17 USCG vessels were loaded on the decks of Military Sea Transport Service (MSTS) ships in the ports of Norfolk, Virginia; New Orleans Louisiana; Long Beach and San Francisco, California; Seattle, Washington; and Galveston, Texas. The Coast Guard crews were trained in weapons use, communications, and survival skills. The cutters and crews joined up again at the U.S. Navy base, Subic Bay (Philippines), and made the 1,000-mile sea journey to Vietnam, refueling and resupplying from large U.S. Navy ships in seas of 15 feet or more, and 35-knot winds.

Upon reaching Vietnam, the Coast Guard patrols commenced. On its first night patrol, the USCGC *Point Orient* (WPB-82319) encountered shoreside enemy machine gun and mortar fire. After that experience, the Coast Guard ordered crews to replace the white paint of its cutters with less visible Navy combat ship colors.[21]

The smallest Market Time seacraft was the 13-foot fiberglass Boston Whaler or "skimmer." Larger Coast Guard patrol boats (WPBs) launched the skimmers from their decks. The small boats maneuvered around sampans and junks, and their armed crews boarded the suspect vessels as the WPBs stood by ready to respond to hostile or evasive actions with fire support. The Boston Whalers were painted gray and outfitted with protective flak shields, signal flares, and a portable radio, and their crews carried small arms. U.S. Navy aircraft patrols searched coastal waters and radioed the location of suspicious watercraft to Navy fast patrol craft (PCFs) and Coast Guard patrol boats.[22]

Operating out of the Vietnamese port of Cat Lo (March 1966), Coast Guard Division Thirteen captured 7 Viet Cong; killed 27; and acquired or destroyed several tons of military weapons, ammunition and other supplies. USCGC *Point White* (Lt. Eugene J. Hickey) and crew rammed a 25-foot enemy junk while under fire and captured a notorious VC leader.[23]

Among the many tragedies of war is the accidental wounding and killing of comrades ashore or at sea by one's own or allied forces, ironically called "friendly fire." Such a tragedy took place in the early morning hours of 11 August 1966 when CGC *Point Welcome* was attacked just off the DMZ between North and South Vietnam. A U.S. Air Force bomber and two F-4C fighter planes bombed and strafed the cutter in a one-hour horror story of futile signals and radio calls and skilled evasive actions by the *Point Welcome* crew. Coastguardsmen were forced into the water to swim for shore while under initial friendly fire from South Vietnamese land forces. The *Point Welcome* crew casualty count was 11 WIA and 2 KIA.[24]

Point Welcome skipper Lt. (jg) David C. Brostrom (USCG), the son of a U.S. Navy commander, and Engineman Second Class Jerry Phillips (USCG) were killed in action. Chief Boatswain Mate Richard H. Patterson (USCG) utilized his seamanship skills and leadership under fire to mobilize the crew and avoid even more serious damage to the patrol boat and crew casualties. BMC Patterson was awarded the Bronze Star with Combat "V" for his heroic actions.[25]

Coast Guard patrol boats put troops ashore in enemy territory and extracted them after their missions and battle. During an extraction of South Vietnamese troops (22 January 1969) CGC *Point Banks*, two U.S. Navy boats, and a USAF C-47 gunship fired on VC positions. Gunners Mate Second Class Willis J. Goff (USCG) and Engineman Second Class Larry D. Villarreal (USCG) guided a small skimmer boat into the night and onto shore. Using their own machine guns to counter VC fire, the Coastguardsmen rescued five South Vietnamese military personnel and returned safely to the *Point Banks*. Their heroism earned GM2 Goff and EM2 Villarreal each a Silver Star.[26]

Captain Alex Larzelere (USCG) graduated from the U.S. Coast Guard Academy, National War College, and Naval War College. Capt. Larzelere commanded five cutters in his career, was a military aid to President Richard M. Nixon, and earned an advanced degree from George Washington University in international affairs. In Vietnam, then Lt. Larzelere commanded two 82-foot WPB patrol boats, CGC *Point Banks* and CGC *Point Comfort*. Capt. Larzelere also wrote a history of the U.S. Coast Guard in Vietnam from 1965 to 1975.

Larzelere's book, *The Coast Guard at War*, chronicled the missions and military actions of the USCG on land and sea using as his sources personal experience, government documents, interviews, primary and secondary works, and more than 70 tape-recorded interviews. The author quoted Gen. Howell M. Estes, Jr., (USAF) on Coast Guard performance: "I am aware of the distinguished record achieved by Coast Guard pilots flying in combat with our

Jolly Greens (helicopters). They are indelibly inscribed in the permanent records of the stirring and moving drama of combat and air crew recovery in Southeast Asia."[27]

Captain Joseph L. Crowe, a Coast Guard lieutenant commander in Vietnam, told Larzelere that in addition to rescues over land, "Coast Guard aviators handled missions at sea when pilots of other Armed Services were not trained in over water navigation, and not familiar with the intricacies of hoisting from a rolling ship."[28]

General Wallace Greene, Jr., the Commandant of the U.S. Marine Corps in the Vietnam era, said in August of 1967, "I want to make sure that the Coast Guard people in Vietnam know that I am hearing about them often and I am pleased with what I hear."[29]

In 1967 Secretary of the Navy Paul H. Nitze "requested that the Treasury Department assist the Department of the Navy by assigning five high endurance (WHEC Coast Guard) cutters to augment Market Time forces" in Vietnam, Larzelere wrote, and from that date on, fast U.S. Army, Navy, and Coast Guard river patrol boats worked together on riverine and coastal missions.[30]

The 378-foot CGC *Rush* (WHEC-723), under the command of Capt. Robert W. Durfey (USCG), joined Coast Guard and U.S. Navy patrol boats and USN radar picket escort ships (DERs) to engage and destroy armed, steel-hulled enemy trawlers bringing ammunition and supplies to Communist forces. Shoot-outs and shrapnel dispersing-explosions increased the mission dangers.

Engaged in these missions was the 255-foot CGC *Androscoggin* (WHEC-68) skippered by Cmdr. William H. Stewart (USCG). His crew joined in action-packed missions with 82-foot Coast Guard patrol craft (WPBs), USN Swift Boats (PCFs), and U.S. Army helicopter gunships. Bullet holes across the bow of the *Androscoggin* gave evidence of the volatility of the encounters.

On 29 February 1968 Cmdr. Herbert J. Lynch (USCG) of the 255-foot *Winona* (WHEC-65) engaged in a gun battle with a North Vietnamese ammunition trawler that resulted in a close-quarters explosion that splattered steel fragments and human body parts from the enemy vessel over the deck of the cutter.

Squadron Three WHECs fired more than 77,000 five-inch shells in Vietnam naval support missions. The oceangoing cutters provided logistical support, berthing, food, supplies and repairs for USN PCFs and USCG WPBs.[31]

Captain Robert Durfey (USCG) later reflected upon his combat tour as skipper of the CGC *Rush*: "We got called on to do all manner of things. And we were never unable to respond to a request or order for a mission." Capt. Durfey concluded that the Coast Guard motto, *Semper Paratus* (Always Ready) was aptly proven in Vietnam.[32]

The U.S. Coast Guard served in Vietnam with the other U.S. Armed Forces and South Vietnamese units for ten years (1965–1975). American combat came to an end with the signing of the Paris Treaty in 1973, but the isolated Coast Guard LORAN navigation station was not deactivated until April 1975.[33]

Paul C. Scotti joined the Coast Guard after four years of duty in the U.S. Air Force. After transferring to the USCG, Gunners Mate Second Class Scotti saw combat action on 82-foot patrol boats in Vietnam from 1967 to 1968. Then GM2 Scotti trained and served as a Coast Guard journalist and was promoted to chief warrant officer and public information officer. CWO4 Scotti retired and wrote the masterful history *Coast Guard Action in Vietnam.* Scotti dedicated the book to Coast Guard combat veterans and their families. The author, a Coast Guard Vietnam veteran, chronicled the service's multi-mission Vietnam responsibilities in port security, law enforcement, SAR, ATN, and riverine and coastal patrols and combat.

Scotti interviewed former U.S. Coast Guard Commandant Paul A. Yost, Jr. As a young officer, Yost commanded U.S. Navy and U.S. Coast Guard units in Vietnam (1969–1970), and then served as Coast Guard commandant from 1986 to 1990. Adm. Yost (USCG, Ret.) reflected on the Vietnam War: "I think we should have been in Vietnam," the admiral stated. "We gave the Vietnamese an opportunity to save their country." But due to official graft and corruption, Yost asserted, and the disinclination of many South Vietnamese "to risk their lives and equipment for their country" and the fact that "the (SV) officer corps often didn't lead (and) was not professional ... they lost the war."[34]

Despite that candid assessment, Adm. Yost was positive about his service experience in Vietnam and proud of the role the U.S. Armed Forces played in general, and the U.S. Coast Guard in particular. The lesson for the Coast Guard from the Vietnam experience was clear to Adm. Paul Yost: "We should be aware of our military mission. The Coast Guard is a capable war-making service in a specialty with the expertise and experience to run patrol boats."[35]

5

Logistics and Tactics in Indochina

In the previous chapter, the impact of the Cold War on the United States after the Korean conflict was considered. Events were discussed, with emphasis on the role of the U.S. Coast Guard in national defense at home and abroad.

The gradual involvement of the Coast Guard in the Vietnam War was described, as well as the mission coordination on land and sea between the Coast Guard, the other U.S. Armed Forces, and the government of South Vietnam. The war was waged to protect South Vietnam from the military forces of the indigenous Viet Cong (VC) and the North Vietnamese Army (NVA).

The logistics and coordinated tactics of the United States Coast Guard (USCG), U.S. Army USA), U.S. Marine Corps (USMC), U.S. Air Force (USAF), and the Army of the Republic of (South) Vietnam (ARVN) and Vietnam Navy (VNN) will be further explored in this chapter.

The Military Channel produced the 50-minutes DVD *Coast Guard at War.* The DVD included magnificent film combat action at sea, on rivers and channels, and ashore on medical, port security and waterways, helicopter search and rescue (SAR), aids to navigation (ATN), and explosives loading (ELD) missions. Compelling and often emotional interviews with Coast Guard commissioned and enlisted combat personnel were also featured.

The Coast Guard was called upon by the U.S. Army, Navy, and Air Force to assist them with the capacities, trained personnel, and air and sea skills that the service was noted for. Coast Guard units assisted and were aided by the other U.S. Armed Forces, ARVN, VNN, and special Army and Navy forces, including the famed U.S. Navy SEALS. To ready themselves for the Vietnam mission, Coast Guard personnel were trained in warfare and survival skills in California at Coast Guard Base Alameda, the U.S. Marine Corps Base at Camp Pendleton, and in the Sierra Nevada mountains.

Coast Guard 82-foot patrol boats (WPBs), medium- and high-endurance oceangoing cutters (WHECs and WMECs), and 180-foot buoy tenders teamed up with U.S. Navy swift boats (PCFs) and destroyers. Volunteer Coast Guard helicopter pilots flew USAF Jolly Green Giant SAR rotor winged choppers over land and sea and behind enemy lines.

Coast Guard cutters carried four-man Boston Whalers (skimmers) to facilitate the dangerous night-and-day boarding of Vietnamese junks and sampans which carried cargo and families and fishing crews, or perhaps enemy infiltrators and contraband such as ammunition, weapons, food and other supplies brought in from North Vietnam to supply VC and NVA troops in South Vietnam. When enemy vessels were discovered, bloody firefights ensued.

More than 1,000 Coastguardsmen served in Vietnam on a variety of cutters. Squadrons One, Two and Three blanketed South Vietnam from the demilitarized zone (DMZ) between North and South Vietnam to the Gulf of Thailand on the western coat of Vietnam. In Squadron One alone, 245 men crewed 17 WPBs.[1]

Gunners Mate First Class Jerry Goff (USCG) served in Vietnam on the CGC *Point Banks* from 1967 to 1969. GM1 Goff patrolled river channels and faced armed VC just yards away. In one incident a VC soldier was killed, and shore exploration discovered a female VC carrying a baby and an AK-47 gun. The woman turned to fire, and Goff regretted the firefight that killed her. The baby was spared and taken aboard the cutter.

Boatswain Mate Third Class Terry Montreuil (USCG) served on the black-hulled 180-foot buoy tender *Blackhaw* on ATN missions in 1967–1968. BM3 Montreuil worked with USN SEALS to check and maintain navigation buoys. The SEALS did underwater surveillance of the buoys and the cutter to thwart the sometimes-successful enemy sappers who placed explosives on the buoys and under merchant and military vessels. The SEALS, Montreuil described, performed their dangerous jobs in murky waters inhabited by the danger of enemy sappers and poisonous sea snakes. The *Blackhaw* (cutter and crew) received U.S. Navy combat awards. Upon his return from Vietnam, BM3 Montreuil paid an emotional visit to the Vietnam Memorial[2] in Washington, D.C., where the names of U.S. Armed Forces personnel killed in Vietnam are forever immortalized in granite.

Lt. Alex R. Larzelere (USCG), captain of the CGC *Point Comfort* and *Point Banks* (1965–1966) and Division Eleven Operations Officer (1966), described crew training, the preparation of the WPBs in the Philippines, and the treacherous 1,100-mile trip across stormy Pacific waters from Subic Bay to the U.S. base and port of Da Nang in South Vietnam. Larzelere, who would later write exemplary histories of Coast Guard combat missions in

World War I and Vietnam, described how, under the command of Adm. Elmo Zumwalt (USN), Navy and Coast Guard riverine patrol boats were ordered to "take it to the enemy."[3]

Gunners Mate First Class William R. Wells II (USCG) served in Vietnam on the CGCs *Point Dumo*, *Point Glover*, and *Point Kennedy* in 1969–1970. GM1 Wells recalled the rigorous survival training he endured at U.S. Coast Guard Station Alameda (Government Island) and the U.S. Marine Corps Base Camp Pendleton.

Boatswains Mate Third Class "Frenchie" Benoit (USCG) served on the CGC *Point Banks* on riverine patrol in 1969. While manning battle station guns, BM3 Benoit was badly wounded by VC shore fire, removed to a USN warship, and taken by helicopter to a military hospital for hip surgery. The extent of his wounds ended BM Benoit's Coast Guard career.

Engineman Second Class A. Taylor Lapham, Jr. (USCG) described service on patrol with the CGC *Point Grey* (1968–1969), and then his transfer to the naval repair base at Cat Lo, Vietnam, in 1969. Gunners Mate Second Class Ray Alger (USCG) performed boarding missions from CGC *Point Orient* in 1966–1967. GM2 Alger explained how dangerous the boarding of fishing sampans and cargo carrying junks was in night missions, not knowing whether the occupants were peaceful civilians or armed VC smuggling contraband to enemy troops on shore. Petty Officer Alger also participated in medical support missions to assist sick and injured Vietnamese civilians in sampans, in junks, and on shore.

Chief Warrant Officer Third Class (CW03) Spencer Herbert (USCG) was associated with the construction and manning of a top-secret coast LORAN station that guided bombers and fighter planes to and from enemy targets and air and sea craft on SAR missions. Gunners Mate Chief Ken Spoor (USCG) was assigned to an explosives loading detachment (ELD) in 1969, and port security and waterways detachment (PS&WD) in 1970 after Coast Guard officials responded to a request for USCG assets from the U.S. Army First Logistical Command at Cam Ranh Bay. GMC Spoor recalled how constant vigilance was required to thwart the attempts of enemy sappers to attach underwater explosive charges to ship anchor chains. Coast Guard and Navy Special Forces (SEALS) swimmers periodically inspected the undersides of merchant and military vessels, including Coast Guard buoy tenders on ATN missions. U.S. Navy and Coast Guard teams periodically tossed hand grenades into the waters around vessels and buoys to kill or deter enemy sapper sabotage missions.[4]

The Coast Guard WPB 82-foot patrol craft were upgraded with 50-caliber machine guns, and at the creative suggestion of a Coast Guard CWO (chief warrant officer), the MGs were attached to 81-mm mortar launchers

USCGC *Point Hudson* (WPB-82322) on patrol on the Saigon River in Vietnam (March 1966). These 82-foot Coast Guard patrol boats inspected Vietnamese boats for contraband and intercepted enemy trawlers carrying weapons and supplies to the Viet Cong.

which provided extraordinarily long range lethal firepower for river and shore firesupport missions and attacks on steelhulled, armed enemy cargo transport junks, a hazardous and essential mission. One captured enemy junk allegedly gave up 250 tons of military contraband.

The CGC *Point White* fired upon a junk. Reciprocal fire ended with the *Point White* crew reverting to the peacetime Coast Guard mission of life saving and taking wounded VC survivors on board. One high-ranking enemy combatant was so grateful for the humane medical treatment he received on *Point White* and at a subsequent medical facility ashore that the then POW revealed valuable strategic and tactical information to his benevolent foes. For his tactical seamanship skills in the shootout, the *Point White,* commander Lt. Eugene J. Hickey (USCG), received the Silver Star. The cutter gun crew also received commendations.[5]

The dangers of combat patrol included unfortunate friendly-fire incidents. The CGC *Point Welcome* was attacked by a U.S. bomber and fighter plane in a one-hour engagement of failed radio communications and evasive tactics that left two fatalities (vessel commander Lt. [jg] David C. Brostrom and Engineman Second Class Jerry Philipps) and every surviving crewmember wounded. *Point Welcome's* executive officer Lt. (jg) Ross Bell steadily gave commands lying on the deck of the destroyed bridge, was rescued from the water by CGC *Point Caution,* and later endured extensive surgery at the USMC field hospital at Phu Bai.[6]

Chief Boatswain's Mate Richard H. Patterson received a Bronze Star and Combat "V" for his skillful maneuvering of the *Point Welcome* under fire and the successful abandon-ship process under VC and then initial friendly Vietnamese fire from shore. The heavily damaged but durable *Point Welcome* was eventually floated free of its shoal grounding and sailed back to Da Nang under its own power.[7]

The Market Time high-endurance cutters (WHECs) sailed offshore on deepwater coastal surveillance and interdiction missions. Armament included a 5-inch 38-caliber deck gun and several machine guns. The WHECs furnished fire support for ground forces. Lt. Ray Houttekier, on the CGC *Chase* (1969–1970), said the five-inch guns could "fire a shell 9 miles for USA or USMC support."[8]

Cmdr. Wayne Caldwell, USCG Squadron Three, served on the CGC *Chase* (1969–1970), provided medical support to troops and civilians, and calculated that the WHEC fired 77,000 rounds of ammunition in support of ground troops.

The heroic story of Lt. Jack C. Rittichier (USCG) was related in the previous chapter. Killed in combat action on a rescue mission flying a USAF Jolly Green Giant helicopter, Rittichier died a hero's death. Lt. Cmdr. Lonnie Mixon, Rittichier's SAR colleague and friend, said the Coast Guard aviators volunteered for SAR slots, and described the missions as "dangerous and rewarding."[9] Lt. Jack K. Stice (USCG) flew Jolly Green helicopter SAR missions in 1972 and recalled how the USAF requested USCG pilots because they were used to flying missions over land and sea. Lt. Stice rescued the two-man crew of a U.S. fighter plane who ejected into the sea following an enemy missile hit. Stice said he and other helicopter rescue pilots dodged rockets, missiles and enemy bullets in the course of their missions.[10]

In the course of the dangerous rescue missions, U.S. Coast Guard SAR pilots were awarded 4 Silver Stars, 16 Distinguished Flying Crosses, and 87 Air Medals.[11] Lt. (jg) Jerry Underwood was in command of the 82-foot WPB *Point Banks* (21–22 January 1969) off the port of Cam Rahn Bay when radio reports of nine ARVN rangers surrounded by VC units reached the cutter. GM2 Willis J. Goff and EM2 Larry D. Villarreal volunteered to take the cutter's 14-foot Boston Whaler into the dark midnight waters and break onto shore through high surf to rescue the rangers. Wearing flak jackets and helmets, Villarreal piloted the boat, and Goff manned the M-60 machine gun. A Navy PCF heard the *Point Banks* radio communications and closed in to offer fire support and SAR potential. GM2 Goff and EM2 Villarreal made two trips to and from the beach giving and taking heavy enemy gunfire under the light of WPB and PCF gunfire. The U.S. Navy awarded citations for Silver Star medals to Villarreal and Goff.[12]

WPB patrol boat combat action kept brave Coast Guard crews challenged and occupied. The USCG helicopter SAR pilots faced similar combat action and diverse danger. On 2 July 1968, two Jolly Green Giant helicopters launched from a forward airstrip south of the DMZ bordering North Vietnam. One of the pilots of the USAF SAR helicopter, Lt. Lance A. Eagan (USCG), endured heavy enemy antiaircraft fire that shook his helicopter as he descended over the last reported position of a downed American fighter pilot. Radio contact revealed that the downed aviator was immobile with a broken back. Airman First Class Joel Talley (USAF) volunteered to descend into the jungle canopy to reach the aviator. Contact was made. Lt. Eagan lowered the cable hoist penetrator chair while in a stationary hover and lifted the para-rescueman and aviator over the treeline as NVA snipers shot through the plexiglass cockpit windshield. As Eagan described the situation, he "took off with the two of them swinging fifty feet below the aircraft." Upon landing at Da Nang, Lt. Eagan's survey of his aircraft revealed 40 bullet hits and damaged rotors. For their conspicuous courage under fire, Lt. Eagan received the Silver Star, and Airman Talley earned the Air Force Cross.[13]

Lt. Cmdr. James M. Loomis (USCG) recalled his training for HH-3E and HH-53-C USAF helicopters at Sheppard Air Force Base in Texas and Elgin Air Force Base in Florida. Fixed-wing aviation, refueling, and survival training were included in the rigorous curriculum, and all of those skills were applied in ARRS (U.S. Air Force Aero- Rescue and Recovery Squadron) combat missions in Vietnam.[14]

Capt. Joseph L. Crowe was a Coast Guard exchange pilot and officer in Vietnam in 1971–1972. Crowe explained how pilots and crews were trained and assigned to different tactical missions in the diverse Vietnam jungle, highland,

and maritime environments. Crowe said Coast Guard pilots were often assigned "missions at sea" and were more experienced than USAF aviators "with the intricacies of hoisting from a rolling ship."[15] While in Vietnam, Lt. Cmdr. Crowe (USCG) was assigned the responsibility of 37th ARRS operational planning officer and was no longer allowed to fly SAR missions because of his knowledge of classified tactical planning and the associated vulnerability to capture by the NVA/VC should his helicopter be shot down.[16]

In 1973, with the signing of the Paris Peace Agreement, POWs were exchanged between North Vietnam and the government of South Vietnam and the United States. Official U.S. combat ended, but support for the GSV continued for a time. The Coast Guard Jolly Green Giant rescue missions ended from bases in South Vietnam and Thailand in July 1973. In the interim between 1973 and 1975, combat between NV and SV continued until the surrender of South Vietnam and unification of Vietnam under Communist control as of 30 April 1975. In that year the remaining LORAN-C stations were evacuated and disestablished in Thailand and Vietnam.[17]

Equally significant and dangerous, if less heralded, missions by port security and waterways explosives loading and aids to navigation detachments contributed enormously to American successes in the Vietnam War. Maj. Gen. C.W. Eifler (USA) of the First Logistical Command reported that Coast Guard ELDs, "despite adverse conditions, maintained port security and explosive safety at our ports at a remarkably high level, and no serious incidents have occurred.... Their accomplishments in the Republic of Vietnam merit the highest praise and add luster to the reputation of the United States Coast Guard."[18]

Adm. Edwin J. Roland, the commandant of the Coast Guard, appeared in Saigon in July 1965 to visit Squadron One cutters and Rear Adm. Norvell G. Ward (USN), the naval advisory group chief. Adm. Ward asked Adm. Roland for a senior Coast Guard port security officer to assist the USN. And on 4 August 1965 the commander of the Military Assistance Command Vietnam (MACV) also requested PS assistance from the USCG to improve port security in Saigon. The Vietnam port security mission was immediately assigned by Coast Guard headquarters (Washington, D.C.) operations chief Rear Adm. William W. Childress to Cmdr. Risto A. Matilla (USCG), chief of the ports and waterways security division. Cmdr. Matilla responded to the Pentagon request for a port security chief in Saigon and subsequently went to Vietnam to work under Adm. Ward (USN). Cmdr. Matilla's investigation of port security and explosives loading in the port of Saigon revealed dangerous discrepancies, inadequacies and pilferage, which subsequent reforms, rigorous inspections, training and supervision ameliorated. Infrastructure improvements and security screening for Viet Cong infiltrators were essential and successful as additional specialized Coast Guard personnel were assigned to the operations.[19]

ATN crews and cutters (buoy tenders) were essential to port, harbor area, and coastal navigational safety and commercial and military ship movements and operations. In its 1971 deployment, the CGC *Blackhaw* was ordered to construct a naval gunfire support buoy in the shallow waters of coastal Thailand. A low shoreline provided a deficient radar image that posed a navigational hazard. And a buoy that reflected radar images was necessary to facilitate gunfire support for military teams in land operations. *Blackhaw* crew members sent a construction party ashore in Viet Cong–controlled territory to set up a radar-reflecting device so the buoy tender could calculate range statistics for naval vessels. After the reflecting buoy was positioned the *Blackhaw* sailed to a strategic island off the Vietnam coast (Paulo Obi), where the crew carried heavy batteries up a mountainside to power a navigation light. Next, at the mouth of the river entrance to a USN Sea float base, *Blackhaw* machine gunners guarded the repair crew as it repaired the dominant station light. Vigilance was constantly necessary to thwart VC operations that sank buoys and shot out navigation lights, and to replace buoys displaced by storms or inadvertently struck by military and commercial vessels. The Coast Guard buoy tenders were up to this combat action task as they went about their ATN responsibilities.[20]

The 180-foot seagoing buoy tenders (WLBs) that served in Vietnam in addition to the USCGC *Blackhaw* (WLB-390) were the CGCs *Basswood* (WLB-388), *Ironwood* (WLB-297), and *Planetree* (WLB-307). The Coast Guard also crewed the cargo vessel CGC *Nettle* (WAK-169).[21] The *Basswood*, *Blackhaw*, and *Planetree* were built at Marine Iron and Shipbuilding Corporation in Duluth, Minnesota, and launched in 1943 during World War II. The CGC *Ironwood* was launched in 1943 at Coast Guard Yard in Curtis Bay, Maryland.[22] The WLBs were also designated as WAGLs (icebreakers).

According to the research list of historian Eugene Tulich, 26 82-foot WPB patrol boats of the USCG were assigned to Coast Guard Squadron One (Divisions 11, 12, and 13) in Vietnam. And 32 WHEC (high endurance ocean-going cutters) served in Vietnamese waters during the war. Several of the WHECs in Vietnam carried famed World War II cutter names and included the *Androscoggin*, *Duane*, *Campbell*, *Bibb*, *Ingham*, *Spencer*, and *Taney*.[23]

The civilian life-saving mission of the Coast Guard was performed well in Vietnam. Coast Guard personnel proved again, as they had throughout the history of the U.S. Revenue Cutter Service and the U.S. Coast Guard, that the lifesavers could also perform professionally as warriors alongside other U.S. Armed Forces units.

The *Point Welcome* incident, discussed previously, illustrated the training, courage and combatant capacity of Coast Guard personnel in Vietnam. Historian Paul C. Scotti described how the CGC *Point Welcome* came under "friendly fire" strafing attacks by a U.S. Air Force B-57 Canberra and F-4 Phantoms near the 17th parallel and DMZ between North and South Vietnam. Scotti said the Coast Guard patrols were not "unusual" and had been occurring "for more than a year as Coastguardsmen sought to intercept enemy movements."[24] The USAF was evidently unaware of U.S. naval activity in the area, and the pilots later said they were told, Scotti reported, that "there were no friendly maritime operations in progress." The USAF error was attributed to "poor information sharing, pilot zealousness, failure to follow recognition procedures, and just plain bad luck."[25]

The importance of the Coast Guard explosive loading detachments (ELDs) in Vietnam, and especially in the Port of Saigon, is revealed by the facts that ships carried 98 percent of the supplies for the Vietnam War and no serious sabotage or explosives incidents occurred under USCG jurisdiction and supervision; and the USCG closely supervised the proper storage of ammunition in warehouses so that "accidental detonations" did not occur.[26] Coast Guard vigilance and courage were exhibited by GM1 Joseph R. Glenn (USCG) who received the Bronze Star Medal for apprehending five Viet Cong attempting to sabotage an ammunition ship in the harbor of Da Nang. GM1 Glenn was alone and armed with just a .45 caliber pistol.[27]

Engineman First Class Robert J. Yered (USCG) is another port security ELD hero in Vietnam. EN1 Yered responded to a VC attack in the port waters of Cat Lai in February 1968. A barge containing mortar ammunition was burning. EN1 Yered climbed into the burning barge armed with a water hose, threw burning shells overboard, and put out the fires despite the risk of explosion. Military police chased the VC away from the surrounding marshes, and a U.S. Army sergeant came to Yered's assistance. The U.S. Army later awarded Petty Officer Robert J. Yered a Silver Star.[28]

U.S. Coast Guard ELDs supervised explosive loading and unloading on military and commercial vessels in port and at sea. Coast Guard and Army personnel worked together to supervise the dangerous cargo process. Coast Guard explosives loading detachments and port security and waterways details (PS&WDs) overlapped and cooperated in these related port security operations. Civilian ships were inspected and crews trained. Safety breaches were monitored, and dangerous behavior could be punished by fines, license revocation and military custody.[29]

By the end of 1968 public support for the war was diminishing, President Johnson had decided not to run for a second elected term, and Richard Nixon was president-elect. Nixon continued Johnson's policy of "Vietnamization," which meant gradually drawing down and withdrawing U.S. forces and training and turning the war over to the Army of South Vietnam (ARVN) and the South Vietnamese Navy (VNN). In South Vietnam, Vice Adm. Elmo Zumwalt (USN) presented U.S. Army commander General Creighton Abrams with the plans for transferring U.S. Navy and Coast Guard assets to the VNN by mid–1970.[30]

Captain Ralph W. Niesz (USCG), a liaison officer at the U.S. Naval War College in NewPort, Rhode Island, developed the plan for turning over several 82-foot Coast Guard patrol boats (WPBs) to the VNN. With his familiarity with Navy operations plans, Capt. Niesz formulated ideas and then briefed Adm. Zumwalt (USN) and Commodore Tran Vann Chon, the VNN operations chief. In January 1969, Capt. Niesz presented his plan of operation for transferring the USCG WPBs to the VNN with the approval and satisfaction of Adm. Zumwalt and Commodore (Vice Adm.) Chon.[31]

Upon President Nixon's June 1969 meeting with President Nguyen Van Thieu in South Vietnam, 14 WPBs were due to be turned over to the VNN. Ten more WPBs and two 311-foot WHEC cutters were included in the $3 billion contribution.[32]

But problems loomed on the horizon, and perceptive U.S. Coastguardsmen noted them. Lt. (jg) Joseph F. Angelico commanded two WPBs (CGCs *Point Jefferson* and *Point Marone*) during the transition and worked with Vietnamese naval crews. Lt. Angelico concluded that the VNN crews "could operate (the WPBs) okay, but to them it was a job, not a career. They didn't run it the way we did.... Once (the) boats were turned over, almost all maintenance ceased. They ran equipment until it stopped running. They ran the electronics until it just didn't work anymore."[33]

Captain Thomas G. Volkle (USCG), a lieutenant commander in Vietnam, said VNN AWOLs were a serious issue during the time of the transfer takeover. Absence without leave problems affected enlisted and officer ranks in the VNN. "At Da Nang," Volkle said, "even commanding officers were dragged back in handcuffs. That's when I began to realize [Vietnamization] just wasn't going to work."[34]

There were reports of VNN crews abandoning cutters for days at a time during national holidays. Master Chief Gunner's Mate William R. Wells (USCG) said that during their vacation jaunts, VNN crews would even steal paint. GMCM Wells contended, "At first we thought we were doing something good and we really tried. But ... the Vietnamese were not 'gung ho' about it. They didn't have experience or willingness and they saw no end to the war.... If the boat didn't work, it meant they didn't have to go out."[35]

U.S. Coast Guard high-endurance oceangoing cutters (WHECs) were also offered to the South Vietnam government. The commander of naval forces in Vietnam, Vice Adm. Elmo R. Zumwalt, requested that Pentagon authorization "be sought for the turnover of two Coast Guard WHECs" to the VNN to "provide a more satisfactory all-weather detection and intercept capability in the outer Market Time patrol areas, enhance the Naval Gunfire Support capability of the VNN, and permit the release of U.S. military ships and men for other duties."[36]

In June 1972, Lt. Cmdr. Homer A. Purdy (USCG) took command of the PS&WD unit in Vietnam in preparation for the turnover of port security activities to the government of South Vietnam and its civilian and military personnel. Cmdr. Purdy was immediately confronted with VC sappers who blew up U.S. Army petroleum and lubricant storage infrastructure at Long Bin, and later a barge. The sabotage activity slowed down, Cmdr. Purdy concluded, when the Paris peace talks commenced. Purdy then managed to get the Coast Guard explosives loading manual published in Vietnamese to assist waterfront workers.[37]

By November 1972 the Coast Guard ELD units were turned over to indigenous personnel. At the end of January 1973 the Saigon PS&WD unit was disestablished at a U.S. Army awards celebration. By the end of the American commitment in Vietnam, more than 11 million tons of munitions and explosives were handled by Coast Guard PS&WD/ELD units without damage to cargoes, ships or infrastructure due to improper or unsafe handling errors.[38]

The PS&WD and ELD units earned three U.S. Army meritorious commendations; several Bronze Star, Silver Star, and Legion of Merit commendations and medals; and other Vietnamese and U.S. awards.[39] The U.S. Coast Guard completed its Vietnam mission with the full appreciation of all of the other U.S. Armed Forces and the government and military forces of South Vietnam. The Coast Guard enhanced its legacy, did honor to its responsibilities, and again proved that the USCG is indeed "Always Ready" ashore and afloat.

6

Cold War, Terror and Interdiction

The Cold War between the Eastern (Communist) Bloc and the Western (non–Communist) Bloc began with the end of World War II and the dissolution of the wartime alliance between the Soviet Union and Euro-America. The Cold War heated up in the Korean and Vietnam wars (covered in previous chapters) and continued on the diplomatic, economic, political, and espionage fronts.

The Cold War missions merged into drug and migration interdiction and the war on terror as the U.S. Coast Guard expanded its maritime mission into the 20th and 21st centuries.

The U.S. Armed Forces and the Western international institutions designed to thwart Soviet and Communist Chinese expansion (NATO and the UN, and various regional trade and military alliances and treaties) managed a general standoff with the Sino-Soviet Bloc and socialist–Marxist Third World. The "mutual assured destruction" posed by the Soviet and American nuclear arsenal exacerbated tensions but also was alleged to have maintained general peace.

The U.S. Coast Guard cooperated with other U.S., Canadian, European, and some Middle East military organizations and intelligence agencies to protect national and regional security as well as to carry out its traditional peacetime missions. On the home front, port security (PS), search and rescue (SAR), aids to navigation (ATN), weather, radio communications, and scientific and oceanic exploration assumed its historic importance. And, in the tradition of that maritime service, the USCG operated generally with too few personnel and too limited a budget. But expanded duties required a gradual increase in personnel and assets ashore and afloat.

Not all Coast Guard Cold War missions resulted in positive results or publicity. On 23 November 1970 when U.S.-Soviet tensions were high, radio operator Simus Kudirka from the Russian-controlled satellite nation of Lithuania attempted to defect to the United States. The Soviet fishing vessel FV *Sovietska*

Litva was moored in New England waters near the ironically named 210-foot CGC *Vigilant* (WMEC-617) off Martha's Vineyard in Massachusetts.

Kudirka made his intentions known to U.S. officials who were visiting on board the Soviet vessel discussing fisheries issues. *Vigilant* officers were unsuccessful in reaching the First U.S. Coast Guard District commander in Boston who was on sick leave. The district chief of staff contacted U.S. Coast Guard headquarters in Washington, D.C., which in turn sought advice from the weekend Foreign Service staff at the U.S. State Department that advised the *Vigilant* crew to do nothing until Kudirka got on board the cutter.

Meanwhile, the ailing First District commander, now informed of the incident, told the acting district commander to deny Kudirka's asylum request because that incident might terminate the fisheries discussions and place U.S. officials on the *Sovietska Litva* in danger. The defector got aboard the *Vigilant*, but district Coast Guard officials ordered Kudirka returned to the Soviet vessel and inexplicably allowed Soviet sailors aboard the cutter to subdue the fisherman and return him to the *Litva* in a Coast Guard small boat.

When President Richard M. Nixon heard of the incident of this concession to Soviet authorities in U.S. waters one mile off the Massachusetts coast, he was outraged, as were anti–Soviet demonstrators in several American cities. U.S. State Department, U.S. Coast Guard, and congressional hearings were conducted that resulted in reprimands, loss of command, and early retirements for several of the involved Coast Guard officers.[1]

U.S. diplomatic pressure contributed to the release of Simus Kudirka after four years in a Soviet prison camp. Kudirka's courageous story was chronicled in a television movie. Kudirka migrated to the United States where he lived for 30 years before returning to his native Lithuania.[2]

Another controversial Coast Guard mission incident involved national defense responsibilities. On 4 April 1997 the suspicious Russian M/V *Kapitan Man* was suspected of tracking and spying on a U.S. Navy nuclear submarine. The Russian vessel was tracked and photographed by a joint Royal Canadian Navy (RCN) and USN crew in a Canadian helicopter over U.S. waters in Puget Sound off the Pacific Northwest coast of Washington State. A Russian crew member is believed to have fired a laser beam at the RCN helicopter that damaged the eyes and affected the careers of the Canadian pilot and a USN intelligence officer.

Sensitive geopolitical considerations allegedly caused the administration of President William J. Clinton and the State Department to cover up the incident, pressure a USN and USCG joint boarding party to superficially search the Russian ship, and let the supposed merchant vessel sail into international waters free of sanctions.

The U.S. Department of Defense favored detaining the *Kapitan Man*, but the U.S. State Department allegedly intervened and warned the Russian embassy in Washington, D.C., of the pending USN-USCG boarding party search. The laser device was never found, and some observers concluded that the alerted Russian crew concealed or confiscated the laser device. Leaked classified documents revealed the Pentagon's conclusion that the laser incident was deliberate. The Russian ship was allowed to sail out of U.S. waters even before the medical exams of the injured Canadian and U.S. military officers were completed.[3]

Lt. Jack Daly, the wounded USN intelligence officer, was pressured not to talk to the news media but later testified that he had been "betrayed and sacrificed by our government for a political agenda, one that assumed our once most feared Cold War foe had become a friend we can trust."[4]

A personal inquiry by this author to the Thirteenth Coast Guard District in Seattle, Washington, revealed more information. Responding in a letter to the author's Freedom of Information Act (FOIA) request about the *Kapitan Man* incident, Cmdr. Michael J. Lodge (USCG) wrote, "no such report or synthesis" of political interference "exists." Cmdr. Lodge referred the author to FOIA district coordinator and assistant legal officer Lt. Melanie Bell (USCG) for further information.

Lt. Bell, a lawyer with expertise in admiralty law, reviewed the 1997 *Kapitan Man* file and suggested the Pentagon and State Department might possess information not available in USCG records. Lt. Bell forwarded to the author "any and all documents related to the 1997 *Kapitan Man* incident" as per a follow-up and more precisely worded request from this author. The documents revealed a very thorough and professional Coast Guard search procedure. The official U.S. Coast Guard reports contained no references to political pressure or federal or Russian obstructionism, although it appeared that some documents had been redacted or withheld.[5]

Coast Guard intelligence teams were effective in Port Security missions in World War I and World War II, and through the Cold War and War on Terror in the 20th and 21st centuries. U.S. military intelligence units cooperated and exchanged information across service lines to protect American in times of war and peace.

The Office of Naval Intelligence (ONI) provided strategic and national security information to federal government agencies and the other military services prior to Pearl Harbor and in subsequent eras. Naval intelligence during World War II expanded to approximately 2,000 personnel in the Joint Intelligence Command Pacific Ocean Area (JICPOA) and included USN, USMC, and USCG personnel.[6]

Coast Guard Intelligence (CGI) operatives worked with ONI personnel in the Pacific and Atlantic theaters and with the Office of Strategic Services (OSS) before that agency became the Central Intelligence Agency (CIA). The OSS utilized Coast Guard signals and information intercepts. Coast Guard regulars and civilian members of the Coast Guard Auxiliary were utilized in port security operations and in swimming, diving, and boat handling missions. Fifty-six Coast Guardsmen worked in the OSS maritime unit in Asia. Field commander Lt. John P. Booth (USCGR) earned the Bronze Star for his mission leadership in Southeast Asia.[7]

Commander Frank Erickson (USCG) instructed Brig. Gen. William Donovan (USA), the OSS director, and Gen. Frank Lowe (USA) about the new Sikorsky helicopter and helicopter aviation. In 1943 Cmdr. Erickson commanded the first military helicopter school at New York Coast Guard Air Station (CGAS), Floyd Bennett Field.[8]

Military intelligence units are trained to gather information with a variety of methods including human observation; map, aerial and ground photography; filmmaking; electronic surveillance; imagery creation and interpretation; interrogation of civilians, migrants, prisoners of war (POW) and other detainees; historical studies of allied and adversary military units; combat and counterintelligence operations; and linguistic experts and interpreters.

During the Cold War, pilotless aircraft (drones) were used for intelligence gathering. In the War on Terror, weaponized drones were used against Middle East terrorists. Cell phones, computers and satellite technology have been utilized. Record analysts and filing systems have been enriched by state-of-the-art technology and computer techniques. Simple and more traditional techniques have been use as well, like pencils, pens, notebooks, sound recordings and telephone taps.[9]

Coast Guard Intelligence is the military intelligence unit of the U.S. Coast Guard. CGI has been active since the World War I era. The Coast Guard stations liaison officers in the Pentagon in Washington, D.C. The service has long cooperated with the other U.S. Armed Forces. The United States Army worked closely with the United States Coast Guard during Prohibition, and ashore and overseas in World War II.

The main U.S. Army Intelligence unit is referred to as G-2. U.S. Army Intelligence (USAI) was an integral part of the national defense system during the Cold War, USAI operations were instrumental in gathering information and protecting America from such Cold War adversaries as the Soviet Union, the People's Republic of China, the Soviet satellite nations of Eastern Europe, and the Communist government of Cuban dictator Fidel Castro.

Neil Sheehan wrote the Vietnam War classic *A Bright Shining Lie.* Sheehan was a war correspondent for United Press International (UPI) and the *New York Times*. From that experience as a reporter, author, and military historian, Sheehan wrote *A Fiery Peace in a Cold War* (2009), the story of General Bernard Schriever (USAAF/USAF). Gen. Schriever was the technical genius who, in the 1950s, led the way in the development of intercontinental ballistic missiles (ICBMs). ICBMs were intended to thwart the Soviet quest for nuclear superiority in the Cold War era and contain the geopolitical expansion of the Union of Soviet Socialist Republics (USSR).

General Schriever flew wartime air combat missions in World War II and believed missiles should and would supplement, if not replace, manned strategic bombers. That conclusion caused serious conflict between Gen. Schriever and the battle-hardened World War II USAAF hero Gen. Curtis LeMay (USAAF/USAF). General LeMay characterized the fledgling Atlas missile as just "a &*^%# firecracker." LeMay had turf and ideology to protect as the head of the Strategic Air Command (SAC) and the massive USAF B-29 strategic bomber force. SAC pilots and crews were trained to protect American territory and launch nuclear attacks in time of war upon Soviet territory. General LeMay ultimately failed in his attempt to isolate and discredit General Schriever.

General Bernard Schriever believed United States naval forces (the U.S. Navy and U.S. Coast Guard) could no longer be the ultimate defenders of the U.S. maritime realm. Naval sea power was no longer sufficient to protect America. Gen. Schriever thought the former USAAF and subsequently the USAF had evolved into the key elements of modern national defense.

U.S. military and political leaders realized the balance-of-power threat posed by the Soviet Union (USSR) after World War II. America had aligned with the USSR to defeat the Nazi and Fascist nations of Germany, Italy, and Japan. The Soviets conquered Eastern Europe during the war and seemed poised to expand further west into non–Communist Europe.

Schriever earned a postgraduate degree in aeronautical engineering and realized the importance of enlisting civilian scientists from industry and academia for ICBM research and testing programs. By 1962 he had earned four stars and had perfected his missiles.[10]

General Schriever persisted even as experimental missiles exploded at the launching sites at Cape Canaveral, Florida. Cape Canaveral is an isolated insular region where, as author Neil Sheehan described, a variety of dangerous predators existed, and "the Coast Guard manned a lighthouse at the end of the Cape where the small crew traveled back and forth by boat."[11] After 1968 when manned space flights occurred, the Coast Guard stayed on site to monitor space shots and assist the U.S. Navy in securing the space shuttles and crews upon their earth landings and splashdowns.

During World War II and the Cold War until 1980, the U.S. government administered a secret program that intercepted and broke Soviet codes and telegraph communications between Moscow and its agents and Communist Party members in the West. The program was initiated in 1943 by the U.S. Army Signal Intelligence Service (USASIS), later called the National Security Agency (NSA). The interception program was called VENONA.

The Soviet intelligence services, known by several historical acronyms, most famously the NKVD, operated within the Soviet government, Navy and Army. From the intercepts, the U.S. government learned that members of the Communist Party of the United States (CPUSA) committed espionage for the USSR and penetrated into the highest levels of the federal government and even the U.S. military. Disgruntled CPUSA members and Soviet agents shared information with the Federal Bureau of Investigation (FBI). Pro-Soviet Americans were found in government, journalism, and academia. Pro-Soviet public servants Alger Hiss (State Department) and Harry Dexter White (Treasury Department) served in the administrations of presidents Roosevelt and Truman.

When the Soviet Communist government fell, the new regime opened its secret files to American scholars. Some of the names of American agents were confirmed from the VENONA project when the files were made available to the public between 1995 and 1997.

Also affirmed was U.S. Senator Joseph McCarthy of Wisconsin, whose contentious and controversial Senate hearings involved testimony, accusations, and the naming of alleged national security threats, CPUSA members, and Soviet agents who either worked in the federal government or received or transmitted classified information. Senator McCarthy was vilified and censored by Senate colleagues and administration figures who resented his belligerent, aggressive tactics and embarrassing assertions. The VENONA files vindicated the deceased senator and revealed that McCarthy had actually underestimated the extent of the national security problem. Several persons exonerated after the hearings had in fact been guilty of the charges. Pro-Communist Americans and Soviet agents had even penetrated the U.S. Navy, U.S. Army, Justice Department, and the OSS.

The Federal Bureau of Investigation was aware of the Communist subversion. FBI Director J. Edgar Hoover cooperated with Senator McCarthy and furnished him classified information. Hoover later became disenchanted with McCarthy for revealing some information too carelessly.

President Harry S Truman was aware of some Communist infiltration into the federal government, but critics say he demeaned the "McCarthyites" for political reasons, as did some of McCarthy's Democratic colleagues in the

Senate. Politicians were vulnerable, and perceived lapses in national security could cause election losses. Truman was aware of the security problem because he had initiated punitive anti–Communist policies with congressional approval even before Senator McCarthy began his notorious "witch hunts" and "red herring" tactics, as his critics alleged.

The Cold War was also waged in Canada. A Communist spy ring was uncovered early in the Cold War in that otherwise peaceful, prosperous and stable nation. Allied with the United States in World War II, and antagonistic to the Soviet threat, Canada became a target for Communist espionage and Soviet recruitment of pro–Communist operatives and government employees.[12]

In September 1945 Igor Gouzenko defected to Canadian security officials from the Soviet embassy in Ottawa. Gouzenko had documents that revealed Soviet espionage in Canada and associated Canadian and U.S. operatives. Gouzenko provided evidence of the pro–Soviet sympathies of Joseph E. Davies, the former U.S. ambassador to the USSR. Davies stated his pro–Stalin feelings in a 19 February 1946 interview in the *New York Times*: "(Russia) in self-defense has every moral right to seek atomic-bomb secrets through military espionage if excluded from such information by her former fighting allies."[13]

The extent to which the Truman administration realized which government employees in the executive branch were pro–Soviet security risks or enemy agents has been debated by historians. There are indications that Truman knew of individuals, disregarded the evidence, and denounced Senator McCarthy for political considerations. FBI Director J. Edgar Hoover shared classified information with Senator McCarthy because he trusted the senator's intentions and shared his concerns. Hoover later withheld information from the senator as evidence of McCarthy's alleged alcoholism and undisciplined behavior became more apparent and classified leaks by McCarthy and his staff became increasingly ill timed and problematic. Hoover gradually distanced himself from the Wisconsin senator and came to depend more on his own FBI agents in investigative and internal security issues and tactics.[14]

The espionage and sabotage threats to the United States and Canada posed by the Soviet Bloc of nations illustrated the need for continued and enhanced U.S. Coast Guard port security missions in American ports, coastal regions, and the Great Lakes like the service did in World Wars I and II.

The Cold War conflicts in Korea and Vietnam required no less vigilance. The geographic proximity of the Soviet Union to Alaska and polar Canada required the cooperation of the U.S. Coast Guard, Army, and Navy; the CIA; and Canadian law enforcement, national security, and military agencies. The

Coast Guard maintained consistent communications and mission articulation with federal, state and local law enforcement, public safety, and customs and immigration agencies, and with their Canadian counterparts.

By 1950, the United States Coast Guard had 23,000 men and women in uniform as frontline protectors of America in its peacetime missions and port security responsibilities in the Cold War on guard protecting home waters against enemy espionage and sabotage. The major concern then and now was that a determined enemy could slip biochemical or nuclear weapons into U.S. ports and destroy economic infrastructures and heavily populated metropolitan areas.

The Coast Guard cooperated with the other U.S. Armed Forces and Canadian military, security, and law enforcement authorities in information sharing and the maintenance and monitoring of the Distant Early Warning (DEW) Line of radar stations pointed toward Soviet territory and over the polar region. Coast Guard cutters explored polar waters, carried out oceanographic and defense missions, and supplied military and civilian stations in the Arctic and Antarctic.

In 1958 the Automatic Merchant Vessel Reporting System (AMVER) was initiated. AMVER serves national security, economic, and SAR needs. Merchant vessels regularly report their positions to the U.S. Coast Guard. Vessels in adjacent maritime locations can be requested by the Coast Guard to assist ships in trouble. Vessels can also be tracked via information exchanges.

Since the 1960s, long-range Coast Guard civilian and commercial aircraft have changed ocean weather station and ice patrol operations. New technologies led to the phasing out of Coast Guard cutter ocean station patrols. Coast Guard air and sea platforms were gradually shifted to the North Pacific, Bering Sea, and North Atlantic regions on conservation, fisheries, SAR, and surveillance patrols as more Russian, Japanese and Chinese vessels plied those waters.

With the emergence of Fidel Castro and Communist Cuba and economic and political chaos in Haiti, the Coast Guard stepped up its immigration and narcotics interdiction missions in the Gulf of Mexico and the Caribbean Sea. The U.S. Navy and U.S. Coast Guard cooperated in these missions with shared crews and assets.[15]

In 1967 President Lyndon B. Johnson created the U.S. Department of Transportation (DOT) and transferred the U.S. Coast Guard from the Treasury Department into the DOT despite the initial objections of Treasury Secretary Henry Fowler and USCG commandant, Adm. Willard Smith. The Coast Guard continued its traditional missions under DOT in subsequent decades, saved thousands of migrants in unseaworthy craft, and confiscated thousands of tons of contraband drugs with commensurate arrests. Coast Guard law enforcement detachments out of Miami, Florida, were busy responding to the increasingly lucrative and dangerous drug trade[16] that required the expanded use of cutters, boarding craft, helicopters, fixed-wing surveillance aircraft, and mission articulation with Immigration, Customs, and Secret Service law enforcement units.

From the Hawaiian Islands to the Pacific Coast of North America, cutters patrolled the seas looking for ships violating pollution control and fisheries laws; protecting marine life; and interdicting narcotics smugglers and illegal immigrants.[17] Abandoned fishing nets and debris and pools of oil pollution had to be contained, retrieved, and tracked back to sources. In the 1990s, the space satellite transmitting Global Positioning System (GPS) was developed. GPS provided instantaneous and accurate tracking systems. The ATN system had been changing since the 1960s when new technology gradually made lighthouses and lighthouse keepers and crews obsolete. GPS led to the final decommissioning of Coast Guard–manned lighthouses. Lighthouses were sold to historical and commercial interests.[18] The U.S. Life-Saving Service Heritage Association (USLSSHA), a nonprofit organization, is dedicated to the historical preservation of lighthouses, lifeboat stations, and lifeboats.

Although challenged by domestic missions, the Coast Guard has always been prepared to cooperate with the other U.S. Armed Forces in international war and peacekeeping missions. When the USSR lost its European satellite states and again became known as Russia, Middle East turbulence attracted international attention. In 1990, Iraq dictator Saddam Hussein invaded oil-rich Kuwait. The United States and several UN members, including Arab states, intervened to restore Kuwaiti sovereignty. Coast Guard law enforcement detachments (LEDETs) joined the other U.S. Armed Forces and articulated with the U.S. Navy to enforce UN sanctions on Iraq and provide port security in harbor areas and secure petroleum refineries.

The Iraq War was divided into phases Operations Desert Shield and Desert Storm and involved 550 Coast Guard Reserve members from three activated port security units (PSUs), and another nearly 1,000 USCG Reservists called up to perform vessel boarding and inspection, and the supervision of explosive loading and other military ordnance. USCG personnel assisted in the capture of 23 POWs. U.S. Coast Guard personnel and assets would later return to the Persian Gulf with the other U.S. Armed Forces in a subsequent war called Operation Iraqi Freedom in 2003.

In 2001, Arab terrorists used domestic U.S. commercial aircraft to attack the United States. More will be covered about 11 September 2001 (9/11) in this and subsequent chapters. President George W. Bush responded to 9/11 by launching preemptive attacks in Afghanistan (2001) and Iraq (2003). In 2001 President Bush established the new cabinet-level Department of Homeland

Security (DHS). On 1 March 2003, U.S. Transportation Secretary Norman Yoshio Mineta oversaw the transfer of the U.S. Coast Guard yet again, this time to the DHS under its new director Tom Ridge.[19]

The Coast Guard role in domestic security was expanded after 2001. To meet the needs of the new missions, the expensive, controversial and long-range Integrated Deepwater System (IDS) program was initiated. The IDS plan was to build new, state-of-the-art Coast Guard shore, air, and sea assets to meet the needs of the 21st-century United States Coast Guard. The commissioned, enlisted, reserve, auxiliary and civilian complement of Team Coast Guard would commensurately be expanded.[20]

Cold War challenges led to Coast Guard administrative reorganization. In the 1980s, maritime defense zones were set up which gave Atlantic and Pacific area coastal defense responsibilities to USCG regional commanders within a USN defense command. Under the National Port Readiness Committee Network, captains of the port networked with Department of Defense (DOD) and Department of Transportation agencies to facilitate the secure transportation of military cargo in U.S. ports. The Special Interest Vessel program tracked and controlled Communist Bloc ships and the ships of various rogue nations in and out of American ports.

U.S. Coast Guard and U.S. Navy teams were involved in overseas port security activities. Coast Guard Reserve units were trained for domestic and overseas port security operations. Port security units were composed of 140 personnel operating well-armed 25-foot fast boats for harbor patrol in cooperation with U.S. Coast Guard and U.S. Navy Harbor defense commands. Port security sweeps even included bicycle patrols that monitored port facilities, pollution control, and boat safety practices.[21] The port security system facilitated successful USCG operations in the Iraq War phases of Desert Shield and Desert Storm. Persian Gulf–area port security and marine safety office detachments secured shore and harbor area facilities to protect military operations against enemy sabotage and to ensure the safe loading and unloading of military supplies. Coast Guard Reserve PSUs were deployed to Saudi Arabia in 1990, the first overseas deployment of USCG PSUs overseas. The PSUs operated under the U.S. Navy Harbor Defense Command.[22]

Since 11 September 2001, armed Coast Guard cutters, helicopters such as MH-68A StingRays, and crews have been assigned port security duties in major U.S. ports over petrochemical production facilities and around naval shipyards. Coast Guard boats and cutters have provided security to U.S. Navy submarines and surface warships entering and exiting U.S. harbors. Offshore oil rigs and civilian cruise liners also come under the surveillance and protection of Coast Guard maritime units.

Coast Guard onshore security protection with U.S. Immigration and Customs Enforcement (ICE) units includes the inspection of vessel shipping containers. The annual numbers are overwhelming. It has been estimated that 8,000 vessels make 51,000 port calls with 6 million shipboard containers per year. This onslaught of commerce provides terrorists the chance to smuggle in chemical, biological and nuclear devices that could be detonated in ports or major urban centers. Coast Guard and customs inspectors use advanced technology and canine patrols to randomly check cargoes for contraband, fluid leaks, radioactivity, and signs of damage or entry.[23]

When the Pentagon was attacked in Washington, D.C., on 11 September 2001, Rear Adm. Jeffrey J. Hathaway (USN) lost several members of his unit in the U.S. Navy Command Center. As Pentagon personnel responded to the 9/11 terror attacks, USCG small patrol and pursuit boats in New York Harbor patrolled the waterways assisting people in distress and forming defensive perimeters against possible attacks.

Coast Guard port security teams were immediately called up for active duty at home and overseas. PSU teams would be sent to the U.S. Navy base

This photograph came from a handout image provided by the USCG taken by a Coast Guard photographer. The photo shows Coast Guard Petty Officer Brett Patterson manning an M-240 machine gun on a Stingray MH-68A Helicopter Interdiction Tactical Squadron (HITRON) patrol over the New York City Harbor on 30 December 2003. The photograph appeared in *Life* on the same date and was attributed to U.S. Coast Guard/Getty Images.

USCG RHIB (rigid-hull inflatable boat) off Manhattan Island, New York City, on 11 September 2001 after the terrorist attacks on the World Trade Center towers. This photograph from the USCG image gallery was taken by Chan Irwin and provided by Mike Harmon.

at Guantanamo in Cuba (called GITMO) to patrol the perimeters of the facility where captured alleged terrorists, labeled "detainees," from Middle East battlefields were incarcerated and interrogated.[24]

Four days after terrorist attacks demolished the Twin Towers in New York City, Coast Guard chaplains were counseling injured and bereaved civilians and courageous police officers, firefighters and paramedics who endured the aftermath. Some rescuers gave up their health and lives in rescue attempts. Coast Guard personnel crawled though dust and debris and destruction monitoring the air pollution levels for the protection and safety of police and firefighters, construction workers, and paramedics in accordance with the standards set by the Environmental Protection Agency (EPA).

Armed Coast Guard patrol craft, including buoy tenders, patrolled New York Harbor areas and the Hudson River for reconnaissance purposes, to protect the valuable and vulnerable waterfront infrastructure and carry out the traditional law enforcement, national defense, search and rescue (SAR), and aids to navigation (ATN) missions the service had long been responsible for. On the day of 9/11 and after, Coast Guard helicopters and other USCG aircraft

USCGC *Juniper* (WLB-201) guards the Hudson River (NYC) on 17 September on port security duty after the 11 September 2001 terrorist attacks on the United States. The 225-foot oceangoing buoy tender's home port is Newport, Rhode Island. The state-of-the-art technology on the *Juniper* makes the cutter capable in all Coast Guard missions.

flew surveillance, SAR, and humanitarian missions, including the transport of medical supplies for injured victims.[25]

Coast Guard boarding crews checked passports and manifests on ships of interest from U.S. waters to the Persian Gulf. Drug enforcement and immigration interdiction in U.S. and international waters are also elements of the USCG national defense mission. Coast Guard helicopters with crews equipped with night-vision goggles thwarted drug and migrant smugglers. Coast Guard sharpshooters shot out the engines of fleeing craft, and small-boat boarding crews from adjacent cutters climbed on board boats, cargo ships, and fishing vessels in the Gulf of Mexico and Caribbean Sea.

Coast Guard crews in armed MH-68A helicopters guarded oil tankers coming into and going out of Alaskan ports. The petroleum and natural gas infrastructure throughout the United States would be guarded from terrorist attacks after the 9/11 tragedies. Armed Coast Guard Maritime Safety and Security Teams made up of regular and reserve Coast Guard personnel patrolled the 361 major U.S. seaports and bridge areas in fast, armed 25-foot reinforced defender class boats; medium- (WMEC) and high-endurance (WHEC) Coast Guard cutters patrolled coastal and international waters and the waters of strategic ports to protect the nation against other terrorist attacks. And Coast Guard divers searched ship hulls, decks and piers beneath the surface of the water for evidence of terrorist espionage. Coast Guard Commandant Thomas H. Collins (2004–2006) and Admiral Vern Clark (USN), chief of naval operations (CNO), signed a National Fleet Policy Agreement that forged integrated policies and operations for the post–9/11 era. Admiral Collins credited his predecessor, Admiral James M. Loy, who had served in the Vietnam War as a combat officer, for having the pre–9/11 foresight to expand Coast Guard national security capacities and training.

Immediately after the 11 September 2001, Adm. Loy called the White House and received permission to call up 5,000 U.S. Coast Guard Reserve (USCGR) members for active duty.[26]

USCG 25-foot Defender-class response patrol boat used in law enforcement, search and rescue, and port security missions.

As the nation confronted the War on Terror (WOT) after 11 September 2001, domestic security was threatened by the drug empire and the violence that ensued from shipping, buying and selling drugs in the chain from Latin America to North America. The War on Drugs (WOD) and the WOT had to be confronted. Drugs, illegal immigrants, and the gun trade threatened peaceful citizens on both sides of the U.S.-Mexican border. U.S. borders were regularly penetrated and had to be guarded on land and sea. The WOD and WOT absorbed limited federal, state, and local personnel and financial resources. The WOT was intertwined with the WOD because anti–American terrorists can just as easily penetrate U.S. borders and territory as do the drug cartels and illegal immigrant smugglers. Money garnered by the drug traders can be put to sinister uses by terrorist groups for bribery, communications, transportation, traditional weapons technology, and the acquisition of bio-chemical and nuclear weapons. The drugs, undocumented aliens, weapons, and terrorist challenges have seriously threatened the land and sea frontiers of the United States. The Coast Guard has teamed up with federal, state, and local agencies to defend America against those threats.

The Coast Guard fights the drug war near the American coasts and far out to sea in national and international waters. A 21-foot rigid-hull inflatable boat (RHIB) may disembark from a cutter and traverse the Sacramento River delta to load marijuana plants from the underbrush. Coast Guard targets and missions usually come from intelligence sources. The missions are often coordinated with the U.S. Drug Enforcement Administration (DEA) and U.S. Customs. Cutters at sea, or a cruising USCG patrol aircraft, might relay intelligence information to supporting units. Cutters chase suspect vessels and pursuit boats off the cutters, along

Adm. James M. Loy, USCG commandant (1998–2002). As commandant, Adm. Loy responded strategically and tactically to the 11 September 2001 terrorist attacks on America. Adm. Loy is a noted authority on leadership. Following his tour as commandant, Adm. Loy occupied various leadership posts in the Department of Homeland Security.

with helicopters and armed crews, take up the chase. USCG crews board the suspect vessels, and have found drugs hidden in hulls and under fish and iron ore cargoes. The armed, well-trained Coast Guard boarding teams impound narcotics, seize the boats and ships, and take the alleged perpetrators into custody and to port.[27]

Narcotics interdiction is a difficult and dangerous task on the high seas. Cargo ships and fishing vessels can offer many enclosed and complex spaces and hostile crews. Coast Guard boarding teams use special high-technology and periscope sighting devices to assist them in the surveillance and discovery process.

Drug smugglers and their ships and fast boats change routes as U.S. Navy, Army, and Coast Guard intelligence, sensors, air assets and boarding teams close in on them. Smugglers have varied their routes and contraband-carrying craft from the Caribbean Sea, Gulf of Mexico, Florida Straits and New England waters. Coast Guard air and sea craft have assisted the DEA in drug interdiction patrols even along the jungle rivers of Colombia.

The Interdiction Operations and Intelligence Center (IOIC) at Seventh District Coast Guard headquarters in Miami, Florida, is especially busy with the high frequency of drug and immigration interdiction cases. There is also a central clearing house for intelligence information at Coast Guard headquarters in Washington, D.C., called the Intelligence Coordination Center (ICC). The Maritime Intelligence Center (MIC) in Miami acquires and disseminates information on national security and economic threats like illegal immigration, fisheries violations, drug smuggling (mostly marijuana and cocaine), and terror activities. MIC coordinates its information and activities with the Department of Defense, federal law enforcement agencies, and foreign governments.

Coast Guard assets include personnel from shore stations, and camouflaged vehicles used in on and off-road situations along the Gulf of Mexico in what is called Operation Gulf Shield. Tense boat- and ship-boarding incidents challenge the U.S. Coast Guard along the maritime boundary in the North Pacific/Bering Sea region where Russian, Chinese, and Japanese fishing vessels meet. The Coast Guard has established cooperative relations and strategies with the naval forces of those nations in policing those geostrategic and economically significant waters.

The Coast Guard marine safety detachment (MSD) at Dutch Harbor, Alaska has used infrared video scope technology to check for heat emissions from the cargo containers of Asian vessels. The heat emissions may indicate stowaway undocumented human cargo from China.[28]

The post–World War II peacetime U.S. Coast Guard traditionally armed

This USCG 45-foot response boat–medium (RB-M) patrol boat participated in a major drug bust with U.S. Customs and Border Patrol out of San Juan, Puerto Rico, in the Caribbean. The successful contraband interdiction occurred on 30 January 2011. A CBP helicopter crew directed the CG patrol boat to the contraband vessel.

its oceangoing cutters and crews, but not the ships and boats on coastal and inland waters or the Great Lakes. It seemed incongruous for a life-saving service to be armed with deck guns, but small arms arsenals could be locked below decks. After 9/11, the arms and ordnance calculation changed.

Drug smugglers were increasingly armed and aggressive, and the threat of terrorism required the potential of armed response to them. With the formation of the Helicopter Interdiction Squadron (HITRON) and its associated armed boats and cutters out of Jacksonville, Florida, its first mission commenced in February 2002 with a more aggressive Coast Guard interdiction posture. In the first 10-month period, HITRON 10, with its new Helicopter MH-68A and support cutters and boats, arrested 90 suspected high-value smugglers. The USCG secured 30 boats that carried more than 2 tons of marijuana and 35 tons of cocaine, with an estimated $2 billion value.

Homeland Security Secretary Tom Ridge assessed the HITRON performance and predicted, "The use of Coast Guard HITRON for armed patrols will increase the level of security in our ports, provide an additional layer of defense, ensure the continued safe flow of commerce, and deter possible acts of terrorism in our nation's key ports."[29]

Throughout its history, the Coast Guard and its predecessor agencies have articulated missions with civilian agencies and the other U.S. Armed Forces. Platforms, assets and crews have interchanged and cross-trained, sharing the heritage and specialties of their separate missions and experiences. Members of the Pacific Area Coast Guard Tactical Law Enforcement Team Bravo, for example, have used U.S. Marine Corps obstacle courses to keep in shape for the challenges and potential confrontations associated with their professional responsibilities.

Cross-cultural missions and technical assistance and support are the watchwords of America's national security agencies. U.S. Coast Guard commandant, Adm. James M. Loy, had just appointed a new Coast Guard Intelligence director when 9/11 occurred.

The USCG was the beneficiary of increased federal funding and Department of Defense assistance in upgrading Coast Guard sensor systems and analytical processes. After the 9/11 attacks on Washington, D.C., and New York City, the Coast Guard joined the National Foreign Intelligence Program. Intelligence information exchanges increased the Coast Guard's ability to track and apprehend drug smugglers, seize formidable weapons caches, and enhance the service's "maritime domain awareness."[30]

To meet its diverse mission requirements, Coast Guard personnel undergo rigorous training. Coast Guard members exchange information with their colleagues in the U.S. Marine Corps, U.S. Navy, U.S. Army, and U.S. Air Force. Members of the USCG benefit from information exchanges and the combat experience of other military and naval personnel.

The USCG has benefitted from the lateral transfers of enlisted and commissioned officer personnel from the other U.S. Armed Forces into the Coast Guard. Service transferees are often motivated by the desire to participate in Coast Guard law enforcement, SAR, ATN, and national defense missions. These exchanges enhance the shared interests of the Defense Department and Department of Homeland Security.

The HITRON teams have shared training and information with Special Forces units of the other U.S. Armed Forces. Coast Guard and U.S. Navy instructors have exchanged training sessions on U.S. Army Apache attack helicopters; Coast Guard HH-65 Dolphins; and U.S. Marine Corps, USN, and U.S. Army helicopter assets. This military exchange and integration enables

A United States Coast Guard HITRON MH-68A helicopter pursues a Go-Fast boat of the type drug runners often use in this narcotics interdiction training scenario. The Stingray helicopter is specially equipped with communications and weapon technology to carry out drug interdiction and port security missions as opposed to traditional search and rescue duties. The crews on HITRON aircraft are trained to use nonlethal weapons to disable the engines of contraband go-fast boats. The helicopters operate off the decks of oceangoing cutters. Small RHIBs are dispatched from the cutters to chase down and board the go-fast boats as well-armed cutters and helicopter crews stand by.

Coast Guard personnel to achieve advanced weapons proficiency. USCG aviation crews have learned to use the M-240 and 7.62 mm machine guns, and RC-50 laser-sighted .50 caliber rifles. These weapons have been used to disable the outboard engines of contraband-carrying speedboats in Gulf of Mexico and Caribbean Sea Operation New Frontier missions.

Mission articulation and cross-training are essential policies because drug and migrant traffickers and terrorists use aircraft, sailboats, motor craft, boats, ships and freighters. The Coast Guard works with U.S. Immigration and Customs officials and has access to multiagency vessels, aircraft, radar and telecommunications networks. Mission articulation and interagency communications are essential elements of effective response strategies and tactics against the threats posed by illegal immigration, the War on Drugs, and the War on Terror.[31]

7

Natonal Defense on the Great Lakes

The interior lakes and rivers of the United States might seem relatively free of external threats and to have little need of surveillance and the protection of American law enforcement, national security and U.S. Armed Forces agencies. But the experiences of World War I, World War II, the Cold War, Vietnam, the Persian Gulf wars and War on Terror, and the drug and immigration interdiction missions suggest the ongoing vulnerability of inland waters to espionage, sabotage, and other national security threats.

The Great Lakes were vulnerable to national security threats and activities in the past, and the strategic shipping, economic, and infrastructure significance of the interior waterways and ports of the United States pose a tempting target for America's enemies and the Islamic extremists and other terrorists who threaten the United States in the air, on land, and sea. Nuclear, biological, chemical and traditional weapons of war are increasingly at the disposal of the adversaries of Western power and values.

In December 2009 on Christmas Day, an Islamic extremist terrorist from Nigeria managed to get on a Northwest Airlines flight from Amsterdam in the Netherlands to the Great Lakes city of Detroit, Michigan. The perpetrator ignited but failed to activate explosives concealed on his person and was subdued by passengers and crew 20 minutes out from landing in Detroit, the center of a large Muslim population.

Former Arizona governor Janet Napolitano, the secretary of Homeland Security, and the Obama administration came under heavy criticism for its perceived failure to react to previous information and warning flags, for initially describing the incident as proof "the system worked," and for claiming the "alleged" perpetrator was just a lone, isolated "extremist," when in fact 23-year-old Umar Farouk Abdulmutallab had been trained by Al Qaeda in Yemen.[1]

The 278 passengers on NWA Flight 273 were spared, but the incident illustrated the vulnerability of the United States to domestic and foreign terrorist threats anywhere within its borders on the ground, in the air, and on its waterways. That the terrorist was then handled as a criminal with civil rights and judicial protections and privileges instead of an enemy combatant illustrated another problematic aspect of the methods used by the federal government in the War on Terror.

Coast Guard law enforcement on the Great Lakes and other inland waters, and on the ocean and seacoasts, contributes to the economic and national defense missions of the service and the security of the United States. In addition to its ATN and SAR missions, the Coast Guard enforces federal maritime, customs, immigration, environmental, public safety and drug laws, and its port security and ship inspection responsibilities contribute directly to domestic legal, economic, and national defense needs. In carrying out these functions on the Great Lakes and other inland waters and river systems, the Coast Guard communicates and articulates with the other U.S. Armed Forces and local, state and federal law enforcement, public safety and national security agencies.

Since the 09/11 terrorist attacks and subsequent threats to America, the strategic responsibilities of the USCG on its own waters and along the maritime borders with Canada have increased. The Coast Guard articulates its maritime sea and land border and port security responsibilities with Canadian military and law enforcement agencies, including the Canadian Coast Guard.

In carrying out its Great Lakes missions, including icebreaking on the Great Lakes and the surveillance of the Sault Ste. Marie ("Soo") Locks and strategic infrastructure along the extensive maritime borders, the USCG coordinates its activities with U.S. Customs, Border Patrol, and DEA; the Departments of Defense, Transportation, Treasury, Interior, and Agriculture; the Bureau of Indian Affairs; and the various agencies and units of the Department of Homeland Security, which the Coast Guard has been part of since the founding of the DHS in 2003. Since 2003 several law enforcement agencies in the DHS have merged and acquired new names. Two examples are Customs and Border Patrol (CBP) and Immigration and Customs Enforcement (ICE). The Immigration and Naturalization Service and the Coast Guard inspect foreign vessels, cargoes, manifests, and crews and enforce compliance with U.S. immigration laws and regulations.[2]

Coast Guard responsibilities on the Great Lakes are extensive in the shipping season and during the several months of the cold, snow and ice of the region's humid continental winters where temperatures can descend to 20 degrees Fahrenheit below zero, with wind chills exceeding even those temperatures.

The extent of Great Lakes maritime activities is illustrated by foreign ship, flag and registry figures from 1969, numbers that have subsequently increased. Foreign cargo vessels and crews visiting the Twin Ports of Lake Superior at Duluth, Minnesota, and Superior, Wisconsin, in order of frequency included Europe, Canada, India, Japan, Africa, Israel, Latin America and the Caribbean, and Southeast and East Asia. The 171 visiting vessels carried more than 6,000 multinational crew members, 106 of whom were denied permission to go ashore because of criminal, immigration, and national security concerns. In that year, eight crew members deserted their ships in the Twin Ports, and all were apprehended.[3]

In 1983 the United States Supreme Court strengthened the maritime law enforcement authority of the USCG and other federal agencies in a decision that stated federal agents could randomly board boats, ships and other watercraft on inland waters adjacent to open waters. The six-to-three Supreme Court ruling decided such boarding and registration checks did not violate the privacy rights of boat operators and crews. The decision overruled a federal appeals court ruling that the random boarding of a vessel by a customs officer and a state trooper violated the Fourth Amendment protection against unreasonable searches and seizures. The U.S. Supreme Court reasoned that the kind of law enforcement spot-checks in roadblocks on land are not feasible on the nation's waterways, so maritime checks, boarding and seizures, by definition and procedure, must be random.

In his investigation of Coast Guard boarding authority in the absence of probable cause, reporter Jack Storey contended that the U.S. Supreme Court's expansion of federal authority in this maritime area reduced constitutional Bill of Rights protections. Storey did credit the Coast Guard with generally using appropriate discretion in its missions and conceded the necessity of random boarding given the lessons from the Prohibition era on the Great Lakes and the kinds of powerful watercraft used by contraband smugglers.[4]

After 1986 the USCG modified its random drug search policy when boaters registered complaints about alleged boarding without cause, and the perception that Great Lakes drug trafficking was negligible. Nonetheless, a Coast Guard official explained that law enforcement patrols would continue to target illegal activities and unsafe boating practices after U.S. Border Patrol (USBP) intelligence revealed increased illegal drug activity from Canada into Minnesota by Asian and Colombian smugglers. The USCG and USBP continued to cooperate with the Royal Canadian Mounted Police (RCMP) and Canadian Customs and share Great Lakes aerial and maritime reconnaissance information.[5]

In 1985 Cmdr. James Hanks, U.S. Coast Guard Group Duluth, informed the media that boarding officers and petty officers would now carry .45 caliber pistols. The new regulation put Great Lakes Coast Guard personnel in compliance with a nationwide law enforcement policy that the service had traditionally resisted but accepted after increased narcotics smuggling became evident.

Cmdr. Stanley Spurgeon of the USCG Marine Safety Office (MSO) in Duluth said Twin Ports officials cooperated with the drug and other contraband searches. But generally the smuggling problem on the Great Lakes was less significant than in South Atlantic, Caribbean and Gulf of Mexico waters because of the long distances between major ports and cities in the Twin Ports region, the relatively few cargo container ships that visited Duluth-Superior, and the three-months-long winters which closed the ports.

Nonetheless, the Coast Guard remained vigilant in boarding and searching private civilian boats and foreign and domestic merchant ships on the Great Lakes. In 1986, Ninth District (Great Lakes) Coast Guard commander, Rear Adm. Arnold Danielson, heralded more extensive cooperation between the USCG, customs, and the DEA in response to increased drug trafficking from Canada.[6]

U.S. Coast Guard and Canadian law enforcement and military authorities have in intelligence, surveillance, and apprehensions since 9/11. The U.S.-Canadian border is porous, and illegal immigrant and terrorist groups have had contacts. Significant Great Lakes urban areas of concern for terrorist group sympathies have included Toronto and Windsor, Canada; Detroit, Michigan; and Buffalo, New York. One suspect was arrested in Dearborn, Michigan, and charged with aiding Hezbollah, a Middle East terrorist organization. A convicted smuggler was arrested in Buffalo and charged with financing the journey of six Americans to an Al Qaeda training camp in Afghanistan.

Rear Adm. Robert J. Papp, as the Ninth District Coast Guard commander, relayed these incidents to the media after his 2005 appointment as district commander. Adm. Papp stressed the importance of the Coast Guard seizures of contraband, profits from which could fund terrorist cells. Contraband seized by the USCG included illegal drugs, alcohol and cigarettes, and weapons and dynamite. Adm. Papp revealed that investigations and apprehensions yielded "hockey bags filled with cash [and contraband with values up to] millions of dollars" on his watch. Adm. Papp said that between 2002 and 2004 Ninth District Coast Guard personnel arrested nearly 2,000 undocumented immigrants, many of whom, the admiral asserted, came "across the northern border from the target counties we are concerned about" and left abandoned rafts.

Responding to the contention that Great Lakes winter ice deters illegal activities, Adm. Papp contended that it was easier for law breakers to come across the ice than to use the warm season waterways where they could be pursued by Customs, Immigration, Canadian and U.S. Coast Guard patrol craft.[7]

Canadian civil, law enforcement, and naval authorities cooperate with the U.S. Coast Guard with a myriad of methods. Shared security and law enforcement missions include "ship rider" joint patrol boat missions that mitigate jurisdictional problems, a program encouraged by Rear Adm. Papp, the former Ninth Coast Guard District commander. Coast Guard and Canadian officials cooperate with surveillance and patrols in strategic choke points like the Soo Locks and around conventional and nuclear power plants and fuel stations. Canadian and U.S. air surveillance missions and information are shared, but Adm. Papp revealed that away from the Ontario, Canada, and Traverse City, Michigan, air stations "at the Western edge of Lake Superior" air cover was inadequate.

On the water, enlisted personnel have patrolled in RBS (rapid response boat–small) Homeland Security boats equipped with machine gun mounts. Historically the presence of armed Canadian and U.S. seacraft has been a problematic issue. Armed government vessels on the Great Lakes have been limited to emergency situations since the signing of the bilateral Rush–Bagot Agreement of 1817 after the War of 1812–14 between the United States and the British Commonwealth (and British Canada). In that time period the U.S. Revenue Marine (or U.S. Revenue Cutter Service), the Coast Guard predecessor, sailed the Great Lakes. As a revenue cutter, and not purely a warship, the armed presence did not alarm the British Canadians.

Since the Rush–Bagot Agreement, subsequent ongoing negotiations have modified the agreements in time of war (the Civil War, World Wars I and II, Korea, and Vietnam), and since the terrorist attacks on 9/11 and the War on Terror.

Joint ship inspections by Canadian and American military, customs and law enforcement personnel have been performed at various ports, including Massena, New York, and Montreal, Canada. International vessels are monitored prior to entry into Canadian and U.S. waters and the strategic St. Lawrence River. The Royal Canadian Navy (RCN) has administered the Maritime Security Operations Center at Halifax, Nova Scotia, and cooperates out of that station with U.S. Coast Guard surveillance and intelligence operations.

Adm. Papp explained that the U.S. and Canada have negotiated periodic "memorandums of understanding" that have allowed Canadian-American cooperation in SAR, icebreaking, law enforcement, and national defense missions, while "sovereignty concerns and Canadian unease with weapons carriage" periodically resurrect national sensitivities that have to be accommodated.[8]

In 2006 the Regular Coast Guard Great Lakes complement (excluding Coast Guard Reserve, Auxiliary and civilian personnel) numbered about 2,200, an increase since 9/11 of 400 people. For his exemplary administration of the Ninth Coast Guard District, in 2006 Rear Adm. Papp was being considered for advancement to the rank of vice admiral and for promotion to the chief of staff position at U.S. Coast Guard headquarters in Washington, D.C.[9]

Adm. James M. Loy (USCG, Ret.) was the first administrator of the Transportation Security Administration on 1 March 2003 after having served as Commandant of the Coast Guard from 1998 to 2002, and showed exemplary leadership in the aftermath of 9/11.

The 1964 U.S. Coast Guard Academy graduate served on six cutters and was a patrol boat commander in combat in Vietnam. Adm. Loy earned numerous Coast Guard and U.S. Navy commendations and awards. With noted leadership expert, author and historian Donald T. Phillips, James Loy coauthored *Character in Action: The U.S. Coast Guard on Leadership* (Naval Institute Press, 2003). In *Leadership*, Adm. Loy described the significance of the Coast Guard mission of Port Security, and the immediate and significant role the USCG played in response to the 11 September 2001 terrorist attacks upon the United States.

Adm. Loy did not neglect the significance of the Great Lakes in the 9/11 attacks and the subsequent role of the Great Lakes Coast Guard in regional port security and overall national security.

James M. Loy described the 1,500 miles of international maritime border between Canada and the United States that the USCG had to protect, and the strategic infrastructure along the shores of the St. Lawrence River and the Great Lakes of Superior, Michigan, Huron, Ontario, and Erie. Every large ship in that region was stopped; with Canadian military and law enforcement agencies, ships were monitored and inspected; and "in Chicago, every nuclear plant, every water intake system, every major coastal facility was secured." Coast Guard officers from District Nine Headquarters in Cleveland, Ohio, Adm. Loy asserted, rushed to New York City, the site of the 9/11 attacks (as was Washington, D.C.) to assist in planning logistical and tactical responses. Great Lakes captains of the port (COTPs) joined their national counterparts in increasing security in major harbor areas, and Great Lakes Coast Guard Auxiliarists and Reservists were called up to work alongside Coast Guard Regulars in maintaining national security. That Team Coast Guard administrative "alliance," Loy explained, allowed "the United States Coast Guard to double its forces overnight."[10]

The vulnerability to the Great Lakes region to potential terrorist and Islamic extremist acts is illustrated by a 2009 incident in which the FBI charged 10 men in Michigan with connections to an alleged "jihad scheme." Luqman Ameen Abdullah, previously known as Christopher Thomas, was shot to death after opening fire and refusing to surrender when FBI agents raided a warehouse in Dearborn, Michigan. Ten associates were arrested and charged with being armed and engaging in violent behavior, according to FBI spokespersons. Abdullah and his compatriots were members, according to the FBI, of a radical fundamentalist Sunni group that sought to establish an independent state governed by strict Islamic Sharia law. Detroit and Dearborn police and the FBI cooperated in a Joint Terrorism Task Force that successfully apprehended the suspects.[11]

In time of war and other threats to national security from the early 19th century to the present, the U.S. Coast Guard has teamed up with the U.S. Navy at home and overseas. And the Coast Guard has played a role in national defense throughout its history. The Great Lakes region contributed greatly to victory in World War II, which lasted in Europe and Asia from 1939 to 1945, and in which the United States was directly and officially involved from 1941 to 1945. The role of the Coast Guard in World War II was traced in chapter 2 of this book and will not be reviewed here except in so far as the Great Lakes region and U.S. Coast Guard District Nine contributed to victory in that war and in subsequent wars and national security threats.

Coast Guard cutters built at Great Lakes shipyards played a significant role in domestic security and in overseas combat theaters. Civilian workers and the U.S. Merchant Marine as well as domestic public safety agencies played an important role in World War II and in subsequent wars and national security events. Keeping commercial lanes open and establishing port and infrastructure security also protected the engines of commerce that fed the world and provided essential supplies to allies and military personnel. Coast Guard captains of the port (COTP) were stationed in U.S. commercial and military ports to protect port and national security in previous wars and in the War on Terror today.

By 1990 USCG Station Duluth had a complement of 100 active-duty and 40 reserve personnel, and included a Marine Safety Office (MSO) and the U.S. Coast Guard cutter *Sundew* (WLB-404), which by 2004 had been replaced by the 225-foot USCGC *Alder* (WLB-216) with a crew complement of 50, including approximately 8 officers and 40 enlisted personnel. The Duluth COTP's office shared a building with the U.S. Army Corps of Engineers

(USACE), and the USCG boat and cutter station is a short distance down shore on Lake Superior.[12]

Great Lakes Coast Guard active-duty (regular) and reserve personnel received orders in January 2003 to deploy for domestic and overseas duty in the Iraq War (Operation Enduring Freedom). Port Clinton (Ohio) Port Security Unit (PSU) 309 sent 117 personnel to join more than 500 deployed Coast Guard men and women assigned to land and sea security missions. Ninth District Coast Guard commander Vice Adm. James Hull explained the USCG–Defense Department coordination in national defense: "These deployments," explained Adm. Hull, "demonstrate how Coast Guard expertise can play an important role in the operation to fight terrorism and prepare for future contingencies."[13]

National security analyst Ben Brandt raised compelling post–9/11 national defense concerns about U.S./Mexico/Canada border security and cited alleged Minnesota and Great Lakes vulnerabilities. Brandt reviewed Minnesota's international airports at International Falls, Minneapolis, and Rochester. Brandt surveyed what he concluded were security weaknesses on Lake of the Woods, Lake Superior, and the Mississippi River. Brandt said the front line of defense in border and national security is the Immigration Service, Border Patrol, Customs Department, and United States Coast Guard.[14]

Coast Guard Station Erie (Pennsylvania) had traditionally welcomed public access and tour groups. After 9/11 the station gates were open only for the delivery of supplies and equipment, vehicles were closely inspected, and the Port of Erie was guarded by private security, the Erie-Western Pennsylvania Port Authority, U.S. Customs and the U.S. Coast Guard. The USCG increased its Great Lakes patrol frequencies with the acquisition of new 47-foot motor lifeboats (MLBs) and 21-foot rigid-hull inflatable boats (RHIBs). After 9/11, Great Lakes Coast Guard personnel were authorized to carry 9 mm handguns and utilize its arrest powers over civilians.

Vessels, companies and ports on the Great Lakes initially received only 2.6 percent of the federal funds appropriated for security enhancement in 2004. Coastal ports received most of the federal funds. Great Lakes port directors claimed they had to spend money on port security enhancement that was needed for infrastructure and technology. The U.S. Customs Service predicted cargo shipments through American ports would significantly increase in coming decades, and port officials could only speculate about how to manage the increased traffic and federally mandated port security enhancements. The USCG estimated that post–9/11 port security plans would cost more than $8 billion in the following decade.[15]

Coast Guard and customs authorities cooperated with port officials on national security, law enforcement, public safety and commercial issues in the Twin Ports and across the nation. A 1981 report issued by the U.S. Department of Commerce and its Foreign Trade Zones Board (FTZB) illustrates the evolving interagency cooperation. Notice was given of the request by the Duluth Port Authority to the FTZB to expand its trade zone region in the Duluth area. As per regulations, the board appointed an Examiners Committee to administer the application process. Committee members included Department of Commerce representatives, the district engineer from the Detroit office of the U.S. Army Corps of Engineers, and Robert W. Nordness, district director, U.S. Customs Service in Duluth.

The Coast Guard and customs and border protection have cooperated in the Twin Ports and commercial ports across the nation and overseas to protect the United States against illegal contraband, illegal immigrants, contaminated food supplies, and terrorism. USCG-CBP coordination was expanded with the Container Security Initiative (CSI) that was designed to monitor and inspect cargo containers that enter the U.S. in domestic and foreign ships, and to prevent the entry and detonation of weapons of mass destruction (WMDs).[16]

The Coast Guard has cooperated with the Duluth Seaway Port Authority (DSPA) in port security, maritime law enforcement, the facilitation of commerce, and national defense. The enormity of Coast Guard responsibilities in the Twin Ports of Duluth-Superior is illustrated by reviewing the structure, activities and geographic jurisdiction of the DSPA. Since 1954 the DSPA served the largest Great Lakes port and has ranked 16th or better nationally in terms of tonnage. In 2000 the Twin Ports of Duluth-Superior exported 91 percent of its cargo overseas.

Ships traveling from the Atlantic Ocean to the Twin Ports navigate the 2,340 miles of water in one week or less. The Twin Ports waterfront is 50 miles in length. In a 2004 DSPA report, it was calculated that the USCG and DSPA monitor and serve more than 1,000 ships annually at the grain, coal and iron ore docks and bulk terminal of the area. The port infrastructure has annually supported $2 billion of transshipped cargo, has had a $200 million regional economic impact, and has directly supported more than 2,000 jobs.

The leadership qualities expected and significance of port officials was illustrated by the 2004–5 appointment of the DSPA commissioner. Port Promotion Manager Lisa Marciniak informed the media that the Duluth City Council appointed General Ray Klosowski (USAF, Ret.), the former commander of the 148th Fighter Wing in Duluth and the Minnesota National Guard. Gen. Klosowski's military background and leadership experience was expected to facilitate effective articulation between the port authority and federal state and local law enforcement and other public safety and emergency response agencies, the myriad of commercial maritime and business interests in the Great Lakes region, and the United States Coast Guard.[17]

The Ninth Coast Guard District includes from east to west the Great Lakes shoreline states of New York, Pennsylvania, Ohio, Indiana, Illinois, Michigan, Wisconsin and Minnesota. The Great Lakes Coast Guard units service more than 3,000 ATNs (fixed aids to navigation lights and buoys); 9 captains of the port (COTPs), and 8 Marine Safety Offices (MSOs). Great Lakes combat-trained port security units (PSUs) have been deployed in conflicts to the Caribbean and Middle East.

In 2003 the Great Lakes District included 92 U.S. Coast Guard units, 48 stations, 188 small boats on shores stretching from Duluth, Minnesota, to New York City, in addition to two LORAN radio communications stations, two air stations, and ten large cutters (mostly buoy tenders and icebreakers) which are defined as boats of 65 feet or more in length which have crew berthing quarters.

The Great Lakes Coast Guard cutters range from 140 to 240 feet in length and are generally since 9/11 armed and technologically equipped for law enforcement, SAR, ATN and national defense missions.

By 2004, District Nine Coast Guard personnel had increased to 2,200 active duty, 1,100 reserve, and 190 civilian personnel, plus a civilian U.S. Coast Guard Auxiliary (USCGAUX) complement of 4,200.

Major shipbuilding facilities in Duluth-Superior and at Sturgeon Bay and Marinette in Wisconsin have built exemplary Coast Guard cutters, boats and other craft. The Ninth District Coast Guard headquarters is located in Cleveland, Ohio. Coast Guard air stations, using mostly helicopters, are located at Detroit and Traverse City, Michigan. Regional Group stations and Marine Safety Offices are located at Buffalo, New York; Sault Ste. Marie and Grand Haven, Michigan; Chicago, Illinois; Detroit, Michigan; Milwaukee, Wisconsin; and Toledo, Ohio. There is a busy Marine Safety and Ship Inspection Station in Sturgeon Bay, Wisconsin. The 225-foot USCGC *Alder* (WLB-216) is home ported at Duluth, Minnesota, and the 240-foot CGC *Mackinaw* (WLBB-30) is at Cheboygan, Michigan. Smaller lifeboat and SAR stations such as at Coast Guard Stations Bayfield, Wisconsin, on Lake Superior adjacent to Chequamegon Bay, and Saginaw, Michigan (on the Saginaw River off Saginaw Bay, an arm of Lake Huron), do ATN, SAR, and pollution control missions and are kept busy during boating and camping seasons.

Coast Guard Group Station Sault Ste. Marie (Michigan) guards the strategic "Soo" Locks as a Great Lakes–St. Lawrence River transit canal. The entire Great Lakes shoreline is filled with strategic infrastructure, power plants, and fuel depots that require vigilance against espionage, sabotage, and terror attacks. In 2005 Coast Guard Group/MSO Sector Sault Ste. Marie administered two MSOs, an ATN TEAM, two electronic support detachments, nine small boat stations, and six USCG cutters.

The Great Lakes Coast Guard air stations play a crucial role in SAR, harbor and lake surveillance, and icebreaking reconnaissance to assist Coast Guard icebreakers in finding vulnerable leads in the winter ice pack. Traverse City Coast Guard Air Station has assisted state and local law enforcement, conservation, and environmental protection agencies in surveillance and apprehension with its five 2006 vintage HH-65A Dolphin rotary-wing helicopters. Each aircraft can carry a trained first-responder crew complement that includes a pilot, copilot, rescue swimmer, and hoist-operator flight mechanic. State-of-the-art technology includes radar, telecommunications equipment, a powerful searchlight, and other life-saving aids. The Dolphins are capable of a 135 mph cruising speed and a 350-mile range.

USCGAS Traverse City has a base crew complement of 28 commissioned and warrant officers, 2 U.S. Public Health Service medical officers, and 100 enlisted personnel. As has been noted, the Great Lakes Coast Guard units coordinate missions and communications with federal, state and local law enforcement agencies and other public safety units and paramedic and firefighting stations, as well as with Canadian law enforcement and military agencies.[18]

Coast Guard missions coordinate with the U.S. Secret Service and contribute to the protection of the president of the United States and other federal officials when they visit maritime locations in the U.S. and Hawaii or on the Great Lakes. The Coast Guard uses cutters and boats to secure shorelines where significant meetings and large crowds assemble.

In 2009 the USCG received criticism for conducting security drills on the Potomac River near the White House on the anniversary of 9/11. In February 2006 the federal government and the USCG restricted air and river traffic on the waterways between Detroit, Michigan, and Windsor, Canada, up to 300 yards offshore at the scene of the National Football League Super Bowl game. Federal, state and local law enforcement agencies cooperated with Canadian maritime security officials in that mission.

Since 9/11 armed Coast Guard cutters and boats patrol waterways adjacent to other strategic and possible terrorist targets, such as in proximity to the Boston, Massachusetts, Airport. And the Coast Guard has acquired another mission from the U.S. Defense Department: the responsibility of armed helicopter patrols around the nation's Capitol (Congress) and the White House in Washington, D.C.

Coast Guard Air Station Detroit (Michigan) on the Great Lakes opened in 1966 and grew into the 2006 personnel complement of around 24 officers, 80 enlisted personnel, and 6 civilian employees. By 2006 USCGAS Detroit maintained five HH-65A Dolphin helicopters which provided 24-hour SAR, law enforcement, icebreaking, and pollution response capabilities along 1,100 miles of shoreline and out into the Great Lakes maritime domain as far as missions dictated. USCGAS Detroit hanger facilities are named after Lt. Jack C. Rittichier who was stationed at the air base from 1966 to 1968. Lt. Rittichier was killed by enemy fire on a USAF SAR mission in Vietnam. The Coast Guard aviator won the Distinguished Flying Cross and the Silver Star for his courage and sacrifice on SAR missions often behind enemy lines.[19]

The USCG MSO in Milwaukee, Wisconsin has been staffed with Regular, Reserve, and Auxiliary personnel. The 50 Reservists and 75 active-duty personnel at Group Milwaukee has operational command over western Lake Michigan from the Indiana coastline through Chicago, Milwaukee, Green Bay, Sturgeon Bay (where Bay Shipyard is located), and the Upper Peninsula of the state of Michigan. Coast Guard Marine Safety Detachment Sturgeon Bay (USCGMSD) is north of the city of Green Bay and the maritime enclosure of Green Bay, an expansive body of water that borders the peninsula between the bay and Lake Michigan, upon which the port of Sturgeon Bay is located.

USCGMSD cooperates with local and state police, Customs and Border Protection, the FBI, and local law enforcement and other public safety units. The Coast Guard MSD boards and inspects vessels in port under construction and repair, those vessels laid up for the winter, and ships in the shipyard and afloat. USCG ship and boat inspections are also administered at the Marinette Marine Corporation and Bay Shipbuilding Corporation in Wisconsin, and the Basic Marine Company in Michigan.

The Coast Guard Marine Safety Unit in Toledo, Ohio is located on the western side of Lake Erie. The Port Operations Department is charged with waterways management, ATN, waterfront facilities inspection, vessel boarding, pollution prevention and control, hazardous material and explosive loading, and harbor patrols.[20]

Post-9/11 security and law enforcement considerations have resulted in the arming of Great Lakes Coast Guard boats with machine gun deck mounts, and cutters with powerful M-60 machine guns (which can be concealed below deck) in addition to the traditional cache of small arms. The 225-foot buoy tender cutters have this armament capacity, as do the 140-foot icebreaking tugs in the Sault Ste. Marie and St. Mary's River region. Gun crews have trained with the M-60s but have incurred the animosity of tourists, inn and lodge keepers, fishing guides, and the mayors of shoreline urban settlements. Diplomatic discussions with Ninth District Coast Guard officials have occurred, and modifications have resulted.

USCGC *Acacia* executive officer Lt. Cary Codwin reported that his cutter was armed with heavy weaponry in 2004, but crews were not permitted to aggressively train with the weapons on the Great Lakes until diplomatic negotiations with Canada were completed. Petty Officer William Colclough, a spokesperson from Ninth District Coast Guard headquarters in Cleveland, told the media that the then new icebreaker CGC *Mackinaw* was scheduled to receive heavy weapon gun mounts "as circumstances require." Senior Chief Petty Officer Jeff Hall revealed that the "necessary circumstance" occurred during the 2006 Super Bowl in Detroit when the Coast Guard was assigned security detail in the maritime area. CPO Hall asserted, "Coast Guard ships and boats have to meet a certain response standard and have weapons on board for when you might need them."

On Wisconsin waters, Coast Guard Station Milwaukee maintained seven 25- to 41-foot patrol boats that could have gun mounts. Coast Guard Station Kenosha had a 25-foot response boat and a 41-foot utility boat, each capable of carrying gun mounts and heavy weapons.[21]

In 2006 the commander of the Ninth Coast Guard District, Rear Adm. John E. Crowley, Jr., reminded Team Coast Guard that the multimission responsibilities of the Coast Guard on the "inland seas" (Great Lakes) were ongoing and required training and vigilance.[22] Adm. Crowley then met with maritime-interested groups and for public relations purposes sought to mitigate the armed cutter controversy by modifying the schedules and suggesting that Coast Guard gunners might achieve their essential training on simulation computers at various instruction sites.

Rear Adm. James D. Hull was commander of the Ninth Coast Guard District when the four 9/11 airline attacks and crashes occurred in the Pennsylvania countryside, at the Twin Towers in New York City, and at the Pentagon in Washington, D.C. Within hours the Great Lakes area commander activated a Crisis Action Center, recalled Coast Guard Reservists to active duty, ordered full alert, and placed active-duty units on extended patrol duty. Adm. Hull formed a regional security task force and upgraded the security command structure across the Great Lakes district at the boat and air station, cutter and group levels.

Ninth District Coast Guard personnel worked closely with Canadian maritime, military and law enforcement agencies, including the Canadian Coast Guard, as well as U.S. Immigration, Customs, Border Patrol, FBI, and state and local public safety and police agencies. Canadian and U.S. Coast

Guard personnel conducted surprise and high-risk vessel boarding. Civilian Coast Guard Auxiliary; personnel supplemented active-duty Coast Guard men and women at small boat stations, air stations and marine safety offices so USCG regulars could get out in the field and conduct patrols, inspections, and public awareness and response activities.

The necessity and extent of the response is illustrated by an analysis of the strategic infrastructure present in the Ninth District: 1,500 miles of international maritime borders; three international bridges; several major ports and international airports; defense shipping through the Sault Ste. Marie Locks and other strategic choke points; the infrastructure and population base of several major Great Lakes cities, including Chicago, Detroit, Milwaukee, Duluth and Superior; and numerous energy and power facilities, including 12 nuclear power plants.[23]

Adm. Thad Allen, USCG commandant (2006–2010). Adm. Allen led the USCG through expanded missions at home and overseas. Adm. Allen's leadership in the Hurricane Katrina disaster in 2005 was a factor in the presidential appointment of then Vice Adm. Allen to Coast Guard commandant. Toward the end of his command, and after his retirement from the Coast Guard, Adm. Allen supervised the disastrous and controversial 2010 Gulf of Mexico oil spill and its complex socioeconomic and environmental repercussions.

On 3 May 2002, Rear Adm. Ronald F. Silva replaced Adm. James Hull as Ninth District commander. Rear Adm. Hull was promoted to vice admiral rank and assumed command of the Atlantic Area, which included the ocean coastal region and the Great Lakes. Adm. Silva graduated from the U.S. Coast Guard Academy in 1971, earned a master of science degree in civil engineering from the University of Illinois and a masters in engineering administration from George Washington University. The engineering specialist served on several cutters and in various headquarters offices.

On 30 May 2002, Adm. Thomas H. Collins became Coast Guard commandant. Adm. Collins has been credited with enhancing the morale and cohesion of Team Coast Guard and upgrading the technology, facilities and air and water platforms of the service. The upgrading of Coast Guard air and sea assets in the proposed Integrated Deepwater Systems Project became a federal priority after 9/11.

Vice Adm. Thad W. Allen (U.S. Coast Guard Academy, 1971) gained national notoriety as the Coast Guard spokesperson in the media and USCG operations commander in New Orleans, Louisiana, after the devastating Hurricane Katrina struck the Gulf of Mexico–U.S. shoreline in 2005. President George W. Bush placed Adm. Allen in charge, declaring, "Adm. Allen speaks for the administration."

Adm. Allen's administrative and communications skills were on display to the devastated region and the nation as he articulated the Coast Guard mission with civilians, local and state and federal officials and agencies, and U.S. Army, Air Force, Marine and Navy leaders and other military personnel. After Katrina, President Bush appointed Vice Adm. Allen to succeed Adm. Thomas Collins as Coast Guard commandant in 2006.

Prior to assuming his duties as U.S. Coast Guard chief of staff in 2002, Adm. Allen was Atlantic Area commander and commander of the Atlantic Maritime Defense Zone. As Atlantic commander, Adm. Allen coordinated Coast Guard operations in the Atlantic and Great Lakes regions immediately after the 9/11 terrorist attacks.

Returning to Hurricane Katrina (2005), Ninth District Coast Guard units provided three SAR iceboats to the unlikely subtropical and tropical Gulf Coast environment for use in the Katrina aftermath. The above-water iceboat fan blades, not the traditional underwater propellers that could get hung up on obstructions and debris, served the purpose as the ice boats patrolled the flood zone in SAR patrols. U.S. Army Airborne officers and enlisted personnel accompanied Coast Guard members on their water patrols.

Ninth District Coast Guard Auxiliary, Regular and Reserve personnel responded to Katrina, as did the skilled USCG helicopter pilots who risked their own lives in storms, winds, and around electric lines and transmitters to rescue hurricane victims. Great Lakes Sector Detroit formed teams of coxswains and crews which joined up with personnel from the Ninth District Stations Saginaw River, Port Huron, St. Claire, Belle Island, Harbor Beach, Toledo, East Tawas, Marble Head, Manistee, Buffalo, Sturgeon Bay, Sault Ste. Marie, the Detroit ATN unit, and other teams.

In all, the USCG rescued more than 33,000 hurricane victims from homes, trees, off rooftops, and from floodwaters during the chaos of the Joint Task Force Katrina mission.

The Katrina mission illustrated again how well-trained Coast Guard officers and enlisted personnel assumed leadership responsibilities and rose to the occasion, adding to the achievements of the service whose motto is *Semper Paratus*, "Always Ready."

The 2005 Katrina Mission, like the 9.11.01 Coast Guard response which we shall explore in detail in a subsequent chapter, illustrated again how well prepared the U.S. Coast Guard is to meet the challenges of national disasters, an especially comforting perspective given the dangers of the era of the War on Terror.

8

Natural Disasters and the War on Terror

The operations of the U.S. Coast Guard in response to the terror attacks upon the United States on 11 September 2001 and to natural disasters such as Hurricane Katrina were briefly explored in chapter 7. The response of the Coast Guard to natural and human-caused public disasters are worthy of more detailed consideration because the training and experiences of the service in responding to devastating events contributes to national defense.

Because the United States Coast Guard has the unique responsibility of exercising law enforcement authority over civilians, the service missions and operations must adhere to civil and criminal law. Therefore, in exercising its law enforcement and maritime safety responsibilities, Coast Guard personnel may be subject to judicial challenges from attorneys for defendants apprehended by the Coast Guard. Court challenges have occurred throughout the history of the service, and did during the Prohibition era, the Cold War, subsequent domestic and overseas conflicts, and during the wars on drugs and terror. Defendants who have had property (boats and contraband) confiscated by the Coast Guard have resorted to court challenges.

During the domestic phase of Prohibition, and the Red Scare period of the Cold War, defense attorneys took issue with the confiscation of licenses and certificates that occurred when Coast Guard investigators concluded that some mariners were public safety and national security risks and when alleged conveyors of contraband were apprehended.

Historian Ellen Schrecker contended that the anti–Communist Cold War period in America was a repressive period of "crimes" committed in the era of "McCarthyism." Schrecker, civil libertarians and attorneys claimed the federal government, including the U.S. Coast Guard, committed civil liberties violations in voiding the licenses of more than 3,000 longshoremen and merchant seamen suspected of radical sympathies. Coast Guard authorities contended that the service mission required the enforcement of national security regulations and laws intended to protect vessels, cargoes, port infrastructures, and people from accidents, fires, sabotage, espionage, labor strikes, and work slow-downs that threatened public safety, commerce, and national security.[1]

During this critical period, the Coast Guard screened 500,000 merchant mariners and denied clearance to 3,700. A third of these decisions were reversed in the appeals process.[2]

The wide reach and border penetration of international gangs, and the danger of these networks communicating with and aiding and abetting terrorists, is illustrated by a successful Minnesota law enforcement operation.

International gangs are evidently operating from the isolated Northern Plains to the ocean shores of the United States. In January 2010 federal Immigration and Customs officials made 26 arrests in the Twin Cities of Minneapolis and St. Paul and adjacent communities.

U.S. Immigration and Customs Enforcement (ICE) officials claimed the arrested suspects had ties to drug-smuggling organizations in Asia, South America and Mexico. The ICE agents worked closely with federal, state and local law enforcement agencies. The operation led to the arrest of 450 suspected gang members in more than 80 cities in the United States. Imprisonment and the deportation of undocumented aliens were expected to follow.[3]

Coast Guard mission responsibilities in natural disasters, the wars on drugs and terrorism, and immigration interdiction keep the small, tightly budgeted service busy. When the Cold War appeared to be over by the end of the 20th century, it seemed the Coast Guard would be concentrating its missions on the domestic scene in its traditional SAR, ATN, ship inspection, drug and immigration interdiction, and responding to natural disasters such as floods and hurricanes. Then the terrorist attacks on 11 September 2001 thrust the Coast Guard into national defense responsibilities and the War on Terror (WOT) at home and then overseas.

In his magnificent book *Rescue Warriors*, David Helvarg chronicled the U.S. Coast Guard's multifaceted roles in drug, immigration, and fisheries enforcement, and the WOT, as well its traditional domestic peacetime missions. Helvarg visited Coast Guard stations and participated in maritime patrols. Mr. Helvarg's interviews with USCG enlisted, commissioned, reserve and auxiliary personnel provide a clear and riveting picture of, in Helvarg's description, "America's forgotten heroes."

When the 9/11 terrorists struck New York City with hijacked passenger airliners, Coast Guard Station Battery Park at the base of Manhattan Island had a front-row seat. That New York USCG station was a center for patrols and civilian rescues and mission articulation with passenger ferries, federal law enforcement agencies, New York and New Jersey paramedics, police officers, and firefighters. Cape Cod (Massachusetts) Coast Guard air station officers ordered an HH-60 helicopter on the one hour-flight to NYC to hopefully take victims off the burning buildings. But the USCG chopper was ordered out of the sky by traffic controllers who warned that USAF and USA aircraft might shoot them out of the sky. The Coast Guard aircrew obeyed the orders but insisted they could have saved some of the victims. Meanwhile, NYC COTP Adm. Richard E. Bennis and his deputies initiated maritime missions with regional Coast Guard units. Armed responders from New York, New Jersey, and New England in a variety of boats, buoy tenders and cutters responded on SAR and security patrols.[4]

In Washington, D.C., Coast Guard vessels closed the Potomac River after the terrorists crashed a plane into the Pentagon building. Adm. Jeffrey Hathaway (USCG) was on duty in the U.S. Navy Command Center where 42 military and civilian personnel were killed. In Boston Harbor USCG officials denied docking privileges to an LNG (liquid natural gas) tanker because of concerns Al Qaeda terrorists might have captured the vessel.

David Helvarg surveyed the 9/11 responses in port security and vessel boarding and tracking by Coast Guard teams in the ports of Boston, Los Angeles, San Francisco, Seattle, and Houston. Coast Guard Commandant James Loy and the U.S. Navy chief of naval operations (CNO) consulted about reciprocal operations in New York Harbor and decided that the immediate presence of Coast Guard cutters and armed small craft was essential to public safety and national security.

Coast Guard strike teams and armed male and female port security personnel manned small boats on the east and west coasts of America. Coast Guard personnel carried M-60 machine guns on 25-foot Boston Whalers and 45- and 47-foot fast boats, harbor tugs, and buoy tenders. Coast Guard vessel tracking system computers at Pacific and Atlantic coast headquarters stations tracked freighters coming into ports. Boarding teams and newly formed units of sea marshals climbed aboard "vessels of concern" and manned the helms of certain vessels coming into port. Strategic and historic coastal infrastructures were protected along coastal waterways,

Coast Guard Investigation Service personnel made computer checks of the documents and certificates held by thousands of mariners to monitor possible terrorist connections. Maritime Safety and Security Teams (MSSTs) patrolled ashore and afloat to protect civilians and infrastructure from further attacks. U.S. Coast Guard MSST and tactical law enforcement units teamed up with U.S. Customs personnel and trained canines. The teams used

USCGC *Tahoma* (WMEC-908) on port security patrol guards the Hudson River (New York City) on 17 September 2001 after the 11 September 2001 terrorist attacks on the World Trade Center towers.

advanced technology to monitor thousands of containers on docked vessels and in warehouses to check for contraband and explosives. Meanwhile, ocean-going cutters pushed out to sea to guard U.S. maritime frontiers and practice firing deck guns, machine guns, and small arms in preparation for the War on Terror.[5]

As David Helvarg observed, "For a rapidly growing force within the Coast Guard, the job and the mission are not primarily about saving lives anymore, but about arming up for violent confrontations in the maritime domain."[6]

Bill Gertz, *Washington Times* national security and defense reporter, analyzed what he considered were the government failures that led to the breakdown of American intelligence and the failure to prevent the 9/11 terrorist attacks on New York City and Washington, D.C. With access to Defense Department and Central Intelligence Agency (CIA) sources and documents, Gertz explained how the defense and intelligence establishments missed critical signs and evidence about the coming attacks and Al Qaeda intentions. Part of the problem was political. Gertz described the animosity of certain Clinton administration officials and members of Congress toward the CIA and officers, erroneous and politically correct assessments and policies, and the refusal to respond effectively to actionable intelligence. Gertz described his assessment of how the CIA failed to penetrate Al Qaeda and Osama bin Laden's terror apparatus, how the FBI was thwarted in its investigations and use of technology, and the excesses of congressional oversight on the security and intelligence communities. In his book *Breakdown*, Gertz suggested reforms to counter the political and national security blunders made by the political establishment, CIA, and the FBI.[7]

Gertz credited U.S. Customs Service agent Diane Dean at the Port Angeles, Washington, border crossing with Canada for discovering bomb-making materials in an Al Qaeda operative's car in December 2009.[8]

The author criticized the CIA for not preventing the bombing of the USS *Cole* in the port of Aden, Yemen, in October 2000, and the Clinton administration for not responding to that and other overseas bombings of U.S. diplomatic and resident sites. Part of the problem, Gertz asserted, was the failure of the CIA to penetrate terrorist organizations instead of relying on the intelligence offerings of foreign embassies and enemy defectors. Gertz deplored the tendency of U.S. presidents to appoint political figures and leaders not experienced in CIA overt and covert operations to head the agency.[9]

Bill Gertz believes that CIA "recruitment of clandestine sources of terrorism information is encouraged in theory, but [wrongly, in his view] discouraged in practice;"[10] that CIA reluctance to engage in covert action is counterproductive; that the CIA was inept in engaging in covet assignments, and that those assignments; "should be transferred to the military Special Operations Command."[11]

In the immediate 9/11 period, some observers contended that a wall of separation had been built between the CIA and the FBI and that terrorism and terrorist suspects during the presidential administrations of Bill Clinton (1993–2001) and Barack Obama (2009–2013) were treated like criminal defendants, given the civil rights of American citizens in American courts, and provided with defense attorneys. Critics of Obama's policies preferred that the detainees be treated as enemy combatants and tried in military courts. During the intervening years of the presidency of George W. Bush (2001–2009), terrorists were tried both in civilian courts and before military tribunals.

The Bush administration constructed a detainee detention center at the U.S. Navy base at Guantanamo Bay (GITMO) on the island nation of Cuba. Alleged terrorists taken in custody by U.S. military forces in Iraq and Afghanistan were transported to GITMO for incarceration and interrogation. Civil libertarians, many Democrats and liberals argued that GITMO incarceration was harsh and a violation of civil liberties. Republicans and conservatives contended that GITMO was like a country club, and Muslim detainees, however dangerous, were treated respectfully and humanely, and were culturally accommodated in a myriad of ways.

Nonetheless, presidential candidate Barack Obama (in 2008) campaigned on his promise to close down GITMO and transfer the detainees to U.S. soil or other nations. President Obama found his policy intentions difficult to implement for political, strategic, and national security reasons. President Obama's objectives were variously postponed, modified or suspended.

Political correctness ("PC") induced a societal reluctance to stereotype Muslims, although the terrorist extremists were invariably followers of the Islamic faith. "PC" may have prevented the proper supervision and incarceration of Maj. Malik Nadal Hasan (U.S. Army), a Muslim-American military psychiatrist who shot and killed 12 and wounded 30 U.S. soldiers at Ft. Hood, Texas, in November 2009. Sergeant Kimberly Munley, a courageous civilian police officer, responded to the scene and shot down Dr. Hasan. Sgt. Munley suffered life-threatening wounds in the process and was immediately cared for by military medics. Major Hasan was badly wounded, survived partially paralyzed, and is scheduled for trial.

Alleged political correctness and jurisdictional confusion interfered with the initial interrogation process of Nigerian terrorist Umar Farouk Abdulmutallab, the Christmas bomber who unsuccessfully tried to blow up a transatlantic Northwest Airlines aircraft over Detroit, Michigan, on 25 December 2009.[12] Passengers and crew subdued the would-be terrorist whose connections with Al Qaeda in Yemen were subsequently discovered, which contradicted President Obama's initial statements that Abdulmutallab acted alone. In fact, the Nigerian's father tried in vain to warn officials at the U.S. embassy of his son's extremist training and propensities.[13]

Thus, subsequent terrorist events since Bill Gertz published *Breakdown* in 2002 would appear to support his thesis and predictions about FBI and CIA procedural shortcomings and the blinders that cultural political correctness posed and would pose to the agencies and personnel tasked with waging the War on Terror. The political correctness regimen was aided and abetted by the "sensitivity sessions" that government employees at local, state and federal levels have been forced to experience since the 1960s.

The politically correct timidity which limited FBI effectiveness is described by Bill Gertz in his appropriately titled *Breakdown* chapter, "The FBI: The Decline of Domestic Intelligence." On 10 July 2001, FBI Special Agent Kenneth Williams wrote a classified "electronic communication" from the Phoenix, Arizona, office to FBI headquarters in Washington, D.C., suggesting that the FBI should accumulate a listing of civil aviation universities/colleges around the country," but it was not acted upon.[14] After Williams had interviewed some radical Islamic aviation students, he became alarmed by the possibility that one or more of them was taking aviation lessons to facilitate an airborne terrorist action in the United States.

The "Phoenix Memo" was not shared nationally by the FBI in Washington but was sent to New York. But FBI agents in Minneapolis, Minnesota, had independently discovered the arrest of radical Islamist Zacarias Moussaoui on illegal immigration charges on a tip from a suspicious flight school employee who wondered about Moussaoui's strange requests as a flight student. After the 9/11 attacks, Moussaoui was discovered to be one of the potential 9/11 perpetrators but had avoided intense pre–9/11 interrogation because the FBI felt its agent lacked the proper evidence to proceed,[15] even after a Minneapolis agent requested access to Moussaoui's home computer and was denied.

Gertz believes that had the FBI acted immediately on the "Phoenix Memo" the 9/11 airliner attacks might have been interrupted and avoided. FBI Director Robert Mueller told the House Select Committee on Intelligence (May 2002) that action on the "Phoenix Memo" would not necessarily have prevented the 11 September 2001 terrorist attacks! Mueller subsequently declared that the FBI would pursue Al Qaeda terrorists to "preserve" terrorist prosecutions. President George W. Bush's attorney general, John Ashcroft, interrupted Mueller to insist, "No, we are not going to 'preserve prosecutions.' We are going to use FBI intelligence to prevent further attacks!"[16] Congress did facilitate the exchange of national security information between federal government agencies, especially by the CIA and the Justice Department, with the passage of the controversial Patriot Act in late 2001.[17]

National defense reporter and author Bill Gertz offered an appreciative and positive perspective on the expanded role of the U.S. Coast Guard in national security responsibilities. Gertz perceptively described the maritime security challenge to protect the nation against terrorists operating from ships or using watercraft to attack harbor and urban infrastructure or other ships.

Gertz mentioned the significant speech that U.S. Coast Guard commandant, Admiral James Loy, gave to a secret intelligence meeting in 2002. Ports and waterways offer valuable economic targets that affect, Adm. Loy asserted, 25 percent of the gross domestic product (GDP) of the United States. Loy described the need for better intelligence on foreign threats and the need of the USCG to acquire intelligence information on ships, potential terrorists, cargo, targets and technology. Information exchange would involve the national and overseas intelligence communities and the cooperation of shipping company operators. Effective information exchange systems require, the commandant insisted, the coordinated efforts of waterways, immigration, airways, and law enforcement experts in the fight against the nation's adversaries in the War on Terror.[18]

Gertz saw a positive movement toward the integration and coordination of national security, defense, and intelligence assets in the War on Terror in the Bush administration with the bipartisan 2002 announcement of the proposed new cabinet-level Department of Homeland Security (DHS) that would be subjected to congressional oversight. Dozens of federal agencies were to be moved into the new national security agency, including the Immigration and Naturalization Service (INS), U.S. Customs Service, Federal Emergency Management Agency (FEMA), Border Patrol, Secret Service, and the United States Coast Guard.

The Border Patrol would be moved into the DHS from the Justice Department, U.S. Customs would come into the DHS from the U.S. Treasury Department, Animal and Plant Inspection Department would come from the U.S. Agriculture Department, and the United States Coast Guard would be shifted from the U.S. Department of Transportation into the DHS.[19] Gertz was supportive of the DHS creation, but he regretted and predicted that, "By leaving out the FBI and CIA, the president is ensuring that the intelligence agencies that need reform the most will not be changed in any fundamental way."[20]

On 24 January 2003 the Homeland Security Act of 2002 activated the U.S. Department of Homeland Security. The DHS missions include protecting the United States against terrorist attacks, protecting the flow of commerce and people on the nation's coastal and inland waterways, and providing citizenship services and natural disaster relief, all elements of national security and defense.

The major agencies that have since been incorporated into the DHS to facilitate its missions are several and significant. The agencies include the Federal Emergency Management Agency (FEMA), U.S. Citizen and Immigration Services (USCIS), U.S. Customs and Border Protection (USCBP), U.S. Secret Service, Transportation Security Administration (TSA), and the United States Coast Guard (USCG).

The TSA was formed by the Aviation and Transportation Security Act of 19 November 2001 and transferred to the DHS in 2003. The TSA is charged with the protection of the transportation systems of the United States and inspects passenger and cargo vehicles to check for weapons and contraband.

Under the Department of Homeland Security, the U.S. Coast Guard is charged with its traditional search and rescue and maritime law enforcement missions, is a branch of the U.S. Armed Forces and part of the U.S. Navy in wartime, suppresses maritime drug and immigration trafficking, inspects maritime vessels, and licenses vessels and merchant mariners. The Coast Guard has continued its icebreaking mission to support maritime commerce in the winter months.[21]

The Coast Guard icebreaker fleet serves commercial, national security and national defense purposes. During World War II, Great Lakes icebreakers kept the lakes open longer in the winter and fall seasons, and earlier in the spring, to facilitate commerce during World War II and today. Adm. Thad Allen was concerned about the expense and necessity of maintaining the Coast Guard icebreaker fleet in the northern polar region, a strategic necessity given the significance of warming and expanding navigable Arctic waters as the region warms up. Canada, Russia, and the United States have shown interest in the region for commercial, search and rescue, and natural resource considerations. The Coast Guard commandant spoke to a maritime symposium in January 2010 and said the nation has to make a decision about the future of the icebreaker fleet,[22] which supports scientific research and transport and supply missions in the Arctic and Antarctic regions.

Adm. Allen quickly responded to the Haitian earthquake tragedy that occurred on 12 January 2010. The commandant sent four 270-foot WMEC (medium endurance) Coast Guard cutters to assist in rescue missions. The cutters *Forward, Mohawk, Tahoma,* and *Valiant*[23] were expected to perform the traditional Coast Guard natural disaster missions of supply, transportation, SAR, and law enforcement. Coast Guard personnel deployed on USCG aircraft and vessels to assist in the rescue and relief operations.[24]

A 120-member Coast Guard port security unit (PSU *307*) from Clearwater, Florida, deployed on a C-17 aircraft on 23 January to bring water, food, weapons and tents to Haiti. The unit would also perform patrol missions on the waters off Port-Au-Prince to secure the maritime domain for transportation recovery teams to rebuild the devastated port. PSU *307* would also be transporting and using four trucks and six 25-foot Coast Guard security boats.[25]

Lt. Cmdr. Elizabeth Fielder (USCG) piloted a giant C-130 cargo and surveillance aircraft out of Coast Guard Air Station Clearwater to Haiti. Fielder radioed operations information back to Coast Guard Station Miami. The 13-year veteran Coast Guard aviator had flown a similar mission over New Orleans, Louisiana, during Hurricane Katrina in 2005. In Hurricane Katrina operations, Cmdr. Fielder assisted in helicopter recovery coordination.[26]

The DHS and USCG experience and responsibilities in natural disaster missions correlate with national defense capabilities to respond to potential terrorist attacks, and nuclear, biological, chemical and pollution incidents. The wide-ranging human and infrastructural devastation associated with natural and man-made (terrorist) disasters must be responded to. Coast Guard strike teams have been trained for and have had experience in similar emergency scenarios.

The 2004 and 2008 hurricane seasons required extensive Coast Guard responses, as did the horrific Hurricane Katrina and its aftermath in late August and early September of 2005. "As the law enforcement and military organization tasked to do search and rescue, environmental response, and maritime commerce support, [the Coast Guard] didn't have to wait," David Helvarg wrote, "for an official disaster decree or federal letter of permit"[27] to respond to Hurricane Katrina in the Gulf region in 2005. The personnel, cutters, boats and helicopters, as well as iceboats (with high, obstruction-proof propellers) from Great Lakes stations responded promptly. In coordination with other U.S. Armed Forces and civilian public safety agencies, the USCG saved over 30,000 lives during Hurricane Katrina and its aftermath. Plus the USCG used its aids to navigation skills to save and secure ships, boats and barges, to replace damaged and missing ATN infrastructure such as buoys, signal signs and lights, and to remove dangerous debris from waterways.

Coast Guard personnel, in cooperation with regional law enforcement agencies, fed flood victims, faced down criminals with guns, and performed dangerous roof rescues dangling from helicopters trying to avoid telephone wires and trees in high winds. All of the brave and skilled Coast Guard rescue swimmers, aviators and air and boat crews deserved the accolades they later received, and 30 Coast Guard helicopter pilots received Distinguished Flying Crosses for their achievements.[28]

Fisheries law enforcement is a Coast Guard priority in the North Atlantic and North Pacific, especially off the coast of Alaska and in the stormy and frigid Bering Sea. The mission is to protect and preserve marine life and safeguard U.S. commerce and fishing within the 200-mile Exclusive Economic Zone (EEZ) in the North Pacific. Coast Guard oceangoing cutters, their associated 25-foot RBS (response boat small) craft, helicopters, and C-130 overhead surveillance and communications aircraft police the seas. Coast Guard crews board ships to check cargoes and netting practices, and keep foreign vessels out of those strategic waters.

There are maritime safety and national security concomitants to the missions, and international incidents have occurred on those waters. The Coast Guard has had reciprocal assistance from Pacific Rim–nation patrol craft on occasion, but not without occasional confrontations. Taiwanese, South Korean, Chinese, Russian and Japanese fishing vessel are monitored, surveyed, boarded, and sometimes chased down. Domestic fishermen appreciate the SAR and safety check functions of the USCG in those dangerous and stormy waters, but not necessarily the Coast Guard inspection of crews, cargoes and ships, especially when contraband is discovered.[29]

The Coast Guard domestic and national defense missions have continued since the USCG was transferred to the newly created Department of Homeland Security in 2003. Michael Chertoff was the Bush administration's secretary of Homeland Security after Tom Ridge. Chertoff described the efficiency and success that occurred after 9/11 with the establishment of the DHS. Chertoff heralded the combining of Customs and Border Protection (CBP), the Transportation Security Administration (TSA) and its air marshals, and the Federal Emergency Management Agency (FEMA). Chertoff said the addition of the U.S. Coast Guard enhanced DHS objectives "by performing its myriad of land, sea, and search and rescue missions; protects our coastlines from preventable disasters; (and performs) prevention ... protection ... preparedness and response."[30]

Hurricane Katrina (2005), in addition to the politically motivated criticisms of Republican president George W. Bush and the federal government in response to the disaster, was not without its controversies. President Bush could have deflected some of the criticism by more frequently highlighting the alleged Democrat leadership failures of the New Orleans mayor and Louisiana governor. The president chose not to do that, but he might have more fully explained the successes of the federal government and the Coast Guard and other U.S. Armed Forces in the Katrina life-saving mission.

Nonetheless, a little-known scenario did occur during Operation Katrina that involved the DHS and U.S. Coast Guard and the notorious Blackwater mercenary army. Blackwater agents had protected American civilian and military leaders in Iraq and engaged in bloody and controversial combat incidents. CNN (Cable News Network) executive producer and author Suzanne Simons reported that Blackwater president Erik Prince offered to lend his all-weather Puma helicopter and armed security personnel to the U.S. Coast Guard and to local and private law enforcement agencies and security teams. New Orleans was in chaos. As people were being rescued from winds, buildings, and floodwaters, criminals and snipers were reportedly firing upon hospitals, security and public safety personnel, and vehicles. Erik Prince claimed his company had trained Coast Guard personnel, and offered to attach his crews to the USCG, Army National Guard, and other agencies. Blackwater claimed they did attach to the Coast Guard, rescued people, and provided security from looters to businesses, institutions, and an oil and gas pipeline.[31]

Reporter and author Jeremy Scahill wrote that Blackwater founder Erik

Prince claimed he donated "aerial support services" to the Katrina relief mission, and "put ourselves under Coast Guard command ... got a Coast Guard call sign ... and saved some 150 people that otherwise would not have been saved."[32] Coast Guard Commander Todd Campbell directed several Katrina operations and questioned Blackwater's rescue claims: "There were legal concerns, so we asked (Blackwater) not to engage in pulling people out." Cmdr. Campbell added, "Blackwater debriefed me every day and no one ever mentioned doing any rescues. If they were out there doing them, it was solely on their own."[33]

Coast Guard search and rescue missions serve national security and national defense interests, especially when military air and sea craft and crews are involved. The Coast Guard has lost its own crews in dangerous SAR missions in inclement weather and treacherous topography. But the storms that befall other craft beckon the Coast Guard out of ports and air stations when mariners and aviators are in distress.

On 25 January 2010, a U.S. Navy training T-34 propeller-driven aircraft flying out of Naval Air Station Whiting Field in Milton, Florida, crashed into Lake Ponchartrain off New Orleans, Louisiana. The training student was rescued two hours after the crash by Coast Guard boats. The U.S. Navy pilot was not found. Air traffic controllers at Lakefront Airport in New Orleans who reported that the plane disappeared from the radarscope had notified the Coast Guard. The Coast Guard launched a helicopter and two boats from Coast Guard Station New Orleans and searched a five by seven mile lake area before calling off the mission at dusk. The Coast Guard was scheduled to resume the search the following morning.[34] The Coast Guard helicopter was an MH-65-C rescue aircraft.[35]

SAR and surveillance for fisheries, drug contraband and immigration violations are risky for air, cutter and boat boarding personnel in fair or foul weather, or calm or heavy seas. On the evening of 29 October 2009, a USCG HC-130 Hercules collided with a USMC AH-1 Cobra gunship near San Clemente Island in the Pacific Ocean off the California coast. A five by twelve mile field of debris was spotted in an area with an ocean depth of 2,000 feet. The HC-130 crew of seven and the Cobra crew of two went missing. Naval officials doubted that the black boxes of the aircraft or the missing crew members would be recovered at those depths. The Hercules was based out of Sacramento CGAS in Sacramento, California.[36]

By 1 November the search had been called off, and military investigators were analyzing airplane and helicopter fragments recovered from the sea. The remains of the eight men and one woman in the aircraft crews had not been found. Air traffic controllers from Naval Air Station North Island in San Diego

Bay had spoken with the HC-130 several minutes before the crash that was observed by another airplane pilot who reported the air collision to the Federal Aviation Administration (FAA) after seeing a fiery ball in the evening sky.[37]

More than 2,500 people gathered at Coast Guard Air Station (CGAS) McClellan (California) to honor the nine USCG and USMC crew members who perished in the aircraft crash. Coast Guard commandant, Adm. Thad Allen, honored and expressed regret for the loss of the brave service personnel. The missing marines were on a training mission out of Camp Pendleton, California. The Coast Guard aircrew out of Sacramento was looking for a lost mariner. Other members of the U.S. Armed Forces, local law enforcement officers, firefighters, relatives and friends paid final tribute to the military heroes as the U.S. Coast Guard Band played "Amazing Grace."[38]

In addition to SAR and interdiction missions at sea, the Coast Guard has been responsible for port security missions at home and abroad since World War I. The port security mission has been intensified and expanded since the terror attacks upon the United States on 11 September 2001 and the War on Terror conducted overseas.

U.S. ports are vulnerable to terrorists on sea and land who might try to smuggle nuclear and biochemical weapons devices into the country. A November 2009 report by the inspector general of the DHS indicated the vulnerability of the United States to such an attack and the limited assets the U.S. Customs and Border Protection (CBP) and U.S. Coast Guard have to respond to the threat. One avenue of terrorist attack, the DHS contends, is the transport of such weapons into domestic ports by merchant vessels.

Port security cargo inspection units have to contend with more than 11 million vessel cargo containers that come into U.S. ports, according to 2008 statistics. CPB and USCG border protection relies on well-trained personnel and the most advanced detection technology.[39]

In its mission to protect and secure the nation's ports and waterways, the multimission Coast Guard has also been assigned to inspect and certify bridges which span the nation's commercial and navigable waterways. The U.S. Coast Guard's Bridge and Administration Division has overseen the process of bridge construction and security since 1967 when the service was in the U.S. Transportation Department (DOT). The supervisory and inspection domain includes more than 20,000 bridges.

The U.S. Coast Guard Reserve (USCGR) assists in the bridge patrol mission. For example, a USCGR unit has been responsible for inspecting the new Interstate 35 bridge in Minneapolis since the old span collapsed on the upper Mississippi River in September 2007 killing 13 and injuring more than 140 people. Some critics contend that the bridge administration responsibilities should be returned to DOT civilian personnel so the Coast Guard can concentrate on its ever-increasing domestic SAR, law enforcement, ATN, and national security missions.[40]

To better secure the nation's ports, harbors and surrounding infrastructure, merchant mariners and port facility employees, dockworkers, truck drivers, and others who have access to maritime facilities and vessels must posses the Transportation Worker Identification Credential (TWIC). TWIC–certified personnel are expected to contribute to port security by utilizing their own independent observation and judgment capacities and informing officials of unusual circumstances. The USCG and the Transportation Security Administration (TSA) manage TWIC.

USCG and TSA officers inspect merchant mariners and maritime facility personnel at port facilities and at waterfront fuel and power plants. Facility personnel are subjected to periodic computer fingerprint identification (ID) checks, and they assist in the monitoring of waterfront activities and personnel to maximize maritime domain awareness. The TWIC certification program allows a "fully vetted" and secure workforce to enhance port security and occupy the front lines of national security.[41]

The 2010 Defense Department Authorization Act provided incentives to increase maritime shipping and relieve some of the trucking burden and congestion on the nation's highways. The Department of Transportation's Maritime Administration (MARAD) was directed to fund much of the shipping project to allow U.S. merchant vessels and shipyards to facilitate and modernize maritime transportation. Truck transportation is expected to increase in the next two to three decades, so the maritime solution will not hurt highway and railway transportation as much as it is intended to better manage highway congestion and environmental pollution.

The Coast Guard will be affected by its increased role in policing and protecting merchant vessels, crews, and maritime security, and issuing and monitoring the credentials of merchant sea personnel. Coast Guard boat crews will coordinate their expanded missions and train with civilian maritime police officers, sheriff's deputies, and other public safety and paramedic specialists. It is expected that the U.S. Merchant Marine academies and officers and crews will be expanded in numbers and become an additional asset in the maritime security realm.[42]

Pollution control on the nation's waterways and seas is another significant Coast Guard mission that contributes to economic growth and national security. Terrorists could inflict significant damage by polluting and influencing traffic and safety on America's navigable waters.

Therefore, constant Coast Guard vigilance and effective responses to pollution incidents in the nation's ports and on the lakes and oceans is a significant task. On Saturday January 23, 2010 an oil tanker headed for the Exxon Mobil Corporation's Beaumont (Texas) refinery was struck by a towing vessel and its two barges. A hole was torn in the hull of the 807-foot oil transport, the M/V *Eagle Otome*, which then spilled an estimated 450,000 gallons of crude petroleum into the Sabine Naches Waterway.

Coast Guard officials reported on the following day (24 January 2010) that the oil spill was confined to a two mile shoreline corridor adjacent to the city of Port Arthur, Texas, due to swift action by civilian and USCG personnel and the tanker crew that managed to shift 69,000 gallons of the remaining crude oil out of the ruptured compartment.

Coast Guard officials who nonetheless predicted that the temporary closing of the waterway would have an economic impact on surrounding communities declared the impacted vessels "stable." An adjacent refinery offered its oil cleanup equipment to supplement Coast Guard technology. Local law enforcement agencies monitored the incident and alerted adjacent communities.[43]

The U.S. Navy and U.S. Coast Guard operate in joint missions to keep America safe and confront America's adversaries overseas. The Coast Guard, with law enforcement authority in U.S. ports, provides security for U.S. Navy warships and submarines as the USN returns to and disembarks from home-port waters. The CGC *Sea Fox*, an 87-foot coastal patrol cutter, escorts USN submarines in and out of U.S. Naval Base Kitsap-Bangor in Washington State, along with its sister ship the CGC *Sea Devil*. The cutters are assigned to Coast Guard Marine Force Protection Unit Bangor and patrol in the maritime domain of the Naval Undersea Warfare Center at Keyport. The submarine base is located in Puget Sound outside of Bremerton, Washington.[44]

The Coast Guard guides USN submarines and other USN vessels to and from American home ports and U.S. Navy bases, including port security patrols at U.S. Naval Station Guantanamo (GITMO), Cuba. A team of 50 Coast Guard personnel assists the USN and the Pentagon in protecting the coasts, port and waterways of the U.S. Navy Base in armed transportable port security boats (TPSBs). The Coast Guard uses these "fast boats" for port security missions and to escort vessels through Guantanamo Bay in proximity to Cuban territory immediately north of GITMO.

Coast Guard detachments provide transportation and escort services and protects vessels and high-profile visitors from potential terrorist attacks. Coast Guard personnel also team up with U.S. Marine Corps security units, and coordinate training and missions with the U.S. Army, Air Force and Navy.[45]

Protecting ports at home and overseas keeps the Coast Guard busy. The USCG cooperates with the U.S. Secret Service to protect the president of the

United States, from the Potomac River in Washington, D.C., to the maritime locations of the president at conferences or on vacation.

When President Barack Obama and his family vacationed in Hawaii in December 2009, the Coast Guard set up a security zone around Obama's residence on the island of Oahu in Kailua Bay. Fines and imprisonment faced any boaters who broached the yellow buoys that marked the security boundary.[46]

Team Coast Guard is composed of civilian auxiliary and support personnel, and reserve and regular enlisted and commissioned men and women. These are the dedicated individuals who have made the U.S. Coast Guard successful in its myriad of responsibilities, training, and missions throughout the history of the service. Descriptions of a few of those individuals are included in the following chapter.

9

Coast Guard Aviation and National Defense

The U.S. Coast Guard pioneered in the field of aviation, an era that began while World War I was raging in Europe. In April 1916 USCG officers and enlisted personnel were accepted into U.S. Navy flight training at Pensacola, Florida. In May 1919, Lt. Elmer Stone (USCG) was the pilot of USN floatplane *NC-4* in the first aircraft transatlantic crossing. In 1920 the first U.S. Coast Guard Air Station was operational at USCGAS Morehead City, North Carolina.

In August 1942, during World War II, a Coast Guard–crewed Grumman *J4F-1 Widgeon* (V-212) sank a German U-boat (submarine) in the Gulf of Mexico. The first mercy mission performed by a helicopter occurred in January 1944 when rotor-wing aviator and helicopter pioneer Cmdr. Frank A. Erickson (USCG) flew a blood plasma supply in a snowstorm to a New Jersey hospital where USN survivors of a torpedoed destroyer explosion were patients. Floyd Bennett Field in Brooklyn, New York, became a Coast Guard helicopter-training base where American and British aviators and mechanics were trained.

In June 1944 the landing of a helicopter on the deck of a combat vessel, the USCGC *Cobb* (WPG-181), occurred off Long Island, New York. The aviator, Cmdr. Frank Erickson (USCG), helped develop helicopter tactics for search and rescue (SAR) and antisubmarine warfare (ASW) operations, and acquainted intelligence and U.S. Army representatives with the rotor-wing aircraft.[1] Aviator and author Lt. Cmdr. Tom Beard (USCG, ret.) is an expert on Coast Guard aviation and helicopter history. Lt. Cmdr. Michael Bennett, a U.S. Coast Guard Academy professor, has done extensive research on Coast Guard intelligence operations and served in the Persian Gulf and War on Terror. Coast Guard aviators flew USN aircraft in Patrol Squadron Six and PBY flying boat patrol bombers on the Greenland Patrol and in the North Atlantic in World War II, and Grumman J2-F seaplanes, the bi-winged floatplanes, on reconnaissance, SAR, iceberg tracking, transportation, ASW, and combat missions.[2]

Between 1945 and 1990 Coast Guard floatplanes were transitioned out of existence, and USCG helicopters evolved from amphibious choppers to land- and cutter-based wheeled aircraft.

Coast Guard sea (float) planes were discussed in chapter 2 during World War II. Emphasis in this chapter will be placed on Coast Guard helicopters and fixed-wing aircraft, defense and SAR missions, challenges, crew skills and responsibilities and successes, and the contributions, dangers and fatalities involved in Coast Guard aviation from the earliest days to the present.

Captain Joseph T. Connell (USAF, Ret.) was a pilot from 1960 to 1966. After pilot training in a variety of aircraft, Connell flew HH-43-B and HH-43-F helicopters for the Air Rescue and Recovery Service (ARRS) in Vietnam (1964–1965). Connell's aviation career and postwar aviation avocation interests have kept him focused on aviation history and contemporary events.[3]

Connell, a retired 34-year IBM employee, constructed and flew his own aircraft. Connell's interest in aviation and respect for the U.S. Coast Guard has motivated him to keep this author informed about his research on aviation, including Coast Guard history and events. A skilled photographer and writer, Capt. Connell provided information about Coast Guard stations visited in his travels. The following discussion about USCG aviation missions in Southeast Asia and Coast Guard aviation missions, downed aircraft, and injuries are courtesy of Capt. Connell. The incidents illustrate the skills and risks associated with peacetime training and peace and wartime flying for aviators and crews of the U.S. Armed Forces. Civilian Coast Guard Auxiliary aviators have also suffered casualties in their missions.

U.S. Coast Guard helicopter pilots served with United States Air Force helicopter pilots in combat rescue and recovery missions in Vietnam between 1968 and 1972. Ten volunteer USCG aviators few out of Da Nang with the 37th ARRS unit. The U.S. Coast Guard aviators (and years of service) were Lt. Richard Butchka (1969), Lt. Cmdr. Joseph Crowe (1971), Lt. Lance A. Eagan (1968), Lt. Robert E. Long (1972), Lt. James M. Loomis (1969), Lt. Roderick Martin III (1971), Lt. Cmdr. Lonnie Mixon (1968), Lt. (jg) Robert T. Ritchie (1969), Lt. Jack C. Rittichier (1968), and Lt. Jack K. Stice (1972). Each of these pilots was inducted into the United States Coast Guard Hall of Fame on 8 November 2005.[4]

Getting experienced SAR helicopter pilots who could operate over land and sea was a challenge in the initial 37th ARRS deployment to Indochina.

ARRS initially met personnel requirements by training fixed-wing aviators for helicopter flying. With the acquisition of Coast Guard SAR helicopter pilots, the transitional staffing was fulfilled by qualified, experienced aviators. The 37th ARRS commander, Lt. Col. Charles R. Klinkert (USAF), described his satisfaction with USCG pilots: "Coast Guard aviators have [contributed] a terrific assist to the Air Force.... I can't say enough about them."[5] MSgt. Jack Watkins (USAF) said, "The crews liked to fly with the Coast Guard pilots ... they were able to adapt to any situation. Flying the helicopter was natural to them (and they passed) along their skills to the other pilots."[6]

General Howell M. Estes, Jr. (USAF commander, Military Airlift Command) affirmed the respect and appreciation USAF personnel had for USCG aviators: "I am personally aware of the distinguished record achieved by the [Coast Guard] pilots flying in combat with our Jolly Greens (USAF helicopters). They have flown many difficult and challenging missions ... [and] ... are indelibly inscribed in the permanent records of the stirring and moving drama of combat aircrew recovery in Southeast Asia."[7]

The ARRS flights were completed by brave USAF and USCG aviators and crews, but not without cost. Helicopters were shot down by enemy fire, and crews and pilots were casualties of war, wounded (WIA) and killed (KIA) in action. U.S. Coast Guard Air Station (USCGAS) Detroit (Michigan) held a memorial service on 9 June 2010 for Lt. Jack C. Rittichier (USCG) who died on 9 June 1968 in the Vietnam War in an attempted rescue of a downed U.S. Marine Corps aviator. Lt. Rittichier was the pilot of an HH-3E Jolly Green Giant USAF helicopter that was shot down near the Vietnam-Laotian border.[8]

Also killed on the Sikorsky HH-3F helicopter (Jolly "23" USAF 67-14710) with Lt. Rittichier were Capt. Richard C. Yeend, Jr. (USAF), SSgt. Elmer Larry Holden (USAF), and Sgt. James Douglas Locker (USAF). The pilots and crew were flying in the 37th Aerospace Rescue and Recovery Squadron out of Da Nang in the Republic of South Vietnam (RSV). The incident location was calculated to be 37 miles west of Hue, RSV. The rescue team was attempting to rescue a USMC fighter pilot reported on the ground with a broken leg and arm. Heavy enemy fire drove the HH-3F away while gunships counterattacked. As Lt. Rittichier returned to recover the Marine pilot, enemy ordnance punctured and set fire to the helicopter, which hit the ground and exploded. Other helicopters flew over the downed and burning HH-3F. No survivors were spotted.[9]

In addition to the loss of Coast Guard helicopter aviator Lt. Jack C. Rittichier, a survey of USCG aircraft crashes in training, transportation, SAR, and national security and defense missions between 1934 and 2009 listed more than 100 fatal incidents. The following discussion of fatal crashes is limited to missions and flights associated with law enforcement, national defense, and national security in the service of the United States.

On 29 May 1934 a flight out of Coast Guard Air Detachment San Antonio (Texas) crashed in the immediate vicinity of Ft. Bliss in El Paso, Texas. Harry L. Sexton (San Antonio U.S. Customs collector) was killed in the crash of the Curtis Falcon biplane (USC 2576).[10] The Coast Guard shared missions and transportation with U.S. Customs Service officials, as both agencies were under the authority of the U.S. Treasury Department.

During World War II, between 1941 and 1943, as might be expected in that time of intense aircraft training, SAR, and patrol activity in the United States and in overseas combat zones, several fatal Coast Guard air crashes occurred.

On 5 August 1941 two Coast Guard aviation machinist mates and a radioman perished when their Douglas RD-4 Dolphin (V126) crashed near the Carillon Islands off USCGAS San Francisco (California). The ironically named airman, AMM1 L.L. Stonerock (USCG), piloted the amphibious plane. The patrol aircraft, flying low over the water due to foggy conditions and poor visibility, struck an emerged rock. Also killed were Coast Guard crewmen RM1 John C. Gill and AMM1 F.D. Hancock. Naval minesweepers on SAR missions discovered the plane wreckage after the aircraft ceased sending radio signals.

A Vought OS2U-Kingfisher (5777) out of USCGAS Salem (Massachusetts) struck the water while on antisubmarine (ASW) patrol against German U-Boats. AMM2 Edward T. Werner (USCG) and RM3 Cecil V. Bratu (USCG) perished. A wingtip was recovered but not the remains of the crewmen.

Lt. Robert J. Lafferty, AMM1 Steven J. Tarapchak, and RM1 William A. Boutillier departed from USCGAS Brooklyn (New York) in an amphibious Grumman JRF-3 (V-190) floatplane on a test flight on 16 April 1942. The Coast Guard aircrew was diverted to Massachusetts Atlantic waters to search for a reported U-Boat off Nantucket in deteriorating weather, darkness, rain and poor visibility. The Grumman JRF-3 crashed into the cliffs on Block Island. There were no survivors.

AMM2 Richard L. Fisher (USCG) flew a PBY patrol bomber out of Naval Air Station (NAS) Pensacola (Florida) on 5 June 1942. PBY-5A Catalina 05023 flew over the Gulf of Mexico with eight USN aviators on board for navigation training. After military authorities determined the PBY was overdue, an unsuccessful search for the aircraft and crew was conducted.

Lt. John A. Pritchard (USCG) and RM1 Benjamin A. Bottoms (USCG) set out on a rescue mission in polar Greenland on 29 September 1942. The Grumman J2F-Duck (V1640) was attached to the 216-foot USCGC North-land (WPG-49). The seaplane aviators successfully located the crew of a downed B-17F U.S. Army Air Force (USAF) bomber. Two survivors were flown back to the *Northland*. Lt. Pritchard and RM1 Bottoms returned one day later to rescue other crewmembers, but extreme weather conditions forced the departure of the Grumman J2F before the mission could be completed. Heavy fog and blinding snow caused Pritchard, Bottoms and Cpl. Loran E. Howarth (USAAF) to crash into a glacier, with the loss of all hands.

A Vought OS2U kingfisher (2270) floatplane out of Naval Air Station San Francisco, California, crashed off San Gregorio Beach, south of the NAS. The flight was returning from an antisubmarine patrol on 9 May 1943. The pilot, Lt. (jg) Dale C. Burroughs (USN), died in the crash. Crewman Henry H. Kind (USCG) survived when Stanford University student Bob Brown swam the quarter-mile distance from the beach to the wreck to save the severely injured Coastguardsman.

Ensign Charles E. Johnson (USCG) was flying a USN PBY-5A Catalina floatplane (08118) that was destroyed upon landing in heavy seas and poor weather off Dutch Harbor (Alaska) on 27 November 1943. Ens. Johnson, Lt. (jg) William Phillips (USN), and ART2c (Aviation Radio Technician Second Class) Ludwig A. Stroesswer (USNR) were killed in the crash. Ensign Johnson was doing baseline tests for the secret LORAN (long range aid to navigation) system and attempted a water landing. The aircraft broke up on impact and sank rapidly.

A consolidated PBY-5A Catalina (05007) crashed in Atlantic waters off USCGAS Elizabeth City (North Carolina) in Albemarle Sound on 23 February 1945. In the training flight while practicing water takeoffs and landings, the PBY-5A hit high waves, sheared a wing, and split open the fuselage. Ensign Walter D. Huston (USCG) and ARM1 (aviation radioman) James A. Wood (USCG) perished in the incident.[11]

The 1950s ushered in the era of the so-called Cold War between the Communist Bloc nations and the West. National security became a domestic political and international geopolitical issue. The Coast Guard participated in the Cold War at home and abroad. At home, port security and protection from the threat of domestic espionage and sabotage by Communist Bloc agents were part of the Coast Guard's extended missions.

The concern about domestic sympathizers with the agendas and expansion of power of the Soviet Union and the People's Republic of China posed national security and civil liberties issues. Overseas, the Coast Guard and the other U.S. Armed Forces and national security agencies confronted Communist nations in the Korean War (1950–1953) and later the Vietnam War (late 1960s to 1973).

On 18 January 1953 a Martin PBM-5G Mariner (84738) took off from USCGAS Detachment Sangley Point in the Philippines on a SAR mission to the Formosa Strait off the coast of the People's Republic of China (PRC). The PBM-5G crew had rescued the survivors of a U.S. Navy P2V aircraft that PRC military forces had shot down. On takeoff, the Coast Guard aircraft went down after being struck by high waves. Casualties included five USCG and four USN military personnel who died in the crash. The Coastguardsmen who perished were the aviator, Lt. (jg) Gerald W. Stuart, and Petty Officers Winfield J. Hammond, Carl R. Tornell, Joseph R. Bridge, and Tracy W. Miller.

Lt. (jg) Edward A. McGee (USCG) was on detached duty from USCGAS Elizabeth City, North Carolina, in a law enforcement mission to help federal officers locate illegal whiskey production sites in Texas. On board the USCG Stinson OY-2 Sentinel (03937) piloted by Lt. McGee was a U.S. Treasury agent. While in a low-flying search pattern over a heavily forested area outside the city of Marshall, the OY-2 had engine failure and crashed into the trees. Lt. McGee was hospitalized with head injuries and then died of pneumonia. The Treasury agent suffered a broken leg.[12]

Dangerous Coast Guard missions and aircraft fatalities took their toll in the following decade in the United States and, as noted above, Vietnam. On 29 June 1961, Coastguardsmen Lt. Cmdr. Stuart T. Scharfenstein, Lt. Cmdr. Charles E. Mueller, and AL1 John R. Doherty perished in Massachusetts. The crew was flying a Sikorsky H04S-3G (HH-19G) 5509 on a training mission. Mayday calls were transmitted after the helicopter experienced what was later surmised as structural fatigue failure. The rotor-wing aircraft fell 1,200 feet before crashing.

Sikorsky HUS-1G (HH-34F) 1336 out of USCGAS St. Petersburg, Florida, was on a SAR mission over the Gulf of Mexico (29 November 1962). The helicopter mistakenly descended too rapidly and crashed into the water killing AD2 Thomas Chastain (USCG) who failed to escape from the sinking aircraft. The rest of the crew survived.

On 8 February 1967, Grumman HU-16E Albatross 1271 was flying law enforcement and LORAN missions out of USCGAS Kodiak (Alaska). As the amphibious aircraft approached LORAN Station St. Paul Island, the crew encountered a low-visibility ceiling and blinding snow. A low fuel level required immediate landing during which one aircraft wing touched the ground and the plane crashed. AT2 Frank R. Edmunds (USCG) perished in the incident.[13]

The formidable bomber-sized Lockheed HC-130H Hercules 1600 was transporting cargo and personnel to USCG LORAN Station Attu Island, Alaska, on 30 July 1982. The HC-130 was out of USCGAS Kodiak (Alaska). The huge propeller-driven aircraft encountered deteriorating weather conditions and diminished pilot visibility and crashed on land. Coast Guard Petty

Officers Brad S. Canfield and Steven D. Berryhill died in the crash. The surviving crewmembers were injured but got clear of the destroyed aircraft.

The treacherous, unpredictable weather of Alaska and the Aleutian Islands in the North Pacific took additional tolls of Coast Guard aircrew members. On 2 November 1986, Sikorsky HH-3F Pelican helicopter 1473, piloted by Lt. Michael C. Dollahite (USCG), was on a SAR mission out of USCGAS Kodiak. The helicopter crashed against a cliff on Ugak Island and burned. Heavy winds, rains and low visibility caused the impact. The entire crew perished. Posthumously honored were the pilot, Lt. Dollahite, and his fellow commissioned officers, Lt. Robert L. Carson, Jr. and Cmdr. David M. Rockmore (M.D., U.S. Public Health Service). The honored enlisted petty officers were ASM2 Kevin M. McCraken, AT3 William G. Kemp, and HS3 Ralph D. King.[14]

Civilian men and women members of the U.S. Coast Guard Auxiliary have given their lives in the line of duty ever since the World War II creation of the organization. The USCGAUX members operate in the air, on land, and sea. On 18 September 1989, Beech Aircraft A35 N566B, a single-wing propeller-driven plane, was on Auxiliary surveillance patrol when it merged into an extensive layer of clouds. The disoriented pilot reportedly lost control of the aircraft at 7,000 feet elevation and went into a spiral dive that caused a stress fracture and separation of the right wing. The aircraft hit the ground in the area of Escondido (California). Killed in the crash were Robert J. Duffield and Gerard B. Rene.[15]

Another USCGAUX aircrew gave their lives in the service of the United States on 12 May 1990. Killed in an Atlantic sea crash off Davis Park, New York, were Charlene J. Huhne, Julie A. Nappi, Russell J. Anderson, and Christopher R. Polimeni. They were flying a routine training flight and were reported lost six hours after takeoff. Radar information indicated that the Bellanca 17–31A N7SF propeller aircraft had flown out over the ocean in a consistent pattern of less than 500 feet in elevation and then circled back toward shore. Three days after takeoff the aircraft wreckage was found on a beach. An investigation of the wreckage indicated that the plane had hit the ocean surface at a high rate of speed. Medical records indicated the aviator had recently suffered a head injury and complained of a headache. Speculation suggested the pilot may have passed out and lost control of the aircraft.[16]

On 24 August 1990 a Coast Guard crew assigned to USCGAS St. Augustine (Florida) was making a landing approach into U.S. Naval Air Station (USNAS) Puerto Rico. The pilot reported a wing fire and hydraulic control problems on the Grumman F2C Hawkeye 3501 after a night law enforcement patrol. The aircraft crashed before touching down on the runway. Lt. Duane

E. Stenbak, Lt. Paul E. Perit, Lt. Craig E. Lerner, and AT1 Matthew H. Baker died in the crash. There were no survivors.[17]

On 31 August 1993, HH-65A Dolphin 6594 flew out of USCGAS Brooklyn, New York, on an aids to navigation (ATN) mission to fly equipment out to the ATN crew on the Ambrose Light Tower. The helicopter approach was short of the landing zone. The HH-65A Dolphin struck the edge of the helipad, rolled over, and fell 100 feet into the ocean. Aviators Lt. Marc C. Perkins (USCG) and Lt. (jg) Mark S. Fisher were killed in the incident.[18]

The 21st century began with the crash of a USCGAUX aircraft, Piper PA-32-300 N99WD on 1 February 2001 off the Florida Keys. Killed in the accident were civilian Coast Guard Auxiliarists Mr. Robert S. Fuller and Mr. Casey A. Purvis. The fliers were on a night law enforcement intercept-training mission with a USCG HU-25 from USCGAS Miami (Florida). The Piper aircraft was assuming the role of a drug-smuggling plane. The Piper pilot described hazy conditions and radioed that he was terminating the mission. After brief communications the radio transmissions ended. The radar record indicated the last nighttime position of the Piper craft was at 1,500 feet, 51 minutes after midnight. The wreckage indicated no evidence of a mechanical malfunction, but analysts concluded the aircraft made a high-speed water entry because only the tail section remained in one piece.

Training exercises are ongoing to prepare the Coast Guard for its missions and *Semper Paratus* (Always Ready) responsibilities. Military training is essential and often dangerous. On 4 September 2008 Coast Guard helicopter HH-65 Dolphin 6505 was practicing hoist operations with a Coast Guard Station Honolulu (Hawaii) 47-foot motor lifeboat (MLB) off USCGAS Barbers Point. The hoist became caught in the structure of the MLB. The cable snapped and damaged the helicopter rotor blade, which subsequently caused the HH-65 Dolphin to fall 450 feet into Mamala Bay. A Honolulu Fire Department Response boat recovered one helicopter crewman already dead, performed medical emergency treatment on the other three crewmen, and evacuated them to a hospital where they did not survive. The search for USCGAS Barbers Point Executive Officer (XO) Cmdr. Thomas G. Nelson was suspended after three days. Killed in the line of duty were HH-65 Coast Guard aviators Cmdr. Thomas G. Nelson and Lt. Cmdr. Andrew C. Wischmeier and petty officers AST1 David Skimin, a rescue swimmer, and AMT2 Joshua Nichols, an aviation maintenance technician.

The risk of air crashes between operating military aircraft is an ever-present danger. On 29 October 2009 a Coast Guard transport and patrol aircraft HC-130-H Hercules 1705 was on a SAR mission 50 miles off San Diego, California, immediately east of San Clemente Island in the Pacific Ocean. At approximately 7 P.M. the HC-130 aircraft collided with a U.S. Marine Corps AH-1W Super Cobra helicopter. The HC-130 had a seven-person crew complement. The Marine helicopter out of Air Group 39 (Third Marine Aircraft Wing) had two crewmen aboard: Major Samuel Leigh (USMC) and 1st Lt. Thomas Claiborne (USMC).

The commissioned Coast Guard crewmembers were pilot Lt. Cmdr. Che J. Barnes and copilot Lt. Adam W. Bryant. The enlisted Coast Guard petty officers were AMTC John F. Seidman (flight engineer), AET2 Carl P. Grigonis (navigator), AET2 Monica L. Beacham (radio operator), AMT2 Jason S. Moletzsky, and AMT3 Danny R. Kreder. No survivors of either aircraft were found. U.S. Armed Forces search teams suspended SAR operations on 1 November. The C-130 black box recorder was later discovered at a depth of 2,000 feet and used as evidence in subsequent military deliberations.[19]

On Tuesday, 24 August, the USN, USMC and USCG released the findings of their investigation of the collision between the Coast Guard HC-130 out of San Francisco and the USMC helicopter out of Camp Pendleton, California. The conclusion: there was no single factor that caused the accident, according to Capt. Michael Eagle (USCG), commanding officer of USCGAS McClellan Park (California), and no professional errors committed by the Coast Guard or Marine aircrews, all of whom perished in the incident, although critics said the accident occurred under the watch of the USN control center in San Diego, California.[20]

Although the official reports concluded that no particular blame could be assessed to the pilots and aircraft involved in the incident, the USCG and USMC did find some reciprocal fault, according to one news organization. In that report, the Coast Guard suggested the acting regional Navy traffic control tower did not follow standard procedure. The Navy concluded the crash had been preventable, better air traffic control–pilot communications could have been followed, and the Naval Air Station in Coronado (California) near San Diego could have more clearly alerted the pilots to the aerial situation. Navy officials added that the aircraft and pilots were required to operate under visual sight rules and were responsible for their own safety analysis. The U.S. Navy controller was also occupied at the time of the crash with the higher priority of monitoring USN fighter jets flying in the region.[21]

Proceedings, the prestigious periodical of the U.S. Naval Institute, featured an article written by Lt. Cmdr. David R. Neel (USCG): "Analysis of a Helicopter Crash in the Bering Sea" (April 2008). Cmdr. Neel described how his helicopter (HH-60 6020) out of USCGAS Kodiak (Alaska) crashed into the frigid Bering Sea during a SAR mission on 8 December 2004. The helicopter went down after being struck by a 100-foot rogue wave in night blizzard conditions during the rescue of the crew of the Malaysian cargo vessel M/V *Selendang Ayu*. The helicopter hit the sea, flipped over and sank. The three USCG crewmembers survived, as did one of the seven rescued merchant seamen. Cmdr. Neel described the harrowing experience of fighting for survival and being rescued by another on-scene Coast Guard helicopter. Cmdr. Neel attributed the survival to superior Coast Guard egress and swim training and the exemplary helicopter technology, equipment, and clothing provided by the Coast Guard. The dangers of Coast Guard defense and SAR missions were illustrated. Lt. Cmdr. Neel subsequently contributed his aviation, instructor and analytical skills after graduating from the National Defense Intelligence College in Washington, D.C., and subsequently serving as Chief of the U.S. Coast Guard Pacific Intelligence Division.[22]

Helicopter aviation is fraught with danger for even the most experienced aviators. Cmdr. Patrick Shaw (USCG) knew about winter storms and high winds as a pilot flying out of Kodiak, Alaska. The decorated aviator had his first aviation accident when his MH-60T Jayhawk helicopter crashed in a Utah snowstorm on 3 March 2010. Cmdr. Shaw was flying home from a security detail at the Winter Olympics from Canada to his new base at USCGAS Elizabeth City (North Carolina). Cmdr. Shaw's skill and experience prevented a worse catastrophe, but Shaw, copilot Lt. Cmdr. Steven Cerveny, and Petty Officer Gina Panuzzi were seriously injured. Two other passengers escaped injury.[23] Ten days after the crash, Cmdr. Shaw, a Juneau, Alaska, native, and crewmembers PO3 Darren Hicks of Oroville, Washington, and PO3 Edward Sychra of Blanchard, Idaho, had returned to USCGAS Elizabeth City (North Carolina). PO2 Gina Panuzzi and Lt. Cmdr. Steven Cerveny remained at University Hospital in Salt Lake and upgraded to fair condition.[24]

The southeastern Atlantic coast of the United States contains a large number of U.S. Armed Forces bases. American aviators do practice missions off the southern Atlantic coast. USCG SAR missions are frequent. On 15 March 2010, U.S. Marine Corps Air Station Beaufort (South Carolina) notified the USCG of a flaming engine failure of an F/A 180 18D fighter jet and the ejection of the aviators 35 miles off the coast on 11 March 2010. The USCG rescued the aviators in an HH-65 Dolphin helicopter out of USCAGAS Charleston (South Carolina) one hour after being notified by the Marine Corps Air Station. The Marine pilots deployed to the jet's survival craft and were safely recovered by the USCG crew.[25]

Coast Guard reconnaissance, SAR, and training missions are essential and not without risk whether in the Gulf, Pacific, Atlantic, or on the Great Lakes. A rescue helicopter conducting a nighttime training exercise crashed into Lake Huron in April 2010. Chief Petty Officer Robert Lanier of the Ninth

(Great Lakes) District public affairs office in Cleveland, Ohio, said the Coast Guard airmen were conducting hoist training when their helicopter crashed around 9:45 P.M. nine miles north of Port Huron (Michigan). A Coast Guard lifeboat picked up all of the crewmen shortly after the crash. The HH-65C's pilot was Lt. Vincent Bukowski of Chicago; Lt. Tasha Hood of Bell County, Texas, was the copilot; and AET3 Samuel Downie of Tyler, Texas, was the flight mechanic on board. Coast Guard officials were expected to interview the helicopter and boat crews and evaluate electronic gauges and electronic transmissions to establish the cause(s) of the crash.[26]

A USCG helicopter crashed at Arcata Airport after flying out of USCGAS Humboldt Bay (California) in late April 2010. The three crewmembers aboard were rescued and not seriously injured.[27] Not so fortunate were the three helicopter crewmen who were killed, and one injured, when a USCG helicopter (MH-60 Jayhawk) crashed in the waters around James Island off LaPush, Washington, in July of 2010. Rear Adm. Gary Blore reported that the helicopter had departed from USCGAS Astoria (Oregon) on its planned flight to Sitka, Alaska. A civilian sailor pulled the injured Coastguardsmen from the sea. The missing crew from the inverted helicopter were being searched for after the incident.[28]

On 8 July 2010, the media reported that the U.S. Coast Guard identified the survivor and three deceased crewmembers of the MH-60 Jayhawk helicopter that creased in the sea off La Push, Washington. Lt. Lance D. Leone survived the crash and was treated for injuries at a Seattle, Washington, hospital. The deceased crewmembers were Lt. Sean D. Krueger, AMT1 Adam C. Hoke, and AMT2 Brett M. Banks. The deceased and surviving crewmembers were all decorated Coastguardsmen. Rear Adm. Gary T. Blore (13th District Coast Guard Commander) expressed his regard for the Coastguardsmen and their service, and remorse to their families for the loss of life and injuries incurred in the line of duty.[29]

10

Homeland Security

In 2001, one month after the 11 September 2001 (9/11) terrorist attacks on the United States, congressional legislation authorized the creation, merger and coordination of a department of Homeland Security which evolved out of more than 40 disparate federal agencies that dealt with national security issues. In 2001 former U.S. Army sergeant, lawyer, congressman and governor Tom Ridge became director of the Office of Homeland Security, and later the first Secretary of Homeland Security (2003–2005).[1]

From its 2001 origins to the present, the Department of Homeland Security (DHS) has managed a plethora of law enforcement and national security agencies mandated to monitor and respond to foreign and domestic threats. Former U.S. Circuit Judge Michael Chertoff served as the second DHS secretary under President George W. Bush from 2005 to 2008. Former governor Janet Napolitano became the third DHS secretary under President Barack Obama in 2009.

Agencies and departments of the DHS include the Federal Law Enforcement Training Center (FLETC) in Glynco, Georgia; U.S. Customs and Border Protection (CBP); U.S. Citizen and Immigration Service; U.S. Immigration and Customs Enforcement (ICE); Federal Emergency Management Agency (FEMA); U.S. Secret Service; Transportation Security Agency (TSA); Domestic Nuclear Detection Office; and the United States Coast Guard (USCG). The USCG was transferred from the U.S. Transportation Department to the U.S. Department of Homeland Security in 2003 where the service continued its multimission domestic and national defense missions in coordination with other DHS agencies and the U.S. Department of Defense.[2]

The Coast Guard DHS mission is a continuation of the service's traditional responsibilities with increased emphasis on national defense. The USCG is mandated to protect U.S. waterways, ports and infrastructure, and public safety; superintend aids to navigation (ATN); interdict illegal immigrants and contraband; and enforce maritime law in home waters and at sea. Environmental protection, natural disaster assistance, and search and rescue (SAR) are additional duties of the multimission Service. Protecting the nation's 360 major ports against sabotage and terrorism is the contemporary priority of the fifth member of the U.S. Armed Forces.[3]

Since 9/11 Congress increased the Coast Guard appropriation to accommodate the acquisition of a modernized, highly technical, coastal and deepwater air and sea fleet. The Coast Guard updated its helicopter and surveillance aircraft; ordnance and armament; and telecommunications technology. HH-65 helicopters were armed and attached to the Washington, D.C., National Capital Region Air Defense (NCRAD) command. In 2007 Congress appropriated $60 million to fund the USCG NCRAD mission.[4]

With its air, sea and land assets, and more than 50.000 civilian, auxiliary, regular, and reserve personnel, the U.S. Coast Guard is ideally suited to be the security watchdog over port, harbor, interior, and sea maritime zones. And with its connections and access to local, state, and federal law enforcement and other public safety agencies and the military forces of the Pentagon, the U.S. Coast Guard is ideally suited for its role as a national security force multiplier.

In 2004, the USCG initiated the Maritime Law Enforcement Academy (MLEA) at the Federal Law Enforcement Training Center (FLETC) in Charleston, South Carolina. Coast Guard investigative and intelligence personnel receive advanced training in investigation, rules of evidence, and other procedures. Port security training and vessel boarding, inspection and escort are important elements of economic and national security. Container inspection ashore and afloat and merchant ship crew inspections are ongoing duties that the Coast Guard coordinates with private security companies and local, state, and federal law enforcement and security agencies.[5]

Coast Guard intelligence and the National Maritime Intelligence Center (NMIC) provide information about ship arrivals, terrorist potential, maritime domain awareness, and smuggling operations. Information is exchanged between the Coast Guard and other U.S. Armed Forces, the U.S. Drug Enforcement Administration (USDEA) and U.S. Customs. The NMIC is a unit of the Office of Naval Intelligence (ONI) in Suitland, Maryland. The intelligence units include specialists from the civilian and military communities.[6]

On 20 October 2010, Homeland Security Secretary Janet Napolitano said upgrading Coast Guard assets and fleet "recapitalization" would be a continued federal priority. Napolitano warned that illegal immigration could have an Al Qaeda link, and the Coast Guard had an important role to play in that issue. Senator Joe Lieberman joined Secretary Napolitano in the U.S. Coast Guard Academy appearance. Senator Lieberman told the audience of staff and cadets that the Coast Guard gave the nation "confidence," and that the USCGA is a "great asset."[7]

After 9/11, the U.S. defense system was modified over North America into the Northern Command that integrates with the North American Aerospace Defense (NORAD). NORAD was a Cold War creation composed of United States and Canadian military forces in land and sea coordination. Canada and the U.S. have joint command responsibilities at NORAD headquarters in Colorado Springs, Colorado. The Coast Guard is associated with the Northern Command in its responsibility to protect America's coastal and internal waters and keep the terrorist threat far out to sea. The USCG mission is pursued within the context of domestic and international law and related agreements between nations.[8]

Congress passed the Maritime Transportation Security Act (MTSA) in 2002. The MTSA was intended to better secure domestic ports and maritime transportation and enforce cargo container regulations. U.S. Customs and Coast Guard officers have been posted at major ports in the United States and overseas. The USCG is the MTSA agency tasked with conducting port security assessments and developing and administering the Automatic Identification System (AIS). AIS technology allows the USCG to track and inspect domestic and foreign ships in U.S. waters and at sea. The associated advanced technology facilitates the inspection of ship cargoes, trucks, railroad cars, port and ship personnel, and suspected terrorist weapons and ordnance such as radioactive and biochemical devices.[9]

Charles S. Faddis was a counterterrorism operative and Middle East station chief in the Central Intelligence Agency (CIA). His experiences in counterterrorism and concerns about what he sees as vulnerabilities in the U.S. Department of Homeland Security and the U.S. Coast Guard are outlined in his book, *Willful Neglect: The Dangerous Illusion of Homeland Security.* Faddis analyzed what he contends are shortcomings and weaknesses in the security operations of key elements of U.S. infrastructure at nuclear, electrical and biochemical power plants; ports, harbors, ocean coasts, inland waterways and dams; petroleum and LNG (liquid natural gas) storage facilities; and on LNG and oil tankers sailing into U.S. waters.[10]

Faddis contends that the proliferation and blending of previously competent and stand-alone law enforcement and security agencies into the unwieldy federal Department of Homeland Security is not pragmatic or efficient. Complacency has set in and even U.S. military bases are not secure, let alone shipping and transportation systems on land, rail and water. Even signage, Faddis observed, not only gives warnings but defines terrorist access points. And civilian security guards are often inadequately trained and poorly armed against determined and suicidal Al Qaeda attackers armed with weapons, explosives, and perhaps missiles and nuclear devices. Strategic infrastructure, the security specialist asserted, needs to be surrounded by secure barriers and not be in proximity to dense population centers where possible.

In 2007, the security analyst recalled, six terrorist operatives were arrested by the FBI in the United States. The foreign-born Muslims were independent actors aligned with Al Qaeda and planned to attack the Fort Dix (New Jersey) U.S. Army Base. The belligerents possessed maps drawn by cohorts who had delivered pizza to the base, taken video photos undetected, and had not been interfered with or questioned.[11]

Military base vulnerability was also demonstrated in the Fort Hood (Texas) U.S. Army Base incident on 11 November 2009. Radical Muslim U.S. Army psychiatrist Maj. Nidal Malik Hasan opened fire killing 12 and wounding 31 soldiers preparing to go to Iraq. The troops were unarmed. The perpetrator was brought down by two civilian patrol police officers.[12]

Faddis elaborated on the danger that LNG on ships or at shoreside terminals posed. The gas is condensed from vapor to liquid for merchant vessel shipping and returned to a volatile vapor state ashore to be stored and transmitted along gas pipelines. Increasing amounts of LGN have been shipped to U.S. facilities from Middle East nations and stored onshore or at offshore receiving terminals in Massachusetts, Maryland, Puerto Rico, Louisiana, Alaska and Texas. More storage facilities were being planned in 2010. Faddis warned that an average LNG tanker carried "an energy content equivalent to several Hiroshima atomic bombs which would make a terrorist-activated ignition potentially devastating.[13]

Middle East pirates seized chemical tankers on the high seas in 2008–2009. Some of the pirates were alleged to have Al Qaeda connections and contacts, Faddis claimed, with Somali Muslims in the United States.[14]

Despite his stated respect for the training, responsibilities, and missions of the U.S. Coast Guard, Charles S. Faddis expressed doubts about the ability of the service to defend against a commandeered terrorist-crewed LNG tanker ship in Chesapeake Bay near the Potomac River and Washington, D.C. Faddis appreciated the ship inspection and escort operations of the USCG but expressed doubts that the service could provide the security and intervention force necessary to monitor all LNG vessels and prevent the potential "floating bomb" LNG tanker attack that dedicated terrorists might initiate.[15]

The former CIA agent conducted his own surveillance of strategic LNG terminals and recorded arrival and docking schedules of LNG tankers on the eastern seaboard. Charles S. Faddis concluded that the published mission statements, intervention plans, and coordinated agency actions assessments between USCG and other federal and private security and public safety agencies were problematic. Most of the planning scenarios, Faddis concluded, were too complex to ensure a rapid, unified, effective response to a dedicated terrorist attack on an LNG tanker or terminal.[16]

The USCG carefully trains personnel to carry out its ship monitoring, surveillance, boarding, and inspection techniques. Ship boarding requires intensive training. Skilled small boat coxswains operate off oceangoing Coast Guard cutters to carry out contraband interdiction, maritime law enforcement, port and national security, and homeland defense missions. Contemporary USCG coxswain skills replicate the successful World War II Coast Guard landing craft operations in the Atlantic, Mediterranean, and Pacific maritime theaters. Skilled coxswains are emphasized and rewarded by the U.S. Coast Guard.

The USCGC *Campbell* (WMEC-909) is stationed at U.S. Naval Shipyard Portsmouth (New Hampshire); Chief Boatswain's Mate John Costabile (USCG), crewmember and coxswain, received the 2009 Douglas A. Munro Inspirational Leadership Award. The award is named after Coxswain SM1 Douglas Munro (USCG), a World War II landing craft coxswain at Guadalcanal and posthumous Medal of Honor recipient. In presenting the award, Cmdr. Scott Clendenin (USCG) described BMC Costabile's courage and seamanship skills in hazardous sea and contraband ship boarding circumstances. Cmdr. Clendenin explained how BMC Costabile's leadership skills were further illustrated by his assignment as underway officer of the deck on the CGC *Campbell*, a duty traditionally assigned to commissioned officers.[17]

Charles S. Faddis expressed legitimate concerns about the potential dangers posed by domestic or Middle East liquid natural gas (LNG) tankers mooring out to sea or coming into U.S. harbors and ports. The Coast Guard is concerned as well and has trained its personnel to plan, monitor and respond to LNG exigencies and the concerns of affected populations and communities in proximal geographic regions.

U.S. Coast Guard officials believe they have security plans that facilitate the safe passage of LNG tankers coming to the United States from the Middle East nation of Yemen into the Port of Boston, Massachusetts. Captain John Healey (USCG), captain of the port (COTP) Boston, responded to the concerns and criticisms of Boston Mayor Thomas Menino and surrounding community leaders who feared explosions of the flammable cargoes, or the presence of terrorists on the tankers. Capt. Healey reported in February 2010 that the shipments due to arrive that month had been reviewed and planned for throughout the previous year, and LNG tankers not meeting security standards would be turned away and out to sea by the USCG. The first LNG tanker from Yemen arrived safely at a remote Texas port the previous week.[18]

Boston Mayor Thomas Menino stated his disappointment with the Coast Guard decision to approve the port docking of Middle East tankers and declared his preference for an offshore unloading terminal. Mayor Menino suggested that the Coast Guard decision might put corporate interests ahead of regional security. Captain Healey, in his meetings with the press and concerned state legislators and community officials, said Yemen's ports met national security standards, tanker crews would be screened, security forces would check the tankers in the Middle East and seven miles off the U.S. shoreline, and USCG personnel would do shipboard and underwater surveillance before the tankers entered harbor waters. Distrigas of Massachusetts, the LNG importer, released a public statement that outlined its own security procedures and cooperation with the U.S. Coast Guard.[19]

In September 2010, the U.S. Coast Guard submitted a recommendation to the Federal Energy Regulatory Commission (FERC) that endorsed a plan to build an LNG terminal and transit facility in Calais, Maine, pending specific security and safety modifications. The tanker transit route would be along the Passamaquoddy Bay and St. Croix River waterways. Captain James McPherson (USCG), Coast Guard COTP for Northern New England, and specialists from Coast Guard Sector New England worked with corporate, public safety, and community representatives in the planning and initiation stages of the project. The Coast Guard reviewed and approved the Calais LNG Waterway Suitability Assessment report. Upon licensure, Calais LNG Corporation would be required to submit safety and security emergency response plans submitted by civilian and USCG security experts.[20]

National security specialists have expressed concern about the vulnerability of tourist cruise ships to terrorist takeover and destruction, and the threat that insurgents disguised as passengers might sail a huge ocean liner into a strategic port and ignite explosives or weapons of mass destruction (WMDs). While that oceanic and port security scenario has not occurred, the following incidents illustrate the possibility of such an attack.

In early November 2010, Carnival Cruise Lines passenger vessel *Carnival Splendor* was stranded without power, electronics, and communications equipment after an engine-room fire disabled the vessel 50 miles off the Mexican coast. Lt. Patrick Montgomery, a Coast Guard spokesperson, said the 952-foot luxury cruise liner carrying 4,000 passengers and 1,100 crew members was scheduled to be towed by tugboats to a Mexican port. Coast Guard crewmembers boarded the *Carnival Splendor* to conduct an investigation. A USCG cutter stationed nearby stood ready to provide all necessary assistance.

Sailors aboard the diverted aircraft carrier USS *Ronald Reagan* readied 65,000 pounds of food and other supplies for helicopter transshipment to the disabled cruise ship. Naval architect William Garzke, an investigator of ship accidents and sinkings, said, "If it was an accident," the fire could have been by a short-circuited electric cable or a burst pipe. In 2006 the *Star Princess* caught fire from a discarded cigarette that resulted in one fatality and 11 injuries. That incident caused Carnival Cruise Lines to limit the number of smoking stations and install more sprinkler systems on its vessels.[21] These incidents illustrate the relative ease with which determined extremists could take hostages and disable or commandeer a cruise liner and pose significant danger at sea or in coastal and harbor areas.

The significance of effective boarding teams and federal agency coordination for national security was illustrated by an early–November 2010 incident that occurred three miles off the Massachusetts coast. Two stowaway passengers were removed from the Liberian-flagged M/V *Prince of Sound*. The migrants were discovered hidden in cargo crates by ship crewmembers. The Middle East migrants were Palestinians. The USCG transferred the prisoners to U.S. Customs and Border Protection (CBP) agents for interrogation and disposition.[22]

Coast Guard and Customs and Border Patrol officers conducted another early November 2010 mission approximately four miles out of San Diego, California. At 2:45 A.M., the 110-foot USCG patrol boat *Edisto* (WPB-1313) noticed a suspicious vessel running northbound out of Mexican waters without navigation lights. CBP maritime interdiction officers and USCG crewmembers intercepted the 20-foot vessel and placed 23 illegal Latin America nationals under arrest for further interrogation and processing. The CBP and USCG, both Department of Homeland Security (DHS) agency team members, conduct joint operations under the Maritime Unified Command.[23]

David Allen is a senior technical engineer at International Business Machines (IBM) in Rochester, Minnesota. Allen, a serious military history student, speaker, military actor and game player, is president of the Scott Hosier World War II Roundtable. Two brothers pursued military careers. David Allen's father, Lt. Col. John C. Allen (U.S. Army), retired in 1968 after serving in World War II and the Korean War, as commander of a defense guided-missile unit, and an intelligence officer.

David Allen took national defense classes at American Military University in 2009–2010. Allen studied national defense and national security and developed an interest in the Department of Homeland Security and the missions of the U.S. Coast Guard. David Allen shared his military studies, research, class materials, professor notes, and perspectives with this author through interviews, e-mails, conversations, and travel to military sites and presentations.[24]

Allen brought his engineering background to the study of terrorist use of cyberspace technology, hacking into defense and infrastructure systems, ignition of weapons with cell phones, and the potential use of missiles to bring down civilian passenger airliners. In a research paper, Allen outlined the possible scenarios of terrorists coming over the vulnerable and sparsely guarded U.S.–Canada border and bringing down vulnerable aircraft at airports in the rural-urban Midwest. Allen described various tower, unmanned aircraft, and counterterrorist electronic and missile defenses that could be used to thwart such attacks.

Allen's security and defense studies at American Military University surveyed the attraction to terrorists and defense measures that must be considered in protecting domestic water supplies, agricultural products, and biochemical plants and products. Also studied were psychological warfare tactics and strategies; the dangers posed by illegal immigrants and drug and gun traffickers and their connections to terror networks; and the siphoning off of money by Islamic extremists from charitable organizations. The importance of courageous civilian and military leadership was considered, as opposed to the vulnerabilities caused by risk-averse leaders, and the undermining of American resolve in the decline of patriotic unity and the corrosive influence of naive political correctness.

Professor notes and Allen's deliberations also focused on the U.S. Coast Guard, its well-trained personnel and multimission responsibilities, and the contradictions and complexities posed by the USCG in civilian law enforcement, national defense, border security, and exemption from the Posse Comitatus Act (1878–1879), which generally prohibits the other U.S. Armed Forces from direct involvement in domestic law enforcement. Also considered was the need for better communication between public safety agencies and civilian security and commercial interests that are the most vulnerable and are the first responders to terrorist attacks.[25]

President George W. Bush signed the Department of Homeland Security into law in 2003, two years after the 11 September 2001 terrorist attacks in his first administration. Bush supporters insisted that in his two terms of office the president kept America safe from post–9/11 domestic terrorist attacks. In contrast, Bush's successor, President Barack Obama, suffered domestic terrorist attempts, both failed and successful, on his watch. Several attack attempts from overseas sources were thwarted by international cooperation in the first two years of Obama's presidency.

To prevent a second attack after 9/11, Bush deployed National Guard troops to airports; tightened up visa application procedures and airport security measures; put federal air marshals on passenger aircraft; and encouraged federal agencies to work more closely with local governments, law enforcement and other public safety agencies, and the private sector. Security was increased at nuclear power plants, other critical infrastructure sites, and seaports. Governor Tom Ridge of Pennsylvania was given a White House post to oversee Homeland Security operations. President Bush saw the need to coordinate the security activities of the U.S. Customs and the Immigration and Naturalization (INS) agencies in the Treasury Department, and the U.S. Coast Guard in the Department of Transportation. Democratic senator Joe Lieberman of Connecticut had been a proponent of the creation of a unified cabinet-level Homeland Security agency and pushed through the necessary legislation. Bush nominated Tom Ridge as the first secretary of the Department of Homeland Security (DHS).[26]

The DHS coordinated 22 previously autonomous federal agencies. The FBI remained in the Justice Department but created a new National Security Branch that focused on antiterrorist activities. The Defense Department established the Northern Command to defend the territorial United States, and the Treasury Department developed methods to monitor and interrupt terrorist financing sources. Policies were established during the Bush years to facilitate CIA antiterrorist operations, develop effective interrogation techniques on captured terrorists, and monitor telecommunications networks to track terrorist communications at home and abroad. Domestic politics, an ever-inquisitive media, and civil libertarians objected and exposed some of these operations, and subjected the security process to judicial intervention. The Bush administration did its best to protect sources, enhance antiterrorist policies, and protect sources against the politicized opponents of the policies and operations.[27]

Bush's national security support team included national security advisor Condi Rice and Secretary of State Colin Powell, whom Rice later succeeded, and Secretary of Defense Donald Rumsfeld whose necessarily aggressive posture and controversial policies and responses antagonized political opponents and elements of the media. Rumsfeld later resigned and was succeeded by Defense Secretary Robert M. Gates.[28]

Hurricane Katrina struck the Gulf Coast states of Mississippi and Louisiana in August 2005. President Bush credited U.S. Armed Forces response teams and courageous U.S. Coast Guard aviation teams that saved thousands of lives in inclement and dangerous conditions. Bush credited the Coast Guard for prepositioning USCG helicopters in critical zones. The federal response was thwarted by domestic politics and initial inadequate decision making, which illustrated the difficulties local, state and federal authorities can face in responding to natural or man-made (terrorist) disasters.[29]

President George W. Bush credited two no-nonsense, highly capable military leaders for their on-scene administrative and communications skills in coordinating military and civilian hurricane relief operations and managing media relations: Vice Admiral Thad Allen (U.S. Coast Guard) and General Russ Honore (U.S. Army). Bush later appointed Adm. Allen commandant of the United States Coast Guard.[30] Gen. Honore and Adm. Allen exemplified the leadership skills and essential role the U.S. military would play in future natural and terrorist disasters when widespread disasters, panic, casualties, and infrastructure damage must be responded to by cooperative federal, state, and local public safety, law enforcement, and military agencies.

11

The Coast Guard in Kosovo, Iraq and the Persian Gulf

Reference has been made in other sections of this book to the U.S. Coast Guard's national defense contributions in war and peace, and in the War on Terror in the United States and overseas. In this chapter the Coast Guard's role in the Muslim world of the Balkans (Kosovo) and the Middle East (Iraq and the Persian Gulf) will be explored in greater detail.

In the spring of 1999, President William Jefferson Clinton sent U.S. Armed Forces into the Eastern European Balkan nation of Kosovo to assist Muslims under attack by Yugoslav-Serbian dictator Slobodan Milosevic. The Serbians initiated the violent "ethnic cleansing" policies to expel Kosovar Muslims out of the region. In his attempt to keep U.S. ground casualties low, Clinton ordered U.S. Air Force jet fighters and bombers to assist the military forces of the North Atlantic Treaty Organization (NATO). Using high technology and generally precise "surgical strikes" to protect Muslims from Serbian soldiers, the U.S.–NATO response was eventually successful,[1] despite a few attack errors that caused civilian "collateral damage" on a railroad bridge and at the embassy of the People's Republic of China.

As historian and author William J. Bennett pointed out, despite the criticism the United States received from extremist Islamic groups during the subsequent War on Terror, for more than two decades "the United States had taken up arms on behalf of Muslims ... from Afghanistan to Kuwait to Somalia to Bosnia and Kosovo,"[2] and one should add Iraq in the George W. Bush administrations (2001–2009).

The USCGC *Bear* (WMEC-901) deployed to the Adriatic Sea in southern Europe in the summer of 1999 to support Operation Noble Anvil and Operation Allied Force and NATO military operations against the former Communist Republic of Yugoslavia and its freshly splintered member states.

The CGC *Bear* served with the USS *Theodore Roosevelt* (CVN-71), the U.S. Navy aircraft carrier and lead ship of the battle group near the Albanian coast. The *Bear* provided surveillance, SAR backup, and combat escort for the U.S. Army transport ships which carried cargo across the Adriatic Sea between Italy and Albania. The *Bear* sailed in waters within enemy surface-to-surface missile range. The *Bear* later cruised into the Black Sea between Turkey and Russia to participate in a ship and aircraft military exercise group that consisted of the United States, France, Greece, and Turkey, and the former Soviet satellites and now sovereign nations of Georgia, Romania, and Bulgaria. The *Bear* later participated in training operations with the African nations of Tunisia and Morocco.[3]

The support that oceangoing Coast Guard cutters lend to U.S. Navy commanders was illustrated by the subsequent deployment of the CGC *Bear* to the Navy Sixth Fleet in the Mediterranean Sea. The *Bear* provided naval escort service to merchant vessels in the Kosovo war. The U.S. Navy utilized the *Bear* because of the cutter crew's training in naval war fighting, functional war weaponry and ordnance, and ship escort and maritime vessel control. In those naval support operations the *Bear* earned the NATO Kosovo Medal and the Kosovo Campaign Medal.[4]

President George W. Bush launched Operation Iraqi Freedom (OIF) in 2003, after Iraqi dictator Saddam Hussein ignored years of United Nations resolutions condemning his vicious regime. Saddam Hussein had refused to comply with international demands to allow international inspectors to fully ascertain the dictator's possession or destruction of weapons of mass destruction (WMDs). Saddam Hussein had previously used WMDs upon his own people and on Iranian troops in the 1980s. UN/U.S. troops and President George H. W. Bush, George W. Bush's father, had thwarted Saddam's invasion of Kuwait in the 1990s. Saddam Hussein later threatened to kill Bush family members.

Relying on international intelligence consensus, George W. Bush ordered the 2003 U.S. invasion of Iraq. After hard fighting in extreme battle and geographic conditions, Saddam Hussein was captured, tried and executed. Bush considered this a victory in the War on Terror.

Democratic and Republican members of Congress and President Clinton had previously asserted their belief that Saddam had WMDs and that the threat he posed to his people and neighbors required "regime change." Later in the war, when large caches of biochemical and nuclear WMDs were not found, the Bush administration was severely criticized at home and abroad for launching the war under deceptive circumstances. Remnants of biochemical weapons and yellow cake were subsequently discovered, however, and some observers continued to assert that Saddam had transported his WMDs into Syria before the U.S. invasion and had maintained the capacity and his intention to restart the WMD program. The former president reiterated in his book *Decision Points*, and in 2010 public interviews, that he had no regrets about the Iraq invasion or displacing Saddam. Bush expressed his appreciation of the "Coalition of the Willing" nations that sent troops to Iraq to assist the United States. The result, Bush asserted, was a more democratic and stable Iraq and a democratic ally in the volatile Middle East. Part of his legacy, Bush contended, was keeping his promise to protect America from a post–9/11 internal terrorist attack.[5]

The Coast Guard performed coastal security and marine interception patrols with the U.S. Navy and coalition (allied nations) naval units to enforce UN sanctions. The USCG blocked the maritime movements of Iraqi officials and military units in Operation Iraqi Freedom. CGC *Boutwell* (WHEC-719), out of the home port of Alameda, California, identified and seized contraband cargo. CGC *Adak* (WPB-1333), out of Sandy Hook, New Jersey, captured the first maritime prisoners of war (POWs) in OIF. Other USCG patrol boats (WPBs) and law enforcement detachments (LEDETs) seized Iraq mine-laying naval vessels to protect cargo vessels in the harbor area of Umm Qasr. LEDET-205 captured Iraqi weapons and military equipment in coastal caves. USCG port security units (PSUs) of Coast Guard Reservists secured Iraqi oil terminals and provided port security in the Arabian and Persian Gulf regions. Coast Guard Maritime Environmental Response Teams (MERTs) were trained to respond to environmental terrorism. The CGG *Walnut* (WLB-205), out of Honolulu, Hawaii, conducted navigation surveys on strategic waterways like the Khor Abd Allah River to Umm Qasr. The CGC *Walnut* maintained ATNs (aids to navigation) such as buoys to secure safe navigation routes for commercial, military, and humanitarian vessels.[6]

At operational maximum in OIF, 1,250 USCG regular and reserve personnel were deployed to the Persian Gulf. The Coast Guard operations included two large 378-foot cutters: CGC *Boutwell* (WHEC-719) and CGC *Dallas* (WHEC-716), out of the ports of Alameda, California and North Charleston, South Carolina respectively; and the 225-foot CGC *Walnut* (WLB-205), a seagoing buoy tender out of Honolulu, Hawaii.

Eight CGC WPB patrol boats served in OIF: *Wrangell* (South Portland, Maine); *Adak* (Sandy Hook, New Jersey); *Aquidneck* (Atlantic Beach, North Carolina); *Baranof* (Miami, Florida); *Grand Isle* (Gloucester, Massachusetts); *Bainbridge Island* (Sandy Hook, New Jersey); *Pea Island* (St. Petersburg, Florida); and *Knight Island* (St. Petersburg, Florida). Six PSUs (305, 307, 308, 309, 311, 313) served in OIF out of their respective home bases of Hampton

USCGC *Wrangell* (WPB-1322) and USS *Reagan* (CVN-76) in the Persian Gulf on 8 March 2006 (USN photograph, taken by an on-duty USN photographer in the public domain).

Roads, Virginia; St. Petersburg, Florida; Gulfport, Mississippi; Cleveland, Ohio; San Pedro, California; and Tacoma, Washington. Tactical law enforcement detachments in OIF were teams from Chesapeake, Virginia; Miami, Florida; and San Diego, California.[7]

Lt. Cmdr. Greg Magee (USCG) wrote an exemplary analysis and summation of Coast Guard operations in the Persian Gulf during Operation Iraqi Freedom (OIF) in his official U.S. Coast Guard history.[8] Cmdr. Magee wrote that as early as October 2002, the U.S. Central Command requested that specialized Coast Guard forces lend support to "possible military action against Iraq" before, as it turned out, the actual 2003 U.S. invasion. The U.S. Navy expressed interest in the application of the USCG areas of specialization and expertise: pollution response in anticipation of Saddam's Hussein's use of oil spills against the U.S. and coalition force allies as the Iraqi dictator had done in the United Nation's Desert Storm military intervention that expelled Iraqi forces from Kuwait; port security operations in harbor areas and around port infrastructure; maritime interdictions and ship boardings by Coast Guard law enforcement detachments to enforce UN sanctions against contraband on enemy vessels; and littoral (shallow-water) warfare operations by Coast Guard patrol boats (WPBs) to maintain a U.S. Navy presence while larger USN vessels patrolled further out to sea.[9]

Operation Iraqi Freedom began on 19 March 2003. The WPBs protected amphibious and mine laying and deactivating naval units. Coast Guard cutters made the first capture of maritime POWs, stopped the escape to sea of more than 70 contraband smuggling vessels, and escorted humanitarian aid ships into Iraqi waters. The U.S. Navy viewed the U.S. Coast Guard as the experts in maritime interdiction operations (MIOs). The Coast Guard combat complement was the largest wartime deployment of the service since the Vietnam War. The USS *Chinook* and USCGC *Adak* jointly boarded an Iraq tugboat and discovered drums containing mine-laying equipment. An Iraqi sea captain blamed the presence of Coast Guard "white patrol boats" for his failure to release mines into the waterways.[10]

PSUs 311 and 313 conducted port security operations in the harbors and ports of Kuwait and the major Iraq port of Az Zubayr. The PSUs provided security teams on offshore oil platforms after U.S. Navy special warfare teams secured the huge infrastructures. Coast Guard National Strike Force (NSF) teams secured and guarded oil platforms before enemy soldiers could release petroleum into the Arabian Gulf. Lt. Cmdr. Magee reported that WPB crews averaged an astounding 900 hours underway on sea patrols each month without major mission breakdowns. Despite the impressive seamanship skills exhibited, extensive maintenance was periodically needed and performed.[11]

Coast Guard Reservist Magazine (May–June 2003) covered USCG operations in Operation Iraqi Freedom in an illustrated article. YN1 Thomas Heavey (USCGR) sent in a report (1 May 2003) about port security unit activities in the Middle East. PSU-311 (San Pedro, California) and PSU-313 (Tacoma, Washington) relieved U.S. Marines of security on two oil and gas platforms in the Persian Gulf that had been liberated from Iraqi military control by U.S. Navy SEALS. The gas and oil platforms (GOPLAT) were identified as the Mina Al Bakr Oil Terminal (MABOT) and Khawr Al Amaya Oil Terminal (KAAOT). Iraqi soldiers still on the platforms were detained as enemy prisoners of war (EPWs) and later boarded ships for transfer to the Iraqi mainland. The platform decks were 20 and 40 feet off the water surface and 1,200 yards long. MABOT had a helicopter landing pad.

Heavy storms threatened PSU 25-foot patrol boats. U.S. Army landing craft brought supplies to the platforms. USN and USCG boats and ships patrolled the six-mile waterways between the GOPLAT. Rear Adm. Mary

Petty Officer First Class (P01) Timothy A. Beard (USCG) stands guard at the Mina al Bakr oil terminal in July 2003 as member of port security unit (PSU) 313. The oil terminal is located in the North Arabian Gulf (NAG) off the coast of Iraq.

O'Donnell (USCGR), the ranking reservist of the Pacific Area, visited the PSUs. The Coast Guard crews made the GOPLAT as clean and livable as possible, including setting up a satellite TV antenna to keep in touch with Fox News and CNN. YN1 Heavey described the security and life-saving missions the Coast Guard performed in the Persian Gulf and described his hope for "liberty to take root" in the historic "birthplace of civilization."[12]

In the same issue of *Coast Guard Reservist* (May–June 2003), Lt. John Garofolo (USCGR) described joint USCG-USN security operations at the captured port of Umm Qasr in Iraq. Humanitarian aid and infrastructure rebuilding were added to the missions after combat incidents diminished. The USCG-USN armed force operated out of Naval Coastal Warfare Group One out of San Diego, California. Naval security forces operated vessels of various sizes, set up .50 caliber machine gun emplacements, and performed anti-terrorist missions in Iraq and Kuwait with British forces. PSU-311 (Long Beach, California) crewed armed small boats, patrolled the Iraq port of Umm

Qasr, guarded the Khawr al Amaya petroleum terminal, and coordinated ship escort missions with U.S. Navy Inshore Boat Unit 14 (St. Louis, Missouri). Lt. Garofolo described operations designed to protect the port, harbor, infrastructure, and personnel against enemy swimmers, divers, and suicide craft.[13]

Master Chief Petty Officer Tom Cowan (USCGR) interviewed Boatswain Mate Chief Ted Cooley for *Coast Guard Reservist* Magazine (May–June 2003) and credited BMC Cooley as the most senior Coastguardsmen deployed in OIF. BMC Cooley served with the USN in San Diego (1959) and joined the USCGR (1981). Chief Cooley's Coast Guard career included duties as a drilling reservist and assignments to Reserve Unit National Strike Force Support, Station Lake Tahoe, and, since 1999, PSU-311. In the 20-month period before May 2003, BMC Cooley served on deployments to strategic U.S. ports and the Middle East nations of Bahrain, Kuwait, and Iraq. Chief Cooley retired on 15 May 2003 at age 62 after 26 years with the USCGR.[14]

PA2 John Masson (USCGR) wrote an article on PSU-305s homecoming for the May–June 2003 *Coast Guard Reservist*. PA2 Masson, public affairs specialist for the U.S. Coast Guard Atlantic Area, described the return to the United States of the 100-member Virginia-based Port Security Unit-305. Among the PSU-305 personnel who landed at Langley Air Force Base was

35. PSU-311 Petty Officer Paul Floge (USCG) on port security duty in 2003 in Operation Iraqi Freedom. PO Floge guards the Iraqi oil terminal at Khawr al Amaya with a .50 caliber machine gun.

professional firefighter Petty Officer First Class Tim Pais (USCGR). PSU-305 served in three deployments over a 20-month period, including immediate deployment to New York Harbor hours after the 11 September 2001 terrorist attacks, five months in port security assignments at U.S. Navy Base Guantanamo Bay (Cuba), and deployment to support OIF with the U.S. European Command in the Global War on Terror. The sailors and PSU-305 commanding officer Cmdr. Robert Grab (USCG) were welcomed home by family and friends and addressed by Rear Adm. Duncan C. Smith III, Atlantic Area deputy commander for mobilization and reserve affairs.[15]

In the Northern Persian Gulf (NPG), three Iraqi sailors became the first prisoners of war (POWs) apprehended by the USCG in OIF. The 24-crew complement of the USCGC *Adak* (WPB-1333) rescued and captured the surviving Iraqi sailors after coalition forces destroyed their patrol boat. The POWs were taken to a secure location for interrogation and confinement.[16]

Basil Tripsas, Patrick Roth, and Renee Fye wrote a primary source analysis of the USCG in OIF for the Center for Naval Analysis (CNA). Dr. Harvey M. Spivak, director of the Maritime Search and Undersea Warfare Team in the Advanced Technology and Systems Analysis Division of the CNA, approved the report for distribution to the Department of Defense (DOD). The conclusions of the center are specifically stated to "represent the best opinion of CNA at the time of issue (October 2004)" and "does not necessarily represent the opinion of the Department of the Navy."[17]

The CNA analysis was done at the request of the U.S. Coast Guard Historian's Office (USCGHO) in Washington, D.C. CNA data was acquired from interviews, situation reports, and reconstructions. Interviews occurred with and were conducted by representatives of the USCGHO, and Coast Guard officials at Atlantic Area/Pacific Area headquarters. Interviews were conducted with USCG OIF participants in and outside the theater of operations after the mission operations. Civilian specialists and U.S. Navy and U.S. Coast Guard officers and enlisted petty officers were consulted.

Coast Guard officers on the USCGC *Boutwell* (Capt. Scott Genovese), the cutter support detachment in the Middle East nation of Bahrain, and the 110-foot patrol boats *Aquidneck* (Lt. Holly Harrison), *Baranof* (Lt. Cmdr. Christopher Barrows), and *Wrangell* (QM1 David Chapman) were interviewed. Also consulted were USN, USNR, and USCG and USCGR officers in Naval Coastal Warfare Group One and the Fifth Fleet U.S. Navy commander, Capt. James Hanna (USN), and Coast Guard Liaison officers Lt. Cmdr. Robert Hanley and Lt. Cmdr. John McKinley.

Coast Guard law enforcement detachment (LEDET-406) officers and petty officers "Lt. (jg) Robert Kinsey; MT1 Gerald Visser; and DC3 Nathan

Brukenthal [*sic*]" described their combat theater experiences.[18] Petty Officer Nathan Bruckenthal was later killed in the line of duty when he and Coast Guard and Navy crew members attempted to stop and board an Iraqi suicide boat in the Persian Gulf.

The CNA summarized the USCG missions as traditional intercept, SAR, port security, ATN, and security patrols closer inshore than the larger USN vessels could operate. CNA concluded that the USCG generally performed its missions effectively, but there were communications technology deficiencies via encrypted radio circuits (SIPRNET: Secure Internet Protocol Network) that the USN and larger USCG cutters used but smaller patrol boats could not.[19]

The CNA report concisely described the different Coast Guard theaters of operations in OIF. The Persian-Arabian Gulf mission was emphasized, but support missions were significant in the Mediterranean Sea region. Coast Guard units provided security escorts for cargo shipments from the Strait of Gibraltar in the eastern Mediterranean through Egypt's Suez Canal. The 378-foot USCGC *Dallas* (WHEC-716) and four USCG 100-foot patrol boats escorted U.S. Navy military supply convoys and aircraft carrier battle groups. The Coast Guard cutters stood SAR watch for USN flight operations and intercepted and boarded vessels that intruded into operational waters.[20] Joining the *Dallas* in the Mediterranean were the Coast Guard patrol boats *Grand Isle* (WPB-1338), *Knight Island* (WPB-1348), *Bainbridge Island* (WPB-1343), and *Pea Island* (WPB-1347), and the port security unit PSU-309.[21]

The 223-foot USCGC *Walnut* (WLB-205), a seagoing buoy tender, carried a 40-crew complement and one 25 mm gun for defense against small craft. The *Walnut* missions included harbor patrol, cargo carrying, SAR, environmental cleanup, installation and maintenance of navigation aids (ATN) such as buoys and other vessel guiding devices, and law enforcement. The cleanup capacity was important in the expected event that Iraqi troops and naval forces released oil into the Gulf as they had in Operation Desert Storm.[22]

Coast Guard law enforcement detachments (LEDETS) operated ship-boarding teams off USN Cyclone-class patrol boats. Coast Guard shore detachments in Bahrain and Iraq supported maintenance, personnel and supply support.[23]

U.S. Coast Guard units were informed about the coming 2003 OIF deployment overseas in October and November of 2002 to provide time for mission-specific personnel training and the installation of functional warfighting technology on Coast Guard boats and cutters.

The CGC *Boutwell* out of Alameda, California prepared for the coming mission and Pacific-Persian Gulf voyage. The cutter was equipped with more secure Internet protocol and network technology (called SIPRNET) used by the U.S. Navy for voice communications, intelligence data, and other information. The CGC *Walnut* was also able to communicate on the channel network. The *Boutwell* added a helicopter to her deck platform in Hawaii. The helicopter was equipped with an infrared system that allowed nighttime observation of possible contraband vessels to be interdicted and boarded.[24]

Transportation logistics for Coast Guard vessels and personnel varied. The CGC *Boutwell*, with some challenges, was able to traverse the Pacific with her diesel and gas turbine engines and keep pace with accompanying naval vessels at a 13–18 knot speed. The CGC *Walnut*, a smaller and slower cutter (13-knot cruising speed), had to commence the sea journey to the Persian Gulf alone and before other cutters and personnel were deployed by the naval Central Command. There was concern, fortunately not realized, that the buoy tender might be targeted as a merchant vessel by pirates in Southeast Asian waters. The *Walnut* arrived in the Arabian Gulf on time to participate in the March 2003 military operations.

The 110-foot Coast Guard patrol boats, too small to sail to OIF from the United States, were carried to the Gulf on the chartered commercial vessel M/V *Industrial Challenger.* The patrol boat crews and PSU personnel were flown to the theater of operations. Their small boats and equipment came in on cargo aircraft. The four Mediterranean theater patrol craft were carried to their operations areas by cargo vessels. After the conflict ended the patrol boats sailed back across the Atlantic Ocean accompanied by the CGC *Dallas.*[25]

Although much of the OIF operations information was still classified, the CNA analysts reported that the U.S. Coast Guard cutters operated effectively within the Navy command. While testifying to that, USN Fifth Fleet staff said some "connectivity (communications) difficulties" with patrol boats might require the installation of SIPRNET capacity on patrol craft to facilitate future USN-USCG operations. The Coast Guard cutters in the geographically expansive Northern Arabian Gulf (NAG) operated at "the tip of the spear," the CNA asserted, because of "the limited threat Iraq forces posed to ships and the fact that smaller (USCG) vessels were exactly the type needed for NAG littoral waters intercepts and boardings."[26]

The CNA analysts contended that the USCG cutters and two USN Cyclone–class patrol boats with Coast Guard LEDET personnel provided essential boarding operations on "uncooperative" vessels. The USCG vessels operated more freely than USN craft could because of the "less threatening nature of a white-hulled Coast Guard ship as opposed to a grey-hull Navy one." This was a significant factor when Iranian navy forces in close proximity border areas had to be dealt with. The Coast Guard vessels in the NAG and

U.S. Coast Guard port security unit 311 on patrol at the Iraq port of Umm Qasar. The crew of a USCG 25-foot patrol boat mans the guns and check out a beached craft in May of 2003.

Mediterranean regions were taken off domestic SAR, narcotics, and fisheries enforcement missions, which necessitated extended duty hours, and patrols for USCG crews in U.S. waters.[27]

CNA analysts surveyed the training and role of U.S. Coast Guard Reserve members in OIF. USCGR personnel had to be trained or refreshed in rules of force, weapons use, and small boat handling at U.S. Coast Guard Training Center Yorktown (Virginia). The Atlantic Area Coast Guard staff modified schedules to accommodate training needs.

Cmdr. Jim Brinkman (USCG), director of mission planning, trained USCGR members as small boat coxswains and in weapons qualifications. Cmdr. Chris Doane (USCG), Atlantic Area port security chief and coordinator of strategy and policy, said Reserve program problems were discovered. Coast Guard responses to security needs in the major out-load ports of Charleston, South Carolina; Jacksonville, Florida; Corpus Christie, Texas; Philadelphia, Pennsylvania; and Norfolk, Virginia, posed logistical and tactical issues. Personnel had to be transferred between various ports, but they generally met the challenges. CNA suggested a more efficient Reserve tracking and training system to maintain the qualifications and readiness of USCGR personnel for future national defense call-ups.[28]

A CNA suggestion for improved "interoperability with the Navy" was for the Coast Guard to send more of its officers to the U.S. Navy Tactical

Training Group in Dam Neck, Virginia, and San Diego, California. The CNA said the USCG did an exemplary job keeping deployed units "supplied and operational," and determined its forces "fit well into the Navy's command and control structure," a conclusion supported by U.S. Navy personnel who affirmed "the valuable and unique contributions the Coast Guard made."[29]

The Coast Guard port security unit (PSU) boats were judged deficient for the mission of gas and oil platform security duty. CNA found the boats too small, vulnerable to damage in high seas while attached to platforms, and insufficiently armed for surveillance and platform defense. But in their general port security operations at key ports, the PSUs were judged to have performed well.

Coast Guard operations in shoal (shallow) littoral waters were an important contribution to OIF because the larger USN ships could not operate safely or effectively in all NAG waters.

The Coast Guard liaison officers to the Fifth Fleet U.S. Navy commander (Capt. James Hanna, chief of staff, USN) were Lt. Cmdr. John McKinley (USCG liaison officer) and Lt. Cmdr. Robert Hanley (assistant USCG liaison officer). The assistant USCG liaison to the Fifth Fleet described the Coast Guard contribution to OIF precisely: "This was a war fought in the littorals. [The U.S. Navy has stated] we have to project power from where the water turns blue to where it turns brown. So here is the Coast Guard with WPB patrol boats and the 378-foot cutter *Boutwell* that were able to allow the Navy to project force in the places it couldn't have gotten to otherwise."[30]

12

Port Security, Pirates and Commandos

Since the 11 September 2001 terrorist attacks, the United States has expanded its activities in domestic security, national defense, and overseas operations. The U.S. Armed Forces have teamed up to coordinate and take the fight overseas to where terrorists operate.

The United States Coast Guard (USCG) has increased its training and missions in port security and national defense missions at home and overseas. The USCG has conducted joint operations against extremists in the War on Terror with local, state and federal public safety, national security, law enforcement, diplomatic and defense agencies.

The USCG and U.S. Navy (USN) have conducted joint missions in the Persian Gulf; against international piracy in African and Asian waters; and against illegal contraband (drugs, weapons, migrants) on ships and boats. The Coast Guard cooperates with other security agencies ashore in the protection of harbor infrastructure from espionage, sabotage, and terrorist attacks.

Those complex operations have involved U.S. Customs and U.S. Immigration units, the Federal Bureau of Investigation (FBI), the Drug Enforcement Administration (DEA), and the security, defense, and law enforcement agencies of the international community of nations.

To protect the territory of the United States, the Coast Guard has enhanced its personnel training and acquired the assets necessary to patrol and secure the interior, coastal, and international maritime domain. The missions have necessitated increased congressional appropriations and the acquisition of expensive and technologically complex air, sea, and shore assets and secure communications systems.

To train its personnel for the age of terrorism, the USCG initiated commando training. Twelve Coastguardsmen were selected for U.S. Navy SEAL integration in 2008. The elite Coast Guard team attended the U.S. Navy Diving and Salvage Training Center in Panama City, Florida. The commando units reflect back to World War II when highly trained Coast Guard personnel joined Office of Strategic Services (OSS) forces to conduct training and clandestine maritime operations in Europe and Asia. By 1944 the OSS (predecessor to the Cold War Central Intelligence Agency or CIA) included more than 100 Coastguardsmen who were attached to training schools and/or participated in firearms, signaling, swimming, boat handling, intelligence, espionage, and sabotage missions during the war.[1]

The OSS precedent "paved the way for Coast Guard participation in modern-day Special Operations," stated Rear Adm. Dean Lee (USCG), the Deployable Operations Group (DOG) commander. Adm. Lee was quoted in the "Coast Guard Commandos" article in *Coast Guard* magazine, written by Lt. James McClay (USCG) and PA1 Adam Eggers (USCG) in 2009.[2]

In 2008, Adm. Thad Allen, USCG commandant, and Adm. Gary Roughead, chief of naval operations, signed the memorandum of understanding that allowed Coast Guard personnel to earn positions on SEAL teams. The training opportunity was an outgrowth of the Cooperative Strategy for 21st Century Sea Power (2007) — signed by the chiefs of the USMC, USN, and USCG — and the innovative leadership of former DOG commander, Rear Adm. Tom Atkin (USCG).

The Coast Guard trainees studied basic underwater demolition and unconventional warfare operations. The successes of the program, and support of special operations instructors in the U.S. Navy and U.S. Army, led the way for future Coastguardsmen to be trained in special military operations at U.S. Armed Forces schools and apply their skills in the War on Terror, port security, and other national defense missions.[3]

The SEAL recruits studied naval special warfare, dive training, and parachuting, according to USCG Deployable Operations spokesperson Lt. James McLay. Command Master Chief Darrick Dewitt (USCG) commented on how exemplary the Coast Guard trainees were. Captain Stewart Elliott (USN), commander of the Naval Special Warfare Center in Coronado, California, said he looked forward to "welcoming" the Coastguardsmen "into the ranks of our nation's elite maritime special operations force."[4] Chief Petty Officer Dewitt (USCG) said the Coast Guard SEAL graduates would serve in the U.S. Navy for at least one tour as instructors, or in other capacities, and eventually choose to remain in the Coast Guard or Navy,[5] or perhaps even liaison petty or commissioned officers between the sea services.

Dr. Joe Durazno III and Chris Duane are retired USCG officers and adjunct professors at the Joint Forces Staff College in Norfolk, Virginia. The authors' exemplary 2010 review of Coast Guard operations in 2009 illuminated the significant role the service plays in narcotics interdiction, national security, and defense missions at home and abroad.

International partnering and maritime theater security operations were extensive in terms of geographic expanse and successful outcomes. More than $5 billion dollars in illegal drugs and 332 perpetrators were interdicted and taken into custody by the Coast Guard. Maritime training, exercises in law enforcement, national security, and antiterrorist operations were conducted with Russia, Georgia, and several Latin American, African, Middle East, and Asian nations. The USCG has long partnered with the British Royal Navy in defense and illegal contraband operations in the Caribbean.

The naval forces of the developing nations are tasked with duties more comparable to U.S. Coast Guard as opposed to U.S. Navy missions. In the smaller nations, coastal (border) defense, law enforcement, and regional security missions are emphasized. An exception was the diplomatic visits by U.S. Coast Guard cutters to the Peoples Republic of China (PRC). The PRC Navy has developed into a significant strategic defensive and offensive force. The USCGC *Boutwell* (WHEC-719) under the command of Capt. Kevin Cavanaugh (USCG) supported U.S. Navy Fifth and Sixth Fleet combatant commanders in successful theater security and antipiracy operations off the Horn of Africa. A *Boutwell* helicopter intercept off the Somali coast drove off a pirate vessel that had targeted a foreign merchant vessel.[6]

In a joint USN-USCG crew mission on the USS *Gettysburg* (CG-64), a suspected pirate ship was boarded off the Somalia coast. Rocket-propelled grenades and assault rifles were found. A joint USN-USCG crew from the USS *Anzio* (CG-68) in the Gulf of Aden confiscated several tons of narcotics.[7]

Lt. Cmdr. Mike Bennett (USCG) is the head of intelligence studies at the U.S. Coast Guard Academy (USCGA) in New London, Connecticut. Coast Guard cadets, as future officers, are trained in national security and intelligence specialties. Classified material is downloaded from secure Internet sources. Visiting specialists in national security visit USCGA classes, as have experts connected to the Central Intelligence Agency (CIA). Lt. Cmdr. Bennett guides academy cadets though national defense and security scenarios, maritime threats, and responses. Cadets are exposed to weapons and situation simulators to practice team coordination, weapons operations, and use-of-force decisions in possible ship and boat confrontations.[8]

Law enforcement is a significant U.S. Coast Guard mission directly related to national security and defense. U.S. Coast Guard officials initiated the rating of maritime enforcement specialist in January 2010. The rate is available to trained and qualified active-duty and Reserve personnel.[9]

Pirate and terrorist attacks on commercial vessels off the East African coast and in the Gulf of Aden prompted the Coast Guard to create a data dissemination system and websites about high-risk international waters. Cmdr. Lee Boone, chief of the Domestic Vessel Compliance Division at U.S. Coast Guard headquarters in Washington, D.C., worked with other experts on vessel tracking, piracy action, and information dissemination procedures.

The USCG issued a maritime security directive in May 2010 that required U.S. flag commercial vessels to have Coast Guard approved security protocols to respond to acts of piracy, armed robbery and terrorism. Cmdr. Chris Keane in the Office of Policy and Integration at Coast Guard headquarters monitors information exchange and interagency coordination with the U.S. Departments of State, Homeland Security, Defense, and the Maritime Administration.

Coast Guard boarding teams have been integrated into the crews of U.S. Navy combat vessels on patrol in the Gulf of Aden and other high-risk maritime regions. The USN and USCG have conducted maritime security operations against suspicious vessels and monitor high-risk waters in the Middle East, Africa, Asia, and Latin America.[10]

Some merchant vessels have placed security personnel on board and trained crews to use water hoses and a variety of nonlethal and lethal weapons to deter or combat pirate attacks. Private security personnel, armed crews, and military units have deterred and fought off pirate and terrorist attacks and captured assailants.

Admiral Mark Fitzgerald (USN), commander U.S. Naval Forces Europe and Africa, held a Pentagon press conference about counterpiracy and international partnerships in April 2010. Adm. Fitzgerald said coalition naval forces cannot guarantee safe commercial shipping and asserted that armed merchant ship guards have been effective.

Private security firms have hired former military personnel to supplement armed merchant vessel crews. Merchant vessel captains must be ready to declare the existence of armed personnel when entering foreign ports. U.S. flagged vessels have used armed and unarmed security forces to comply with Coast Guard protocols and provide time for multinational military and naval forces to respond by air and sea to incidents.

Civilian and coalition naval and military personnel have successfully responded to pirate attacks. This cooperative international partnership will likely continue as long as extremist terrorist and pirate groups use aggression on the high seas to fund their interests and activities.[11]

Interagency and international cooperation is essential to combat and defeat maritime terrorists and pirates. Captain Bruce B. Stubbs (USCG, Ret.)

applied his maritime experience to the responsibilities as Department of Defense (DOD) executive agent for maritime domain awareness (MDA). Capt. Stubbs and his office (created in 2008) assumed the responsibility of coordinating MDA programs and policies with the DOD and integrating U.S. Navy and U.S. Coast Guard missions on the high seas.

Before being named MDA director, Capt. Stubbs advised the secretary of the U.S. Navy on naval and regional maritime security issues. Stubbs explained that one MDA priority was to find technologies to facilitate the acquisition and analysis of data about crew lists, vessels and people of interest, cargo manifests, and the transfer of cargo from ship to shore and ground transportation. Stubbs described the importance of ongoing "war-fighting" conversations between Navy and Coast Guard leaders about national security and defense and the emphasis of U.S. Customs officials on cargo.

Captain Stubbs worked to blend MDA concerns and policies with the operations of foreign security and military officials. The MDA director explained the success and significance of the presence of USCG law enforcement and boarding detachments on U.S. Navy vessels that operate globally on the high seas, and the reciprocal utilization of the assets and platforms of both sea services in national security and defense operations.[12]

A crucial element of national defense on the home front is port security. The Coast Guard is responsible for the protection of harbors and ports, cargoes, and shore infrastructure. The USCG carries out that mission in coordination with civilian port authority officials, U.S. Customs and Immigration, and local and federal public safety and law enforcement officials. The Coast Guard performs search and rescue and, in the northern climates, icebreaking missions to keep harbor areas safe and commerce flowing.

Since the terrorist attacks upon the United States on 11 September 2001, military and civilian authorities have been concerned about and designing strategies to prevent or respond to terrorist and sabotage threats in major ports.

Captain Jim Howe (U.S. Coast Guard, Ret.) has written about his concern that terrorists might attack ports, fuel terminals, and power company infrastructure with elusive, small recreational craft, and not, as has usually been feared, commandeer large cruise and cargo vessels for attacks in the domestic maritime domain.[13]

In the past decade, terrorists have employed small, explosive-packed vessels to damage, destroy and control commercial cargo vessels and tankers in Middle East and Asian waters. Capt. Howe listed several examples of attacks upon foreign cargo and tanker vessels, and the 500-foot missile-equipped destroyer USS *Cole* (DDG-67). The USS *Cole* was attacked on 12 October

2000 by an Al Qaeda suicide boat in the Middle East port of Aden, in Yemen. The explosion took the lives of 17 USN sailors and injured more than 30 crew members.

Capt. Howe (*Proceedings*, October 2010) contended that terrorist will try maritime attacks in U.S. ports, pondered what can be done about it, reviewed failed or inconsequential federal meetings and policies about port security, and offered his solutions. Howe asserted that the U.S. is a vulnerable target of terrorist opportunity, and the Department of Homeland Security (DHS) and Coast Guard are under equipped and lack the personnel to provide the visible presence, patrols, and response teams to deter domestic port security threats. Essential deterrents, Capt. Howe contends, are sophisticated intelligence and technological assets to detect and interrupt unusual maritime events and patterns.[14]

The initial Small Vessel Security Strategy policy established by the DHS after 9/11 has not been adequately funded or supervised in Capt. Howe's opinion. The proposed fiscal year 2011 federal budget inexplicably recommended reducing USCG personnel by 1,000, and decommissioning 12 Maritime Safety and Security Teams (MSSTs) specifically trained to respond to maritime threats in coastal and port regions. Captain Howe recommended that Coast Guard technological assets, personnel, and maritime patrols be increased to deter or stop threats which will increase as aircraft and land border security regimens are enhanced.[15]

Lt. Cmdr. Brian LeFebvre (USCG) responded to Capt. Howe's "Forgotten Threat" article in the December 2010 issue of the U.S. Naval Institute magazine, *Proceedings*. Cmdr. LeFebvre concurred with Capt. Howe's concerns and analysis and attributed the minimal response to port security threats to the emphasis on commandeered airplanes because of 9/11 legacies. The emphasis led to increased budget and personnel complements for the Customs and Border Protection (CBP) and Transportation Security Administration (TSA) agencies.

Budget and staffing issues prevented the USCG from fully responding to the potential security threats in the maritime domain of the United States. Lt. Cmdr. LeFebvre said more MSSTs, increased Coast Guard air assets, and increased maritime patrols are essential defense strategies. LeFebvre offered an innovative merger plan as an efficient multiplier of federal resources and assets: "integrating Customs and Border Protection's Air and Marine Division into the Coast Guard."[16]

To enhance and update port security defense tactics and strategies, the Coast Guard, with contributions from allies and industry, has been immersed in research and development. With increased boat and cargo vessel traffic at

American ports, the USCG has remained at the head of the curve in developing underwater imaging systems, high-frequency sonar, and high-resolution imaging. Enhanced imaging has been effective in murky channels, ports and piers and has supplemented the work of divers, small boat patrols, and cameras.

The Coast Guard Research and Development Center in New London, Connecticut, has pioneered in port security strategies since 9/11. Progress has been significant in technological development, computer applications, and information systems. Increased cargo container traffic at sea and in major U.S. ports has posed new security challenges. The new high-resolution sonar imaging technology systems are mobile enough to be mounted on the sides of Coast Guard port security vessels and efficiently prepared and shipped to other vessels and port facilities.[17]

The Coast Guard identified several terrorist threats to U.S. ports: enemy swimmers, semisubmersible watercraft, and hostile surface boats and ships. The Coast Guard Office of Counterterrorism and Defense Operations, created in 2003, worked with strategic USCG sectors to develop underwater antiterrorist strategies. Underwater technology, including remotely operated watercraft and sonar, have been utilized and improved. Computer software systems have been developed to detect and differentiate targets (and debris and marine life) up to 1,000 meters. The technology was utilized by regionally dispersed Coast Guard Maritime Safety and Security Teams (MSSTs) at major maritime locations. Strategically placed and deployable port security units (PSUs) composed of active-duty and Reserve Coast Guard personnel were trained for extended emergency service. But in 2011, federal budget cutters aroused opposition within the Coast Guard and Congress for proposing the decommissioning of five MSST units at the ports of New York/New Jersey; Kings Bay, Georgia; New Orleans, Louisiana; San Francisco, California; and Anchorage, Alaska.[18]

The U.S. Navy and the U.S. Coast Guard have coordinated their assets in the missions of national defense and the War on Terror. The cooperation has included the mixing of crews and joint patrols in the domestic and overseas maritime domains.

Rear Adm. Philip H. Greene, Jr. (USN) was the director of irregular warfare in the Office of the Chief of Naval Operations when interviewed by *Seapower* magazine in the spring of 2010. Adm. Greene has communicated and cooperated with the U.S. Coast Guard and the navies and coast guards of nations in developed and developing maritime nations. The U.S. Merchant Marine Academy graduate had commanded USN patrol boats, a destroyer, and a destroyer squadron.

Rear Adm. Greene identified the national security challenges that faced the United States and other nations: piracy, weapons proliferation, contraband trafficking, and other illegal activities that take place in littoral zones. Those activities, Adm. Green said, threatened the stability and safety of third world nations and maritime commerce and facilitated the recruitment of disgruntled youth by radical Islamist militants.

Among the solutions to the problem of international terrorism and regional instability, Adm. Greene asserted, is the USN strategy of "preventative security" through international relationships and training within the framework of "development, diplomacy and defense."[19] "The partnership stations [in allied nations] supported through our combatant commanders leverage the capacity and capability," Greene explained, "of the Navy, Marine Corps, and the Coast Guard in providing persistent presence, relationship development [and] tools that respond to [allied] needs in maritime security and safety."[20]

Rear Adm. Greene listed the U.S. Navy assets (specialized ships, submarines, aircraft, missile defense, intelligence sharing, and training) available to protect the West, and to instruct and defend African, Asian, Middle Eastern, and Latin American nations. The global partnerships, Greene said, help allied nations more effectively respond to the militant threats that exist in their maritime regions and strengthen the security of all nations.[21]

Under Obama administration fiscal guidelines, the post–9/11 Coast Guard Maritime Safety and Security Teams (MSSTs) posted at strategic U.S. harbors would be decommissioned. Some of the saved money from the proposal would be transferred to support the USCG Deepwater Program to replace aging and outmoded air and sea craft and supportive infrastructure. The reallocated funds would also be used to expand law enforcement detachment (LEDET) units, some of which are assigned to U.S. Navy ships for vessel boarding in narcotics interdiction and national defense missions. Some budget-cutting proponents speculated that the MSST mission could be assigned to Coast Guard Reserve units and other federal agencies. Congressional and Coast Guard opponents of MSST defunding believed the elimination of the MSST units would be a devastating threat to national maritime and port security.[22]

U.S. Senator Chuck Schumer, a New York City Democrat, publicly criticized Department of Homeland Security Secretary Janet Napolitano and asked her to cancel the Obama administration plan to defund Coast Guard MSSTs. In his letter to Secretary Napolitano, Senator Schumer expressed concern about the elite 90-member MSST unit that had guarded New York Harbor since the 9/11 terrorist attacks. Senator Schumer threatened to block the defunding plan in Congress and said the entire New York congressional delegation would unite against it. "If there ever was a plan that was penny wise and pound foolish," Schumer exclaimed, "this is it."[23]

Port security defense zones include waterways adjacent to ports and port entrances, port waters, piers, warehouses, transportation facilities and vehicles, power plants, and other proximal infrastructure. The Pilgrim Nuclear Power Station in Plymouth, Massachusetts, on Cape Cod Bay illustrates the challenges of security zone protection.

Since 9/11, the nuclear plant has been considered a potential terrorist and sabotage target. After 9/11, the Coast Guard imposed a public "no-go" zone with buoy markers on the waterway outside the plant. In October 2009, the Coast Guard clarified regulations for the security zone, and changed the designated coordinates around the plant. No swimmers or boats may enter the security zone without the permission of the captain of the port in Boston.

The president of the Duxbury nuclear watch group Pilgrim Watch, Mary Lampert, criticized Coast Guard policies and the superfluous buoy barrier which critics have called a boater "slalom course." Lampert said the Coast Guard patrols the security zone infrequently. Pilgrim Watch has advocated for a permanent anchored fence structure or chain barriers all the way to the ocean floor, similar to what U.S. Navy bases use to guard ships and docks. Lampert concluded that permanent barriers would prevent surface and submersible watercraft and explosives from drifting too close to the Pilgrim nuclear plant. "I'm suggesting," Lambert said, "beef it up."[24]

The necessity of constant personnel training to keep security forces competent is not without its dangers and costs. In October 2010, a U.S. Coast Guard member fell from a vessel and drowned while undergoing antiterrorism training in Virginia. Petty Officer Third Class Shaun Lin (USCG) was being trained in ship boarding on Chesapeake Bay. PO3 Lin climbed out of a 25-foot craft onto a 175-foot Coast Guard cutter and fell into the water carrying 60 pounds of tactical gear. Lin's body was later found, but it was not determined whether his life vest inflated or was properly operated. PO3 Lin had previously served on the USCGC *Maui* (WPB-1304) in the North Arabian Gulf.[25]

The Exclusive Economic Zone (EEZ) extends 200 miles off the coast of the United States. The 14th Coast Guard District (with stations in Hawaii and Guam) is tasked with covering the 12 million square miles of ocean in that vast insular region. The maritime realm includes the United States island territories of the Northern Marianas, Jarvis, Wake, and Howland/Baker. The U.S. Navy and U.S. Coast Guard do joint patrols, and the two U.S. naval services patrol with other nations that have possessions, sovereignty, and interests in the maritime region: France, New Zealand, Australia, and Micronesia.[26]

In June 2009, 14th District U.S. Coast Guard law enforcement officers teamed up for the first time with the crew of the 453-foot guided-missile frigate USS *Crommelin* (FFG-37). Fourteenth District Marine Resources Chief, Lt. Cmdr. Jay Caputo (USCG), said USN ships and aircraft provide essential technological assets to supplement Coast Guard national security, antidrug, and fisheries enforcement missions, and to monitor foreign vessel movements in Oceania.[27]

In October 2009, U.S. Navy vessels joined U.S. Coast Guard and Canadian naval units to practice maritime security operations off the Washington coast in the Pacific Northwest. This and continued joint missions were designed to coordinate and strengthen military operations between Canada and the United States.[28]

Canada's Special Operations Forces Command (CANSOFCOM) was established to monitor and respond to maritime terrorism. The counterterrorism unit works with Canadian military and naval units, and domestic law enforcement agencies, including the Royal Canadian Mounted Police (RCMP). CANSOFCOM is mandated to defend Canada against terrorist threats on the maritime approaches to Canada and to prevent attacks upon such shore infrastructure as power plants and petroleum and natural gas facilities. Canadian Special Operations units have coordinated practice missions with foreign special forces, most often the United States. Canada's Special Operations Forces practiced beach landings, ship boardings from armed rigid-hull inflatable boats, and port security operations.

Canada has conducted joint training exercises with U.S. Navy SEALS and the British Special Boat Service (SBS). Canadian special forces units have integrated with Royal Canadian Navy (RCN) operations and assets. Operations and assets have included offshore patrol boats, Arctic missions, and coordination with Canada's Victoria-class submarines. In 2007, Canadian Joint Task Force Two personnel conducted practice training operations with the U.S. Navy, U.S. Coast Guard, and the Royal Canadian Navy in a hijacked cruise liner scenario that used the HMCS *Preserver* (AOR-510), an RCN supply ship.[29]

Chief Petty Officer Glenn Wilson (USN, Ret.) shared his professional experience with USN/USCG joint missions with this author. In a 27 March 2010 e-mail exchange, CPO Wilson explained an incident where the U.S. Navy was requested to support a U.S. Coast Guard drug interdiction mission because, as Wilson said, "we had superior electronic snooping equipment." The USS *Mississippi* (CGN-40) and USS *Arkansas* (CGN-41) were escorting the aircraft carrier USS *Nimitz* (CVN-68).

The U.S. Navy had been listening to Caribbean radio communications and sent an aircraft to survey a 90-foot shrimp boat called the *Recife*. The fishing vessel was miles from shrimp areas, CPO Wilson explained, and exhibited no nets out, but a heavy load of cargo as indicated by the boat's low draft in the water. The two U.S. Navy cruisers chased down the *Recife* to check registration and manifest, but got no response. After a blank shell was shot across the bow, the *Recife* cut back its speed and claimed Haitian registry, a dubious proposition.

The U.S. Coast Guard informed the Navy that the registration claim was false and sent a helicopter out to the USS *Mississippi* with a law enforcement boarding crew. The USS *Mississippi* caught up to the *Recife* again at about midnight, but the shrimp boat would not stop. Wilson said the USN commanding officer ordered gun crews to man the "forward and aft 50-caliber machine guns [and] fired a real shell across her bow, missing intentionally." The Coast Guard boarding crew found 50 tons of marijuana and 55 kilos of cocaine and heroin, plus stashes of cash and guns. The *Recife* crew "offered no resistance." Chief Wilson recalled that the "first USN-USCG was in 1984." Chief Wilson served on the USS *Mississippi* from 1982 to 1985. After that, the USN chief served on the USS *South Carolina* (CGN-37) and participated in a "bust" on a yacht that was carrying 1,100 kilos of cocaine.[30]

Lt. Col. Edward W. Novack (USMC) advised the U.S. Marine Corps, a service historically "rooted in the sea," to return to the naval maritime realm. In the last decade the Marines fought in Iraq and Afghanistan in the War on Terror. Lt. Col. Novack said the Marine Corps is planning for future national security challenges with sophisticated technology against radical extremists and rogue and opposition nation states. Col. Novack described the Marine Corps Service Campaign Plan 2009–2015 (MCSCP) and the analysis of U.S. Marine Corps commandant, General James T. Conway. A key theme in the MCSCP is the commitment of the USMC to strengthen "its long-standing ties with the U.S. Navy ... and increasingly with the U.S. Coast Guard."[31]

General Michael W. Hagee (USMC, Ret.) was the U.S. Marine Corps commandant from 2003 to 2006. General Hagee subsequently served as president and CEO of the Admiral Nimitz Foundation, and the National Museum of the Pacific War in Fredericksburg, Texas. In his letter of 11 September 2010, Gen. Hagee responded to the author's previous book, *The United States Coast Guard in World War II*. Gen. Hagee was familiar with the articulated missions of the USCG, USN, USMC and U.S. Army in the Pacific War and wrote, "I have been to the [Guadalcanal] location where [USCG landing craft coxswain SM1 Douglas] Munro's actions earned him the Medal of Honor. The Marines have always enjoyed working with the USCG."[32]

General Michael W. Hagee (USMC, Ret.) and Admiral James M. Loy

(USCG) were the respective commandants of the Marine Corps (2003–2006) and Coast Guard (1998–2002) during their active-duty careers. Adm. Loy and Gen. Hagee issued a joint statement about the significance of both the military and civilian communities in defending national security. They concluded that transnational challenges would have to be met by both military force and civilian policies of economic development and diplomacy. Terrorism must be fought, the former commandants concluded, by boosting up failing states and economic infrastructures, fighting diseases, responding to natural disasters, and controlling the proliferation of weapons and nuclear materials. Gen. Hagee and Adm. Loy stated their belief that "our military depends on having strong civilian components of national power."[33]

In his April 2010 testimony before the U.S. House Subcommittee on Homeland Security, Rear Adm. Vincent Atkins (USCG) discussed Coast Guard air and maritime security operations, mission and technology articulation between the USCG and other federal agencies, and economic (cost and investment) challenges and strategies.[34]

Adm. Atkins explained Coast Guard cooperation with the U.S. Customs and Border Protection (CBP) Office of Air and Marine, and the joint interagency maritime alien migrant and drug interdiction missions. The admiral described the unique maritime expanse of Coast Guard law enforcement, inspection and ship-boarding authority in U.S. waters and on the high seas; and the provisions of the U.S. Code (14:2 and 89) that are the basis of USCG boarding, inspection, investigation, arrest, and seizure authority.

Rear Adm. Atkins concisely articulated the joint mission tactics and strategy to the assembled Congressional committee members: "The Coast Guard and CBP Office of Air and Marine deploy maritime patrol aircraft ... [and the USCG] assigns our largest cutters, which carry helicopters, small boats, and boarding teams to the transit zone. Additionally, we deploy our law enforcement [detachment] boarding teams [LEDETS] onboard U.S. and allied naval ships as force multipliers in the transit zone."[35]

The maritime agencies patrol "arrival zones" in the Gulf of Mexico, the southeast coast of the United States, and coastal California. The Coast Guard intercepted $5 billion worth of illegal drugs in 2009. Coast Guard armed helicopter interdiction units (HITRON), Adm. Atkins contended, spotted a record number of contraband vessels for maritime boarding in 2009 and continued that record pace in 2010. Adm. Atkins attributed the successes to the unified command air and sea task forces of CPB, the National Security Agency (NSA), Department of Justice (DOJ), Department of Defense (DOD), Department of State, and law enforcement and military liaison officials from cooperating nations. U.S. Navy, Coast Guard, and allied nation aircraft and

The USCG/CBP Caribbean drug interdiction that involved the 45-foot RB-M and CBP helicopter netted the 95 bricks (kilos) of cocaine shown here.

ships cooperated in boarding, reconnassaince, and intelligence operations. Foreign embassy officials cooperated with the Coast Guard in foreign flag vessel incidents to validate registry and support use of force and boarding missions in accordance with established bilateral diplomatic agreements.[36]

The interdiction of illegal migrants who attempt to cross into the United States by land or sea constitutes significant law enforcement, socioeconomic, and national security functions. Undocumented aliens strain the nation's economic, legal, educational, and medical systems, Drug smugglers migrate from Latin America, often from Colombia and Mexico, and pose threats to immigration, customs, and other law enforcement officers and law-abiding citizens, some of whom have been injured or killed in the line of duty or murdered by miscreants. Illegal migrants pose a national security threat because their success at transgressing porous borders has encouraged potential terrorists to follow the migrants into the United States. Anti-American terrorists may emulate the strategies of illegal migrants and assimilate with nonviolent undocumented aliens who desire to enter the U.S. to seek jobs and better opportunities for themselves and their families.

Rear Adm. Atkins informed the members of the House Subcommittee on Homeland Security that illegal drugs and immigration activities in America's maritime domain pose a definite threat to national security. Coast Guard migrant interdictions are humanitarian (search and rescue) and law enforcement actions and often take place in the heavy traffic of the Florida Straits. Contraband smugglers who operate fast, high-powered boats constantly challenge the Coast Guard, the admiral explained, and run million-dollar operations. To address the technology, acquisition, and maintenance requirements of the missions, the Department of Homeland Security Boat Commodity Council has confiscated, purchased, shared, and exchanged air and sea craft, weapons, and communications assets with its military, national security, and law enforcement partners.[37]

The Coast Guard partners include civilian and private law enforcement and port security agencies; the U.S. Navy, Air Force, and Marine Corps; and the Department of Defense Special Forces.[38]

13

Budgets, Assets, Missions and Training

Since its origins, the U.S. Coast Guard has been tasked with a plethora of missions, with limited funding interspersed with periodic increases and cuts. Within those fiscal constraints, the Coast Guard has acquired, built, and maintained its shore, air and sea assets; expanded its missions, personnel complement, inventory, and technology; and trained its enlisted and commissioned regular and reserve personnel.

In addition to it traditional maritime law enforcement, search and rescue, and environmental protection tasks, since the 11 September 2001 ("9/11") terrorist attacks upon the United States, the USCG has fought terrorism overseas, guarded oil pipelines in Iraq, and cooperated with the USN in antipirate and drug and migrant interdiction patrols on the high seas. The multimission service has experienced "strained resources" and the repair and replacement of an aging fleet of oceangoing cutters that averaged more than twice the age of USN ships. The deterioration of the fleet threatened crew safety, according to former Coast Guard commandant, Adm. Thad Allen (USCG, Ret.).[1]

Some critics of the U.S. Coast Guard's expanded international role since the service was transferred from the Department of Transportation to the Department of Homeland Security in 2003 believe the marine safety and ship inspection missions have been comparatively diminished in frequency and personnel experience and competence.[2]

Rep. Gene Taylor, Democratic congressman from Mississippi, headed the House Armed Services Committee on Sea Power and Expeditionary Forces in 2009. Rep. Taylor served in the USCG Reserve (1971–1984) as a SAR boat commander. Taylor also served on the House Transportation Subcommittee, which has oversight over Coast Guard and maritime transportation issues. Congressman Taylor advocated having armed teams on board commercial

164

vessels to thwart piracy threats, and advanced shipyard technology to compete with overseas shipbuilders.[3]

Congressman Taylor asserted that the Coast Guard had been assigned too many mission responsibilities for the limited funding and personnel (less than 40,000 men and women) assigned to the service. Rep. Taylor explained that the conflicts he endured between his balanced-budget philosophy and the material needs of the sea services (USN, USCG, USMC) required meeting assigned defense and national security responsibilities. Taylor stated he was more concerned about a rogue nation or group smuggling a destructive weapon in a cargo container or on a ship into the United States than he was about a potential weapon that, say, Iran might develop. Hence the importance of the national defense port security mission. And the further offshore the Coast Guard makes those maritime checks, Taylor concluded, the better it is for American security.[4]

In October 2009 an appreciative U.S. Congress increased the Coast Guard budget to accommodate funding for new oceangoing cutters, patrol boats, and aircraft to support the asset upgrades of the Deepwater Program. Deepwater commenced in 2002, and was plagued with cost overruns and hull engineering problems. The $10 billion Coast Guard budget request, which came out of Senate and House appropriations committees, totaled $8.7 billion, an increase over the Obama White House proposal. The congressional budget allowed for completion of the fourth national security cutter *Hamilton* and the start of construction on a fifth NSC. The Senate and House committees supported a $243 million expenditure for the continuation of construction on several Sentinel-class fast response cutters (FRCs) and requested a report from the DHS to assess the resource needs for enhancing Coast Guard protection of liquid natural gas (LNG) tankers and associated harbor facilities.[5]

The 418-foot NSC *Waesche* (WMSL-751) and its sister ships were intended to replace the 1960s-built 378-foot Hamilton-class cutters. The "378s" had replaced the legendary World War II–era Treasury/Secretary class "327s." The *Waesche*, a Legend-class cutter (named after World War II Coast Guard commandant, Adm. Russell R. Waesche), successfully completed acceptance trials in October 2009. The U.S. Coast Guard and U.S. Navy Board of Inspection and Survey (INSURV) inspected the cutter.

The first NSC was the *Bertholf* (named after Ellsworth P. Bertholf, the U.S. Revenue Cutter Service captain-commandant and first U.S. Coast Guard commandant, ca. 1915). The third NSC cutter was the *Stratton* (named after Captain Dorothy Stratton, USCG, the World War II founder of SPARS, the Coast Guard Women's Reserve).[6]

The challenges of evolving nautical engineering, expanding Coast Guard mission requirements, and escalating maintenance and construction costs were revealed by the hull deterioration scenario on USN Cyclone-class coastal patrol craft (PC). Naval inspections in 2010 revealed that the 170–180-foot PCs used by the USN and USCG in U.S. coastal waters and the Persian Gulf suffered severe structural deterioration from decades of hard use. Corrosion and hull buckling were discovered on the PCs that threatened the lives of the 150-member crew complements in heavy seas.

The Navy has come to depend on coastal littoral water patrol boats to meet the requirements of contraband and insurgent warfare. The Coast Guard has long emphasized littoral patrol craft and is expected to rely on the emerging fast response cutters (FRCs). Professor Milan Vego, military operations instructor at the Joint Military Operations Department of the Naval War College (Newport, Rhode Island), stated that the PCs were essential to contemporary naval defense missions. Professor Vego said the USN needs the smaller boats to give junior officers vessel command experience,[7] a responsibility the multimission U.S. Coast Guard has long required of its officers.

In its requested 2011 Department of Homeland Security (DHS) budget, the proposed $10.2 billion Coast Guard expenditure was a 3 percent reduction from the 2010 fiscal year. The national security cutter (NSC) and fast response cutter (FRC) constituted the balance of the Coast Guard budget. The response boat–medium (RBM) and maritime patrol aircraft (MPA) expenditures were expected to be reduced.

The budget proposals and reductions were problematic because of extended Coast Guard missions in natural disaster responses, Persian Gulf operations, and antipiracy patrols off the northeast coast of Africa. The service extended its Deepwater upgrade and continued production of the eight NSC cutters at the Northrop Grumman shipyard in Pascagoula, Mississippi. The second NSC, the USCGC *Waesche*, was stationed at Coast Guard Island in Alameda, California.[8]

The USCG obtained $121 million for 22 response boat–medium (RBM) boats in 2010 and requested $42 million for 10 RBMs to be constructed at Marinette Marine Corporation (Marinette, Wisconsin). The 2011 budget request covered maritime patrol helicopters and other aircraft, and included HC-144A, C-130-J, C-130H, HH-65 and H-60 construction and maintenance programs. Unmanned Aircraft System (UAS) projects were considered in the research and development (R & D) stage by Coast Guard officials and put on hold.[9]

The Sentinel-class patrol boat was scheduled to replace the Island-class patrol craft in 2011. The Sentinel craft was built to offer more complete and sophisticated maritime domain functions than its predecessor. Among its assets are more advanced command, control, communications, computers, intelligence, surveillance, and reconnaissance (C4ISR) technologies that can operate with USCG assets and the technology of the DHS and Department of Defense. The 153-foot boats (or cutters) were tabulated to cost $60 million each and to last 20 years. The Sentinel craft have speeds of 28 knots and armament that includes a stabile remote-operated 25 mm chain gun, four crew-manned .50 caliber machine guns, and a crew complement of 22. The boats will initially operate out of Miami, Florida and patrol Caribbean and Florida Strait waters.[10]

The USCGC *Waesche* (WMSL-751) was the first national security cutter to be built (2006), formally named (2008), and commissioned (2010) and is considered the flagship of the modern Deepwater Coast Guard Fleet. The 418-foot NSC cutter was designed to support maritime security missions and the operations of the joint U.S. Armed Forces combatant commanders.[11]

USCG 45-foot all-aluminum response boat–medium (RB-M) class patrol boat and Dolphin HH-65 helicopter team up for law and treaty enforcement, environmental, and defense operations missions. The RB-M communications technology allows communication with other Homeland Security, federal, and state and local law enforcement and defense agencies.

President Barack Obama's wife, First Lady Michelle Obama, christened the third NSC cutter in July 2010. Mrs. Obama paid tribute to the cutter's namesake, Capt. Dorothy Stratton, as "the first woman to serve as a commissioned officer in the United States Coast Guard."

The 418-foot USCGC *Stratton* (WMSL-752) honors the World War II officer who organized the SPARS, the U.S. Coast Guard Women's Reserve. The SPARS acronym came from the letters of the USCG motto, *Semper Paratus*. The *Stratton* has a 28-knot speed, 12,000-mile range, automated weapons, and advanced command and control systems that are interoperable with the U.S. Department of Homeland Security and the U.S. Defense Department. The *Stratton* was built in Pascagoula, Mississippi, at Northrop Grumman shipyards.[12]

Coast Guard stations, vessels, and aircraft offer a sense of security with the visual images of public safety, search and rescue, law enforcement, natural disaster, national security and defense missions, migrant and drug interdiction, and port security operations on the ocean coasts and internal waterways of the United States.

When Coast Guard units are disbanded or moved from established stations, citizens and political leaders notice and protest. U.S. Senator Chuck Schumer, as previously noted, criticized Homeland Security Secretary Janet Napolitano for announcing, as a potential cost-cutting measure, the displacement of Coast Guard maritime security teams from the New York City port and harbor region. Mayors of port cities have complained about dangerous cargo and weapons of mass destruction potentials upon their waterways and economic infrastructure.

New Bedford, Massachusetts mayor Scott Lang requested that a displaced Coast Guard unit return to his port city. The incident that stimulated his concern occurred in November 2010 when two Middle East (Palestinian) stowaways were found hiding aboard an inbound cargo ship. Crewmembers of a Liberian freighter found the illegal passengers when the vessel was three miles off the Massachusetts/New Bedford coast. U.S. Customs officers questioned the migrants who claimed they intended to go to Canada, a nation with allegedly more lenient immigration requirements than the United States has.

Mayor Scott Lang informed the media that the incident indicated the Coast Guard should return to its former New Bedford station. In 2003 the Coast Guard transferred two cutters from New Bedford to Portsmouth (New Hampshire) Naval Shipyard.[13]

The U.S. Coast Guard has utilized civilian and U.S. Navy shipyards for the construction, maintenance, and repair of its small craft, boats and cutters. The Coast Guard has also utilized its own government-operated shipyard on

Curtis Bay in Arundel County, Maryland. The facility is called United States Coast Guard Yard, or simply Coast Guard Yard. The Yard has been in existence since 1899, when the boats and ships were built and repaired for the USCG predecessor, the U.S. Revenue Cutter Service (USRCS).[14]

In the World War II era (1939–1949), Coast Guard Yard, or the "Depot," as the Yard was also called, experienced significant shore and harbor expansion and infrastructural and technological upgrades to accommodate wartime requirements. The Depot was officially named "Coast Guard Yard" and acquired a force of 3,100 skilled civilian employees. In subsequent decades, the Yard expanded its technology, infrastructure, and production to meet the Coast Guard's increased multimission needs. From 1989–1999 to the present, Coast Guard Yard replaced the aging dry docks, utilized more environmentally friendly and efficient procedures and operations, and accommodated the advanced weapons and nautical innovations necessary for the diverse missions of the 20th and 21st centuries.[15]

The following testimonials describe the significance and quality production associated with Coast Guard Yard and its working motto: "Since 1899 — Servicing the Fleet that Guards our Coasts." Coast Guard Yard has "built, repaired, and renovated ships in Baltimore Maryland for the U.S. Coast Guard. It is the Service's sole shipbuilding and major repair facility, and an essential part of the Coast Guard's core industrial base and fleet support operations. Coast Guard Yard has enjoyed an enviable reputation for the quality of its work and productivity of its work force and is a winner of several awards for its commitment to customer satisfaction and quality improvement."[16]

The quality of the production of Coast Guard Yard is a function of the exemplary leadership exhibited by the Coast Guard commanders who have administered the base. In 2010–2011, Captain Richard Murphy (USCG) served as commanding officer, U.S. Coast Guard Yard. The exemplary professional record of Capt. Murphy illustrates the quality, achievements and responsibilities of key Coast Guard officers.

Captain Murphy graduated from the U.S. Coast Guard Academy with a bachelor of science degree in civil engineering. Murphy served in the Acquisition Directorate as a cutter and boat project manager; commanding officer of a civil engineering unit at USCG Base Miami (Florida); and in civil engineering leadership capacities at Coast Guard Yard (Baltimore) and U.S. Coast Guard headquarters (Washington, D.C.); and officer of the deck on the USCGC *Chilula* (WMEC-153).

Besides having earned a master of science degree in civil engineering (University of Illinois), Capt. Murphy received a master's degree in national strategic strategy from the National Defense University Industrial College in

Washington, D.C. Captain Murphy was the recipient of numerous service, commendation, and achievement medals and the Legion of Merit.[17]

The controversies over naval ship construction, functions, funding, missions and interoperability were ongoing. Cmdr. John Patch (USN, Ret.) wrote a compelling analysis in the U.S. Naval Institute magazine *Proceedings* in 2011.[18]

Cmdr. Patch brought his experience as a surface warfare officer and intelligence analyst to the fore. At the time of the interview, Cmdr. Patch was a professor of strategic intelligence at the U.S. Army War College (Carlisle, Pennsylvania) and at American Military University (Charles Town, West Virginia).

Commander Patch concluded that the littoral combat ships (LCSs) the U.S. Navy had constructed, and was scheduled to build, were unaffordable, too technologically complex, inefficient, top-heavy, and too vulnerable and limited in littoral combat zones and heavy seas. Cmdr. Patch said the Navy could learn from and apply the construction and function of Coast Guard patrol boats and cutters to the legitimate littoral combat needs of the USN. Commander Patch was critical of the "failure of the Coast Guard and Navy to conduct a combined effort to design a new cutter/corvette-sized vessel"[19] and said the U.S. Navy should "cancel the [LCS] program and shift funds to a corvette based on the Coast Guard's National Security Cutter hull with basic surface warfare, self defense, and helicopter-support capabilities."[20]

The United States Coast Guard Academy is one of the five federal military academies in the nation. The USCGA is located in New London, Connecticut, on the Thames River. The undergraduate students, called cadets, are selected through difficult competitive examination, not by congressional nominations like the other service academies. The academy motto is *Scientiae cedit mare* (The sea yields to knowledge). In 1947 the academy acquired the 295-foot-tall sailing barque *Horst Wessel* as a World War II reparation from Germany. The vessel was renamed the USCGC *Eagle* (WIX-327) and serves as a training vessel for cadets and officer candidates in the Coast Guard Academy Officer Candidate School (OCS).

The USCGA traces its origins to the School of Instruction (1876) of the Coast Guard predecessor agency, the U.S. Revenue Cutter Service (USRCS) and then to the foundation date of the U.S. Coast Guard (1915). The academy prepares commissioned officers for the multimission service. The cadet complement is around 1,000 students, with about 200 annual graduates who assume a five-year active-duty obligation. The cadets graduate as ensigns.[21]

The rigorous academy curriculum covers law, history, environmental science, marine engineering, naval architecture, computer analysis, electrical engineering, mechanical engineering, civil engineering, seamanship, environmental and other sciences, liberal arts, management, and government.

Military and physical training are of course emphasized. Strong music and athletic programs round out the list of elective courses and activities.[22]

The military colleges and universities have updated their program, classes, and curricula to cover national security threats and countermeasures, terrorism, and intelligence. The U.S. Coast Guard Academy (USCGA) has modified its curriculum since the 11 September 2001 terrorist attack on the United States. Coast Guard cadets study radioactive material detection, national security policies and operations, and applicable federal and constitutional laws. The Naval Postgraduate School in Monterey, California, administers the Center for Homeland Defense and Security. National security experts contend that military schools must teach information about emerging (developing) nations, terrorist groups and operations, and nuclear and weapons proliferation.[23]

The USCGA has offered more than 300 courses in terrorism, strategic intelligence, emergency environmental response, Arctic Ocean policy, remote sensing, and hazardous materials. Captain Kurt Colella (USCG, Ret.), USCGA academic dean, said information sharing and urgent strategic needs have led to Coast Guard course additions for its 1,000 officer candidate cadets.

Coast Guard members attending classes at the Naval Postgraduate School study national security issues alongside their U.S. Army and U.S. Navy colleagues. The U.S. Naval Academy (Annapolis, Maryland) has also increased its national defense and security curriculum and added critical language studies, including Arabic and Chinese. The U.S. Marine Corps University (Quantico, Virginia) has also offered national security, strategy, and joint (military) warfare courses.[24]

U.S. Department of Homeland Security courses, programs and certificates encompass the topics listed above, and such Coast Guard mission specialties as dangerous cargo and explosive detection on cargo vessels, aircraft, and other modes of transportation; port and coastal infrastructure security; emergency management; and drug and immigration interdiction.[25]

Three academic courses were designed for cadets at the U.S. Coast Guard Academy to meet Department of Homeland Security (DHS) academic "core requirements of an operational Coast Guard officer." The description by the DHS for the strategic intelligence component of the Coast Guard Academy curriculum requirement stated the following:

> The Coast Guard has assumed a key role in the collection, analysis, and dissemination of maritime information and intelligence in the post 9/11 world. The Coast Guard is responsible for ensuring relevant information is available to decision makers. [That information dissemination] requires critical thinking skills and an understanding of the maritime domain. Coast Guard officers must have the foundation for strategic, operational, and tactical intelligence to effectively execute the various safety, security, and national defense missions in the ever-changing national security environment.[26]

The importance of properly educated, trained, and informed U.S. Coast Guard officers has traditionally required the U.S. Coast Guard Academy (USCGA) to offer the best curriculum, faculty, and administration possible. The national and international reputation of the USCGA has indicated the consistent success of the service in accomplishing that objective.

In December 2010, Rear Adm. Scott Burhoe, the outgoing USCGA superintendent, announced the 2011 transfer of his command to Rear Adm. Sandra L. Stosz. Admiral Stosz would become the first female chief of a U.S. military academy. Admiral Robert J. Papp, U.S. Coast Guard commandant, selected Stosz, whose previous assignments were commander of the U.S. Coast Guard Training Center in Cape May, New Jersey, and director of recruitment, training, and support of the 8,000-member complement of U.S. Coast Guard Reservists. Adm. Stosz commended Rear Adm. Burhoe, under whose leadership the USCGA increased minority admissions and was ranked first among the colleges in the Northeastern United States by *U.S. News and World Report*. Rear Adm. Stosz had also served on the Commandant's Leadership Advisory Committee and the USCGA Board of Trustees.[27]

14

The Arctic and National Security

The United States Coast Guard was assigned the responsibility of carrying out its missions in the polar regions with the U.S. purchase of Alaska from Russia in 1867. The challenges of law enforcement, natural resource protection, icebreaking, search and rescue, and national defense fell to the brave seafaring personnel of the sailing and later coal-powered vessels of the U.S. Revenue Service (1867) and later the U.S. Coast Guard (1915 to present).

The service personnel served as federal law enforcement officers and provided transportation, supply, and mission support for the U.S. Armed Forces, Alaskan natives, settlers, and territorial, state, and federal officials on the mainland, Bering Sea, Aleutian Islands, and off the north coast of Alaska.

The challenges have included ice, fog, snowstorms, gale-force winds, and heavy seas of 20 feet and more. During World War II, the Coast Guard joined the U.S. Army, Navy, and Marines and British-Canadian military forces to wage war against invading Japanese naval, air and ground forces in the forbidding insular and maritime domain.

In more recent times, the USCG has sent its personnel and assets into Alaskan waters on environmental, economic, national defense, and scientific missions, and to establish a presence in competition with other nations, including Canada and Russia. As climatic change expanded the maritime domain, Coast Guard sea and shore presence increased. The enhanced USCG presence has posed logistical and tactical challenges and increased personnel, expenditures, and assets.

Reported climate change will require a cooperative polar maritime presence and expanded missions for the U.S. Coast Guard, U.S. Navy, and U.S., Marine Corps. It is expected that maritime calls for relief and rescue assistance from commercial vessels, crews, and recreational boaters will increase,[1] as will the presence of foreign commercial and perhaps naval vessels from allied and adversary nations, and concomitant national defense and security issues.

173

Force structures to match increasing population, defense, and economic growth issues will need to be accommodated. Issues of governance, international agreements, and political stability are expected to evolve. Complex weather systems, melting ice, and rising sea levels will exacerbate problems.[2]

In August 2010, the USCGC *Healy* (WAGB-20), a 420-foot icebreaker, teamed up with the Canadian Coast Guard ship *Louis S. St-Laurent* in a joint-mission Arctic Ocean continental shelf survey. Melting ice will increasingly facilitate access to oil, natural gas, and other regional resource deposits. The Arctic border nations of the United States, Denmark, Canada and Russia are staking claims and asserting territorial sovereignty rights in the maritime region. International conferences have been and will be held to clarify claims and missions. The Coast Guard has established and is expected to expand its onshore port presence, fueling depots, and other infrastructure at Dutch Harbor and (Point) Barrow, Alaska.[3]

U.S. Coast Guard and Navy officials have cooperated in the assessment of Arctic region issues and exigencies. The sea services (USCG, USN, USMC) have been commended for their joint concerns and participation in conferences and symposiums, and for their 2007 *Cooperative Strategy for 21st Century Seapower*. U.S. Navy Secretary Ray Mabus clearly described the significance of the Arctic missions: "Demand for energy continues to rise ... add in the additional pressures [of] a summer Arctic free of ice [and] access to clean water ... and you have a potential powder keg of security challenges that need to be confronted."[4]

An affirmation of the challenges of polar mission conditions was provided in an October 2010 flight above northern Alaska in a Coast Guard C-130 transport aircraft en route to the Arctic Ocean. Rear Admiral Christopher C. Colvin (USCG) shared his perspectives with a news reporter on the flight.

Adm. Colvin said the Russians were aggressively working to create shipping routes in the Arctic, and it was essential for the Coast Guard to keep icebreakers operating in the region. The Russians sailed oil and natural tankers from East Asia through the Bering Strait into the Arctic, asserted the admiral, who concluded "we [the U.S.] must have a presence up there to protect our future sovereignty and continental shelf claims.... There is one way in and out of the Arctic Ocean for over half the world, and that's the Bering Strait."[5]

Rear Adm. Colvin, in command of Coast Guard operations in Alaskan waters, said the Bering Strait will be the main access route to the Arctic and lamented the fact that the CGC *Healy* was his only operational icebreaker. Its Arctic predecessors, the CGC *Polar Sea* (WAGB-11) and CGC *Polar Star* (WAGB-10), were undergoing maintenance in Seattle but were speculated to be back in service respectively in time frames ranging from June 2011 to 2013. Icebreaker

USCG HC-130 cargo and reconnaissance plane in taxi position directed by an Army National Guard member at an Alaskan National Guard airport hanger in Juneau for a joint USCG–USA Operation Arctic Crossroads mission in August 2010.

renovation and new purchases, all prohibitively expensive, were described as essential options if scientific expeditions are to be continued on those platforms.

Adm. Colvin said the closest USCG base from northern Alaska is at Kodiak, 1,000 miles south of Barrow. Rear Adm. Colvin said a base and hangar for C-130s and H-60 helicopters must be built in Barrow because freezing weather had caused damage and expensive maintenance costs when a C-130 aircraft was left outside on a runway for just one night. Oil exploration is likely in the Beaufort Sea off the Alaskan north coast. Adm. Colvin revealed that Shell Oil Corporation had already applied for exploration permits.[6]

In October 2009 a 644-foot passenger condominium cruise ship visited Nome, Alaska, in the Bering Sea and tundra region of Alaska. The shrinking ice cap allowed that and three other such vessels to visit Nome along new shipping channels. The U.S. Coast Guard began to deploy small Arctic patrol boats as scientific teams and gas and oil seeking survey ships traversed the waters.

The Bering Strait town of less than 10,000 people has spent several million dollars to modify its port and infrastructure to enhance its emerging role as a maritime frontier town. Barrow and Kotzebue have also planned to become cargo and tourist attractions for foreign and domestic entities. The

USCGC *Polar Sea* (WAGB-11) in the Arctic on one of the many scientific expeditions the 399-foot icebreaker supported between 2008 and 2010. The *Polar Sea* is homeported out of Seattle, Washington; it carries 3 boats and a helicopter aviation detachment, a crew complement of approximately 140, and up to 32 scientists. The missions include scientific exploration, transportation, and other USCG economic, support, and national interest missions.

Coast Guard has begun to manage maritime regulation, search and rescue, pollution control and national security and defense missions in the icy polar seas in response to expected economic and demographic expansion.[7]

The Arctic Ocean floor has not been extensively mapped. The Coast Guard has only two icebreakers capable of operating in these treacherous waters. Kodiak, Alaska, is eight hours away by rescue helicopter for response to the several thousand ships which are expected to ply polar waters increasingly open to navigation between the Northwest Passage route across northern Canada between Atlantic and Pacific waters, and the Northeast Passage off the northern coast of Russia.

Mineral resources beneath the water and Alaskan shores include oil, natural gas, and coal. The Canadian Arctic contains reserves of iron ore that could be transported to U.S and European steel mills. Offshore Alaskan-Arctic waters may be open to drilling that would require federal[8] and state executive and legislative cooperation. Opposition from environmental protection interests would be expected.

Canadian Ice Service and U.S. Coast Guard officials expect melting and ice floe problems to cause dangerous navigational difficulties along with the challenges of climate change, economic expansion, and national defense and security factors. Coast Guard officials believe a large USCG operations base is necessary in the region. Some regional analysts believe that base should be built in Nome.[9]

The changing Arctic maritime domain will impact the global economy and geopolitics. In other words, the changes will have geostrategic significance. Satellite measurements and sonar measurements from U.S. Navy submarines indicate, despite claims of global warming, the Arctic ocean remains largely ice covered during the year which impacts operational vulnerabilities, restrictions and regulations for polar vessels, and naval and commercial vessels with limited icebreaking capability. Commercial cargo, passenger, and armed naval patrol vessels in Arctic waters will have to be reinforced to be ice capable during seasonal weather changes and in shifting ice floes.

Nonetheless, the Arctic Ocean is expected to become increasingly navigable as international organizations study ways to protect the economies and traditions of sparse native populations. Scientific teams and shipping interests from the U.S., Canada, Denmark, Norway, Finland and Sweden conducted continental shelf exploration and shared technical information and assessments in 2009–2010. Two nuclear-powered icebreakers furnished convoy escorts in Russian waters. Arctic maritime nations are also under the jurisdiction of the United Nations Convention on the Law of the Sea. International councils have cooperated and crafted marine safety and search and rescue policies and have been hosted by the U.S. State Department and U.S. Coast Guard. The International Maritime Organization (IMO) held discussions on standards for ship construction and ice navigation standards and training.[10]

The costs of icebreaker maintenance and escort and related service fees may not be economically efficient, according to Capt. Lawson W. Brigham (USCG, Ret.), polar ice commander and university geographer. Captain Brigham writes that, "globalization, climate change, and geopolitics (international diplomacy and relations) continue to shape the future of the maritime Arctic. The Arctic Council and International Maritime Organization have awakened to the urgent need to protect Arctic people, the marine environment ... and address marine infrastructure ... strategic interests [and] future oil and gas discoveries."[11]

The 225-ft USCGC *Alder* (WLB-216) steamed out of its Duluth, Minnesota, homeport on 12 July 2010 for a two-month deployment into the Canadian Arctic. The mission trained Coast Guard personnel for potential security threats, economic and climate change contingencies, and international mission cooperation with the U.S. Navy, Royal Canadian Navy, and the Royal Danish Navy.

USCGC *Alder* (WLB-216) a 225-foot oceangoing buoy tender homeported in Duluth, Minnesota. The *Alder* participated in Operation Nanook 2010, a national security, natural disaster, and scientific Arctic training expedition in partnership with the Royal Canadian Navy, Canadian Reserve, Canadian Rangers and Canadian Coast Guard; the Royal Danish Navy; and the U.S. Navy.

The 1,800-mile voyage from Duluth into the Canadian Polar Region and eastern Greenland included mission experience in diving, search and rescue (SAR), and simulated oil spill drills. Lt. Cmdr. Mary Ellen Durley commanded the *Alder* through the mission and the cutter's 9 September 2010 return to Duluth after the 56-day voyage. The Great Lakes oceangoing buoy tender crew prepared to return to aids to navigation (ATN) and icebreaking duties on Lake Superior after, as Cmdr. Durley described, the cutter "navigated more than 8,500 miles through fog, rain, and heavy seas, amongst icebergs and whales, while witnessing beautiful fjords and a quick glimpse of a polar bear."[12]

The CGC *Alder* Arctic mission was part of international exercise Operation Nanook with the U.S. Navy, Canadian Coast Guard, and the navies of Canada and Denmark. The *Alder* crew traversed the freshwater Great Lakes and St. Lawrence Seaway, and the salt waters of the Atlantic and Arctic Oceans. The CGC *Alder* had to test its SAR skills when it participated in the rescue of a Canadian Navy small boat crew that was swept onto rocks of the coast of Labrador, Canada. The *Alder* engaged in joint missions with the HMCS *Goose Bay* and HDMS *Rasmussen* in live weapons and tactical ship maneuvers and numerous other drills.[13]

With the melting of Arctic ice, the United States is tracking, mapping, and charting changes in ice thickness and gradually expanding open waters. Federal civilian and military officials have responded to protect American security, defense, and commercial interests in the region, as are other nations in proximity to the polar regions.

The Government Accountability Office was reported to have concluded that the USCG lacks the funding, infrastructure and equipment for patrolling, policing, and administering Arctic waters. It has been estimated that 25 percent of the world's unexploited natural resources are located in the region, and new waterway passages could reduce transport and naval shipping distances by almost 50 percent from traditional routes and time frames.

President George W. Bush and President Barack Obama stated national security was a significant element of U.S. Arctic policy and planning, but some military officials said their requests for additional Arctic mission infrastructure and resources have been ignored,[14] given the debt, deficit, and fiscal challenges that faced the United States in the early 21st century. More than 150 nations ratified the UN Convention on the Law of the Sea, the only international treaty that considers the Arctic Region. U.S. officials helped write the treaty, but Congress failed to ratify it because of possible infringements on American sovereignty.[15]

In December 2010, Homeland Security Secretary Janet Napolitano announced the DHS was forming the Climate Change and Adaption Task Force to respond to the impact of climate change on domestic security missions and operations. Among the concerns and possible mission assignments, Napolitano explained was, "What assistance can the Coast Guard bring to bear to assist remote villages in Alaska which have been negatively affected by changes up in the Arctic?"[16]

The task force report stated, "Many USCG and Customs and Border Protection facilities, by their mission, are located in the coastal zone which will be adversely impacted by sea level rise. Costs will increase for protecting existing facilities from the impacts of sea level rise and some facilities might have to be abandoned in the longer term."[17] The previous June 2010 DHS Strategic Sustainability Performance Plan stated, "climate change has the potential to accelerate and intensify extreme weather events which threaten the nation's sustainability and security."[18]

Those concerns and statements illustrate the necessity of a USCG Arctic presence to continue its historic missions: the protection of life and property in the maritime domain, and Coast Guard cooperation with the other U.S. Armed Forces and allies in national security and national defense.

Congressional and DHS oversight and management of U.S. Coast Guard funding and operations requires that informed lawmakers and federal and USCG administrators are placed in decision-making capacities.

Captain Chip Cravaack (USNR, Ret.) appeared to be that kind of qualified decision maker. Congressman Cravaack was elected to office from northeast Minnesota in 2010.[19] Cravaack's Eighth Congressional District includes Coast Guard Station Duluth, the home port of the USCG cutter *Alder*.

The Republican representative was assigned to three subcommittees with jurisdiction over transportation, maritime and infrastructure issues. The former U.S. Navy and Northwest-Delta Airlines pilot was named vice chairman of an aviation subcommittee. Representative Cravaack was appointed to the subcommittees on Coast Guard and Maritime Transportation, and Water Resources and Environment, and the Homeland Security Committee.[20]

The multimission Coast Guard and the Department of Homeland Security must integrate enormous responsibilities with civilian and governmental agencies and the executive and legislative branches of the federal government. Effective and timely congressional oversight and communications between those agencies and the U.S. Coast Guard are essential elements of mission compliance and success. Those interrelationships and communications assure that the Coast Guard will always be true to its motto: *Semper Paratus* (Always Ready).

15

The Coast Guard Heritage

The U.S. Coast Guard heritage of multimission responsibilities in law enforcement, protection of life and property at sea, aids to navigation, and national security is significant. The contributions of the service to national defense and national security have become singularly important. The national defense and security missions of the U.S. Coast Guard in the 21st century have been emphasized in this book.

The Coast Guard has carried out its national defense missions at home and overseas, ever true to its service motto: *Semper Paratus* (Always Ready). The USCG has performed its traditional missions through its predecessor agencies (Revenue Marine, Revenue Cutter Service, Life Saving Service, Lighthouse Service) down through the ages, and since the formation of the modern U.S. Coast Guard in 1915.

C. Douglas Kroll concisely traced and illuminated the heritage of the Coast Guard and its agency predecessors in his book, *A Coastguardsman's History of the U.S. Coast Guard.*[1] Especially enlightening was Capt. Kroll's history of well-earned Coast Guard "battle streamers" from 1790 to the present. The first battle streamer credited the U.S. Revenue Marine for its maritime protection of the New Republic (1790–1797).

The Revenue Marine (Revenue Cutter Service) was the post–Revolutionary War federal republic's first navy. The U.S. Navy was not operational until 1798, when the USN and Revenue Marine battled French warships in the quasi-war with France (1798–99). Subsequently, the USRCS engaged in the War of 1812, pirate wars, slave trade patrol, Indian Wars in the Florida Everglades, Mexican War, Civil War, and Spanish American War.[2]

The Coast Guard battle streamers earned in the 20th and 21st centuries, the period covered in this book, include World War I (1917–1918); Yangtze (China) Service (1926–1927, 1930–1932); American Defense Service (1939–1941); World War II American and Pacific Campaigns (1941–1946); Philippine

Defense, Liberation, and Independence (1941–1945); Philippine Presidential Unit Citation (1941–1942, 1944–1945); World War II Europe, Africa, Middle East Campaigns (1942–1945); French Croix de Guerre, World War II (1944); World War II Victory (1941–1946); and the Navy Occupation Service battle streamer (during and after World War II).[3]

The post–World War II Coast Guard battle streamers include Korean Service (1950–1954); China Service (1917–1939, 1945–1957); Navy Unit Commendation; National Defense Service; Armed Forces Expeditionary; Vietnam Service; Coast Guard Unit Commendation; Coast Guard Meritorious Unit Commendation; Army Meritorious Unit Commendation; Navy Meritorious Unit Commendation; Republic of Vietnam Armed Forces Meritorious Unit Citation; Republic of Vietnam Meritorious Unit Citation Civil Actions Medal; Southwest Asia Campaign; Kosovo Campaign; Department of Transportation Secretary's Outstanding Unit Award; Global War on Terrorism Expeditionary; Global War on Terrorism Service; Coast Guard Presidential Unit Citation; Afghanistan Campaign; and the Iraq Campaign (Iraq War, Second Gulf War, and Operation Iraqi Freedom).[4] The campaign ribbon references include all of the War on Terror Persian Gulf missions. Mediterranean support activities are considered part of War on Terror operations as well.

Professor Kroll magnificently summarized the Coast Guard missions and chronologies associated with each of the historical battle streamers. Commander Kroll quoted then commandant, Adm. Willard J. Smith (USCG), on that officer's explanation of the significance of the battle streamers on the 178th anniversary of the Coast Guard (4 August 1968):

> They commemorate Coast Guard heroic actions in naval engagements throughout the history of the Service, serving as reminders of sacrifice ... and a proud heritage ... they provide a summary of operational battle history ... a lasting tribute to our gallant personnel who, by their deeds and heroic action, served the Coast Guard and nation with glory and distinction.... These Battle Streamers, together with others which may be bestowed on the Coast Guard at some future date, will adorn [USCG ceremonial colors] whenever and wherever unfurled.[5]

The heritage of brave Coast Guard men and women who have died in service of the nation is continuously expanded, and the contributions made are monitored and assessed. Among the heroes who died in World War II action was Lt. John H. Pritchard (USCG). Pritchard flew Arctic Greenland rescue missions off the USCGC *Northland* (WPG-49) in a J2F-4 Grumman floatplane. Pritchard achieved heroic rescues of downed Canadian and U.S. aviators. In his final rescue mission in November 1942, Lt. Pritchard, his radio operator Benjamin Bottoms, and a U.S. Army airman perished in an Arctic blizzard. Pritchard and Bottoms posthumously received the Distinguished Flying Cross.[6]

In August 2010, more than 60 years after the J2F-4 Grumman float biplane crew perished, a recovery team continued the attempt to locate the aircraft and its glacially entombed crew members. Master Chief Petty Officer John Long (USCG) conceived the recovery mission three years earlier. Long assumed the leadership of a 15-member unit seeking to recover the aircraft and bodies before the ice moves out to sea.

Helicopters, GPS devices, ground-penetrating radar, ice-melting equipment, and cameras to photograph ice fissures were part of the high-technology equipment inventory needed to probe the six most likely glacial sites. Challenging weather conditions periodically delayed operations. In 2008, Chief Long ordered a survey using ground-penetrating radar and electromagnetic waves from a P-3 Orion aircraft. MCPO Long said, "any branch of service wants to recover their fallen members if they can. It is the right thing to do."[7]

As World War II veterans pass from the scene, it is essential to preserve their contributions to national defense. Among those veterans is Lee Smith, 85 years of age in 2010. The Salisbury, Maryland, resident was a radioman third class in the U.S. Coast Guard during the war, assigned to the USS *Lowe* (DE-325). RM3 Smith was among the first naval personnel to "capture by Morse Code" Admiral Karl Doenitz's public statement on the surrender of Germany in May 1945.

Petty Officer Lee Smith experienced the trauma and responsibility of guarding a ticking German U-boat torpedo at an isolated pier in Hampton Roads, Virginia. The unexploded torpedo had struck a USN destroyer. The 18-year-old Coastguardsman was assigned custody of the weapon while military authorities prepared to disarm and examine it. RM3 Smith said military authorities told him, "If it stops ticking, I should run and then call them!"[8]

PO Smith served on patrol in a USCG-USN "killer group" of 1 Coast Guard and 3 USN manned ships that targeted German U-boats in the North Atlantic. RM3 Smith, who suffered hearing loss in a gun-firing incident, proudly recalled, "We got credit for sinking a submarine near Nova Scotia [Canada]."[9]

Captain Alex Larzelere (USCG, Ret.) authored books about Coast Guard national defense missions in World War I and Vietnam. In *The Coast Guard in World War I*, Larzelere explained how in 1928, U.S. Treasury Secretary Andrew Mellon, U.S. Navy Secretary Curtis D. Wilbur, and U.S. Coast Guard commandant, Rear Adm. Frederick C. Billard (USCG), dedicated a monument to the 192 Coastguardsmen killed during the Great War (1914–1918).

The monument at Arlington National Cemetery (Virginia) also commemorated the victims of the German U-boat attack on the convoy escort ship USCGC *Tampa*. The 1918 Annual Report of the U.S. Navy secretary stated that the sinking of the CGC *Tampa* in Bristol Channel off the coast of Wales

(United Kingdom) was the largest loss of life in a single naval combat incident in the war. Of the 131 fatalities on that 26 September 1918 evening, 111 were Coast-guardsmen, and the other victims were U.S. Navy personnel and British subjects.[10]

In November 2010, Homeland Security Secretary Janet Napolitano and Admiral Robert J. Papp, the U.S. Coast Guard commandant. commemorated the Coast Guard heritage in World War I. The occasion was a wreath-laying ceremony at the U.S. Coast Guard World War I memorial in Arlington Cemetery. The memorial was constructed to honor the crews of the Coast Guard cutters *Seneca* and *Tampa* that were sunk in September 1918. The World War I memorial contains the names of all of the members of the U.S. Coast Guard who perished in the war.[11]

U.S. Coast Guard Station Lake Worth Inlet (West Palm Beach, Florida) hosted a December 2010 ceremony honoring veterans killed in action (KIA) whose bodies were never recovered. The remembrance commemorated several hundred battle sites and ships from military conflicts including World War II, Korea, Vietnam, the World Trade Center (9/11), and other locations. Public affairs officer Ed Greenfield (USCG Auxiliary) reported that all the U.S. Armed Forces were represented, including the U.S. Army, Navy, Marines, Air Force, Coast Guard, POWs, MIAs, and the U.S. Merchant Marine. Military representatives were scheduled to embark on a Coast Guard cutter to the Palm Beach Inlet and set a commemorative wreath adrift.[12]

Because the Coast Guard has law enforcement authority over civilians and carries out a variety of civilian contact missions like fishing enforcement, search and rescue, ship inspections, narcotics and immigration interdiction, and environmental pollution enforcement and response, some observers do not perceive the Coast Guard as a military service. Many people are unaware of the national defense role and articulation with the other U.S. Armed Forces the Coast Guard performs. Add to that the limited geographic concept engendered by the word "Coast" in the service name, and the fact that the Coast Guard has been under the jurisdiction of the Treasury, Transportation, and now Homeland Security departments, and not permanently under the Defense Department. The nonmilitary conception of the USCG is understandable.

President Barack Obama slipped into the stream of omission, or experienced a mental lapse, while speaking to U.S. military forces in Afghanistan in December 2010. Obama proudly declared, "I think we have every service here tonight," and enumerated the U.S. Army, Navy, Air Force and Marines. Then someone in the audience shouted, "Coast Guard!" Obama responded, "Coast Guard? Is that what I heard?" After his own and audience laughter, Obama remarked, "Here in Afghanistan, all of you are part of one team, serving and succeeding together."[13]

Petty Officer First Class Middleboro Jones (USN/USNR, Ret.) is the director of the *USNavyJeep* Internet blog site. Jones commented on President Obama's speech and how Obama "forgot to thank the Coast Guard for their efforts in Afghanistan ... funny as there is no *coast* in Afghanistan."[14]

Middleboro went on to describe his U.S. Navy experience while serving the flight line at Kandahar (Afghanistan) Airfield. He saw two men come off an aircraft in Navy Desert uniforms and called out, "How's it going, Navy?" The officer said, "I'm not Navy," and showed Middleboro the U.S. Coast Guard emblem. Petty Officer Middleboro politely inquired, "What COAST are you guarding? There is no coast" in Afghanistan. After further amiable conversation, Petty Officer Middleboro concluded, "We in the Blue Water Navy welcome our Coastie cousins ... as it is One Team–One Fight."[15]

The Coast Guard missions in the Arabian Gulf and Afghanistan were unique, and further testimonial to the multimission skills and national defense responsibilities of the service. President Obama did not forget the U.S. Coast Guard later in December 2010 and made a holiday call to a USCG unit in the Persian Gulf nation of Kuwait.

Petty Officer 2/C Class Dustin Monroe (USCG) received the call from the commander in chief and was honored by the experience. PO2 Monroe explained elements of the Coast Guard missions in the Persian Gulf (Kuwait and Iraq) and the landlocked nation of Afghanistan in the War on Terror. President Obama called a second Coastguardsman who was on a patrol boat in the Arabian Gulf.

PO2 Monroe, a Montana native, explained to the president that he was completing a yearlong deployment to the region as a hazardous materials (HAZMAT) inspector. Monroe said he proudly shared his conversation with President Obama "with my Coast Guard and Army teammates."

Monroe was assigned to the Coast Guard Redeployment Inspection Assistance Detachment that was embedded with U.S. Army units. The Coast Guard detachment was assigned to inspect and clear Army equipment and personnel for return to the United States.[16]

U.S. Armed Forces Medal of Honor (MOH) recipients were honored and commemorated by the USCG in a visit to U.S. Coast Guard Station Juneau (Alaska) in January 2011. Major Drew Dix (U.S. Army, Special Forces, Ret.), Col. Jay Vargas (USMC, Ret.), and M/Sgt. Richard Pittman (USMC, Ret.) spoke with U.S. Coast Guard personnel. The visitors ranged in age from 65 to 73. As inspirational as their heroic stories and presence were to Coast Guard members, the Medal of Honor recipients in turn extolled the significance and courage of USCG personnel exhibited in their multimission responsibilities.

Dix, Vargas, and Pittman were en route to USCG Station Kodiak

(Alaska) for a ceremony to honor SM1 Douglas Munro. The heroic World War II landing craft coxswain earned a posthumous Medal of Honor for using his LC and machine gun to shield U.S. Marines from Japanese gunfire on Guadalcanal (27 September 1942). The Kodiak ceremony would feature a bust of Petty Officer Munro presented on the 378-foot USCGC *Munro* (WHEC-724) at the cutter's home port. The MOH recipients were then scheduled for a patrol run on a 47-foot fast response boat.[17]

Captain Melissa Bert, U.S. Coast Guard Sector Juneau commander, said, "Hearing their (the MOH recipients') stories is such a connection to our history."[18] USCG Station Juneau officer in charge, Senior Chief James Greenlief, added, "For the District to ask us to open the station and show them what we do is an honor [because of] what they endured and what they did."[19]

Since 11 September 2001 and the commencement of the War on Terror, the multimission Coast Guard has been stretched to the limit in missions, assets, personnel, budgets, and training. In a January 2011 media interview, Adm. Robert J. Papp, Jr., the USCG commandant, expressed concern about finding "the right balance" in missions with an aging maritime fleet.

Adm. Papp, a native of Norwich, Connecticut, spoke about expanded mission requirements, concern about priorities and "balance," and the responsibility the USCG has to meet its mandated statutory responsibilities.[20]

In the Coast Guard commandant's February 2011 "State of the Coast Guard Address," Adm. Papp expressed concern about mission stretch, overextension of personnel tasks and responsibilities, and the rise in mission-related injuries and deaths. Adm. Papp attributed the casualties to resource and budge shortages and mission creep. In the preceding two years, Papp asserted, the USCG lost one Marine Safety and Security Team (MSST) member and 14 aviators, "largely during routine missions."[21]

Adm. Papp said, "I've spoken at too many memorial services. We have also had several serious boat accidents. This is unprecedented [and] unacceptable. And we've got to do something about it."[22] The increase in high-technology equipment and complex skill sets imposed on the Coast Guard since 11 September 2001, Papp explained, may require the USCG "to reduce the number and range of capabilities until properly resourced." In the future, Papp concluded, mission assignments will require cost evaluations and mission training with assurances that "we understand their full ramifications."[23]

Domestic border security is a critical element of national defense. The U.S.–Canada and U.S.–Mexico land and water routes provide vulnerable and porous border access into the United States for criminals, weapons, narcotics, undocumented migrants, and terrorists. Despite the diligent and professional efforts of the U.S. military, naval, and law enforcement communities, the success of maritime drug trafficking has illustrated the permeability of U.S. borders. Border control is an essential element of national sovereignty and public safety.

The U.S Coast Guard seized more than 90 tons of contraband cocaine in 2010, with an estimated value of $3.5 billion. The seizures constitute a commendable achievement, but unfortunately it accounts for only about one-quarter of the alleged total amount of 350 tons that comes into the United States annually.[24]

In their attempts to evade U.S. Navy, Coast Guard, and Customs enforcement, the narcotics traffickers have used "go-fast" boats instead of more easily spotted aircraft. The boats can carry more cargo than most private aircraft can. Contraband can be more easily jettisoned overboard from a boat than an aircraft. And the boats are fast enough to challenge and outrun larger maritime law enforcement craft.

The USCG and U.S. Customs often rely on patrol aircraft flown from shore bases, or Coast Guard helicopters flown from the decks of oceangoing cutters. Once the contraband boats are located, Coast Guard fast boats released from Coast Guard cutters pursue the traffickers. Coast Guard helicopter gunners and sharpshooters can disable go-fast engines as a prelude to apprehension by law enforcement boarding teams.

Narcotics traffickers have continually escalated the drug wars with new technology and assets (as have U.S. law enforcement agencies and partner allied nations). In the last few decades, contraband traffickers have used hard to spot and apprehend camouflaged semi-submersible craft. In their problematic attempts to elude or deceive

20. Adm. Robert J. Papp, U.S. Coast Guard commandant (2010–). Adm. Papp succeeded Adm. Thad Allen. Adm. Papp is responsible for maintaining the expanded Coast Guard missions at home and abroad within the context of limited budgets and the essential upgrading and modernizing of the air and sea fleets, shore stations, and the U.S. Coast Guard and other training centers while articulating USCG missions with federal, state, and local law enforcement and the Defense Department.

U.S. Coast Guard, Navy, and Customs patrols, traffickers (in drug and human smuggling) have plied their trade on cargo vessels, fishing boats, and pleasure craft.[25]

The open border problem is usually attributed to the U.S. border with Mexico. But in February 2011, two senators on the Senate Homeland Security and Governmental Affairs Committee asserted that the 4,000-mile Canada-United States border is just as vulnerable, if not more so. Committee hair, Senator Joe Lieberman independent from Connecticut, and Republican Senator Susan Collins (Maine) claimed that only about 32 miles of the northern border is securely covered and under "operational control" by the federal government. The rest of the border is "grossly underprotected" from contraband smugglers and terrorist penetration.[26] That border porosity is significant because of Canada's more lenient immigration policies and processes, and the tremendous expanse of land and Great Lakes waterways between the two nations.

Department of Homeland Security (DHS) spokesman Matt Chandler responded that the DHS is working to improve and enhance support technology and infrastructure in the northern border regions, hire more Border Patrol agents, and better coordinate security operations with Customs and Immigration personnel. Senators Lieberman and Collins had previously requested that cooperation and information exchange be improved between the DHS and Canadian and U.S. law enforcement agencies at national, state and local levels.[27]

That law enforcement coordination request was interesting because in 2010–2011 the state of Arizona was sued by the Obama administration for empowering its local law enforcement officers to enforce illegal immigration law. The Arizona law was crafted by the state legislature in response to what Republican state governor Jan Brewer and border county sheriff departments contended was a federal failure to enforce the law, close the border to illegal migrants, and mitigate the resultant socioeconomic costs, crime, violence, and national security issues.

The Coast Guard's contributions to national defense are exemplified by the service's national security missions in the Middle East in the War on Terror. Commander Brenden Kettner (USCG) participated in urban operations training at Ft. Dix, New Jersey. Cmdr. Kettner completed a monthlong training program in 2011 at the Expeditionary Combat Readiness Center in preparation for his second tour of duty in Iraq. The Coast Guard commander trained with U.S. Air Force, U.S. Army, and U.S. Navy personnel. Cmdr. Kettner, a certified Combat Life Saver, was assigned to Multi-National Forces Iraq, as a port advisor and officer in charge.[28]

The responsibilities assigned to Cmdr. Kettner included antiterrorism training, improved port security measures, and the advancement of international ship and port infrastructure security. In his first Iraq tour, Cmdr. Kettner was the international port security liaison officer to Iraq (2007) and directed policy planning to help Iraq ports contribute to the economic growth of the nation. Cmdr. Kettner commended the Coast Guard men and women who were sacrificing to preserve and extend freedom and concluded, "As the furthest deployed units in our service, (the USCG missions) are key in achieving our nation's strategic and operational goals."[29]

The training and professionalism Coast Guard personnel experience and exhibit accounts for the successful completion of the service missions. The leadership and competencies of the noncommissioned enlisted members, and warrant officer and commissioned officer personnel, ensures that the Coast Guard stays true to its motto, "Always Ready."

Among the exemplary noncommissioned officer leaders is Master Chief Petty Officer Warren Benson (USCG). MCPO Benson enlisted in the Coast Guard in 1980 after completing three years of college, at the suggestion of his father, a U.S. Army colonel. During his 25-year career, CPO Benson served at a LORAN station in the Arctic; in emergency communications at the USCG manned National Response Center in Washington, D.C.; in commercial vessel safety; as a training school chief; in port security and antiterrorism; in forecasting and analysis; and as a Coast Guard recruiting supervisor. Chief Benson's leadership skills have been applied to sports, coaching, and competitive martial arts. MCPO Benson has been inspired by other Coast Guard personnel and has been enriched by "helping other military members excel, sharing my experiences with others."[30]

The United States Coast Guard Academy (USCGA) is the premier training institution for cadets preparing to assume commissioned Reserve and Regular officer ranks in the service. The USCGA is located in New London, Connecticut, along the Thames River. The main USCG enlisted recruit basic training school is located at Cape May, New Jersey. The Coast Guard offers advanced training in a variety of specialties for noncommissioned petty officers at various sites across the nation. Coast Guard enlisted personnel and officers also attend U.S. Navy schools, other U.S. Armed Forces institutions and training centers, and various war and national defense schools and colleges in the United States.

U.S. Coast Guard headquarters is located in Washington, D.C. The national headquarters, as opposed to regional district Coast Guard headquarters, was scheduled to be rebuilt on a southeast Washington, D.C., site in multiphase, billion-dollar projects scheduled for completion by 2016. The headquarters would have multiple floor levels terraced into an excavated hill-side. The completed Department of Homeland Security (DHS) campus would accommodate more than 20 separate DHS agencies and include several renovated buildings on the historic 19th-century St. Elizabeth Hospital campus.[31]

The Coast Guard heritage was continued by a 2010 workforce of more than 34,000 enlisted, 8,200 commissioned, 7,800 civilian, 7,000 reserve, and 30,000 auxiliary personnel. The active-duty complement was 87 percent male and 13 percent female. Assets included approximately 250 cutters, 1,800 boats, and 200 aircraft. The 2010 U.S. Coast Guard budget was $10 billion.[32] Coast Guard assets, budgets, and personnel support the following missions: aids to navigation; search and rescue; marine resources and environmental protection; marine safety; drug and migrant interdiction; ice operations; maritime law enforcement; port, waterway and coastal security; and defense readiness.[33]

Appendix A.
Team Coast Guard and
Commandants to 1990

The civilian support staff and the volunteer civilian members of the U.S. Coast Guard Auxiliary (USCGAUX) perform important administrative, boat safety, and SAR mission tasks for the USCG. Those contributions allow the uniformed part-time active-duty Reserves; enlisted active-duty nonrated and rated (petty officers and chief petty officers); and the warrant and commissioned officer ranks to tend full-time to the multimission functions of the U.S. Coast Guard.

The men and women of the U.S. Coast Guard are part of the personnel establishment called "Team Coast Guard." The talent, training and dedication exhibited by Team Coast Guard explains the reputation and mission success of the sea service and has served the USCG motto: *Semper Paratus* (Always Ready).

Since its founding as the Revenue Marine in 1790, and subsequently the U.S. Revenue Cutter Service (USRCS), and then the U.S. Coast Guard in 1915, the service has benefited from the professionalism and heroism of Team Coast Guard, some of whose members have given their lives in the line of duty in times of peace and war.

The general public and the other U.S. Armed Forces usually appreciate Coast Guard missions. But Coast Guard activities have not gone unchallenged, without criticism or litigation. Court challenges and public protests against USCG mission tactics occurred during Prohibition, the Cold War, and the War on Terror (WOT). During the WOT, Great Lakes Coast Guard cutters began gunnery practice and incurred the animosity of the tourist and fishing communities. Then, public criticism occurred in 2009 when Coast Guard fast boats practiced antiterrorist tactics and boarding drills on the anniversary of the terrorist attacks of September 11, 2001.

Several of these controversies have been and will be further discussed in this book. Coast Guard missions and controversies during Prohibition (1920–1933) will be considered in more detail in this chapter.

The USCG was ordered by Congress to enforce the laws that prohibited the manufacturing, selling and consumption of alcohol, as per the Volstead Act of 1919. Because the USCG was then under the jurisdiction of the U.S. Treasury Department, the service assisted federal revenue agents of the U.S. Internal Revenue Service, and local, state and federal law enforcement agencies in enforcing Prohibition laws. The Coast Guard assignment to interdict illegal alcohol was consistent with the Service's duties and the precursor of the illegal drug and immigration interdiction mission the USCG would carry out from the Prohibition era to the present.

Given the unpopularity of Prohibition, it was inevitable that the Coast Guard was not fully supported by the public, the alcohol distributors who were part of organized crime syndicates; civil liberties groups, and certain judges and juries. The corruption of public officials influenced by threats and bribes made the already dangerous enforcement challenges even more problematic, and Coast Guard and other law enforcement officials suffered and caused casualties in the process. Coast Guard commandants prepared and monitored the service in the execution of its orders and duties.

A closer look at the USCG experience in Prohibition law enforcement is in order because the mission related to national security and defense; prepared the Coast Guard in technology, assets, and seamanship for its port security and overseas missions in World War II; and prepared it for its expanding drug interdiction responsibilities from the 1920s to the present.

Prohibition (1920–1933) and the national economic dislocation of the Depression (1929–1939) presented new challenges for the Coast Guard because it represented federal authority when it was unpopular, challenged, and often defied. The Volstead Act (1919) prohibited the production, transportation and consumption of intoxicating liquor and provided for the enforcement of the 18th (Prohibition) Amendment. As has happened so often in history, a new national crisis resulted in the expansion of the Coast Guard mission.

Millions of dollars of federal appropriations were used to enforce Prohibition laws, and thousands of arrests and convictions occurred, some challenged by civil liberties groups and defense attorneys. Among the litigants were federal agencies and officers, including the Coast Guard. Federal agents, the Coast Guard included, were wounded and killed in the enforcement process on land and sea. The Wickersham Commission Report (1931) concluded that the laws could not be enforced and that the well-intentioned moral crusade had failed. Congress repealed the 18th Amendment with the 21st Amendment (1933), but not before considerable cultural damage had been done, including defiance of the law, and the bribery and corruption of local, state and federal officials by criminal elements, which led to further defiance and contempt for the law and legal processes. The revenues generated from the sale of illegal alcohol in a supply-and-demand buyer's market intensified the power, violence, and wealth of organized crime syndicates that reinvested its profits into gambling, prostitution, and drug smuggling.

The Prohibition Bureau was placed under the Treasury Department, which ordered its subordinate agencies (revenue agents and the USCG) to enforce the law. The USCG was active on the high seas in alcohol interdiction because the flow of illegal spirits came from Canada and the West Indies. Contraband boats and ships plied the waters of the Caribbean, Atlantic, Pacific, and the Great Lakes and came into coastal, lake and river ports with their precious cargo. Liquor-laden watercraft, aircraft, and land vehicles traversed jurisdictional boundaries with ease. Detroit was alleged to have made as much money from liquor transferred from Ontario province in Canada as it did from the manufacture of trucks and automobiles.

Dedicated federal, state and local law enforcement personnel, including Coastguardsmen, carried out the law despite threats to their lives, dangers associated with apprehension and arrest, and a few corrupt colleagues in the criminal justice fraternity.

The Coast Guard "Rum Fleet" chased the "rumrunners" with the assistance of the border patrol, customs agents, local and state police, and Treasury Department agents. The government agents were called "G" men. The Coast Guard enforcement fleet consisted of watercraft ranging from small coastal and inland patrol boats to the 20 destroyers transferred to the USCG by congressional action in 1924. Coastguard crews gained experience in running destroyer-sized vessels and USN craft, and the oceangoing cutters of the service. Coastguardsmen also learned to use a favorite gang and law enforcement weapon, the Thompson submachine gun.[1] That training proved useful in World War II.

Foreign rumrunners generally stayed outside the three- and twelve-mile U.S. territorial boundaries policed by Coast Guard boats, cutters and destroyers. The oceangoing cutters and destroyers reported the location of speedboats that off-loaded the liquor. The contraband boats tried to outrun the Coast Guard patrol boats that stopped the speedboats, boarded, seized evidence, and confiscated contraband. Suspect foreign and American vessels were boarded and seized by Coast Guard port security personnel in U.S. ports.

Rear Admiral Frederick C. Billard, the U.S. Coast Guard commandant (1924–1932), reluctantly accepted and carried out the Prohibition enforcement mission and observed that the total annual value of alcohol contraband seizures compared closely with the annual federal appropriations for the USCG. Unfortunately, the dangers Coast Guard crews faced chasing down contraband vessels and criminal crews were ignored by some judges and law enforcement officials who chose to treat lawbreakers leniently and released seized vessels, that quickly returned to the illicit and profitable trade.[2]

The danger of drug enforcement is illustrated by an incident that occurred in the Florida Straits in 1927. Rumrunners had bought liquor in the British Bahamas islands with counterfeit United States currency. Chief Boatswain's Mate Sydney Sanderlin (USCG), the commander of patrol boat *CG-249*, was on patrol with seven crew members and U.S. Secret Service agent Robert K. Webster. *CG-249* stopped a suspected vessel after firing warning shots over the bow of the boat off Fort Lauderdale, Florida. One hundred cases of liquor were found, and the smugglers were placed under arrest. A gun battle ensued on the Coast Guard cutter. Chief Petty Officer Sanderlin and SS agent Webster were killed. Using hand tools, the Coast Guard crew overwhelmed and apprehended the two smugglers. Subsequently, one of the smugglers was found guilty of murder in the confrontation and hanged at U.S. Coast Guard Base Fort Lauderdale.[3]

Prohibition was active and dangerous on the Great Lakes between Canada and the United States. In 1919, in anticipation of its role in Prohibition law enforcement, Coast Guard patrol boats were prepared for the mission. As an agency of the U.S. Treasury Department, the USCG was called upon to enforce Prohibition laws on the Atlantic, Gulf, and Pacific coasts, and on the Great Lakes. Using patrol boats, cutters and destroyers on loan from the U.S. Navy, the USCG carried out its dangerous and unpopular missions, and suffered casualties and court adjudications.

Prohibition enforcement on the Great Lakes and U.S. coastal regions required increased federal appropriations for personnel increases, more patrol boats, enhanced technical support systems and updated radio communications equipment. The winter Great Lakes ice on the St. Claire and Detroit rivers allowed liquor and beer laden cars and trucks to drive on plowed lanes between Canada and the United States. Coast Guard icebreakers carved ice channels to deter alcohol smuggling operations and kept commercial shipping channels opened.

Great Lakes maritime historian Frederick Stonehouse chronicled the Prohibition era and Coast Guard operations in his thoroughly researched book, *Great Lakes Crime: Murder, Mayhem, Booze and Broads* and the many incidents of intrigue and danger on cold Great Lakes nights. Rumrunning small craft crossed the Detroit River. Rumrunners killed each other in turf wars and engaged in reciprocally dangerous gunfights, carnage and casualties with Treasury, Customs, and Coast Guard law enforcement teams.

Rumrunning boats had armor plating and were equipped with aircraft engines that propelled the craft at speeds in excess of 45 miles per hour. Coast Guard craft ranged from 35- to 75-foot picket and patrol boats, and 300-foot destroyers loaned by the USN to the USCG.

Contraband-carrying aircraft landed on Minnesota farm fields. Boats visited ports and depots on Great Lakes shores and on Isle Royale in Lake Superior. Shoot-outs occurred in harbors and on the normally peaceful Apostle Islands tourist haven north of Ashland, Wisconsin. Contraband vessels were seized and sold at auctions or became part of the maritime arsenal of the U.S. Customs, Border Patrol and Coast Guard. Unfortunately the war on alcohol and the enormous money supply generated by illegal contraband led to the corruption and prosecution of a few members of the above-named federal agencies and civilian law enforcement officers and judges.

The Coast Guard armed arsenal matched their federal colleagues and included the aforementioned Thompson machine ("Tommy") guns, as well as revolvers and rifles. Coast Guard boats and cutters carried a variety of small arms and ordnance, and larger vessels carried deck cannons. An estimated 1,550 criminals were killed in the alcohol wars, along with more than 70 Treasury agents, Customs inspectors and Coast Guard personnel.

In his investigative article about Coast Guard boarding policies and authority, reporter Jack Storey expressed concern about probable cause issues, Bill of Rights protections, and a U.S. Supreme Court decision that expanded federal boarding authority. Storey conceded the necessity of maritime boarding authority and the generally judicious use of that legal power by the Coast Guard given the experience of Prohibition and the kinds of watercraft used by contraband smugglers then and in the contemporary period of drug smuggling and the War on Terror.[4]

International law challenged Coast Guard alcohol interdiction and law enforcement efforts. A court ruled that the "hot pursuit" claim of the Coast Guard in the capture of a Canadian rumrunner was invalid because two cutters were involved at different times before the vessel was finally captured in international waters. Arbitration eventually resolved the dispute and clarified the court's problematic interpretation.

Coast Guard diligence was illustrated in December 1922 when the USCGC *Acushnet* towed a schooner with 2,000 cases of alcohol into Boston (Massachusetts) Harbor, and in June 1925 when the CGC *Redwing* and 75-

foot patrol boat *CG-237* coordinated the joint seizure of a contraband vessel.

The U.S. Congress funded a USCG request for faster cutters and the acquisition of aircraft for surveillance and rescue missions. In 1934 Henry Morgenthau, President Roosevelt's treasury secretary, designated the USCG responsible for coastal and inland maritime border surveillance and assisting the U.S. Border Patrol.

Treasury Department aviation missions were assigned to the Coast Guard. To achieve the aviation missions the USCG acquired 15 aircraft from the U.S. Customs Service and 6 from the U.S. Navy, along with air stations in San Diego, California; San Antonio, Texas; and Buffalo, New York. The sea and air assets acquired by the Coast Guard for its Prohibition enforcement mission were later used in World War II.

Among the Coast Guard aircraft assets acquired in the 1920s were two Chance Vought biplane seaplanes with "U.S. Coast Guard" prominently lettered on the fuselage of each aircraft. Forty-six "off-shore patrol boats" were acquired by the service in 1926–1927 and named after U.S. Revenue Cutter officers and cutters. The new boats, long enough to be called "cutters," were 100 to 125 feet in length, diesel-powered, twin-screw (propeller), steel-hulled vessels with three-inch .23 caliber guns. Some patrol craft were acquired from the seizure of contraband vessels. Boats taken into the Coast Guard were given a CG number on the hull based on whether they were more or less than 40 feet in length.

The USCG used radios for intelligence gathering and communications between sea and shore stations, and between aircraft and air stations. Because rumrunners learned to monitor Coast Guard radio frequencies, new codes had to be developed. The radio codes were initially based on U.S. Navy systems until Major William F. Friedman, a U.S. Army cryptographer, and his wife Elizabeth Friedman, developed unique Coast Guard ciphers.

By the end of Prohibition in 1933 the USCG was operating 15 destroyers that were returned to the USN in 1934. By June 1933 Coast Guard headquarters in Washington, D.C., reported progress in the war against alcohol smuggling on the Great Lakes and along the Atlantic, Gulf, and Pacific coasts. Public demand for the illegal contraband and the creative countermeasures employed by domestic and foreign traffickers made it impossible for federal authorities to completely terminate the lucrative liquor trade.

Adm. Frederick Billard, the U.S. Coast Guard commandant, dedicated himself to improving the morale of Coast Guard personnel posted at isolated stations or serving on long, monotonous, and dangerous sea voyages. Libraries and correspondence courses were established, along with athletic equipment, films, radios, and phonograph record players. Correlated with those supportive activities was the founding of the League of Coast Guard Women that promoted the morale of USCG personnel through contacts and gifts, and through aiding sick, distressed, and needy personnel and their families.

The USN assisted Adm. Billard's personnel mission by making USN correspondence courses available to Coast Guard members. The U.S. Marine Corps extended its educational facilities to Coastguardsmen and established a model for the Coast Guard Institute at the U.S. Coast Guard Academy in New London, Connecticut. The institute graded advanced rating examinations and awarded certificates and correspondence course graduation diplomas.

Adm. Billard had served as the USCGA's superintendent and used his authority to encourage members of Congress and Connecticut officials to improve academy facilities and purchase the land necessary to expand activities and infrastructure. Treasury Secretary Andrew Mellon and federal architects were instrumental in the construction of Alexander Hamilton Hall, a fitting tribute to the first treasury secretary and founder of the Revenue Marine, latter called the U.S. Revenue Cutter Service. Captain Quincy B. Newman (USCG) was appointed head of the Department of Engineering at the USCGA, and revised the courses and curriculum to match the leading laboratories, colleges, and universities and give Academy cadets the knowledge to meet the technological needs of the service.

In 1928–1929 Adm. Billard was able to build several "Lake-class" cutters so called because they were named after large U.S. lakes, including the *Champlain*, *Mendota*, *Ponchartrain*, *Tahoe*, and *Itasca*. Even in the early years of the Depression (1932–1939) the cutters *Escanaba*, *Tahoma*, *Mohawk*, *Onondaga*, *Comanche*, and *Algonquin* were launched. Several of these cutters served on the front maritime lines in World War II.

Some naval historians believe the origin of the Coast Guard use of the letter *W* to designate its cutters is lost in obscurity. For example, the letters WHEC identifies a high-endurance oceangoing Coast Guard cutter. WMEC indicates a medium-endurance cutter. Coast Guard historian Robert Erwin Johnson credited Adm. Billard with advocating use of the *W* to distinguish Coast Guard cutters from U.S. Navy ("USS") ships. Professor Johnson did not reveal what the *W* literally stood for but suggested it was chosen as a definitive and easily recognized letter.

Perhaps *W* designated a Weather (Ocean) Station cutter, a significant and hazardous duty cutters performed in heavy Atlantic seas. Whatever the meaning of the *W*, the designation identified the valiant oceangoing cutters and crews that confronted America's nautical enemies in World War II at great costs and losses to vessels and crews. The *W*'s served admirably in the national defense of the United States in World War II, Korea, and Vietnam, and subsequently in interdiction missions and the War on Terror.[5]

The multimission U.S. Coast Guard owes its successes to the civilian, auxiliary, reserve, and active-duty enlisted and commissioned personnel of the service. The leadership skills of noncommissioned officers (NCOs), chief petty officers (CPOs), warrant and commissioned officers, and the Coast Guard commandants define and guide the missions that all members of Team Coast Guard contribute to and carry out. Several Coast Guard commandants have been mentioned in this narrative, but a chronological review of several of the commandants who served the Coast Guard and the nation so well in the 20th and 21st centuries is in order.

From the time of the U.S. Revenue Marine (USRM) and U.S. Revenue Cutter Service (USRCS), from 1790 to 1915 and the origin of the U.S. Coast Guard, several of the service directors were civilians in the Revenue Marine Bureau, U.S. Life-Saving Service, U.S. Customs Service, and U.S. Treasury Department. Commissioned USRC officers who assumed the highest leadership position were called captain-commandants.

Captain-Commandant Ellsworth P. Bertholf (1911–1919) directed the USRCS into its transition into the U.S. Coast Guard, led the USCG through World War I and the immediate postwar transition period, and was head from the service's wartime connection to the U.S. Navy back to the U.S. Treasury Department and postwar demobilization. Rear Adm. William E. Reynolds led the Coast Guard in the early years of Prohibition.[6] Adm. Reynolds, the former commander of the Bering Sea Patrol Fleet, was appointed by the president of the United States, confirmed by the U.S. Senate in September 1919, and assumed office in October. Under Commandant Reynolds, the number of U.S Coast Guard Academy cadets expanded from 23 in 1920 to 72 in 1923.[7]

Coast Guard Commandant Reynolds was succeeded by Rear Adm. Frederick C. Billard (1924–1932) whose leadership achievements were surveyed in this chapter. Rear Adm. Harry G. Hamlet, commandant from 1932 to 1936, led the USCG in the early period of the Depression (1929–1939) and the termination of Prohibition. The Depression-era economy forced Adm. Hamlet to reduce officer promotions and officer and enlisted ranks. Nonetheless, under Hamlet's leadership, the cutter and seaplane fleets expanded.[8]

Admiral Hamlet was succeeded by the exemplary World War II commandant, Adm. Russell R. Waesche (1936–1946). Adm. Waesche served Presidents Franklin D. Roosevelt and Harry Truman and prepared the U.S. Coast Guard for its World War II missions on the domestic front and in every theater of war on U.S. Navy, Army, and Coast Guard vessels and USCG aircraft.

Adm. Waesche integrated U.S. Navy and Coast Guard operations in consultation with the chief of naval operations and helped design schools of instructions and exchanges with Coast Guard and Navy personnel and instructors to take advantage of the experience, assets, and missions of the respective sea services. Adm. Waesche earned awards, commendations, and medals in the line of duty, and the praise of commanders of each of the U.S. Armed Forces and civilian wartime leaders.

Coast Guard Women Reserves (SPARS), Temporary Reservists, Auxiliary and civilians in the USCG performed their duties on the home front to release other Coast Guard members for overseas duty. After the war,

Admiral Russell R. Waesche, commandant U.S. Coast Guard, World War II. Adm. Waesche served for 10 years. He prepared the USCG to enter the war and earned commendations from political and military leaders for his innovative leadership and ability to articulate Coast Guard missions with the other U.S. Armed Forces.

Adm. Waesche superintended postwar demobilization and returned the Coast Guard from USN control to the U.S. Treasury Department and its traditional domestic and national defense missions.[9]

Succeeding the legendary World War II commandant, Adm. Russell R. Waesche, was no easy task for the less charismatic Adm. Joseph F. Farley (1946–1949). But Farley's achievements were significant and included the postwar demobilization of service personnel; effective management of the Bureau of Marine Inspection and Navigation, Ocean Stations, and the LORAN system; and sustaining the support of Congress with the statutory clarification and expansion of Coast Guard domestic and national defense missions.[10]

Commandant Merlin O'Neill led the USCG from 1949 to 1954 in the embryonic stages of the Cold War and concomitant domestic and overseas national security threats. Vice Adm. O'Neill (USCGA 1921) commanded the attack transport *Leonard Wood* in World War II and earned the Legion of Merit and led the Coast Guard in the expansion of fixed-wing and rotary air assets and air stations.

The Coast Guard had sent a small detachment to South Korea in 1946 to establish a Korean Coast Guard (later Navy) service. With the outbreak of the Korean War (1950–1953), Adm. O'Neil administered a small Coast Guard contingent that ran a LORAN station and several cutters in weather station and support missions. President Truman expanded the traditional domestic USCG port security mission by executive order in October 1950. Under Adm. O'Neill, the USCG achieved its then highest peacetime complement of 29,154 military and 4,963 civilian personnel, and played a national defense role at home and overseas during the Cold War confrontation of the Korean War.[11]

Admiral Alfred C. Richmond was the Coast Guard commandant from 1954 to 1962. Adm. Richmond had been the senior Coast Guard officer on the staff of the U.S. Naval Forces commander in Europe in 1945, commanded the USCGC *Haida*, and served as a legal and budget specialist at U.S. Coast Guard headquarters in Washington, D.C. Commandant Richmond diplomatically and successfully opposed President Eisenhower's plan to merge the U.S. Coast Guard Academy (New London, Connecticut) with the U.S. Merchant Marine Academy (King's Point, New York) for supposed economic efficiencies. Adm. Richmond assembled a committee to do a feasibility study of the proposal. The study concluded that the differential missions of the sea service academies would lead to inefficiencies and increased costs. The opposition of the Connecticut and New York congressional delegations helped sink the proposal. Adm. Richmond's tenure as commandant increased the efficiency and visibility of the Coast Guard and paved the way for the appointment of Rear Admiral Edwin J. Roland as the next USCG commandant.[12]

Commandant Edwin J. Roland (1962–1966), a 1929 USCGA graduate, was an accomplished athlete and academy coach and instructor. In World War II Adm. Roland served as the commander of Destroyer Escort Division 45, and later as the skipper of the icebreaker *Mackinaw* that kept the Great Lakes transportation network open for the crucial wartime transit of ships and cargo. Adm. Roland attended the Naval War College (New Port, Rhode Island) and served as the Atlantic Area commander. On Commandant Roland's watch, Coast Guard North Atlantic and Bering Sea fisheries patrols were increased and supplemented with three WMEC (medium-endurance) cutters to cope with the increased presence of Japanese and Soviet commercial fishing vessels. In the Caribbean and Gulf regions, Coast Guard immigration interdiction patrols were increased to deal with the numbers of Cubans fleeing Fidel Castro's Communist dictatorship into the Florida Straits.

The Coast Guard helicopter fleet grew to include HH-52A boat-hull amphibian floating rotor-wing aircraft ideally suited for SAR missions and water landings. Besides the Sikorsky helicopters the Coast Guard air fleet was supplemented by huge Lockeed C-130 Hercules cargo and surveillance aircraft that were admirably suited for long-range iceberg-tracking patrols. New USCG 378-foot WHEC (high-endurance) cutters came on line to supplement the oceangoing fleet. Large USCG icebreakers supplemented the U.S. Navy Arctic and Antarctic scientific and surveillance patrols so well that the USN later transferred all of its icebreakers and missions over to the Coast Guard.

By 1965 the Vietnam War was heating up, and Adm. Roland made sure the USCG was involved by supporting U.S. Navy requests for assistance with Secretary-class oceangoing cutters and river patrol boats in the escalating conflict. The USCG role in Vietnam was covered in chapters 4 and 5.[13]

Adm. Roland and Treasury Secretary Henry H. Fowler vociferously objected, to no avail, when President Lyndon B. Johnson decided to transfer the U.S. Coast Guard from Treasury to the new Department of Transportation (DOT).[14] Commandant Roland acquiesced when assured that the USCG would maintain its military role under the DOT. Roland's successor, Adm. Willard J. Smith (1966–1970), solidified the Coast Guard national defense and military missions as the service got more involved in the Vietnam War.

Admiral Willard John Smith (USCGA 1933) was the first USCG aviator to become commandant, and, as would be expected, he kept a watchful eye over the expanding Coast Guard air arm. Commandant Smith also oversaw the application of the unique slanted orange and blue "Coast Guard stripes" that adorned Coast Guard cutters, boats, watercraft, aircraft, land vehicles, and shore station signage and stationary. Deck guns were removed from domestic cutters and replaced with .50 caliber machine guns and small arms, although Coast Guard patrol boats in Vietnam made use of heavier armament and ordnance, as well as mortar and grenade launchers.[15]

Admiral Chester R. Bender served as USCG commandant from 1970 to 1974. Commandant Bender changed the traditional sailor uniform worn by enlisted personnel to match the visor dress cap and chief petty officer style that he thought gave marine law enforcement personnel a more authoritative appearance. Dress uniforms were also changed on Adm. Bender's watch to a "royal blue." Female Coast Guard personnel were admitted to the U.S. Coast Guard Academy for cadet and officer training in 1973. Admiral Bender increased the Coast Guard role in pollution control and the policing of oil tankers for safety and environmental control[16] which eventually correlated with the sea service's national security and defense responsibilities in the War on Terror.

From 1974 to 1986 the respective Coast Guard commandants were Admirals Owen W. Siler, John B. Hayes, and James S. Gracey. The three commandants confronted narcotics interdiction on the nation's coasts, but especially in the Coast Guard Seventh District of the southeastern and southern United States in proximity to the Gulf of Mexico, Caribbean, and Latin America. Since the Prohibition era, Coast Guard personnel acquired the right to board vessels in international waters beyond the traditional 12-mile zone of sovereignty of oceanic America.

Boarding permission can be granted by the master of an oceangoing vessel, or through the nation of the ship's flag or registry through communication with the U.S. State Department. If the suspect vessel is "stateless" it is subject to U.S. jurisdiction, or if boarding permission is not received, the Coast Guard cutter commander may track the ship into U.S. waters and then board it, or let the vessel steam on its way.[17] The tactics and strategies developed and expanded by the USCG since the Prohibition era have applicability to contemporary narcotics and immigration interdiction and the War on Terror, with the coordination and asset contribution of federal law enforcement agencies and the U.S. Navy.

Appendix B.
Team Coast Guard and
Commandants, 1990–2010

Admiral Paul Alexander Yost, Jr., became the 18th U.S. Coast Guard commandant in May of 1986 and served in that capacity until 1990. Prior to that assignment, this Vietnam War veteran served as Atlantic Area commander and commander Third Coast Guard District in New York City.

In his capacity as Atlantic Area commander, Adm. Yost administered law enforcement and SAR missions in the Atlantic, Gulf of Mexico, and Great Lakes and was responsible for maritime coastal defense under the United States Navy Atlantic Fleet commander. Adm. Yost's career included three years as the Eighth District commander headquartered in New Orleans, Louisiana, in the 1980s. From the 1960s to the 1980s, Yost was commander of the USCGC *Resolute* (WMEC-620) out of San Francisco; was operations chief for the Seventeenth District in Alaska; headed a combat command in Vietnam; was captain of the port (COTP) in Seattle, Washington; and served at U.S. Coast Guard headquarters in Washington, D.C.

Adm. Yost's eclectic intellect is illustrated by his academic achievements: master's degrees in mechanical engineering (University of Connecticut, 1959) and international affairs (George Washington University, Washington, D.C., 1964) and graduation from the Naval War College (Newport, Rhode Island, 1964).

Commandant Yost's Coast Guard mission emphasis was on maritime safety, law enforcement (emphasizing illegal drug interdiction), and defense readiness. Adm. Yost added harpoon missile launchers to WHEC (high-endurance) oceangoing Coast Guard cutters and increased communication and cooperation with the U.S. Drug Enforcement Administration, U.S.

Customs, and the Department of Defense. The USCG also assisted the U.S. military in the Persian Gulf during the Iran-Iraq War.

Commandant Yost did not neglect domestic SAR, pollution control, and natural and human-caused disaster assistance. The USCG responded to hurricanes, the 1989 California earthquake, and two tanker oil spills: the MV *American Trader* (off southern California) and the gigantic MV *Exxon Valdez* spill in Alaska's Prince William Sound. Such tragic oil spills led to increased USCG responsibilities in tanker regulation and environmental protection, and to passage by Congress of the Oil Pollution Act of 1990.

Adm. Yost earned several military medals and citations in his career but was criticized for the increased militarization of the Coast Guard in ordnance and weapons, elements of which were reduced by his successors.[1]

That ironic refutation was ameliorated after the terrorist attacks on the United States on 11 September 2001. In 2003 the USCG was transferred from the Department of Transportation to the newly formed Department of Homeland Security (DHS) and an expanded national defense role.[2]

Admiral J. William Kime was the 19th USCG commandant from 1990 to 1994. After graduating from the U.S. Coast Guard Academy (USCGA) second in his class (1957), Kime served aboard the USCGC *Casco* (WAVP-WHEC 370). Lt. (jg) Kime was commander of the long-range aid to navigation station (LORSTA) at Wake Island in the Pacific in 1960–1961.

William Kime's technical intellect was exhibited by his acquisition of a master's degree in naval architecture and marine and naval engineering from the Massachusetts Institute of Technology (MIT) in 1964. Kime was later in charge of structural engineering design for the large Polar-class icebreakers and was the engineer officer on the 378-foot CGC *Boutwell* (WHEC-719). Kime served in various Coast Guard administrative positions at shore stations and U.S. Coast Guard headquarters, and he provided innovative leadership in marine safety, environmental protection, chemical spill response tactics and technology, drug interdiction, and merchant marine technology.

Adm. Kime led the USCG during the challenging periods of change from the Cold War to the termination of Communist governments in Eastern Europe and the former Soviet Union. The commandant administered Coast Guard support missions during the U.S. military operations of Desert Shield and Desert Storm in the Persian Gulf.

After his tenure as Coast Guard commandant, Adm. Kime served in leadership and advisory capacities in the maritime industry in the United States and overseas.[3]

The twentieth commandant of the U.S. Coast Guard was Admiral Robert E. Kramek (1994–1998). Congressional budget polices required Kramek to streamline Coast Guard operations, a difficult task for the leader of the multimission service that has historically been stretched in its budget, asset, and personnel capacities.

The USCGA honors graduate (1961) took advanced courses at the University of Michigan, Johns Hopkins University, the University of Alaska, and the U.S. Naval War College in Newport, Rhode Island. The national defense responsibility of Coast Guard leaders illustrates the significance of Naval War College studies, from which Kramek graduated with distinction.

Commandant Kramek had enhanced his leadership skills to be commander of the USCGC *Midgett* (WHEC-726); commander of the U.S. Coast Guard base at Government (now "Coast Guard") Island, Alameda, California; commander of two Coast Guard districts (7 and 13); and regional coordinator of migration and drug interdiction missions. Before his appointment as U.S. Coast Guard commandant, Adm. Kramek served as chief of staff at U.S. Coast Guard headquarters in Washington, D.C.

In his postretirement career, Adm. Kramek applied his maritime knowledge in leadership roles at the American Bureau of Shipping (1998–2006) in Houston, Texas.[4]

The U.S. Naval Institute (USNI) has performed the exemplary service of preserving naval history through its publicly funded oral history project. Among the oral history interviews scheduled for completion in 2010 listed in the USNI periodical *Proceedings*, was that of "Admiral Robert E. Kramek, USCG (Ret.) — a former Commandant of the Coast Guard."[5]

Admiral James Milton Loy succeeded Adm. Robert E. Kramek as commandant of the Coast Guard and served in that position from 1998 to 2002. Following his tenure as the top Coast Guard leader, Loy was appointed deputy secretary of the Department of Homeland Security (2003–2005), and acting secretary of Homeland Security in 2005, succeeding former Pennsylvania governor Tom Ridge. Michael Chertoff succeeded Loy as DHS secretary. Adm. Loy would serve as an administrator of the Transportation Security Administration (TSA) and direct its assimilation into the DHS.

As the 21st commandant of the Coast Guard, Adm. Loy ably responded to the 11 September terrorist attacks on the New York City World Trade Center towers and on the Pentagon in Washington, D.C. Loy immediately shut down major U.S. ports after the attacks, later resumed maritime port operations, and initiated the 2004 International Ship and Port Facility Security Code.[6]

As commandant, Adm. Loy was responsible for the initiation of the $24 billion Deepwater Program, the objective of which was to build a fleet of new Coast Guard cutters to replace the aging ships that were deployed 50 miles or more offshore. Concerns about crew safety in cutters that were facing obsolescence motivated Loy to allow competing maritime corporations to build the cutters and support technology in autonomous, relatively oversight-free operations.

The resulting cost overruns and production of several unseaworthy cutters led to contentious congressional oversight hearings that embarrassed the service and the Coast Guard officers who were called to testify. Admiral Loy's subsequent post–Coast Guard employment by a maritime lobbying group and a deepwater contractor caused the decorated Vietnam veteran's integrity to be unfairly questioned and elicited a caustic response from the former commandant to a journalist who broached the topic.[7]

Adm. James M. Loy and Donald T. Phillips coauthored *Character in Action: The U.S. Coast Guard on Leadership*, published in 2003 by the Naval Institute Press. The authors used Loy's experience in the U.S. Coast Guard to highlight leadership training and operations, as well as a plethora of examples of the initiative and courage exemplified by civilian, enlisted and commissioned personnel.

Loy's experience as a combat patrol commander in Vietnam, the many commendations he earned in his career, and his tenure as Coast Guard commandant, gave the retired admiral the background and credibility to write the book.

Loy and Phillips traced Coast Guard history and mission responsibilities, the role of the Coast Guard in national defense with emphasis on the 9/11 terrorist attack response, the motivational foundations of leadership training, and the execution of responsibilities. Team spirit and individual motivation are key elements to mission success, according to the authors.

Among the building blocks of leadership and mission success, Loy and Phillips assert, are establishing and living values, teamwork, cultivating relationships, effective communications, continual learning, and knowing and honoring the history and traditions of the organization in order to instill understanding, pride, and unity.[8]

The 22nd commandant of the USCG was Adm. Thomas H. Collins (2002–2006). From 2000 to 2002 Collins was vice commandant after having served as Pacific Area commander, 11th District (Eastern Pacific) commander, and 14th District commander in Honolulu, Hawaii. Admiral Collins served at Coast Guard headquarters in Washington, D.C., where he managed the Integrated Deepwater System project to modernize the ships, aircraft and technology used on ocean missions.

Other Coast Guard assignments included Lt. Collins's tenure on the USCGC *Vigilant* (WMEC-617) and as commander of the 95-foot USCGC *Cape Morgan* (WPB-95313) out of Charleston, South Carolina. Commandant

Collins also had shore assignments as group commander, captain of the port (COTP), and member of the Humanities Department at the U.S. Coast Guard Academy in New London, Connecticut. Adm. Collins earned a variety of medals, commendations, awards and decorations in his diverse career.[9]

Tucson, Arizona, native Thad W. Allen was the 23rd Coast Guard commandant (2006–2010). The commandant's father, Chief Damage Controlman Clyde Allen, was a career Coastguardsman and World War II veteran. Thad Allen graduated from the U.S. Coast Guard Academy in New London, Connecticut, in 1971 after distinguished performance on the USCGA football team. Adm. Allen went on to earn the master of public administration degree from George Washington University and a master's degree in management from the Massachusetts Institute of Technology (MIT).

Holding sea and shore commands, Adm. Allen led law enforcement, marine safety and security, and environmental missions; served on the cutters *Gallatin* (WHEC-721) and *Androscoggin* (WHEC-68), and was commander of the *Citrus* (WLB-300). Allen was a group commanding officer and COTP, and commanded a long-range aid to navigation (LORAN) station in Lampang, Thailand, during the Vietnam War.

Adm. Allen was also commander of the Seventh Coast Guard District (Southeast United States and the Caribbean) and Atlantic Area commander of the U.S. Maritime Defense Zone, where he directed defense operations on the U.S. Gulf and Atlantic coasts, and the Great Lakes after the 11 September 2001 terrorist attacks. From 2002 to 2006 Adm. Allen was chief of staff at USCG headquarters in Washington, D.C.

In 2005 President George W. Bush placed Allen in command of the Hurricane Katrina search and rescue and recovery efforts in the Gulf region. Admiral Allen represented the USCG and federal government in the media. The skill with which Adm. Allen handled that assignment led to his nomination and appointment as Coast Guard commandant. In his storied career, Allen earned several service medals, Gold Stars, commendations, and achievement awards from federal and civilian agencies and organizations.[10]

In his book *Rescue Warriors*, author David Helvarg made clear why *U.S. News and World Report* named Thad Allen one of "America's 20 Best Leaders." Helvarg traveled "on the road" with Allen for several weeks and featured the commandant in his 2009 tribute to Coast Guard heroes. The following observations and analyses are Helvarg's.

As commandant, Allen issued action orders to transform the modern Coast Guard. The admiral "created a single Acquisitions Directorate to oversee fleet and asset growth so the service [no longer] needs to outsource its future to private contractors again as occurred under Deepwater."[11]

All equipment and assets for the Coast Guard, in Allen's action orders, were in standardized supply and operational cycles. Planning for international, industrial and environmental incidents was ongoing. And Allen brought to bear his commanding voice and presence to issue orders and explain policies in concise, fast-talking, clear, no-nonsense language. Allen represented the service well in public and private intraservice panels and meetings with the heads of the other U.S. Armed Forces. His service as a Coast Guard liaison officer with the Drug Enforcement Administration gave Allen the training and contacts to enhance Coast Guard drug interdiction missions. And his command of the USCGC *Citrus* on fisheries patrol trained Allen for another of the many maritime law enforcement and SAR missions of the USCG.[12]

Helvarg was also impressed with Adm. Allen's understanding of global environmental and geostrategic issues and the possibility of repercussions from alleged global warming and "Arctic meltdown." Helvarg quoted the commandant: "I'm agnostic on climate change and science and everything else," Allen responded to the media. "All I know is," he continued, "there is water where there didn't used to be, and I have statutory responsibilities to operate there."[13]

As Atlantic commander, Helvarg explained, Allen masterfully diverted seagoing Coast Guard cutters "into U.S. ports within 24 hours of the 11 September 2001 attacks, clinching a security belt around the continental homeland."[14]

Commandant Allen's vice admiral, and second in command in the USCG hierarchy, was Vice Commandant Vivien Crea. A helicopter pilot, Adm. Crea exhibited a congenial and collaborative side to Helvarg, who found her "whip smart" and confident, traits one would expect from a military leader at the top of the command charts. Adm. Crea completed Officer Candidate School (OCS) and became a commissioned officer in 1973.

Adm. Crea broke several minority "glass ceilings" and was the first female aircraft commander who flew the giant USCG C-130 Hercules cargo plane, a Gulfstream executive jet aircraft, an HH-65 Dolphin rotor-wing (helicopter) aircraft, and was USCG air station commander. Admiral Crea attributed her independent spirit and professional achievements to her upbringing "as an Army brat."[15] Crea, whose husband is a former USCG captain, retired in 2009. Admiral Thad Allen presided over Adm. Crea's retirement and change of command.

Adm. Allen scheduled his final state of the Coast Guard address at the National Press Club in Washington, D.C., on Friday, February 12, 2010. The address was to be broadcast nationally on the C-SPAN cable channel. In his presentation Adm. Allen addressed the fiscal year 2011 budget, the capitalization needs of the USCG fleet, and the relief efforts in earthquake-torn Haiti.[16]

As Coast Guard commandant, Adm. Allen led the largest agency in the Department of Homeland Security (DHS), composed of 42,000 active-duty men and women; 8,000 Reservists; 7,000 civilian employees; and 34,000 volunteer civilian members of the U.S. Coast Guard Auxiliary (USCGAUX). In addition to running the Coast Guard, Allen was a member of the Council on Foreign Relations. In 2007 the National Graduate School of Quality Systems Management on Cape Cod in Falmouth, Massachusetts, granted an honorary doctorate of science to Commandant Allen.[17]

Coast Guard icebreakers have played a significant role in U.S. national defense and economic security and productivity. During World War II, President Franklin D. Roosevelt (FDR) ordered the Coast Guard icebreaking fleet to keep the Great Lakes (Inland Seas) open to lengthen the commercial shipping season. Freshwater and saltwater freighters unloaded and loaded food grains, mineral resources, and manufactured goods. Great Lakes and inland river shipyards built troop transportation, cargo, and combat vessels that steamed to European and Asian ports and combat theaters to support the Allied war effort against the Axis Powers.

FDR ordered the U.S. Coast Guard to police Danish Greenland and adjacent Arctic and North Atlantic seas to protect its minerals, build bases, establish communications, deprive the German military of strategic posts and communications assets, and keep polar waters open for transportation, commerce, and national defense. The courageous sailors of the U.S. Merchant Marine delivered essential supplies across the Great Lakes and icy ocean waters to U.S. and Allied military forces and civilians, at great risk and with significant wartime casualties.[18]

Coast Guard Commandant Thad W. Allen sought to maintain the USCG icebreaking cutter fleet on the Great Lakes and in the polar regions of the Arctic and Antarctic maritime realms. Allen stressed the significance of the icebreakers in their performance of national defense, oceanographic research, transportation, and economic missions. The Coast Guard icebreaking missions have had a history of geostrategic, scientific and economic significance. The history of the USCG "ice captains" in the Bering Sea, Alaskan waters, and the North Atlantic/Greenland theater in World War II has been chronicled in several exemplary Coast Guard histories.[19]

The Great Lakes icebreaking cutters ranged from just over 100 feet in length to the traditional 180-foot lengths of the traditional "black-hull" buoy tenders, and the 225- to 240-foot lengths of the modern Great Lakes icebreaking cutters.[20] The "Polar-class" cutters are in a distinctive size, function and missions class.

The Coast Guard planned to have a third Polar-class icebreaker on station and back in service in 2013 after a $62 million overhaul and upgrade, ready for the expanding responsibilities of the service in the Arctic and Antarctic high-latitude seas.

In March 2010 Admiral Thad Allen reported that the 399-foot icebreaker *Polar Star* (WAGB-10) would steam from its port at the Seattle, Washington, Coast Guard Station to the adjacent Todd Pacific Shipyards and a three-year restoration project.

The objective is to maintain the service of the giant icebreaker for a decade more of service while the USCG and federal authorities decide whether to build a new generation of very expensive icebreakers for expanded and problematic missions. Adm. Allen stated that the USCG presently had three polar icebreakers in its inventory. The *Polar Star*, commissioned in 1976, had been laid up and taken out of service since 2005 because of its exorbitant operational costs. That left just two giant icebreakers, the USCG cutter *Polar Sea* and the USCGC *Healey*, each operating out of Seattle.[21]

The 399-foot CGC *Polar Sea* (WAGB-11) was commissioned in 1978, has a 141-crew complement, and carries two HH-65C Dolphin helicopters.[22] The 420-foot CGC *Healey* was commissioned in 1999, carries a 76-crew complement and 50 scientists, and two HH-65A Dolphin helicopters on its flight deck.[23]

In his 11 March 2010 presentation, Adm. Allen explained how the polar icebreakers are needed for maritime safety and search and rescue, scientific studies, environmental protection, national defense, economic development, and assertion of sovereignty, given the presence of Russia and other nations in the region interested in the acquisition of natural resources. The scientific research is important for the expansion of geographic knowledge, assessing the impact of climate change on marine life and resources, and the shipping of natural gas, petroleum, and other goods in the newly opening waters, as well as potential tourism.

Commandant Allen speculated how nations will be competing and attempting to resolve resource and territorial claims beyond traditional sovereign boundaries on the continental shelf beyond the 200-mile Exclusive Economic Zone (EEZ). The CGC *Healey*, Allen asserted, was scheduled to sail off the North Slope of Alaska and gather data to support U.S. territorial claims.[24]

The British Petroleum (BP) Gulf oil spill delayed Adm. Allen's retirement. President Barack Obama asked Allen, whose term as Coast Guard commandant was ending, to serve as the national incident commander for the British Petroleum oil spill in the Gulf of Mexico.

David Helvarg, author of *Rescue Warriors: The U.S. Coast Guard, America's*

Forgotten Heroes (2009), interviewed Allen for the natural resource journal *OnEarth* in the Summer 2010 issue. Helvarg asked the straight-talking Coast-guardsman about the significance of the sea service's environmental mission. Allen responded, "We protect men from the sea and the sea from men," and the Coast Guard has enforced environmental and natural resource laws since "the early 19th century ... and after [the United States] acquired Alaska [in 1867]."[25]

Adm. Allen had gained national praise for his management of Hurricane Katrina in the administration of President George W. Bush. In his interview with David Helvarg, Adm. Allen said a national ocean policy and task force, which the commandant helped establish, is necessary because "the oceans are the last global commons for energy production, fishing, shipping, [and] recreation." Allen said "the ice diminished Arctic" will be a frontier for "eco-tourism and oil and gas development," and the Coast Guard has jurisdiction in the Polar Regions for "search and rescue, law [and fishing] enforcement, oil spill response, and national sovereignty issues."[26]

President George W. Bush and his administrative federal agencies were criticized for the allegedly slow and limited response to Hurricane Katrina. However, the USCG was logistically and tactically on scene and prepared in the hours before the hurricane hit the Gulf Coast.

President Barack Obama and his administration were criticized for an allegedly slow and even detached response to the BP Gulf oil spill. In fact, the spill was called "Obama's Katrina." Although the federal bureaucracy is limited in how effectively it can respond to national and natural disasters, there was enough blame to go around, including, of course, BP and Coast Guard responses.

Nonetheless, the USCG was on scene, and the president placed the USCG and Adm. Allen in charge of communications and mission coordination. But the Coast Guard had to deal with bureaucratic infighting and a chain of command in its own operations.

Coast Guard experts, as later revealed in USCG logs acquired by the Center for Public Integrity, quickly understood the devastating threat and potential ecological and economic consequences of the 20 April 2010 BP explosion aboard the *Deepwater Horizon* drilling rig. Within hours of the disaster, the Coast Guard analyzed the significance of events that later, allegedly, were omitted from official White House and Obama administration timelines.

The federal government's first official acknowledgement of the sea floor leak came four days after the explosion that was later blamed on the failure of a "blowout preventer,"[27] lax federal regulatory oversight, and BP profit-sensitive shortcuts, according to several analysts and the Congressional House Oversight and Government Reform Committee.

Admiral Allen had distinguished himself and the Coast Guard in Hurricane Katrina in the Gulf (2005). The admiral brought additional credit to the service and his leadership skills in the BP–Halliburton oil spill of 2010. Allen had been ironically well served by the fortuitous planning exercise for a possible future Gulf oil spill he led out of New Orleans in 2002. Allen initially and correctly predicted that the oil spill, one of the largest in history, could go on for 45 to 90 days or more.[28]

Considering the intricacies of combating the Gulf oil spill, U.S. Coast Guard Rear Adm. Mary Landry and U.S. Environmental Protection Agency (USEPA) administrator Lisa P. Jackson held a 24 May 2010 press conference call to explain BP chemical dispersant operations. Landry and Jackson believed the dispersants, if mixed and disseminated properly, could be functional and less toxic than the petroleum on the water. However, the USEA and USCG representatives directed BP to limit the amounts used and to focus on underwater applications because the oil company's analysis of the environmental impact of the dispersants on marine life had been inadequate.[29]

Coast Guard boat and helicopter crews were deployed from stations across the nation to assist in the Gulf oil cleanup. In June 2010, U.S. Coast Guard Air Station Traverse City (Michigan) deployed one HH-65C Dolphin rescue helicopter and Great Lakes crew to the Gulf of Mexico. The Michigan aircrew would fly aerial reconnaissance flights to follow the oil flows and track the spill locations to civilian and military boat crews tasked with skimming the petroleum off the sea surface. Hundreds of Coast Guard personnel were involved in the Gulf cleanup mission.[30]

The USCGC *Aspen* (WLB-208) out of San Francisco was deployed in June to assist with the Gulf oil spill. The 225-foot CGC *Aspen* would use its surface pump and a floating boom to skim oil off the water. The cutter steamed from San Francisco in the Pacific Ocean and through the Panama Canal to Pensacola, Florida, to join other rescue teams and maritime assets.[31]

Coast Guard Reservists from Great Lakes District Nine out of Marine Safety Office (MSO) Cincinnati (Ohio) joined more than 1,000 colleagues in the Gulf region. MSO Cincinnati Reservists handled security and supervised and assisted civilian employees in applying rubber water barriers to protect shorelines and in cleaning oil-soaked marine and terrestrial wildlife. The Great Lakes unit patrolled Grand Isle, Louisiana, marshlands in iceboats normally used on icy lakes in Northern winters. The flat-bottomed iceboats were readily adaptable to marsh and swamp conditions.[32]

The national incident commander of the Gulf Coast oil spill, recently retired Coast Guard Commandant Thad Allen, had the authority correspondent with his significant responsibilities. Admiral Allen released to the media his order to BP to pay for the cost of five new barrier islands to protect Louisiana marshes from the creeping oil spill. Governor Bobby Jindal had been pleading for the barriers, but the governor and the admiral were frustrated by federal agencies and bureaucrats with fishing and environmental jurisdiction, refusing or delaying the plans and then giving intermittent approval.

Adm. Allen informed Governor Bobby Jindal of the arrival of additional Coast Guard patrol boats, helicopters, and cutters to assist in the spill cleanup, and that response teams were getting to affected sites as quickly as possible. The cutters were the *Cyprus* (WLB-210), *Elm* (WLB-204), and *Tampa* (WMEC-902). The CGC *Tampa* had a helicopter flight deck that permitted aircraft to refuel at sea. The Coast Guard helicopters would transport officials and survey the coastal regions of Louisiana, Mississippi, Alabama and Florida.[33] The 225-foot USCGC *Sycamore* (WLB-209) and its 40 crew members out of Cordova, Alaska, were scheduled to join Coast Guard colleagues in the Gulf for a several-month period to aid in the oil spill cleanup.[34] The cutter, armed with two .50 caliber machine guns for law enforcement and national defense missions, was launched at Marinette Marine Corporation (Marinette, Wisconsin) in 2001.

The appointments of Admiral Thad Allen as incident commander Hurricane Katrina (2005) and commandant of the Coast Guard (2006) by President George W. Bush, and incident commander Gulf oil spill (2010) by President Barack Obama, testify to the confidence federal officials had in him.

Seapower magazine editor in chief Amy L. Wittman, an expert in naval issues, exhibited the same confidence in her testimonial about the Coast Guard commandant in an April 2010 article. Wittman credited Adm. Allen with making "great strides to modernize, stream-line operations, improve acquisition transparency and accountability — all while meeting the demands of an ever-expanding mission portfolio."[35]

Wittman attributed Allen's leadership skills to three efficient administrative changes: renaming the Atlantic Area Command to the Coast Guard Operations Command; changing the Pacific Area Command to the Coast Guard Force Readiness Command; and promoting the deputy commander for operations to three-star rank and the vice admiral to four-star rank. Wittman concluded that the changes would facilitate better mission coordination, command and control; greater flexibility and economic efficiency; and better preparation of the service to meet future challenges and responsibilities.[36]

Among the national defense coordination and efficiencies exhibited by the Coast Guard is its historic and increasing mission partnership with the United States Navy. In June 2010, for example, Lt. Andrew Vanskike (USCG) and Lt. Nick Anderson (USCG) communicated with Cmdr. Kevin Parker (USN), commander of the USS *Crommelin*. Vanskike and Anderson, law enforcement and intelligence liaison officers with U.S. Coast Guard District 14, worked with Cmdr. Parker and other USN surface warship commanders in enforcing maritime law in maritime areas of joint responsibility.[37]

The USN has cooperated with USCG law enforcement teams in drug interdiction missions in the Pacific Ocean and Caribbean Sea, and fisheries enforcement patrols in the central and western Pacific. The Coast Guard also engages in economic and national security missions with key Pacific insular nations, Australia, France, and New Zealand, in a consistent mission presence of surveillance for maritime security.[38]

The leadership skills and reputation enjoyed by Adm. Allen did not spare him from criticism in the administration of the oil spill response. Some critics said the Coast Guard was overwhelmed. An Alabama mayor said the Coast Guard had five weeks to get ready for the oil spill spread and was still not ready. Although Adm. Allen exhibited his usual calm, confident demeanor, critics said he gave BP too much on-scene autonomy, trusted its erroneous oil spill estimates, and did not get federal assets on scene soon enough. Louisiana officials complained of federal agency overlap, contradictory information, and slow approval scenarios. Adm. Allen did call in local fisherman and shrimp boat captains and crews, referring to the civilian flotillas as "vessels of opportunity."[39]

The Coast Guard came under criticism from Louisiana officials for grounding several oil-sucking barges in the Gulf of Mexico that had been working to clean up the oil spill. A regional Coast Guard commander and the New Orleans captain of the port grounded the barges when the USCG found no certificates of inspection for firefighting and other safety equipment. Despite complaints, Coast Guard officials said they could not neglect the water safety inspections or overlook questions about the stability of the watercraft. The barges were later allowed to resume their operations. There was also a report that Coast Guard vessels had run over oil barrier booms that Louisiana officials had put in place without federal approval along Gulf shorelines.[40]

Given the expanded responsibilities of the multimission U.S. Coast Guard since its transfer to the Department of Homeland Security (DHS), three months before the Gulf oil spill, the Obama administration and DHS Secretary Janet Napolitano inexplicably proposed downsizing and cutting USCG pollution strike teams. Coast Guard officers ironically warned against a predictably weakened catastrophic response capacity. The Gulf oil spill caused an understandable reassessment of the downsizing. Commander Stephen Flynn (USCG, Ret.), president of the Center for National Policy, replied, "Whether it's an accident of man or an act of terrorism, it requires almost the same skill set to clean it up."[41]

The BP oil spill illustrates the vulnerability of oil platforms to terrorist attack and explains the presence of U.S. Navy and U.S. Coast Guard security teams during the Persian Gulf wars and around domestic nuclear, petroleum and natural gas infrastructure in the United States.

Yet some defense analysts question whether the Coast Guard and the Interior Department's Mineral Management Service have the expertise and capacity to match, monitor and inspect the complex oil industry infrastructure.

President Obama's $10 billion proposed Coast Guard budget plan would have cut funding and personnel by an estimated 3 percent, displaced 1,000 USCG personnel, and decommissioned the National Strike Force Coordination Center (NSFCC) in Elizabeth City, North Carolina. Supporters of the budget cuts asserted that the NSFCC-NC unit would have been transferred and absorbed at another site. The NSFCC is part of a national command structure that assigns experts and equipment to on-scene incident commanders.

The petroleum industry is ultimately responsible for having and using the essential assets necessary to respond to oil spills. Coast Guard inspection teams are charged with assessing whether the oil companies are capable of effective responses. Cmdr. Tina Cutter (USCG) has said "the elimination of the national command element could lead to a reduction in core competencies in capabilities needed in a crisis" and result in "degraded responder skills."[42]

Ken Wells, chief executive officer of the Offshore Marine Service Association, which represents U.S.–flagged vessels that carry the equipment and crews for drilling rig support, believes the USCG needs competent experts, not oil infrastructure assets: "It is intellectual capital rather than equipment" the Coast Guard should invest in, Wells said. "The government does not own things very well."[43]

U.S. Representative Hal Rogers enunciated a cautionary note on the proposed Coast Guard budget cuts. The Kentucky congressman, a ranking Republican on the House Appropriations Homeland Security Subcommittee, concluded, "If we are going to rely on the Coast Guard to secure our borders, stop Caribbean drug traffickers, respond to [natural disasters], counter terrorist threats, and stop one of the largest oil spills in American history, we had better resource these frontline agencies appropriately."[44]

Coast Guard aficionados and members of Congress on USCG funding, transportation and national security committees expressed concern and outrage when Vice Adm. Robert J. Papp, Jr., the presidential nominee to replace Coast Guard Commandant Thad Allen, was tied to a leaked and controversial internal memorandum.

In response to President Obama's proposed budget cuts, Vice Adm. Papp outlined budget reduction priorities that included the reduction of counterterrorism and narcotics interdiction patrols and training and a reemphasis on the traditional Coast Guard search and rescue (SAR) mission. In response to suggestions by critics of the downsizing, a USCG spokesperson said the memo included possible budget cut speculations in response to U.S. Coast Guard headquarters requests for ideas and were not necessarily Adm. Papp's preferences.

Responding to the memo, Texas U.S. Representative Pete Olson said the proposals would impede the national security missions of the Coast Guard and that he was concerned about the Obama administration's choice to succeed Adm. Allen. Representative Hal Rogers of Kentucky, the ranking Republican on the Homeland Security Appropriations Committee, said the Papp proposals were "dead on arrival."[45]

In response to questions from media sources that had obtained the Papp memo, Homeland Security Secretary Janet Napolitano replied that the leaked memo, marked "sensitive — for internal Coast Guard use only," was only a draft, and she and the Obama administration did not support devastating the Homeland Security budget. Napolitano added that no final decisions on the matter had yet been made. But in the memo, Adm. Papp wrote, "What I offered is just a fraction of what is needed, and I am prepared to go further."[46]

At the time of these responses, the date for Adm. Papp's Senate nomination hearing had not been established. Texas U.S. Representative Pete Olson advised Napolitano to reconsider the Papp nomination because, Olson alleged, the admiral's ideas could put the nation at risk. Napolitano declined to speak further about the memo because, she explained, it was an internal document draft.[47]

Admiral Robert J. Papp cleared the Senate nomination hurdle with a unanimous vote and assumed command as the 24th commandant of the U.S. Coast Guard on 25 May 2010. Admiral Sally Brice-O'Hara, who held various district commands and an advanced degree in national security from the National War College of National Defense University (Ft. McNair, Washington, D.C.) was appointed second in command as vice commandant of the USCG.

Defense Secretary Robert Gates awarded outgoing commandant Adm.

Thad Allen the Defense Distinguished Service Medal. Homeland Security Secretary Janet Napolitano presided over the change of command ceremony and presented Adm. Allen with the Homeland Security Distinguished Service Medal.[48]

Admiral Papp had previously served as commander, Ninth Coast Guard District, Great Lakes, with headquarters in Cleveland, Ohio. Great Lakes operations and Rear Adm. Robert J. Papp were considered in this author's previous book, *The U.S. Coast Guard on the Great Lakes: A History* (2007), briefly reviewed below.

After the 9/11 terrorist attacks on the United States and the transfer of the Coast Guard from the Transportation Department to the DHS in 2003, the Great Lakes became an unlikely frontier zone in the War on Terror (WOT). The USCG, civilian Canadian Coast Guard (CCG), Royal Canadian Navy (RCN), Royal Canadian Mounted Police (RCMP), Canadian Customs, and law enforcement and other public safety agencies in both nations have cooperated with the United States in Great Lakes area patrols, surveillance, and apprehensions.

Vice Adm. Sally Brice-O'Hara is vice commandant of the USCG (2010–) and supervises senior operational and mission support commanders and the staff at USCG headquarters in Washington, D.C. Prior to her appointment as vice commandant, Adm. Brice-O'Hara was commanding officer of Training Center Cape May, New Jersey.

Urban centers of concern and terrorist or Middle East sympathies, connections, and support existed in Toronto and Windsor, Canada; Detroit, Michigan; and Buffalo, New York. As of March 2006, law enforcement authorities held 160 terrorist suspects. One suspect was arrested in Dearborn,

Michigan, and charged with aiding Hezbollah, a Middle East terrorist organization. A smuggler was arrested in Buffalo and charged with financing the journey of six Americans to an Al Qaeda terrorist training camp in Afghanistan.[49]

Rear Adm. Robert J. Papp, the Ninth Coast Guard District Commander, relayed these incidents to the media after his 2004 appointment to head the Great Lakes district. Adm. Papp stressed the importance of the Coast Guard seizure of contraband, profits from which could fund terrorist cells. Adm. Papp encouraged joint maritime and winter-season ice patrols with Canadian naval and police agencies. Adm. Papp reported that surveillance and investigations yielded stashed "hockey bags filled with cash" on his watch. Strategic infrastructure on the Great Lakes required Coast Guard surveillance and patrols. U.S. Coast Guard and Canadian aviation and sea assets cooperated on maritime patrols and in ship inspections. U.S. Coast Guard and Canadian authorities have periodically and pragmatically adjusted Great Lakes naval presence and armament exigencies in times of national defense threats that have required tweaking of the bilateral Rush-Bagot Agreement of 1817.

In 2006 Rear Adm. Papp was considered eligible for advancement to vice admiral and chief of staff at U.S. Coast Guard headquarters in Washington, D.C.[50] Papp went on to become commander, Coast Guard Atlantic Area out of Portsmouth, Virginia, and commander Defense Force East in 2008, and he provided mission support to the Defense Department. Vice Admiral Papp served as U.S. Coast Guard chief of staff, and before that (2002) director of the U.S. Coast Guard Reserve (USCGR), and then commandant in 2010. Papp graduated from the USCGA in 1975 and earned master's degrees in national security and strategic studies (United States Naval War College) and management (Salve Regina College, New Port, Rhode Island). Adm. Papp served at sea on six USCG cutters and commanded three cutters and the USCGA training barque USCGC *Eagle* (WIX-327).[51]

A survey of the history of United States Coast Guard commandants illustrates the diverse training, experience, administrative talent, and enormous responsibilities of the top leaders of the USCG, and the significant role these leaders have played, and will continue to play, in carrying out the domestic and overseas responsibilities of the multimission service in maritime safety, law enforcement, and national defense.

Appendix C.
Always Ready:
Coast Guard Personnel

Members of the United States Coast Guard train, perform, and live by the service motto: *Semper Paratus*, "Always Ready."

U.S. Coast Guard personnel in the civilian Auxiliary, the Reserve, and the regular enlisted and officer ranks have been surveyed throughout this book. Team Coast Guard includes dedicated civilian employees and military personnel. In this section, the diverse backgrounds, training, education, missions, and achievements of the men and women of the U.S. Coast Guard will be further illustrated.

The Coast Guard and its agency predecessors have welcomed women into their ranks from the days of the U.S. Lighthouse Service and U.S. Life-Saving Service of the 18th and 19th centuries to the present. Female Coast Guard personnel are considered in this section and other chapters of this book. Women of the Coast Guard have served at home and overseas; at sea, ashore, and in the air; and in peace and war.

On 2 August 1990 dictator Saddam Hussein's Iraqi troops invaded the nation of Kuwait. President George W. Bush ordered U.S. Armed Forces into the Persian Gulf to expel the invaders and protect oil-rich Saudi Arabia. The U.S. Navy requested the U.S. Coast Guard to assist in a naval blockade, board suspect vessels in search of contraband, and establish a port security operation around petroleum facilities and in harbor areas.

Lt. Jane Hartley (USCG, Ret.) and her colleagues stationed in the port of Wilmington, North Carolina, were assigned to assist in the code-named operations Desert Shield and Desert Storm. Despite the USN request for male combat crews, the USCG insisted that its female personnel were trained for

219

port, patrol boat, and cutter command missions and vouched for their professional fitness and competence.[1] Lt. Hartley attributed her command success at home and in the Persian Gulf to parents who encouraged her to accept challenges, and to the USCG command structure that trained for leadership, individual initiative, and responsibility.[2]

Lt. Holly Harrison (USCG) served in the Persian Gulf as commander of the 110-foot CGC *Aquidneck* (WPB-130). Lt. Harrison and Lt. (jg) Matt Michaelis commandeered an Iraqi tugboat before the enemy vessel could release floating mines into a heavily trafficked river waterway. The *Aquidneck* and three other cutters had been transported to the Persian Gulf on large container ships.

Before disembarking to the Middle East, Lt. Harrison and the *Aquidneck* crew had escorted U.S. Navy submarines and liquid natural gas (LNG) and ordnance carrying ships from the port of Wilmington, North Carolina, and along the Cape Fear River on their way to the Gulf region.[3]

Lt. Harrison had prepared her crew for any contingency in the War on Terror including responses to terrorist attacks, mines, and biochemical attacks. The CGC *Aquidneck* teamed up for mission support and surveillance with the Coast Guard cutters *Adak* (WPB-1333), *Baranof* (WPB-1318), and *Wrangell* (WPB-1332). The cutters coordinated missions with U.S. Navy, British, and Australian combat vessels in the Khawr Abd Allah River between Kuwait and Iraq.[4]

Coast Guard patrol boat crews boarded and searched vessels for terrorists, and interdicted contraband weapons, ordnance, and petroleum while sailing in murky, mined and unchartered shoal waters. CGC *Aquidneck* crew members boarded one partially submerged and abandoned trawler and discovered provisions, ship drawings, maps, and weapons probably left behind by enemy agents.[5]

Lt. Harrison reported that her diligent crew worked long hours in dangerous waters and were sleep deprived on the small, crowded cutter. Vessels were boarded by crews on the alert for escaping Iraqi officials, including Saddam Hussein. The CGC *Aquidneck* guided U.S. Navy minesweepers into mined waters where just a single detonation would likely have sunk the cutter. The *Aquidneck* was armed with .50 caliber machine guns, rifles, and small arms as it discovered, dodged, and detonated floating mines.

Vessel identification was problematic and challenging. In one instance Lt. Harrison ordered her gun crews to hold their fire as a zigzagging boat approached the *Aquidneck* and veered away without signaling or identifying itself. It was later discovered that the boat was crewed by a U.S. Navy SEAL team of special forces that might have been fired upon with tragic results had the cutter commander panicked.

In July 2003, Lt. Harrison received the Bronze Star for her gallantry and leadership in the Gulf War. The ceremony took place at USCG headquarters in Washington, D.C., and included award recipients from the *Aquidneck* and crew members from other Coast Guard cutters who served in the Persian Gulf theater of operations. Lt. Harrison went to other leadership positions ashore and afloat and exemplified the training, responsibilities and talent of Coast Guard personnel serving at home and abroad in law enforcement, national security and defense missions.[6]

On 24 April 2004, a naval team from the USS *Firebolt* (PC-10), piloting an RHIB (rigid-hull inflatable boat), attempted to intercept a suspicious fishing vessel (dhow). Petty Officer Third Class Nathan B. Bruckenthal (USCG) gave his life defending America, as did two other members of the U.S. Navy–Coast Guard boarding team: Michael J. Pernaselli (USN) and Christopher E. Watts (USN). The surviving crew members suffered wounds.

The dhow was speeding toward a petroleum facility. The suicide bombers ignited their boat offshore from the Khawr Al Amaya oil terminal as the naval team attempted to board it. PO3 Bruckenthal was buried at Arlington National Cemetery the following month[7] and posthumously awarded the Bronze Star with Valor, Combat Action Ribbon, Armed Forces Expeditionary Medal, Purple Heart, and Global War on Terror Expeditionary Medal. PO3 Bruckenthal was among several Jewish members of the U.S. Armed Forces killed in action in the Gulf War and War on Terror.[8]

Coast Guard regulars and reservists participated in the Gulf wars. The 140 members of U.S. Coast Guard port security unit 301 returned from Kuwait to Cape Cod, Massachusetts, in January 2010. Members of PSU-301 returned to the applause of 600 spectators to commence 96 hours of leave time before returning to duty. PSU-301 was organized in 2005 to support overseas humanitarian and military missions. The unit performed six months of active duty in Kuwait around the port area of Mina Ash Shu'aybah and provided escort protection and ammunition supply missions for military operations. Among the returning PSU-301 members was PO2 Sergio Maldonado, Jr. (USCGR), who happily greeted his family at Coast Guard Air Station Cape Cod.[9]

The Coast Guard has traditionally encouraged the promotion of women to the highest rates and ranks in the service, from petty officer specialties though the ranks of warrant and commissioned officers up to flag officer (admiral) rank. Several exemplary female Coast Guard officers and enlisted personnel have been previously mentioned in this book.

Rear Admiral Sally Brice-O'Hara was the first woman commanding officer from Training Center Cape May (New Jersey) to earn flag rank. Former Coast Guard Commandant Adm. Thad Allen revealed in August 2009 that

Capt. Sandra L. Stosz, a former Cape May commander, and then Cape May commander, Captain Cari B. Thomas, were recommended for advancement to admiral.

Approval by the president of the United States and confirmation by the U.S. Senate are necessary steps in the process. Captain Thomas, a 1984 U.S. Coast Guard Academy graduate, said she chose the Coast Guard because it opened its rates and ranks to women before the other services (1976–1978) and expanded the openings to women in Officer Candidate School (OCS). Captain Sandra L. Stosz considered the U.S. Naval Academy, as had Adm. Thomas, but went to the USCGA because the USCG allowed women to serve on ships. The USN did not allow female sailors on ships until the 1990s.[10] Admirals Thomas and Stosz achieved their flag ranks and were pictured in the "Flag Officer Coast Guard" section of the prestigious naval periodical *Seapower Almanac* in 2010.[11]

As part of her advancement to admiral rank, Cari Thomas was scheduled to take a six-weeks course in strategic studies for flag and general officers at the Department of Defense in Washington, D.C., that would include national and international travel and a meeting with the service chiefs of the other U.S. Armed Forces. During the frocking ceremonies for promotion to rear admiral (lower half), Vice Commandant David P. Pekoske (USCG) commended the achievements of the flag officer nominee and explained that the Coast Guard had 41,000 active-duty male and female personnel, and only 1 percent of the service complement is promoted to rear admiral, lower half. Commander Gary Thomas (USCG) was present at the Cape May ceremonies honoring his wife Cari's promotion.[12]

Admiral Cari Thomas has illuminated the significant national security and defense roles of the United States Coast Guard. As director of response policy, Adm. Thomas guided training, policy, and maritime missions in law enforcement, defense, and counterterrorism operations. The 1984 USCGA graduate served at sea on the Coast Guard cutters *Valiant* and *Vigorous* and was commander of the CGC *Manitou*, operational officer at Group Air Station Atlantic City (New Jersey), and head of response operations in the Miami Florida Sector. Adm. Thomas participated in USCG–Department of Defense (DOD) operations along the Atlantic and Gulf coasts, and in the Caribbean. Rear Adm. Thomas graduated with honors from the Naval War College in strategic and national security studies and received numerous medals and commendations, as well as campaign and unit awards.[13]

Commander Gary M. Thomas (USCG) and Adm. Kari B. Thomas are a married Coast Guard couple. Cmdr. Thomas, a 1986 USCGA graduate, earned a B.S. in mathematics at the academy, had three duty tours at sea, sailed with U.S. Navy and British Royal Navy combatant units, and was the commanding officer of the CGC *Padre* (WPB-1328) out of Key West, Florida. Cmdr. Thomas served as a liaison officer to the U.S. Customs Service where he created and administered computer information systems. After the 11 September 2001 terrorist attacks on the United States, Cmdr. Thomas led Maritime Safety and Security Teams (MSSTs).

Cmdr. Thomas's technical and mathematical skills led to his graduation from the University of Miami (Florida) with honors, a master's degree in computer information systems (CIS), and graduate telecommunications certification. Cmdr. Thomas's exemplary technical and defense background was supplemented with his graduation from the Staff College Joint Forces Combined Warfighting School. Commander Gary M. Thomas has earned several meritorious service and commendation medals, Coast Guard achievement medals, the Armed Forces Service Medal, and other citations.[14] In 2010 Cmdr. Gary M. Thomas was the commanding officer of the USCG LORAN support unit (LSU) in Wildwood, New Jersey.

The future of LORAN is problematic. Some experts think the system is obsolete and should be replaced by the satellite Global Positioning System of direction finding. But some space scientists have speculated, as a space technology engineer did to this author, that the GPS satellite system is vulnerable to breakdown, accidents, and enemy nation or terrorist attacks, and therefore the LORAN system should be maintained in limited form as a backup system. Other radio and telecommunications experts have suggested that elements of the LORAN system be kept in place for communications and SAR contacts with the LORAN partners Canada and Russia.[15]

The Department of Homeland Security (DHS) has ordered the termination of the LORAN radio navigational safety because it concluded that the LORAN-C system, used by civilian and commercial mariners after its World War II origins, is expensive and obsolete. Some U.S. Senators and other concerned observers think LORAN should be maintained as a backup to the modern satellite GPS systems that will replace LORAN. The Department of Homeland Security ordered the LORAN signals turned off between February and March of 2010 and predicted nearly $200 million in cost savings in the following five years. The Coast Guard claims it would mean a 256-person job loss for the service.

Maritime state U.S. senators Susan Collins and Olympia Snow (Maine), and Joe Lieberman (Connecticut), objected to the LORAN shutdowns. Erik Johannessen, president of Megapulse Inc., a GPS and LORAN equipment manufacturer, favored an enhanced "e-LORAN" network to back up GPS. Johannessen contended that GPS could be disabled and negatively affect air and sea navigation, power grids, and cell phones.[16] That scenario could impact military and civilian operations and have economic and national defense implications. DHS said it would consider the creation of a GPS support system.[17] The U.S. Coast Guard planned to end transmissions from its Quincy (Washington State) LORAN station in February 2010 after 33 years of broadcasting. However, the USCG intended to continue LORAN Station Quincy broadcasts to Canada in accordance with international agreements.[18]

In 2010 Admiral Robert Papp was appointed U.S. Coast Guard commandant to succeed Adm. Thad Allen. Papp and Allen have been covered throughout this book (see index) and shall not be emphasized in this section.

However, the tribute Adm. Papp gave to the civilian men and women of the U.S. Coast Guard Auxiliary (USCGAUX) at their August 2010 convention merits mention, as do the SAR, port security, and boat safety education and inspection duties of the organization. Adm. Papp honored the CGAUX members at the Flagstaff, Arizona, conference and heralded their Coast Guard support missions, their response to the *Deepwater Horizon* oil spill in the Gulf of Mexico that year, and the aid Auxiliarists provided in the Haitian earthquake. Adm. Papp enumerated CGAUX contributions in lifesaving, national security, communications, and logistical support.

In 2010, CGAUX members saved 250 lives, assisted 1,400 people in distress, and saved almost $10 million in property. The commandant reviewed CGAUX history back to its World War II origins when the Auxiliary patrolled American coasts, protected ports from espionage and sabotage, and freed up regular and reserve Coast Guard personnel for wartime missions at home and overseas.[19]

The United States Coast Guard Academy (USCGA) in New London, Connecticut, educates and trains cadets for their role as Coast Guard commissioned officers. The academy also has an Officer Candidate School (OCS) to prepare its students for Reserve and Regular assignments. Cadets are chosen by competitive examinations, unlike the other U.S. Armed Forces service academies, which use congressional recommendations and competitive exams to determine student selections.

The USCGA instructors come from enlisted, warrant officer, commissioned officer, and civilian backgrounds. The academy superintendents are chosen from Coast Guard officer personnel, traditionally USCGA graduates, who serve for limited terms, often prior to retirement.

Admiral James C. Van Sice (rear admiral, upper half) was the 38th U.S. Coast Guard Academy superintendent. Adm. Van Sice retired in 2007 after serving as the Academy head and then briefly as director of personnel management. The career of Adm. Van Sice included naval flight training at

Pensacola, Florida; command of USCG Air Station Borinquen Puerto Rico; deck and antisubmarine warfare (ASW) officer on the USCGC *Munro* (WHEC-724); commander of C-131, HU-25 Falcon, and rotor-wing (helicopter) aircraft; and chief of staff for the Eighth Coast Guard District (New Orleans, Louisiana). Van Sice also served as deputy director of operations, United States Northern Command, at Peterson Air Force Base in Colorado. In the latter position, Van Sice advised Northern Command military officers on methods to deter or defeat threats and aggression against U.S. sovereign territory on land, air and sea, and provided advice and support on security issues to civil officials.[20] Van Sice, a 1974 USCGA graduate, earned graduate degrees in engineering and business and was director of USCG Reserve training and an advisor to the secretary of defense. Rear Adm. Van Sice was the recipient of numerous commendations, awards and medals.[21] The career of Adm. Van Sice exemplifies the extensive education, training, and diverse assignments given to Coast Guard leaders and the responsibility they have in carrying out traditional and national defense missions.

Rear Adm. J. Scott Burhoe assumed command of the U.S. Coast Guard Academy on 5 January 2007. Burhoe had previously been assigned to U.S. Coast Guard headquarters in Washington, D.C., as assistant commandant for government and public affairs. Prior to that, Adm. Burhoe served as alternate (assistant) captain of the port (ACOTP) in New London, Connecticut. Adm. Burhoe (OCS, 1977) successfully dealt with sensitive administrative issues at the USCGA that involved alleged management, discrimination, and sexual controversies.[22] Although he was not, as his predecessors had been, a U.S. Coast Guard Academy graduate, J. Scott Burhoe had earned his stripes, so to speak, in a variety of assignments, including as commanding officer of Station Ft. Lauderdale (Florida) and group commander, Sandy Hook (New Jersey). Adm. Burhoe earned a master's degree in public administration and was awarded meritorious service medals and commendations by the U.S. Coast Guard.[23]

And while Adm. Burhoe was at the helm of the U.S. Coast Guard Academy, the military institution earned honors as the top regional college in the Northern United States in the "Best Colleges 2011" issue of *U.S. News and World Report* (August 2010) and was named one of the best U.S. colleges to work for in terms of employee satisfaction by the *Chronicle of Higher Education*. The USCGA was also mentioned among the best U.S. colleges and universities in the 2010 editions of *Princeton Review* and *Forbes* magazine.[24]

Chief Warrant Officer Michael J. Brzezicki, instructor emeritus as of September 2010, illustrates the diversity and talent of the U.S. Coast Guard Academy faculty. Separated from the U.S. Navy in 1976, CWO Brzezicki joined the U.S. Army National Guard in Tennessee (1982), then the U.S. Coast Guard Reserve (1984); he was selected Reservist of the Year (1996) and was promoted to CWO (1998). CWO Brzezicki was an instructor at the USCGA Leadership Development Center (2004–2010). After retirement, CWO Brzezicki became the USCG Auxiliary liaison to the USCGA leadership and management school.[25]

Commander James Espino (USCG) is a supervisor in the Coast Guard office of communications, computers, information, surveillance, and reconnaissance in Moorestown, New Jersey. Cmdr. Espino (USCGA, 1994) previously had served as deck watch officer on the USCGC *Morganthau*, lead law enforcement officer Pacific Area, and operations officer on the USCGC *Hamilton*. Cmdr. Espino acquired a master's degree in information technology from the Naval Postgraduate School and had a stint at U.S. Coast Guard headquarters in Washington, D.C. Cmdr. Espino described as a particularly memorable mission "the drug interdictions and arrests of drug smugglers" aboard the CGC *Hamilton*.[26]

Lt. Cmdr. Nicole Carter is project manager at the Sensitive Compartmented Information Facility (SCIF) in the U.S. Coast Guard Acquisition Directorate. Lt. Cmdr. Carter, a 1995 USCGA graduate, had served as executive officer on the USCGC *Elm* and CGC *Resolute*, and as military aid to the Eighth District (New Orleans, Louisiana) Coast Guard commander. Lt. Cmdr. Carter was on the leadership team that installed "the SCIF enclosed sensitive classified information system on the first four National Security Cutters, including the first new NSC, USCGC *Bertholf*."[27]

Lt. (jg) La'Shanda Holmes was one of 85 female aviators out of the 1,200 pilots in the Coast Guard, and the first black female helicopter pilot according to Lt. Cmdr. Elizabeth Booker, Los Angeles (California) Coast Guard Station operations officer. Lt. (jg) Holmes flies SAR missions in the Southern California region. Lt. Jeanne Menze (USCG), the first black female fixed-wing Coast Guard pilot, mentored Lt. (jg) Holmes.[28]

Lt. Cmdr. Derek Smith, financial analyst in the U.S. Coast Guard Acquisition Directorate at Washington, D.C., headquarters, previously served on the USCGC *Buckthorn* and then as storekeeper in the 17th Coast Guard District office in Alaska. Lt. Cmdr. Smith graduated from the enlisted rates to commissioned officer rank, having joined the USCG out of high school in Minnesota where he recalled the iconic Great Lakes cutters *Woodrush* and *Mackinaw*. Lt. Cmdr. Smith's memorable missions included SAR and drug interdiction.[29]

Major James H. Eddy (USMC, Ret.) has shared with this author his pride in and the mission activities of his son, Chief Petty Officer Christopher Eddy

(USCG, Ret.). Major James Eddy, political science Ph.D. and professor emeritus at Winona State University in Minnesota, corresponded with the author by mail and over lunch for several years. Major Eddy explained CPO Eddy's responsibilities as lead command center controller, senior duty officer, and command duty officer in the District Seven (Florida and the Gulf) Area of Responsibility (AOR). CPO Eddy directed operations at the Rescue Coordination Center in the Miami SAR Region. Chief Eddy trained personnel for and planned and participated in law enforcement, immigration and drug interdiction, and national defense missions in the AOR.[30]

Chief Petty Officer Christopher Eddy retired from the USCG in October 2006 and was recruited and hired by the Department of Homeland Security (DHS) that same month. Eddy, promoted to federal civil service position GS-12, planned and directed operations out of his office and reported to a Coast Guard admiral.[31]

The skills, courage, and operational leadership rewarded by the U.S. Coast Guard are not restricted to commissioned and warrant officer ranks. Enlisted rated petty officers regularly receive awards. Coast Guard senior chief petty officers selected USCG Maritime Enforcement Specialist Third Class Jonathan Palmer as the Juneau (Alaska) Area Enlisted Person of the Quarter in October 2010. Captain Melissa Bert, Sector Juneau commander, said PO3 Palmer accepts responsibilities above his pay grade and carries out those duties in exemplary fashion.

After graduating from basic training at Cape May, New Jersey, Petty Officer Palmer was assigned to the U.S. Coast Guard Honor Guard in Washington, D.C., where he marched, laid wreaths at the Tomb of the Unknown Soldier, guided foreign officials, and represented the U.S. Armed Forces at military funerals. PO3 Palmer has boarded vessels in port and at sea, done fisheries patrols, and trained as a gunner's mate at USCG Training Center Yorktown (Virginia). PO3 Palmer's next career objective was to join the U.S. Coast Guard Investigative Service.[32]

It was my pleasure to jointly address the National World War II Museum with Rear Admiral Roy A. Nash on the USGC anniversary August 4, 2011. Adm. Nash is the commander of CG District 8 (New Orleans) and task force 189.8.

Chapter Notes

Chapter 1

1. Thomas P. Ostrom, *The United States Coast Guard, 1790 to the Present* (Oakland, OR: Red Anvil/Elderberry Press, 2006), 21–29, 31–40.

2. Ibid., 21.

3. Alex R. Larzelere, *The Coast Guard in World War I: An Untold Story* (Annapolis, MD: Naval Institute Press, 2003), 144–146. Capt. Larzelere (USCG, Ret.), commanded five Coast Guard cutters, served in Vietnam and wrote a book about it, and earned the Bronze Star.

4. Ostrom, *Coast Guard, 1790 to the Present*, 21.

5. Larzelere, *Coast Guard, World War I*, ix.

6. Ibid., 47–49.

7. Ibid., 58.

8. Ibid., 25–28.

9. Donald L. Canney, *U.S. Coast Guard and Revenue Cutters, 1790–1935* (Annapolis, MD: Naval Institute Press, 1995), 56, 66–68.

10. Ibid., 67–68.

11. Ostrom, *Coast Guard, 1790 to the Present*, 43.

12. Larzelere, *Coast Guard in World War I*, 34, 67.

13. Ibid., 67–68.

14. Ibid, 90–92.

15. Ibid., 97–99.

16. Ibid., 104–105.

17. Ibid., 106.

18. Ibid., 128–130.

19. Ibid., 167–169.

20. Ibid., 170–171, 179–180, 185.

21. Thomas P. Ostrom, *The United States Coast Guard in World War II: A History of Domestic and Overseas Actions* (Jefferson, NC: McFarland, 2009), 87.

22. Ibid., 103–104.

23. Ostrom, *Coast Guard, 1790 to the Present*, 43.

24. *Coast Guard History, Frequently Asked Questions* (Washington, DC: United States Coast Guard Historian's Office, June 3, 2004), 1–2.

25. Ostrom, *Coast Guard, 1790 to Present*, 43.

26. Robert E. Johnson, *Guardians of the Sea: A History of the U.S. Coast Guard, 1915 to the Present* (Annapolis, MD: Naval Institute Press, 1987), 57–68.

27. Larzelere, *The Coast Guard in World War I*, 237–239.

Chapter 2

1. Thomas P. Ostrom, The *United States Coast Guard in World War II: A History of Domestic and Overseas Actions* (Jefferson, NC: McFarland, 2009), 29–37.

2. *Coast Guard History: Frequently Asked Questions*, U.S. Department of Homeland Security, United States Coast Guard, June 2004, 1–2.

3. Ostrom, *Coast Guard in World War II*, 5.

4. Ibid., 6.

5. Ibid., 6–7.

6. Ibid., 7.

7. Ibid., 13.

8. Ibid.

9. Ibid., 14–15. The USCG-OSS material came from the Foundation for Coast Guard History (FCGH) periodical *The Cutter* (Spring 2007) and the research of Lt. Cmdr. Michael Bennett (USCG), author of *Guardian Spies: The U.S. Coast Guard and OSS Maritime Operations During World War II*. This author (Ostrom) received an e-mail copy of Cmdr. Bennett's article (pp. 1–12) in July 2010.

10. Rear Adm. Edwin T. Layton (USN, Ret.), Capt. Roger Pineau (USNR, Ret.), and John Costello, *And I Was There: Pearl Harbor and Midway—Breaking the Secrets* (New York: Morrow, 1985), 111.

11. James F. Dunnigan and Albert A. Nofi,

The Pacific War Encyclopedia (New York: Checkmark, 1998), 478–479.

12. Ibid., 480–483.

13. Richard P. Klobuchar, *Pearl Harbor: Awakening a Sleeping Giant* (Bloomington, IN: lst Books Library, 2003), 46–47.

14. Ibid., 105, 249–250.

15. Barrett Thomas Beard (Lt. Cmdr. USCG, Ret.), *Wonderful Flying Machines: A History of U.S. Coast Guard Helicopters* (Annapolis, MD: Naval Institute Press, 1996), 1–3.

16. Ibid.

17. Allen Gwenfread, *Hawaii's War Years, 1941–1945* (Honolulu: University of Hawaii Press, 1950), 40–41, 89–90, 222.

18. Ibid., 365; John W. Chambers II, ed., *The Oxford Companion to American History* (New York: Oxford University Press, 1999), 669; Sally Van Wagenen Keil, *Those Wonderful Women in Their Flying Machines: The Unknown Heroines of World War II* (New York: Rawson Wade, 1979), 270.

19. Lt. Malcolm F. Willoughby (USCG-TR), *The United States Coast Guard in World War II* (Annapolis, MD: Naval Institute, 1957/ 1989), 51, 53, 55–56, 62–63, 71, 150–168, 169–171, 177, 334.

20. Interview with Paul Inden on August 21, 2009.

21. Richard A. Russell, *Project Hula: Secret Soviet-American Cooperation in the War Against Japan*, The U.S. Navy in the Modern World Series, no. 4 (Washington, DC: Naval Historical Center, Department of the Navy, 1997), 1–44.

22. David Hendrickson, "The Official Site for the Patrol Frigate Story," in e-mail correspondence with the author, Tom Ostrom, July 2010; download at http://www.davidhhenrickson.com (July 18, 2010).

Chapter 3

1. Thomas P. Ostrom, *The United States Coast Guard, 1790 to the Present* (Oakland, OR: Red Anvil/Elderberry Press, 2006), 73–75.

2. Ibid., 76.

3. Ibid., 77.

4. Robert E. Johnson, *Guardians of the Sea: A History of the U.S. Coast Guard, 1915 to the Present* (Annapolis, MD: Naval Institute Press, 1987), 285–286.

5. Ibid., 305–307.

6. "Coast Guard History: Frequently Asked Questions," U.S. Coast Guard Historian's Office, June 3, 2004, 1–2.

7. John Whiteclay Chambers II, ed., *The Oxford Companion to American Military History* (New York: Oxford University Press, 1999), 368.

8. Carter Malkasian, *The Korean War* (Great Britain and New York: Osprey Publishing, 2001), 7–9.

9. Ibid., 90–92.

10. Chambers, *Oxford Companion*, 373–374.

11. Scott T. Price, "The Forgotten Service in the Forgotten War: The U.S. Coast Guard's Role in the Korean Conflict," U.S. Coast Guard website, November 10, 2008, 1–2, http://www.uscg.mil/history/articles/Korean_War.asp.

12. Ibid., 2.

13. Ibid., 2–5.

14. Ibid., 5–6.

15. Ibid., 7–9.

16. Ibid., 12–13.

17. Malcolm F. Willoughby, *The U.S. Coast Guard in World War II* (Annapolis, MD: Naval Institute Press, 1957/1989), 150–155.

18. Thomas P. Ostrom *The United States Coast Guard in World War II* (Jefferson, NC: McFarland, 2009), 33–34, 37, 57, 148, 158.

19. Price, "The Coast Guard's Role in the Korean Conflict," 13–14.

20. "The United States Coast Guard in the Korean War," fact sheets, U.S. Coast Guard Historian's Office (accessed January 26, 2009), 1–4.

21. Ibid., 4.

22. Price, "The Coast Guard Role," 14–15.

Chapter 4

1. Thomas P. Ostrom, *The United States Coast Guard, 1790 to the Present* (Oakland, OR: Red Anvil/Elderberry Press, 2006), 73–80.

2. Robert E. Johnson, *Guardians of the Sea: A History of the Coast Guard, 1915 to the Present* (Annapolis, MD: Naval Institute Press, 1987), 320–321, 331.

3. Ostrom, *Coast Guard, 1790 to the Present*, 82.

4. Ibid., 82–84.

5. Coast Guard Historian's Office, "Frequently Asked Questions," 2009, 1.

6. Spencer C. Tucker, *The Encyclopedia of the Vietnam War: A Political, Social and Military History* (New York: Oxford University Press, 1998), 420.

7. Edward J. Marolda, *By Sea, Air, and Land: An Illustrated History of the U.S. Navy and the War in Southeast Asia* (Washington, DC: Naval Historical Center, 1994), 146, 276–278.

8. Barry Gregory, *Vietnam Coastal and Riverine Forces* (Northamptonshire, UK: Patrick Stephens, 1988), 23–24.

9. Alex Larzelere, *The Coast Guard at War: Vietnam, 1965–1975* (Annapolis, MD: Naval Institute Press, 1997), 137–144.

10. "Lieutenant Jack Rittichier's Vietnam Rescue Missions, 1968," Coast Guard Oral History Program, First-Person Accounts of Coast Guard History, U.S. Coast Guard Historian's Office (accessed October 14, 2009), 1–16.

11. Tom Beard, Jose Hanson, and Paul C. Scotti, *The Coast Guard* (Seattle, WA: Founda-

tion for Coast Guard History, and Hugh Lauter Levin Associates, 2004), 307, 344.

12. Ibid., 344.

13. James F. Dunnigan and Albert A. Nofi, *Dirty Little Secrets of the Vietnam War* (New York: St. Martin's Griffin, 1999), 152–153.

14. Tucker, *Encyclopedia of the Vietnam War*, 420.

15. John Whiteclay Chambers II, ed., *The Oxford Companion to American Military History* (New York: Oxford University Press, 1999), 146.

16. Tucker, *Encyclopedia of the Vietnam War*, 421.

17. Harry G. Summers, *The Vietnam War Almanac* (Novato, CA: Presidio Press, 1999), 125.

18. Marc Leepson, *Webster's New World Dictionary of the Vietnam War* (New York: Macmillan, 1999), 71.

19. Summers, *Vietnam War Almanac*, 365.

20. Leepson, *Webster's Vietnam War Dictionary*, 451–452.

21. Thomas J. Cutler, *Brown Water, Black Berets: Coastal and Riverine Warfare in Vietnam* (Annapolis, MD: Blue Jacket Books, Naval Institute Press, 2000), 84–85.

22. Ibid., 91–93.

23. Ibid., 112.

24. Ibid., 112–114.

25. Paul C. Scotti, *Coast Guard Action in Vietnam: Stories of Those Who Served* (Central Point, OR: Hellgate Press, 2000), 104–111.

26. Ibid., 177.

27. Larzelere, *Coast Guard at War: Vietnam*, 137.

28. Ibid., 147.

29. Ibid., 24.

30. Ibid., 121.

31. Ibid., 121, 124–126, 128–133.

32. Ibid., 136.

33. Ostrom, *Coast Guard, 1790 to the Present*, 90–91.

34. Scotti, *Coast Guard Action in Vietnam*, 200–201.

35. Larzelere, *The Coast Guard at War*, 68.

Chapter 5

1. *Coast Guard at War*, Military Channel DVD (Silver Spring, MD: Discovery Communications, n.d.).

2. Ibid.

3. Ibid.

4. Ibid.

5. Ibid.

6. Alex Larzelere, *The Coast Guard at War: Vietnam 1965–1975* (Annapolis, MD: Naval Institute Press, 1997), 24–28.

7. *Coast Guard at War*, Military Channel DVD.

8. Ibid.

9. Ibid.

10. Ibid.

11. Ibid.

12. *Coast Guard at War*, Military Channel DVD; Larzelere, *Coast Guard at War: Vietnam*, 84–86.

13. Larzelere, *Coast Guard at War: Vietnam*, 138–140.

14. Ibid., 142–143.

15. Ibid., 147.

16. Ibid., 148–149.

17. Ibid., xxiv–xxv.

18. Ibid., 151.

19. Ibid., 154–155.

20. Ibid., 222–224.

21. Eugene N. Tulich, "The United States Coast Guard in Southeast Asia During the Vietnam Conflict," United States Department of Homeland Security, United States Coast Guard (accessed October 14, 2009), 27.

22. Robert L. Scheina, *U.S. Coast Guard Cutters and Craft, 1946–1990* (Annapolis, MD: Naval Institute Press, 1990), 141, 148.

23. Tulich, "United States Coast Guard in Southeast Asia," 25–26.

24. Paul C. Scotti, "Attack on Point Welcome," *The Coast Guard* (Seattle, WA: Foundation for Coast Guard History, and Hugh Lauter Levin Associates, 2004), 93. *The Coast Guard* editor in chief was Lt. Cmdr. Tom Beard, USCG (Ret.).

25. Ibid., 94.

26. Tom Beard, *The Coast Guard*, 246.

27. Ibid., 247.

28. Ibid., 252.

29. Ibid., 248–249.

30. Larzelere, 229.

31. Ibid., 230.

32. Ibid., 234.

33. Ibid., 235.

34. Ibid.

35. Ibid., 236–237.

36. Ibid., 241.

37. Ibid., 261–262.

38. Ibid., 263.

39. Ibid.

Chapter 6

1. Robert E. Johnson, *Guardians of the Sea: A History of the U.S. Coast Guard, 1915 to the Present* (Annapolis, MD: Naval Institute Press, 1987), 363–364.

2. Thomas P. Ostrom, *The United States Coast Guard, 1790 to the Present* (Oakland, OR: Red Anvil/Elderberry Press), 2006, 97.

3. Bill Gertz, *Betrayal* (Washington, DC: Regnery, 1999), 7–30, 219–225.

4. Ibid., 25.

5. Ostrom, *U.S. Coast Guard, 1790 to the Present*, 109–110, and appendix F, 245–252.

6. Thomas P. Ostrom, *The United States*

Coast Guard in World War II: A History of Domestic and Overseas Operations (Jefferson, NC: McFarland, 2009), 14.

7. Ostrom, *Coast Guard in World War II*, 15.

8. Ibid., 66.

9. "Military Intelligence Specialists," CIA Film Library, National Archives Records Administration, Military History CD (ARC 1938 135, TF30 3030), 1961.

10. Neil Sheehan, *A Fiery Peace in a Cold War: Bernard Schriever and the Ultimate Weapon* (New York: Random House, 2009), xv–xix, 130–142, 268–269, 412–413, 470–471.

11. Ibid., 332.

12. Herbert Romerstein and Eric Breindel, *The Venona Secrets: Exposing Soviet Espionage and America's Traitors* (Washington, DC: Regnery, 2000), 3–28, 50–53, 115, 161, 289–299, 300–301, 307, 432–435, 451–452, 454–455. Herbert Romerstein was the head of the Office to Counter Soviet Disinformation at the United States Information Agency (1983–1989). He served as a staff member on the House Intelligence Committee and the House Committee on Un-American Activities. Eric Breindel studied at Harvard College, the London School of Economics, and Harvard Law School. Breindel was a syndicated columnist, television moderator, editorial page editor of the *New York Post*, and a staff member of the U.S. Senate Intelligence Committee.

13. Romerstein and Breindel, *Venona Secrets*, 12–13.

14. Arthur Herman, *Joseph McCarthy: Reexamining the Life and Legacy of America's Most Hated Senator* (New York: Free Press, 2000), 165, 212, 243–244. At the time of the publication of *McCarthy*, Arthur Herman was adjunct professor of history at George Mason University and coordinator of the Western Civilization Program at the Smithsonian Institution in Washington, D.C.

15. Tom Beard, ed., *The Coast Guard* (Seattle, WA: Foundation for Coast Guard History, and Hugh Lauter Levin Associates, 2004), 90–91.

16. Beard, *The Coast Guard*, 95–96.

17. Ibid., 96.

18. Ibid.

19. Tom Ridge was the former governor of Pennsylvania, a staff sergeant in Vietnam, county prosecutor, and member of Congress. Tom Ridge, with Lary Bloom, wrote *The Test of Our Times: America Under Siege ... and How We Can Be Safe Again* (New York: Thomas Dunne Books 2009). On September 11, 2001, near Shanksville, Pennsylvania, one of the hijacked planes crashed at the hands of brave passengers who challenged the terrorists. The aircraft, United Flight 93, had targeted Washington, D.C., perhaps the White House or Capitol Hill. Ridge paid tribute

to the Coast Guard and federal law enforcement agencies that were brought into the DHS. Ridge explained how bureaucratic infighting had to be met head on, and how security alert systems and learning curves were mastered. Ridge and Bloom described the challenges of meeting the threats of biological, chemical and nuclear weapons. Port security and infrastructure threats had to be mitigated. Ridge and Bloom emphasized the necessity of maintaining American civil and legal rights in the face of terrorist threats from adversaries who had contempt for those values. Ridge stressed the importance of working in a global partnership to thwart and end the terrorist movement.

20. Ibid., 96–99.

21. Beard, *The Coast Guard*, 251.

22. Ibid.

23. Ibid., 254–255.

24. Ibid., 308–313.

25. Ibid., 315–335.

26. Ibid., 338–357.

27. Ibid., 256–265.

28. Ibid., 268–273.

29. Ibid., 272.

30. Ibid., 274–275.

31. Ibid., 276–278.

Chapter 7

1. "The Terror This Time," *Wall Street Journal*, December 28, 2009, A16.

2. Thomas P. Ostrom, *The United States Coast Guard on the Great Lakes* (Oakland, OR: Red Anvil/Elderberry Press, 2007), 133.

3. Ibid., 133–134.

4. Ibid., 134–135.

5. Ibid., 135.

6. Ibid., 134.

7. Ibid., 137–138.

8. Ibid., 138–139.

9. Ibid., 139.

10. Donald T. Phillips and Adm. James M. Loy, *Character in Action: The U.S. Coast Guard on Leadership* (Annapolis, MD: Naval Institute Press, 2003), 160, 164–165.

11. Ben Schmitt, Niraj Warikoo, and Robin Erb, "Radical Muslim Leader Killed in Raid," *Detroit Free Press*, Associated Press, and *USA Today*, October 29, 2009, 3A.

12. Ostrom, *Coast Guard on the Great Lakes*, 141–143.

13. Ibid., 143.

14. Ibid., 144.

15. Ibid.

16. Ibid., 145–146.

17. Ibid., 146–147.

18. Ibid., 149–152.

19. Ibid., 152.

20. Ibid., 153–154.

21. Ibid., 159–160.

22. Ibid., 168.
23. Ibid., 163.

Chapter 8

1. Thomas P. Ostrom, *The United States Coast Guard, 1790 to the Present* (Oakland, OR: Red Anvil/Elderberry Press, 2006), 75–76.
2. Robert E. Johnson, *Guardians of the Sea: A History of the U.S. Coast Guard, 1915 to the Present* (Annapolis, MD: Naval Institute Press, 1987), 282.
3. Steven John, "In Nationwide Operation, ICE Arrests 26 in the Twin Cities," Minnesota Public Radio News, January 28, 2010, http.// Minnesota.publicradio.org/display/web/2010/01 /28/ice.
4. David Helvarg, *Rescue Warriors: The U.S. Coast Guard, America's Forgotten Heroes* (New York: Thomas Dunne Books, 2009), 77–79.
5. Ibid., 79–98.
6. Ibid., 99.
7. Bill Gertz, *Breakdown: How America's Intelligence Failures Led to September 11* (Washington, DC: Regnery, 2002), 1–6, 157–170.
8. On 2 February 2010, a three-judge federal panel declared the 22-year sentence for Al Qaeda trained terrorist Ahmed Ressam, who planned to blow up Los Angeles International Airport, and assigned the case to another judge in Washington State (*USA Today*, "Sentence Too Lenient," 3 February 2010, 3A).
9. Ibid., 60–61.
10. Ibid., 67.
11. Ibid., 76–77.
12. The author's synthesis of names, places, events and personal perspectives based on a variety of print and electronic media sources and his own notes compiled between November 5, 2009, and January 31, 2010.
13. Ibid.
14. Gertz, *Breakdown*, 83.
15. Ibid., 83–85.
16. Ibid., 85–87.
17. Ibid., 87–88.
18. Ibid., 155–156.
19. Ibid., 123–124.
20. Ibid., 125.
21. John W. Wright, ed., *The New York Times 2010 Almanac* (New York: Times Books, Penguin, 2009), 153–154.
22. "Allen Urges Icebreaker Talks," *Seapower* (February 2010), 10.
23. Ibid.
24. "Disaster Strikes Haiti," *Proceedings* (February 2010), 91.
25. Michele Sager, "Coast Guard Unit Headed to Haiti to Assist Aid Effort," *Tampa Bay Tribune*, January 23, 2010, http://www2.tbo.com/content/2010/jan/23/coast-guard-unit-headed-haiti-assist-aid-effort/.

26. Ed O'Keefe, "Coast Guard Crews Got Early Look at Haiti Quake Devastation," *Washington Post*, January 18, 2010, http://www.washingtonpost.com/wpdyn/content/article/2010/01/17AR2010011702319.html.
27. Helvarg, *Rescue Warriors*, 4.
28. Ibid, 13, 15, 17, 18, 21, 23, 25, 29.
29. Ibid., 216–218, 244–248.
30. Michael Chertoff, *Homeland Security: Assessing the First Five Years* (University of Pennsylvania Press, 2009), 145–146.
31. Suzanne Simons, *Master of War: Blackwater USA's Erik Prince and the Business of War* (New York: HarperCollins, 2009), 127–130.
32. Jeremy Scahill, *Blackwater: The Rise of the World's Most Powerful Mercenary Army* (New York: Nation Books, 2007/2008), 393.
33. Ibid., 393–394.
34. Sarah Aarthun and Sarah Pratley, "Navy Pilot Presumed Dead After Crash in Lake Pontchartrain," CNN News, January 25, 2010, http://www.cnn.com/2010/US/01/25/louisiana.pilot.search/index.html.
35. "One Rescued, One Missing After Navy Plane Crashed in Louisiana Lake," Fox News and the Associated Press, January 24, 2010, http://www.foxnews.com/story/0,2933,583776,00.html.
36. Kit Bonner, "USCG C-130 Collides with USMC AH-1," *Sea Classics* 43 no. 2 (February 2010): 6.
37. Rebecca Cathcart, "Search Called Off for 9 Missing After Crash," *New York Times*, November 1, 2009, http://www.nytimes.com/2009/11/02/us/02crash.html.
38. Cynthia Hubert and Robert D. Davila, "McClellan Service Honors 9 Downed Coast Guard, Marine Fliers," *Sacramento Bee*, November 7, 2009, 3B, sacbee.com. http://www.sacbee.com/2009/11/07/2311311/mcclellan-service-honors-9-downed.html.
39. Fred Lucas, "Biological and Chemical Threats May Go Undetected at Nation's Seaports, Report Says," CNS News, November 11, 2009, http://cnsnews.com/news/article/56966.
40. Patricia Kime, "Bridge Work," *Seapower*, October 2009, 40–41.
41. Daisy R. Khalifa, "Unescorted Access," *Seapower*, February 2010, 38–41.
42. Roxanna Tiron, "Easing Congestion," *Seapower*, February 2010, 42–44.
43. Angel Gonzalez and Naureen Malik, "Collision Causes Crude Oil Spill in Texas," *Wall Street Journal* and Associated Press, January 24, 2010, http://online.wsj.com/article/SB10001424052748704562504575021540843701582.html.
44. "Second Coast Guard Cutter Protecting Bangor Subs," *Kitsap Sun* (Kitsap County, WA), September 21, 2009, http://www.kitsapsun.com/news/2009/sep/21/second-coast-guard-cutter-protecting-bangor-sub/?partner=RSS.

45. Kathleen T. Rhem, "Patrolling Guantanamo Bay," *American Forces Press Service*, February 21, 2005, http://usmilitary.about.com/od/coastguard/a/cubapatrol.htm.

46. "Coast Guard Setting Up Security Zone in Waters Around Obama's Hawaii Vacation Home," ABC News and Associated Press, December 24, 2009, http://abcnews.go.com/US/wirestory?id=9420151.

Chapter 9

1. Thomas P. Ostrom, *The United States Coast Guard in World War II: A History of Domestic and Overseas Actions* (Jefferson, NC: McFarland, 2009), 15, 17, 195–198. See the bibliography for further aviation and intelligence sources: aviator and author Lt. Cmdr. Barrett Thomas Beard (USCG, Ret.), *Wonderful Flying Machines: A History of U.S. Coast Guard Helicopters*; Lt. Cmdr. Michael Bennett, *Guardian Spies: The U.S. Coast Guard and OSS Maritime Operations During World War II*. Lt. Cmdr. Bennett is the Director of Strategic Intelligence Studies at the U.S. Coast Guard Academy in New London, Connecticut, and has done extensive research in intelligence and Coast Guard intelligence history. In 2010 Cmdr. Bennett was serving in the Persian Gulf in the War on Terror.

2. Ostrom, *Coast Guard in World War II*, 36–37.

3. Joe Connell, "Memories: Reliving the Past with the T-37 Tweet," *War Birds*, June 2010, 30.

4. U.S. Air Force, "Coast Guard Aviation in Vietnam: Combat Rescue and Recovery," May 8, 2010, 1–2, http://www.rotorheadsrus.us/documents/388.html.

5. Ibid., 2.
6. Ibid.
7. Ibid.
8. "Rittichier Honored by U.S. Coast Guard Air Station Detroit," Kent State (University) Athletic Communications, June 14, 2010, 1, http://kentstate.prestosports.com/sports/fball/2009-10/releases/20100722enhxbp.

9. "Coast Guard Aircraft Accidents," U.S. Coast Guard, Check-Six.com, March 3, 2010, 26, http://www.check-six.com/lib/Coast_Guard_Aviation_Casualties_html.

10. Ibid., 1.
11. Ibid., 7–10, 12.
12. Ibid., 17, 21.
13. Ibid., 22, 24.
14. Ibid., 31–32.
15. Ibid., 32.
16. Ibid., 32–33.
17. Ibid., 33.
18. Ibid., 34.
19. Ibid., 35–37.

20. Suzanne Phan, "Mid-Air Collision Report: No One at Fault, No One to Blame," News 10, KXTV, Sacramento, California, August 25, 2010, http://news10.net/news/local/story.aspx?storyid=92429&catID=2.

21. Elliot Spagat, Associated Press, "Navy, Coast Guard Trade Blame for Midair Crash," United States Coast Guard, *Blue Water Journal*, August 25, 2010, 1, http://uscgbluewater.blogspot.com/2010/08/navy-coast-guard-trade.

22. David R. Neel (Lt. Cmdr., USCG), "Analysis of a Helicopter Crash in the Bering Sea," *Proceedings*, April 2008, 76–77.

23. Sheena McFarland, "Pilot of Crashed Copter No Stranger to Rugged Weather," *Salt Lake Tribune*, March 4, 2010, 1, http://www.sltrib.com/news/ci_14512849.

24. "Three in Coast Guard Helicopter Crash Back at NC Base," Associated Press, March 8, 2010, 1, http://seattletimes.nwsource.com/html/nationworld/2011284233_apushelicoptercrash.html?syndication=rss.

25. Susy Rabon, "Charleston Based Coast Guard Crew Rescues F/A-18D Pilots," *Military Community Examiner*, March 11, 2010, 1, http://www.examiner.com/military-community-in-national/charleston-based-coast-guard-crew-rescues-f-a-18d-pilots.

26. Christine Ferretti, "U.S. Coast Guard to Investigate Helicopter Crash in Lake Huron," *Detroit News*, April 21, 2010, 1, http://detnews.com/article/20100421/METRO/4210390&templ.

27. "USCG Helicopter Crashes at Arcata," KCRA-TV News, Sacramento, CA, April 29, 2010, 1, http://www.kcra.clm/news/23311168/detail.html.

28. "U.S. Coast Guard Helicopter Crash Kills Three," CNN News, July 7, 2010, 1, http://www.cnn.com/2010/US/07/07/washington.helicopter.crash.

29. "U.S. Coast Guard Identifies MH-60 Helicopter Crew," *Oregonian*, July 8, 2010, 2, http://www.oregonlive.com/pacific-northwest-news/index.ssf/20.

Chapter 10

1. "Tom Ridge, Homeland Security Secretary, 2003–2005," Department of Homeland Security, http://www.dhs.gov/xabout/history/editorial_0586.shtm.

2. Charles P. Nemeth, *Homeland Security: An Introduction to Principles and Practice* (Boca Raton, FL: CRC Press, 2010), 28–49.

3. Ibid., 45–49.
4. Ibid., 96–98, 100–101.
5. Ibid., 359–375.
6. Ibid., 238–239, 245.
7. James Mosher, "Napolitano Pledges to Continue Coast Guard Capitalization Efforts," *Norwich Bulletin*, October 20, 2010, http://

www.norwichbulletin.com/news/x2048880722/
Napolitano.

8. Paul R. Viotti, Nicholas Bowen, and Michael A. Opheim, *Terrorism and Homeland Security: Thinking Strategically About Policy* (Boca Raton, FL: CRC Press, 2008), 83–84.

9. Ibid., 216–220.

10. Charles S. Faddis, *Willful Neglect: The Dangerous Illusion of Homeland Security* (Guilford, CT: Lyons Press, 2010).

11. Ibid., 18–19.

12. "Gunman Kills 12, Wounds 31 at Ford Hood," NBC News, November 5, 2010, http://www.msnbc.msn.com/id/336788801 (accessed November 9, 2010).

13. Faddis, *Willful Neglect*, 96–97.

14. Ibid., 105–107,

15. Ibid., 109.

16. Ibid., 110–115.

17. "Cutter Campbell Crew Member Earns Prestigious Honor," *Portsmouth Herald*, November 09, 2010, http://www.seacoastonline.com/articles/20101109-NEWS-1011.

18. "Coast Guard OKs Yemen LNG Deliveries to Boston," WCVB Boston (ABC) and AP News, February 3, 2010, http://www.thebostonchannel.com/r/22416434/detail.html.

19. Ibid.

20. "Coast Guard Signs Letter of Recommendation for Maine LNG Facility," *Coast Guard News*, September 21, 2010, http://coastguardnews.com/coast-guard-signs-letter-of-recommendation.

21. Timothy W. Martin, "Thousands Stranded on Disabled Cruise Liner," *Wall Street Journal*, November 10, 2010, A6.

22. "Two Stowaways Found on Boat Off New Bedford," WLNE TV 6 ABC News, New Bedford, Massachusetts, November 13, 2010, http://www.abc6.com/Global/story.asp?S=13497736&clienttyp.

23. "DHS Partners Foil Maritime Smuggling Attempt: 23 Illegal Aliens Stopped at Sea aboard 20 Ft. Vessel," *Cypress Times* (Cyprus, Texas), November 13, 2010, http://www.thecypresstimes.com/article/News/National_News/DHS_PARTNERS_FOIL_MARITIME_SMUGGLING_ATTEMPT_23_ILLEGAL_ALIENS_STOPPED_AT_SEA_ABOARD_20_VESSEL/36178.

24. David Allen interview by author, Rochester, MN, April 1, 2010; e-mail exchange September 15, 2010; and subsequent casual conversations at the Rochester (MN) World War II Roundtable and trips to military history events. Allen took online courses from the American Military University that is part of American Public University and the American Public University System (APUS). The office contact location of AMU/APU is Charlestown, West Virginia. AMU/APUS is accredited by the Higher Learning Commission (HLC) of the North Central Association of Colleges and Schools and nationally accredited by the Accrediting Commission of the Distance Education and Training Council. David Allen's professors included Larry M. Forness and Joseph F. Hulsey. Among the nationally distinguished APUS faculty is Dr. James Reilly, a geologist and former NASA astronaut who flew three space shuttle missions. AMU literature claims the institution is "the number one provider of education to the U.S. military and civilian adults interested in national and Homeland Security and public safety. Admission fees are waived for active duty, guard and reserve members."

25. Ibid.

26. George W. Bush, *Decision Points* (New York: Crown, 2010), 155–157.

27. Ibid., 175–181.

28. Ibid., 82–83, 90–91, 93–94, 185.

29. Ibid., 312–317.

30. Ibid., 323–324, 326, 328.

Chapter 11

1. William J. Bennett, *A Century Turns* (Nashville, TN: Thomas Nelson Publishers, 2009), 136–137.

2. Ibid, 153.

3. "Kosovo (1999): Federal Republic of Yugoslavia-Kosovo War: Operation Allied Force," The Coast Guard at War: National Security and Military Preparedness, General Overviews, U.S. Department of Homeland Security, http://www.uscg.mil/history/h_militaryindex.asp (accessed November 20, 2010).

4. Ibid.

5. Bush, *Decision Points*, 158, 226–258, 261–271, 375–382, 396–397, 476.

6. "Operation Iraqi Freedom," U.S. Department of Homeland Security, http://www.uscg.mil/History/articles/OIF_Units_Deployed.asp (accessed November 1, 2010).

7. Ibid.

8. Greg Magee, "Operation Iraqi Freedom & the U.S. Coast Guard: Official History," U.S. Department of Homeland Security, United States Coast Guard, http://www.uscg.mil/history/articles/OIF_History.asp, 1–3 (accessed November 19, 2010).

9. Ibid., 1. Operations Desert Shield/Desert Storm occurred from August 1990 to March 1991. Operation Iraqi Freedom occurred from March through May 2003.

10. Ibid., 2–3.

11. Ibid., 3.

12. Thomas Heavey (USCGR), "The U.S. Coast Guard & Operation Iraqi Freedom," U.S. Coast Guard History, U.S. Department of Homeland Security, *Coast Guard Reservist Magazine* 50, no. 3 (May–June 2003): 2–9, http://

www.uscg.mil/history/articles/OIF_USCGR_
Article.asp (accessed January 19, 2010).

13. John Garofolo (USCGR), "Coast Guard,
U.S. Navy Provide Security at Iraqi Port," *Coast
Guard Reservist Magazine*, May–June 2003, 10–
13, http://www.uscg.mil/history/articles/OIF_
USCGR_Article.asp (accessed January 19, 2010).

14. Tom Cowan (USCGR), "One Last Patrol: BMC Ted Cooley of PSU-311 in the Persian
Gulf," *Coast Guard Reservist Magazine*, May–
June 2003, 14, http://www.uscg.mil/history/ar
ticles/OIF_USCGR_Article.asp (accessed January 19, 2010).

15. John Masson (USCGR), "PSU 305 Returns Home," *Coast Guard Reservist Magazine*,
May–June 2003, 16–17, http://www.uscg.mil/
history/articles/OIF_USCGR_Article.asp (accessed January 19, 2010).

16. "Iraqi War Briefs: *Adak* Takes Iraqi
POWs," *Coast Guard Reservist Magazine*, May–
June 2003, 18, http://www.uscg.mil/history/ar
ticles/OIF_USCGR_Article.asp (accessed January 19, 2010).

17. Basil Tripsas, Patrick Roth, and Renee
Fye, "Coast Guard Operations During Operation Iraqi Freedom," Center for Naval Analysis,
Alexandria, Virginia, D0010862.A2/Final, October 2004, 1–53. The Copyright (2004) is
under the CNA Corporation. Copies can be obtained by calling the CNA Document Control
and Distribution Section at 703-824-2123.

18. Ibid., 1–7.

19. Ibid., 1, 2, 3–4.

20. Ibid., 2.

21. Ibid., 9.

22. Ibid., 11–12.

23. Ibid., 14.

24. Ibid., 17.

25. Ibid., 19–20.

26. Ibid., 26–28.

27. Ibid., 33–34.

28. Ibid., 35–37.

29. Ibid., 40–41.

30. Ibid., 6, 41–42.

Chapter 12

1. James McLay and Adam Eggers, "Coast
Guard Commandos," *Coast Guard*, no. 3, 2009,
10–11. Lt. McLay (Deployable Operations
Group) and PA1 Eggers are active-duty members
of the USCG.

2. Ibid.

3. Ibid.

4. Patricia Kime, "Coasties to Join Navy
SEAL Teams," *Seapower*, June 2010, 26–27.

5. Ibid.

6. Joe DiRenzo III and Chris Doane, "U.S.
Coast Guard in Review," *Proceedings*, May 2010,
90–96.

7. Ibid., 92.

8. Ibid., 95. Lt. Cmdr. Bennett and this author have corresponded by e-mail. Lt. Cmdr.
Bennett is an expert on U.S. Coast Guard history, national security and defense, and intelligence operations and has published articles in
those areas. Lt. Cmdr. Bennett is an instructor
at the U.S. Coast Guard Academy and served
with the USCG in the Persian Gulf.

9. Ibid., 93.

10. John C. Marcario, "Armed with Information: Pirate Attacks Spur Coast Guard Team
to Ramp Up Data Dissemination About High-
Risk Waters, Trouble Spots," *Seapower*, February
2010, 26–28.

11. Larry Cosgriff and Edward Feege, "Arms
and the Merchantman," *Proceedings*, December
2010, 36–41.

12. John C. Marcario, "Expanding MDA:
Stubbs Leads Effort to Bring Whole-Government Approach to Maritime Domain Awareness," *Seapower*, February 2010, 30–33.

13. Jim Howe, "The Forgotten Threat," *Proceedings*, October 2010, 34–38.

14. Ibid., 35–37.

15. Ibid., 37–38. Captain Jim Howe, USCG
(Ret.), brings extensive experience to the issues
of maritime security after serving 11 years at sea
with 5 years as a cutter commander, and with
service as an assistant secretary for legislative affairs in the Department of Homeland Security.

16. Brian LeFebvre, "The Forgotten Threat,"
Comments, *Proceedings*, December 2010, 6–7.
Lt. Cmdr. LeFebvre (USCG) was a program an-
alyst in the Department of Homeland Security's
Office of Program Analysis and Evaluation.

17. John C. Marcario, "Port Technology R
& D," *Seapower*, May 2010, 34, 36.

18. John C. Marcario, "Underwater Security:
9/11 Attacks Prompt Coast Guard Emphasis on
Subsurface Threats," *Seapower*, March 2010, 24–
25.

19. Richard R. Burgess, "Controlling the
Chaos: Focus and Versatility Are Keys to Adapting to Irregular Threats," *Seapower*, March 2010,
34–35.

20. Ibid., 35.

21. Ibid., 35–37.

22. Patricia Kime, "MSSTs on the Block,"
Seapower, June 2010, 22–24.

23. Lore Croghan, "Senator Schumer Calls
Out Napolitano Over Elimination of Antiterrorist Coast Guard Unit," *New York Daily News*,
February 7, 2010, http://www.nydailynews.com/
ny_local/2010/02/07/2010-02-07/local/270556
06_1_schumer-anti-terrorist-napolitano.

24. Robert Knox, "Coast Guard Amending
Rules for Pilgrim N-Plant," *Boston Globe*, October 11, 2009, http://www.boston.com/news/
local/articles/2009/10/11/coast_guard.

25. Alison Gendar, "New York Coast Guard
Member Fell Overboard to His Death During

Nighttime Antiterrorism Training," *New York Daily News*, October 15, 2010, http://www.ny dailynews.com/ny_local/2010/10/14/2010-10-14.

26. Craig Collins, "USN/USCG Partner for EEZ Enforcement," *The Year in Defense*, October 5, 2010, http://theyearindefense.com/naval/usnuscg-partner-for-eez-enforcement.

27. Ibid.

28. "Naval Exercises to Occur Along the Washington Coast," *Seattle Times*, October 18, 2009, http://seattletimes.nwsource.com/html/localnews/2010089882_webcoastguardbrief18.html.

29. David Pugliese, "Force of Last Resort: Canada's Special Operations Forces Command Faces Challenges of Maritime Counter-Terrorism," *Seapower*, June 2010, 18–20.

30. Glenn Wilson, Chief Petty Officer (USN, Ret.), personal e-mail communication to author, "USN/USCG Joint Interdiction Operations," March 27, 2010.

31. Edward W. Novack, "Return Marines to Their Naval Roots," *Proceedings*, May 2010, 44–45. Lt. Col. Novack, an infantry officer, was nearing the end of a three-year assignment at the Strategy and Plans Division in the Operations Department at U.S. Marine Corps headquarters. The *Proceedings* article was forwarded to me by retired Winona (Minnesota) State University political science professor Dr. James H. Eddy. Major Eddy served in the USMC and USMCR. Dr. Eddy's son, Chief Petty Officer Christopher Eddy (USCG, Ret.) served out of USCG Station Miami on drug enforcement and national security missions. After his retirement, CPO Christopher Eddy worked with the Department of Homeland Security.

32. "General Michael Hagee," personal letter of communications to author, "The Coast Guard in World War II," September 11, 2010.

33. Michael Hagee and James Loy, "National Security Rests on Civilian Shoulders," U.S. Global Leadership Coalition, March 23, 2010, http://www.usglc.org/2010/03/23/national-security-rests-on-civilian-shoulders.

34. Vincent Atkins (Rear Adm., USCG), "Testimony of Rear Admiral Vincent Atkins, U.S. Coast Guard, Before the House Subcommittee on Homeland Security, on Department of Homeland Security Air and Marine Operations and Investments," Washington, DC, release date April 19, 2010, 2–10, http://www.dhs.gov/ynews/testimony/testimony_12716903150 07.shtm.

35. Ibid., 3.

36. Ibid., 4.

37. Ibid., 5–7.

38. Ibid., 7–8.

Chapter 13

1. Joe Stevens and Mary Pat Flaherty, "More Tasks Put Coast Guard at 'Breaking Point,'" *Washington Post*, printed in the *Duluth News Tribune*, August 14, 2010, A7.

2. Ibid.

3. John C. Marcario, "Finding the Funds," *Seapower*, November 2009, 42–45.

4. Ibid.

5. John C. Marcario, "Strings Attached," *Seapower*, November 2009, 22, 24.

6. Megan Scully et al., "Waesche Hits Milestone," *Seapower*, November 2009, 10.

7. Patricia Kime, "Buckling Hulls: Damage Due to Extended Use Takes Navy Coastal Patrol Boats Out of Action," *Seapower*, November 2010, 40–41.

8. John C. Marcario, "Balancing Act: Coast Guard Tightens Its Belt in 2011 Budget Request," *Seapower*, November 2010, 24–25.

9. Ibid., 25. Coast Guard Island in Alameda was formerly called Government Island when this author was in basic and advanced training at the USCG base in 1961.

10. John C. Marcario, "Sentinel Moves Forward," *Seapower*, December 2009, 48, 50.

11. "USCGC Waesche (WMSL-751)," Department of Homeland Security, United States Coast Guard, http://www.uscg.mil/pacarea/CGCWaesche (accessed May 6, 2010).

12. "Michelle Obama Christens National Security Cutter Stratton," Department of Homeland Security, United States Coast Guard, Acquisition Directorate, http://www.uscg.mil/acquisition/newsroom/updates/nsc072310.asp (accessed July 24, 2010).

13. "Mayor of Mass. Port City Seeks Coast Guard Return," *Standard-Times* (New Bedford, MA), Associated Press, and *Boston Globe*, November 15, 2010, http://www.boston.com/news/local/massachusetts/articles/2010/15/mayor_of_mass_port_city_seeks_coast_guard_return/ (accessed November 15, 2010).

14. "United States Coast Guard Yard," *Wikipedia*, 1–2, http://en.wikipedia.org/wiki/United_States_Coast_Guard_Yard (accessed January 2, 2011).

15. Ibid., 3, 5.

16. "U.S. Coast Guard Yard," U.S. Department of Homeland Security, United States Coast Guard, http://www.uscg.mil/hq/cg4/yard/ (accessed December 11, 2010).

17. "Captain Richard Murphy: Commanding Officer, U.S. Coast Guard Yard," U.S. Department of Homeland Security, United States Coast Guard, http://www.uscg.mil/hq/cg4/yard/co.asp (accessed January 2, 2011).

18. John Patch, "The Wrong Ship at the Wrong Time," *Proceedings*, January 2011, 16–19.

19. Ibid., 17.

20. Ibid., 19.

21. "United States Coast Guard Academy," *Wikipedia*, 1–2, http://en.wikipedia.org/wiki/United_States-Coast_Guard_Academy (accessed January 2, 2011).

22. Ibid., 4, 6–7.

23. John C. Marcario, "Ahead of the Curve," *Seapower*, December 2010, 38–40.

24. Ibid., 38–39.

25. Ibid., 40.

26. "Strategic Intelligence Studies," U.S. Coast Guard Academy, Homeland Security, http://www.cga.edu/display.aspx?id=10239.

27. "Coast Guard Selects U.S. First Female Military Academy Chief," WTOP-FM Radio, Washington, DC, December 14, 2010, http://www.wtop.com/?nid=25&sid=2200479 (accessed December 14, 2010).

Chapter 14

1. Patricia Kime, "The Climate Challenge," *Seapower*, May 2010, 56–60.

2. Ibid.

3. Ibid., 58.

4. Ibid., 60.

5. "AP Interview: CG Admiral Asks for Arctic Resources," Associated Press and National Public Radio, http://www.npr.org/templates/story/story.php?storyId=130638506 (accessed October 18, 2010).

6. Ibid.

7. Kim Murphy, "Arctic Shipping," *Los Angeles Times* and *San Francisco Chronicle*, A2, October 18, 2009, http://www.sfgate.com/cgi-bin/article.cgi?file=/c/a/2009/10/18 (accessed October 19, 2009).

8. Ibid.

9. Ibid.

10. Lawson W. Brigham, "The Fast Changing Maritime Arctic," *Proceedings*, May 2010, 54–57. Capt. Brigham, USCG (Ret.), distinguished professor of geography and Arctic policy at the University of Alaska in Fairbanks, was the commanding officer of the USCGC *Polar Sea* (WAGB-11) on Arctic and Antarctic missions. Capt. Brigham also chaired the Arctic Council Arctic Marine Shipping Assessment in 2005–2009.

11. Ibid., 59.

12. "Alder Returns from Canadian Arctic," *Duluth News Tribune*, September 11, 2010, B1. Paul J. Skamser, Jr., of Superior, Wisconsin, sent the article to the author. Skamser was a reporter and editor for the Superior, Wisconsin, *Evening Telegram*.

13. "The *Alder* Comes in from the Cold," *North Star Port*, Duluth Seaway Port Authority, Fall 2010, 6–7. Wilfred N. Robertson, of Superior, Wisconsin, sent the article to the author.

14. Jacquelyn Ryan, "As Arctic Melts, U.S. Ill-Positioned to Tap Resources," *Washington Post*, January 9, 2011, http://www.washingtonpost.com/wp-dyn/content/article/2011/01/09/AR2011010903400.html.

15. Ibid.

16. J. Bradley Howell, "Napolitano Says DHS to Begin Battling Climate Change as Homeland Security Issue," CSN News, December 17, 2010, http://cnsnews.com/print/79190 (accessed December 20, 2010).

17. Ibid.

18. Ibid.

19. "Cravaack Appointed to Three Congressional Subcommittees," *Northland's NewsCenter*, January 20, 2010, http://www.northlandsnewscenter.com/news/local/Cravaack-Appointed-To-Three-Congressional-Subcommittees-114294569.html (accessed January 20, 2011).

20. Ibid.

Chapter 15

1. C. Douglas Kroll, *A Coastguardsmen's History of the U.S. Coast Guard* (Annapolis, MD: Naval Institute Press, 2010). Despite the title, Kroll chronicles the contributions of enlisted, commissioned, active duty, Reserve, Auxiliary, and civilian male and female members and employees of the Coast Guard. A Coast Guard Academy graduate, Cmdr. C. Douglas Kroll (USCG, USNR) earned a Ph.D. in history and teaches at the College of the Desert in Palm Desert, California. Professor Kroll is the author of *Ellsworth P. Bertholf: First Commandant of the Coast Guard*. Cmdr. Kroll's two sons are in the USCG: Lt. (jg) Timothy N. Kroll (USCGR) and Lt. (jg) Matthew M. Kroll (USCG).

2. Ibid., 178–183.

3. Ibid., 183–188.

4. Ibid., 189–197.

5. Ibid., 178.

6. Thomas P. Ostrom, *The United States Coast Guard in World War II* (Jefferson, NC: McFarland, 2009), 36, 78.

7. Monique Mugnier, "Race Against Time to Find U.S. Air Heroes' Icy Greenland Grave," September 26, 2010, NEWS.Scotsman.com http://news.scotsman.com/news/Race-against-time-to-find.6550852.jp.

8. Candice Evans Latshaw, "Assignment: Guard Armed, Ticking Torpedo," *Daily Times* (Salisbury, Maryland), December 11, 2010, http://www.delmarvanow.com/article/20101211/NEWS01/12110332.

9. Ibid.

10. Alex R. Larzelere, *The Coast Guard in World War I* (Annapolis, MD: Naval Institute Press, 2003), 45–49. Capt. Larzelere (USCG, Ret.) served on several cutters and was the commander of five. Larzelere attended the Naval War College, National War College, and National

Defense University. Capt. Larzelere, a patrol boat commander in Southeast Asia, earned the Bronze Star with Combat V and is the author of the acclaimed book *The Coast Guard at War: Vietnam 1965–1975* (Annapolis, MD: Naval Institute Press, 1997).

11. "Secretary Napolitano and U.S. Coast Guard Commandant Admiral Robert Papp to Honor Veterans at a Wreath Laying Ceremony," U.S. Department of Homeland Security Media Advisory, United States Coast Guard, November 10, 2010, http://www.wadisasternews.com/go/doc/786/94863/ (accessed November 15, 2010).

12. Bill Dipaolo, "Ceremony Will Honor Soldiers Whose Bodies Were Never Recovered," *Palm Beach Post*, December 10, 2010, http://www.palmbeachpost.com/news/ceremony-saturday-will-honor-soldiers-whose-bodies-were-1112155.html (accessed December 10, 2010).

13. Matt Negrin, "Obama Forgets the Coast Guard," *Politico*, December 3, 2010, http://www.politico.com/politic044/perm/1210/is_that_i_heard_60e2e663-3a68-4616-a7ee-2413fe2c3461.html (accessed December 3, 2010). *Politico* is a subscription newspaper published in Arlington, Virginia, and available in Washington, D.C. Politico.com is a website.

14. Middleboro Jones, "Let's Not Forget the Coast Guard ... Like the President Did When He Went to Afghanistan Recently," December 4, 2010, http://usnavyjeep.blogspot.com/2010/12/lets-not-forget-coast-guardlike.html (accessed December 4, 2010).

15. Ibid.

16. "Coast Guardsman Gets Holiday Call from Commander in Chief," *Coast Guard News*, United States Coast Guard, December 25, 2010, http://www.weshallneverforget.com/coast-guard-news/coast-guardsman-gets-holiday-call-from-commander-in-chief.html (accessed December 27, 2010).

17. Michael Penn, "Medal of Honor Recipients Visit Juneau," *Juneau Empire*, January 5, 2011, United States Coast Guard, U.S. Department of Homeland Security, http://juneauempire.com/stories/010511/loc_765565221.shtml (accessed July 16, 2011).

18. Ibid.

19. Ibid.

20. James Mosher, "Coast Guard Chief Worries About Balance, Terrorism," *Norwich Bulletin*, January 07, 2011, http://www.norwichbulletin.com/newsnow/x389483785/Coast-chief-worries-about-balance-terrorism#axzz1RYt8Enpr.

21. Sarah Mimms, "Coast Guard Hurries to Address Recent Rise in Mission-Related Deaths," *Government Executive*, February 11, 2011, http://www.govexec.com/dailyfed/0211/021111s1.htm.

22. Ibid.

23. Ibid.

24. Ashley Milburn, "Maritime Drug Trafficking," *Navy News Online*, http://www.lookoutnewspaper.com/top-stories.php?id=405 (accessed January 1, 2011). Ashley Milburn filed the story out of the Office of Asia Pacific and the Canadian Forces Base (CFB) Pacific Fleet at Esquimalt, British Columbia, where the Royal Canadian Navy is stationed.

25. Ibid.

26. Seth McLaughlin, "Senators Say U.S.–Canada Border Is Grossly Underprotected," *Washington Times*, February 7, 2011, 12.

27. Ibid.

28. Sondra-Kay Kneen, "Coast Guard Commander Returns to Iraq," *Coast Guard News*, January 14, 2011, http://coastguardnews.com/coast-guard-commander-returns-to-iraq (accessed January 16, 2011). The article was written by Petty Officer Second Class Sondra-Kay Kneen (USCG).

29. Ibid.

30. Warren Benson, "In My Own Words: U.S. Coast Guard Master Chief Warren Benson," *Seapower*, February 2011, 64.

31. Andy Medici, "Coast Guard HQ Rising on Future DHS Site in Southeast D.C.," *Federal Times*, January 17, 2011, http://www.federaltimes.com/article/20110117/DEPARTMENT (accessed January 17, 2011).

32. "Coast Guard 2011 Calendar Edition," *U.S. Coast Guard Military Magazine*, no. 1, 2011.

33. Ibid.

Appendix A

1. Jon Guttman and Gregory Proch, "Power Tool: Thompson Submachine Gun Favored by the Coast Guard, Cops, and Capone," *Military History*, May 2010, 23.

2. Thomas P. Ostrom, *The United States Coast Guard, 1790 to the Present* (Oakland, OR: Red Anvil/Elderberry Press, 2006), 47–49.

3. Ibid., 49.

4. Thomas P. Ostrom, *The United States Coast Guard on the Great Lakes* (Oakland, OR: Red Anvil/Elderberry Press, 2007), 15–16, 36–37, 135, 171. Other sources consulted and listed in the bibliography are Frederick Stonehouse, *Great Lakes Crime* (Gwinn, MI: Avery Color Studios, 2004), 37–88; Jack Storey, "A Drug Highway Could Exist," *Sault Evening News*, Marine Beat, June 12, 1987 (University of Wisconsin–Superior, Jim Dan Hill Library, Maritime Archives, "Coast Guard Operations"); Michael T. O'Brien, *Guardians of the Eighth Sea: A History of the U.S. Coast Guard on the Great Lakes* (Washington, DC: Public Affairs Office and Coast Guard Historian's Office, 1976), 67.

5. Ibid., 47–51. Other references were also reviewed for the discussion of the Coast Guard in the Prohibition era, and are listed in the bibliography. They include John Mack Faragher, p.

749; T. H. Johnson, p. 660; Paul Johnson, pp. 680–683; Kaplan and Hunt, pp. 49–57; and Robert Erwin Johnson, pp. 89–93, 108–110, 115–125.

　　6. "Commandant of the Coast Guard," *Wikipedia*, http://en.wikipedia.org/wiki/Commandant_of_the_Coast _Guard (accessed February 15, 2010).

　　7. Robert Erwin Johnson, *Guardians of the Sea: History of the United States Coast Guard, 1915 to the Present* (Annapolis, MD: Naval Institute Press, 1987), 63, 68.

　　8. Ibid., 144–145, 148.

　　9. Thomas P. Ostrom, *The United States Coast Guard in World War II: A History of Domestic and Overseas Missions* (Jefferson, NC: McFarland, 2009), 61–65.

　　10. Johnson, *Guardians of the Sea*, 29–260, 278–279.

　　11. Ibid., 280–281, 294.

　　12. Ibid., 295–296, 318–319.

　　13. Ibid., 320–331.

　　14. Ibid., 340–341.

　　15. Ibid., 341–343, 345.

　　16. Ibid., 345–349.

　　17. Ibid., 355.

Appendix B

　　1. "Paul A. Yost, Jr., 1986–1990," U.S. Department of Homeland Security, United States Coast Guard, February 26, 2010, 1–2, http://www.uscg.mil/history/people/PAYostBio.asp.

　　2. "Paul A. Yost, Jr.," *Wikipedia*, February 25, 2010, 1, http://en.wikipedia.org/wiki/Paul_A._Yost,_Jr.

　　3. "J. William Kime," *Wikipedia*, February 25, 2010, 1–2, http://en.wikipedia.org/wiki/J._William_Kime.

　　4. "Robert E. Kramek," *Wikipedia*, February 25, 2010, 1–2, http://en.wikipedia.org/wiki/Robert_E._Kramek.

　　5. "Call for Oral History Support," *Proceedings*, April 2010, 94.

　　6. "James Loy," *Wikipedia Encyclopedia*, February 15, 2010, 1–2, http://en.wikipedia.org/wiki/James_Loy.

　　7. Ibid., 2; David Helvarg, *Rescue Warriors: The U.S. Coast Guard, America's Forgotten Heroes* (New York: Thomas Dunne Books, 2009), 248–249, 259, 262–263.

　　8. Donald Phillips and Adm. James M. Loy, *Character in Action: The U.S. Coast Guard on Leadership* (Annapolis, MD: Naval Institute Press, 2003), 9, 26, 51, 66, 121, 140, 149.

　　9. "Thomas H. Collins," *Wikipedia*, February 15, 2010, 1–2, http://en.wikipedia.org/wiki/Thomas_H._Collins.

　　10. "Thad W. Allen," *Wikipedia Encyclopedia*, February 15, 2010, 1–5, http://en.wikipedia.org/wiki/Thad_W._Allen.

　　11. Helvarg, *Rescue Warriors*, 308–309.

　　12. Ibid., 309–311.

　　13. Ibid., 321.

　　14. Ibid., 322.

　　15. Ibid., 323–325.

　　16. "State of the Coast Guard Address," Office of Coast Guard Auxiliary Mailing List, February 10, 2010, 1–3, chdiraux-I@cgls.uscg.mil.

　　17. "Admiral Thad W. Allen, Commandant U.S. Coast Guard," U.S. Department of Homeland Security, September 28, 2009, 1, http://www.uscg.mil/flag/cg00.asp.

　　18. Thomas P. Ostrom, *The United States Coast Guard in World War II: A History of Domestic and Overseas Actions* (Jefferson, NC: McFarland, 2009), 2, 7, 24, 46, 49, 55, 57–58, 80, 82, 100.

　　19. Coast Guard icebreakers and missions have been chronicled in three of my books: Thomas P. Ostrom, *The United States Coast Guard in World War II* (McFarland, 2009); *The United States Coast Guard on the Great Lakes: A History* (Oakland, OR: Elderberry/Red Anvil Press, 2007); and *The United States Coast Guard, 1790 to the Present* (Oakland, OR: Elderberry/Red Anvil Press, 2006). Other comprehensive USCG icebreaking mission histories are Dennis Noble and Truman Strobridge, *Captain "Hell Roaring" Mike Healy: From American Slave to Arctic Hero* (2009) and *Alaska and the U.S. Revenue Cutter Service, 1867–1915* (1999); Irving H. King, *The Coast Guard Expands, 1865–1915* (1996); C. Douglas Kroll, *Commodore Ellsworth P. Bertholf: First Commandant of the Coast Guard* (2002); Thaddeus D. Novak (author) and P. J. Capelotti (editor), *Life and Death on the Greenland Patrol, 1942* (2005); and Charles W. Thomas, *Ice Is Where You Find It* (1951).

　　20. Thomas P. Ostrom, *The United States Coast Guard on the Great Lakes: A History* (Oakland, OR: Elderberry/Red Anvil Press, 2007), 105–118.

　　21. George Tibbits, "Coast Guard Sees Increasing Need for Icebreakers," Associated Press, March 11, 2010, 2, http://www.cnsnews.com/news/article/62635.

　　22. "USCG *Polar Sea* (WAGB-11)," *Wikipedia*, June 17, 2010, 1–4, http://en.wikipedia.org/wik/USCGC_Polar_Sea_(WAGB-11).

　　23. "USCGC *Healey* (WAGB-20)," *Wikipedia*, June 17, 2010, 1, http://en.wikipedia.org/wiki/USCGC_Healey_(WAGB-20).

　　24. Tibbits, "Coast Guard Sees Increasing Need for Icebreakers," 2.

　　25. David Helvarg, "Veteran Defender of the Seas Tapped to Protect Gulf Coast," *OnEarth*, May 6, 2010, 1–2, http://www.onearth.org/article/on-the-waterfront?page=all.

　　26. Ibid., 2–3.

　　27. "Coast Guard Logs: U.S. Knew Early

Gulf Spill's Severity," *USA Today*, June 03, 2010, 1, http://content.usatoday.com/communities/greenhouse/post/2010/06/coast-guard-logs-us-knew-early-gulf-spills-dangers/1.

28. Brad Johnson, "Thad Allen: 'It's Logical to Assume the Oil Will Hit the Beaches,'" *Wonk Room*, May1, 2010, 1–2, http://wonkroom.think progress.org/201005/01/thad-allen-beaches/.

29. Alton Parrish ed., "Gulf Oil Spill: EPA and USCG Consider BP's Scientific Analysis of Alternative Dispersants Insufficient," *IDL*, May 24, 2010, 1, http://beforeitsnews.com/news/49/024/Gulf-Oil_Spill:_EPA_a. *IDL* refers to the process of Interactive Data Language, a system that specializes in data visualization, analysis and software.

30. "USCG Crew Deployed to Gulf," WPBN TV News, Traverse City, MI, June 3, 2010, 2, http://www.upnorthlive.com/news/story.aspx?id=465687.

31. Chris Filippi, "Bay Area Coast Guard Ship Headed to Gulf," KCBS News, San Francisco, CA, June 4, 2010, 1–2, http://www.kcbs.com/print_page.php?contentId=6229010&cont....

32. Steve Kemme, "Coast Guard Reservists Fight Oil," *Cincinnati Enquirer*, June 10, 2010, 1–2, http://news.cincinnati.com//fdcp/?1276215724274.

33. Major Garrett, "Oil Spill Commander Orders BP to Build Five Additional Louisiana Barrier Islands," Fox News, June 2, 2010, 3, http://whitehouse.blogs.Foxnews.com/2010/06/02/breaking-oil-spill.

34. "Alaska-Based Coast Guard Cutter Deployed to Help with Gulf Spill," *Anchorage Daily News*, June 26, 2010, 1, http://www.adn.com/2010/0626/1342783/alaska-based-coast-guard.

35. Amy L. Wittman, "Editor's Note: Acting on USCG Authorization," *Seapower*, April 2010, 4.

36. Ibid.

37. "Navy Supports USCG in Fisheries Patrols," *Seapower*, April 2010, 8–10.

38. Ibid.

39. Ben Evans, "Adm. Allen in Hot Seat Over Spill," Associated Press, June 11, 2010, 1–2, http://news.yahoo.com/s/ap/20100611/ap_on_bi_ge/us_gulf_oil....

40. Jonathan Strong, "Coast Guard Defends Grounding Oil-Sucking Barges in Gulf," *Daily Caller*, 2–3, June 18, 2010, http://dailycaller.com/2010/06/18/coast-guard-defends-grounding. The *Daily Caller* is a web news site founded on January 11, 2010.

41. Spencer S. Hsu, "Critics Say Plan to Cut Coast Guard Personnel Will Harm Readiness for Crises," *Washington Post*, May 28, 2010, p. 1 in online version, http://www.washingtonpost.com/wp-dyn/content/article/2010/05/27/AR2010052705577.html.

42. Ibid., 2.

43. Ibid.

44. Ibid.

45. "U.S. Coast Guard Nominee Would Reduce Terror Hunt," *USA Today*, February 25, 2010, 1, http://www.usatoday.com/news/washington/2010-02-25-coast-guard-nominee_N.htm.

46. Eileen Sullivan, "Coast Guard Pick Wants to Refine Homeland Mission," Associated Press, February 26, 2010, 2, http://www.google.com/hostednews/ap/article/ALeqM5h7mD.

47. Ibid.

48. "U.S. Coast Guard Changes Leadership During Oil Spill," WAFF48News, May 25, 2010, Washington, DC, http://www.waff.com/Global/story.asp?S=12541444. The *Navy Times* (*Navy News*) reported on Wednesday, June 30, that Adm. Allen officially retired from the USCG but chose to remain in his Gulf of Mexico oil spill oversight role at the request of President Obama and DHS Secretary Janet Napolitano, http://www.navytimes.com/news/2010/06coastguard_allen_retire _063010w/.

49. Thomas P. Ostrom, *The United States Coast Guard on the Great Lakes: A History* (Oakland, OR: Elderberry/Red Anvil Press, 2007), 137.

50. Ibid., 137–139.

51. "Robert J. Papp, Jr.," *Wikipedia*, February 25, 2010, 1–2, http://en.wikipedia.org/wiki/Robert_J._Papp_Jr.

Appendix C

1. Evelyn M. Monahan and Rosemary Neidel-Greenlee, *A Few Good Women: America's Military Women from World War I to the Wars in Iraq and Afghanistan* (New York: Knopf, 2010), 343–346.

2. Ibid., 344–345. Authors Monahan and Neidel-Greenlee are ideal writers to chronicle the contributions of women in the U.S. Armed Forces. Monahan, a psychologist, served in the U.S. Army (1961–1967) and the U.S. Department of Veterans Affairs (1980–1996). Neidel-Greenlee served as a nurse in the USN (1962–1965), the USNR (1989–1991), and at the U.S. Veterans Affairs Medical Center in Atlanta, Georgia (1981–2002).

3. Kristen Holmstedt, *The Girls Come Marching Home* (Mechanicsburg, PA: Stackpole Books, 2009), 107–109. The author holds degrees in journalism and creative writing. Holmstedt has testified before Congress spoken to business, college, and military groups and appeared on numerous television and radio news programs.

4. Ibid., 110–111.

5. Ibid., 112–114.

6. Ibid., 116–121.

7. "Department of Defense Identifies Navy,

Coast Guard Casualties," Department of Defense, April 26, 2004, 1–2, http://www.arling toncemetery.net/nbbruckenthal.htm, 1–2 (accessed October 20, 2010).

8. "Nathan Bruckenthal," *Wikipedia*, 1–3, http://en.wikipedia.org/wiki/Nathan_Brucken thal (accessed October 20, 2010).

9. Aaron Gouveia, "Cape Coast Guard Unit Returns from Kuwait," Cape Cod Media Group, January 25, 2010, 1, http://www.capecodonline.com/apps/pbcs.dII/article? AID=/20100124/NE WS/1240326.

10. Degener, Richard, "Coast Guard Center Making Women Admirals," *Press of Atlantic City*, August 18, 2009, 1–2, http://www.pressofatlan ticcity.com/news/press/cape_may/article568822 2d-33d5-517e-800f-7ebd746961e9.html.

11. "Flag Officers Coast Guard," *Seapower Almanac 2010*, January 2010, 191.

12. Fichter, Jack, "Coast Guard Training Center Cape May Capt. Thomas Promoted to Rear Admiral," *Cape May County Herald*, January 21, 2010, 1, http://www.capemaycountyher ald.com/article/58423-coast+guard+tracen+ cape+may+capt.+thomas+promoted+rear+admi ral.

13. "Rear Admiral Cari B. Thomas: Director of Response Policy, U.S. Coast Guard," U.S. Department of Homeland Security, United States Coast Guard, July 23, 2010, 1, http://www.uscg.mil/flag/cg53.asp.

14. "Commander Gary M. Thomas, U.S. Coast Guard," U.S. Department of Homeland Security, United States Coast Guard, 1, http://www.uscg.mil/hq/su/commandingofficer.asp (accessed September 29, 2010). Cmdr. Gary Thomas and this author corresponded by e-mail in July and August of 2010. Cmdr. Thomas was the commander of the USCG LORAN support unit in Wildwood, New Jersey. Cmdr. Thomas, an executive board member of the Foundation for Coast Guard History (FCGH), was kind enough to attend this author's presentation at the U.S. Navy Memorial Foundation, Naval Heritage Center, on August 4, 2010, the USCG anniversary.

The presentation was based on my book, *The United States Coast Guard in World War II* (Jefferson, NC: McFarland, 2009). The USCG developed the LORAN communications system during the war. Cmdr. Thomas joined me at the lectern to explain the history, function, and operation of the LORAN (long-range aid to navigation system) and its U.S. Armed Forces applications in communications and triangulation location in the air, on land, and at sea during World War II and to the present.

15. "LORAN Support Unit, Wildwood, New Jersey," U.S. Department of Homeland Security, United States Coast Guard, January 7, 2010, 1, http://www.uscg.mil/hq/Isu/Isufact

sheet.asp; "LORAN Support Unit, Background Information: LORAN Termination," U.S. Department of Homeland Security, United States Coast Guard, January 8, 2010, 1, http://www.uscg.mil/hq/Isu/. See acknowledgements for the LORAN-GPS space satellite assessment by a critical space technology engineer.

16. Clarke Canfield (Associated Press), "GPS Trumps LORAN: Govt. to Pull Plug on Outdated Navigation System for Mariners, Pilots," *Los Angeles Times*, January 17, 2010, http://www.latimes.com/news/nationworld/nation/wire/sns-ap-u....

17. Ibid.

18. "Coast Guard Pulling Plug on Quincy LORAN Station," Associated Press/*Seattle Times*, February 2, 2010, http://seattletimes.nwsource.com/html/localnews/2010961192_apwaquincyl oranstation.html.

19. Glynn Smith (Cmdr., USCG), "Adm. Papp Thanks Auxiliary at National Conference," *Coast Guard Compass*, August 30, 2010, 1–3, http://coastguard.dodlive.mil/index.php/2010/0 8/adm-papp-thanks-auxiliary-at-national-con ference/. *Coast Guard Compass* is the official blog of the USCG.

20. "James C. Van Sice," *Wikipedia*, 1–2, http://en.wikipedia.org/wiki/James_C._Van_Sice (accessed October 24, 2010). This and other *Wikipedia* notes in this book generally used United States Coast Guard sources in its articles.

21. Ibid., 2.

22. "Rear Adm. Burhoe Assumes Command of the Coast Guard Academy," *Coast Guard News*, January 5, 2007, 1–2, http://coastguard-news.com/rear-adm-burhoe-assumes-com mand-of-the-coast-guard-academy/2007/01/ 05/. This author corresponded with USCGA Superintendents James C. Van Sice and J. Scott Burhoe. Adms. Van Sice and Burhoe were kind enough to commend the Coast Guard books I authored and offered to place them in the USCGA Library.

23. "Superintendent's Welcome," *Superintendent's Biography*, United States Coast Guard Academy, 1, http://www.uscga.edu/display1.aspx?id=335 (accessed October 24, 2010).

24. Connie Braesch (Lt., USCG), "Coast Guard Academy Named Top College," *Coast Guard Compass*, 1–2, August 19, 2010, http://coastguard.dodlive.mil/index.php/2010/08/coast-guard-academy.

25. "Brzezicki Retires from Coast Guard," *The Bristol* (Connecticut) *Press*, September 24, 2010, http://www.bristolpress.com/articles/20 10/09/24/life/doc4c9cd4a5a21cd551367386.txt.

26. "Cmdr. James Espino," *Seapower*, February 2010, 64.

27. "Lt. Cmdr. Nicole Carter," *Seapower*, October 2010, 56.

28. "Coast Guard Appoints First Black Female Helicopter Pilot," WMBF News, Myrtle Beach (Florence) South Carolina, October 13, 2010, http://www.wmbfnews.com/story/133163 15/us-coast-guard-appoints-first-black-female-helicopter-pilot.

29. "Lt. Cmdr. Derek Smith," *Seapower*, June 2010, 56.

30. "Christopher Eddy, CPO USCG," Lead Command Center Controller GS-0301-12, SDO, CDO, correspondence from Maj. James H. Eddy (USMC, Ret.), CPO Christopher Eddy's father, with author Thomas P. Ostrom, received from Winona, Minnesota, dated October 2009.

31. Ibid. Letter received from Maj. Eddy by author dated November 3, 2009.

32. Klas Stolpe, "USCG Maritime Enforcement Officer Palmer Receives Enlisted Honor," *Juneau Empire*, Juneau, Alaska, October 29, 2010, 1–2, http://www.juneauempire.com/stories/102910/loc_727786639.shtml.

Bibliography

Aarthun, Sarah, and Sarah Pratley. "Navy Pilot Presumed Dead After Crash in Lake Pontchartrain." *CNN News*, January 25, 2020. http://www.cnn.com/2010/US/01/25/louisiana.pilot.search/index.html.

"Admiral Thad Allen, Commandant U.S. Coast Guard." U.S. Department of Homeland Security, September 28, 2009. http://www.uscg.mil/flag/cg00.asp.

"Alaska Based Coast Guard Cutter Deployed to Help with Gulf Spill." *Anchorage Daily News*, June 26, 2010. http://www.adn.com/2010/0626/1342783/alaska-based-coast-guard.

"Alder Comes in from the Cold." *Northstar Port*, Fall 2010, 6–7.

"Alder Returns from Canadian Arctic." *Duluth News Tribune*, September 11, 2010, B1.

"Allen Urges Icebreaker Talks." *Seapower*, February 2020, 10.

Atkins, Vincent. "Testimony of Rear Admiral Vincent Atkins, U.S. Coast Guard, Before the House Subcommittee on Homeland Security, on Department of Homeland Security Air and Marine Operations and Investments." Washington, DC, release date April 12, 2010, 2–10.

Beard, Barrett Thomas. *Wonderful Flying Machines: A History of U.S. Coast Guard Helicopters*. Annapolis, MD: Naval Institute Press, 1996.

_____, Jose Hanson, and Paul C. Scotti. *The Coast Guard*. Seattle, WA: Foundation for Coast Guard History, and Hugh Lauter Levin Associates, 2004.

Bennett, Lt. Cmdr. Michael (USCG). "Guardian Spies: The U.S. Coast Guard and OSS Maritime Operations During World War II." *Central Intelligence Agency*, August 18, 2010. https://www.cia.gov/library/center-for-the-study-ofintelligence/.

Bennett, William J. *A Century Turns*. Nashville, TN: Thomas Nelson, 2009.

Benson, Warren. "In My Own Words: U.S. Coast Guard Master Chief Warren Benson." *Seapower*, February 2011, 64.

Bonner, Kit. "USCG C-130 Collides with USMC AH-1." *Sea Classics*, February 2010, 6.

Braesch, Connie. "Coast Guard Academy Named Top College." *Coast Guard Compass*, August 19, 2010. http://coastguard.dodlive.mil/index.php/2010/08/coast-guard-academy.

Brigham, Lawson W. "The Fast Changing Maritime Arctic." *Proceedings*, May 2010, 54–57.

"Brzezicki Retires from Coast Guard." *Bristol Press*, September 24, 2010. http://www.bristolpress.com/articles/2010/09/24/life/doc4c9cd4a5a21cd551367386.txt.

Burgess, Richard R. "Controlling the Chaos: Focus and Versatility Are Keys to Adapting to Irregular Threats." *Seapower*, March 2010, 34–35.

Bush, George W. *Decision Points*. New York: Crown, 2010.

"Call for Oral History Support." *Proceedings*, April 2010, 94.

Canfield, Clarke. "GPS Trumps LORAN: Gov't. to Pull Plug on Outdated Navigation System for Mariners, Pilots." Associated Press and *Los Angeles Times*, January 17, 2010. http://www.latimes.com/news/nationworld/nation/wire/sns-ap-u.

Canney, Donald L. *U.S. Coast Guard and Revenue Cutters, 1790–1935*. Annapolis, MD: Naval Institute Press, 1995.

"Captain Richard Murphy: Commanding Officer, U.S. Coast Guard Yard." U.S. Department of Homeland Security, U.S. Coast Guard. http://www.uscg.mil/hq/cg4/yard/co.asp (accessed January 2, 2011).

Cathcart, Rebecca. "Search Called Off for 9 Missing After Crash." *New York Times*, November 1, 2009. http://www.nytimes.com/2009/11/02/us/02crash.html.

Chambers, John Whiteclay, II, ed. *The Oxford Companion to American Military History*. New York: Oxford University Press, 1999.

Chertoff, Michael. *Homeland Security: Assessing the First Five Years*. Philadelphia: University of Pennsylvania Press, 2009.

"Coast Guard Admiral Asks for Arctic Resources." Associated Press and National Public Radio. http://www.npr.org/templates/story/story.php?storyId=130638506 (accessed October 18, 2010).

"Coast Guard Aircraft Accidents." U.S. Coast Guard, Check-Six.Com, March 3, 2010, 26. http://www.check-six.com/lib/Coast_Guard_Aviation_Casualties_html.

"Coast Guard Appoints First Black Female Helicopter Pilot." WMBF News, Myrtle Beach, South Carolina, October 13, 2010. http://www.wmbfnews.com/story/13316315/us_coast-guard-appoints-first-black-female-helicopter-pilot.

Coast Guard at War. Military Channel DVD. Silver Spring, MD: Discovery Communications Inc., n.d.

"Coast Guard History: Frequently Asked Questions." Washington, DC: United States Coast Guard Historian's Office, June 3, 2004, 1–2.

"Coast Guard Logs: U.S. Knew Early Gulf Spill's Severity." *USA Today*, June 3, 2010. http://content.usatoday.com/communities/greenhouse/post/2010.

"Coast Guard OKs Yemen LNG Deliveries to Boston." WCVB Boston (ABC) and AP News, February 3, 2010. http:/www.thebostonchannel.com/r/22416434/detail.html.

"Coast Guard Pulling Plug on Quincy LORAN Station." Associated Press and *Seattle Times*, February 2, 2010. http://seattletimes.nwsource.com/html/localnews/201096 1192_apwaquincyloranstation.html.

"Coast Guard Selects U.S. First Female Military Academy Chief." WTOP-FM Radio, Washington, DC, December 14, 2010. http://www.wtop.com/?nid=2&sid=2200479 (accessed December 14, 2010).

"Coast Guard Setting Up Security Zone in Waters Around Obama's Hawaii Vacation Home." ABC News and Associated Press, December 24, 2009. http://abcnews.go.com U.S./wirestory?id=9420151.

"Coast Guard Signs Letter of Recommendation for Maine LNG Facility." *Coast Guard News*, September 21, 2010. http://coastguardnews.com/coast-guard-signs-letter-of-recommedation.

"Coast Guard 2011 Calendar Edition." *U.S. Coast Guard Military Magazine*, no. 1 (2011).

"Coastguardsman Gets Holiday Call from Commander-in-Chief." *Coast Guard News*, December 25, 2010. http://www.weshallneverforget.com.coast-guard-news-coast-guardsman-gets-holiday-call-from-commander-in-chief.html.

Collins, Craig. "USN/USCG Partner for EEZ Enforcement." *The Year in Defense*, October 5, 2010. http://theyearindefense.com/naval/usnuscg-partner-for-eez-enforcement.

"Commandant of the Coast Guard." *Wikipedia*. http://en.wikipedia.org/wiki/Commandant_of_the_Coast_Guard (accessed February 15, 2010).

"Commander Gary M. Thomas, U.S. Coast Guard." U.S. Department of Homeland Security,

United States Coast Guard. http://www.uscg.mil/hq/su/commandingofficerasp (accessed September 29, 2010).

"Commander James Espino." *Seapower*, February 2010, 64.

Connell, Joe. "Memories: Reliving the Past with the T-37 Tweet." *Warbirds*, June 2010, 30.

Cosgriff, Larry, and Edward Feege. "Arms and the Merchantman." *Proceedings*, December 2010, 36–41.

Cowan, Tom. "One Last Patrol: BMC Ted Cooley of PSU-311 in the Persian Gulf." *Coast Guard Reservist Magazine*, May–June 2003, 14. http://www.uscg.mil/history/articles/OIF_USCGR_Article.asp (accessed January 19, 2010).

"Cravaack Appointed to Three Congressional Subcommittees." Northland's NewsCenter, January 20, 2010, http://www.northlandsnewscenter.com/news/local/Cravaack-Appointed-To-Three-Congressional-Subcommittees-114294569.html (accessed January 20, 2011).

Croghan, Lore. "Senator Schumer Calls Out Napolitano Over Elimination of Antiterrorist Coast Guard Unit." *New York Daily News*, February 7, 2010. http://articles.nydaily news.com/2010-02-07/local/27055606_1_schumer-anti-terrorist-napolitano.

Cutler, Thomas J. *Brown Water, Black Berets: Coastal and Riverine Warfare in Vietnam.* Annapolis, MD: Blue Jacket Books, Naval Institute Press, 2000.

"Cutter Campbell Crew Member Earns Prestigious Honor." *Portsmouth Herald*, November 9, 2010. http://www.seacoastonline.com/articles/20101109-NEWS-1011.

Degener, Richard. "Coast Guard Center Making Women Admirals." *Press of Atlantic City*, August 18, 2009. http://www.pressofatlanticcity.com/news/press/cape_may/article 5688222d-33d5-517e-800f-7ebd746961e9.html.

"Department of Defense Identifies Navy, Coast Guard Casualties." Department of Defense, April 2004. http://www.arlingtoncemetary.net/nbbruckenthal.htm (accessed October 20, 2010).

"DHS Partners Foil Maritime Smuggling Attempt: 23 Illegal Aliens Stopped at Sea Aboard 20 Ft. Vessel." *Cyprus Times* (Cyprus, TX), November 13, 2010. http://www.thecy presstimes.com/article/News/National-News/DHS_PARTNERS_FOIL_MARI TIME_SMUGGLING_ATTEMPT_23_ILLEGAL_ALIENS_STOPPED_AT_SEA_ ABOARD_20_VESSEL/36178.

Dipaolo, Bill. "Ceremony Will Honor Soldiers Whose Bodies Were Never Recovered." *Palm Beach Post*, December 10, 2010. http://www.palmbeachpost.com/news/ceremony-saturday-will-honor-soldiers-whose-bodies-were-1112155.html.

DiRenzo, Joe, III, and Chris Doane. "U.S. Coast Guard in Review." *Proceedings*, May 2010, 90–96.

"Disaster Strikes Haiti." *Proceedings*, February 2010, 91.

Dunnigan, James F., and Albert Nofi. *Dirty Little Secrets of the Vietnam War.* New York: St. Martin's Griffin, 1999.

_____. *The Pacific War Encyclopedia.* New York: Checkmark Books, 1998.

"Eddy, CPO Christopher (USCG)." Correspondence from Maj. James H. Eddy (USMC, Ret.), CPO Christopher Eddy's father, from Winona, Minnesota, to author in letters received on October 2009 and November 3, 2009.

Evans, Ben. "Adm. Allen in Hot Seat Over Oil Spill." Associated Press, June 11, 2010, 1–2.

Faddis, Charles S. *Willful Neglect: The Dangerous Illusion of Homeland Security.* Guilford, CT: Lyons Press, 2010.

Faragher, John Mack, ed. *The American Heritage Encyclopedia of American History.* New York: Henry Holt, 1998.

Ferretti, Christine. "U.S. Coast Guard to Investigate Helicopter Crash in Lake Huron." *Detroit News*, April 21, 2010, 1. http://detnews.com/article/20100421/METRO/4210 390&templ.

Fichter, Jack. "Coast Guard Training Center Cape May Capt. Thomas Promoted to Rear Admiral." *Cape May County Herald*, January 21, 2010. http://capemaycountyherald. com/article/58423-coast+guard+tracen+cape+may+capt.+thomas+promoted+rear+ad miral.

Filippi, Chris. "Bay Area Coast Guard Ship Headed to Gulf." KCBS NEWS, San Francisco, June 4, 2010. http://www.kcbs.com/print_page.php?contentId=6229010&cont.

"Flag Officers Coast Guard." *Seapower Almanac 2010*, January 2010, 191.

"Frequently Asked Questions." U.S. Coast Guard Historian's Office, U.S. Coast Guard Headquarters, Washington, DC, 2009, 1.

Garofolo, John. "Coast Guard, U.S. Navy Provide Security at Iraqi Port." *Coast Guard Reservist Magazine*, May–June 2003, 10–13. http://www.uscg.mil/history/articles/ OIF_USCGR_Article.asp (accessed January 19, 2010).

Garrett, Major. "Oil Spill Commander Orders BP to Build Five Additional Louisiana Barrier Islands." Fox News, June 2, 2010. http://whitehouse.blogs.foxnews.com/2010/ 06/02/breaking-oil-spill.

Gendar, Alison. "New York Coast Guard Member Fell Overboard to His Death During Nighttime Antiterrorism Training." *New York Daily News*, October 15, 2010. http://www.nydailynews.com/ny_local/2010/10/14/2010-10-14.

Hagee, Michael. "The Coast Guard in World War II." Personal letter of communication to author, September 11, 2010.

———, and James Loy. "National Security Rests on Civilian Shoulders." U.S. Global Leadership Coalition, March 23, 2010. http://www.usglc.org/2010/03/23/national-secu rity-rests-on-civilian-shoulders.

Gertz, Bill. *Betrayal*. Washington, DC: Regnery, 1999.

———. *Breakdown: How America's Intelligence Failures Led to September 11*. Washington, DC: Regnery, 2002.

Gonzales, Angel, and Naureen Malik. "Collision Causes Crude Oil Spill in Texas." *Wall Street Journal* and Associated Press, January 24, 2010. http://online.wsj.com/article/ SB10001424052748704562504575021540843700582.html.

Gouveia, Aaron. "Cape Coast Guard Unit Returns from Kuwait." Cape Cod Media Group, January 25, 2010. http://www.capecodooline.com/apps/pbcs.dIIarticle?AID=201001 24/NEWS/1240326.

Gregory, Barry. *Vietnam Coastal and Riverine Forces*. Northamptonshire, UK: Patrick Stephens, 1988.

"Gunman Kills 12, Wounds 31 at Fort Hood." NBC News, November 5, 2010. http:// www.msnbc.msn.com/id/336788801/ (accessed November 9, 2010).

Guttman, John, and Gregory Proch. "Power Tool: Thompson Submachine Gun Favored by the Coast Guard, Cops, and Capone." *Military History*, May 2010, 23.

Gwenfread, Allen. *Hawaii's War Years, 1941–1945*. Honolulu: University of Hawaii Press, 1950.

Heavey, Thomas. "The U.S. Coast Guard in Operation Iraqi Freedom." U.S. Coast Guard History, U.S. Department of Homeland Security, *Coast Guard Reservist Magazine* 50, no. 3 (May–June 2003): 2–9. http://www.uscg.mil/history/articles/OIF_USCGR_ Article.asp (accessed January 19, 2010).

Helvarg, David. *Rescue Warriors: The U.S. Coast Guard, America's Forgotten Heroes*. New York: Dunne Books/St. Martin's, 2009.

———. "Veteran Defender of the Seas Tapped to Protect Gulf Coast." *OnEarth*, May 6, 2010. http://www.onearth.org/article/on__the_waterfront??page=all.

Herman, Arthur. *Joseph McCarthy: Reexamining the Life and Legacy of America's Most Hated Senator*. New York: Free Press/Simon & Schuster, 2000.

Holmstedt, Kristen. *The Girls Come Marching Home*. Mechanicsburg, PA: Stackpole Books, 2009.

Howe, Jim. "The Forgotten Threat." *Proceedings*, October 2010, 34–38.

Howell, J. Bradley. "Napolitano Says DHS to Begin Battling Climate Change as Homeland Security Issue." CNS News, December 17, 2010. http://cnsnews.com/print/79190 (accessed December 20, 2010).

Hsu, Spencer S. "Critics Say Plan to Cut Coast Guard Personnel Will Harm Readiness for Crises." *Washington Post*, May 28, 2010, A22, 1. http://www.washingtonpost.com/wp-dyn/content/article/2010/.

Hubert, Cynthia, and Robert D. Davila. "McClellan Service Honors 9 Downed Coast Guard, Marine Fliers." *Sacramento Bee*, November 7, 2009, 3B. http://www.sacbee.com/2009/11/07/2311311/mcclellan-service-honors-9-downed.html.

"Iraqi War Briefs: *Adak* Takes Iraqi POWs." *Coast Guard Reservist Magazine*, May–June 2003, 18. http://www.uscg.mil/history/articles/OIF_USCGR_Article.asp (accessed January 19, 2010).

"J. William Kime." *Wikipedia*, February 25, 2010. http://en.wikipedia.org/wiki/J._William_Kime.

"James C. Van Sice." *Wikipedia*. http://en.wikipedia.org/wiki/James_C._Van_Sice (accessed October 24, 2010).

"James Loy." *Wikipedia Encyclopedia*, February 15, 2010. http://en.wikipedia.org/wiki/James_Loy.

John, Steven. "In Nationwide Operation, ICE Arrests 26 in Twin Cities." Minnesota Public Radio News, January 28, 2010. http.//Minnesota.publicradio.org/display/web/2010/01/28/ice.

Johnson, Brad. "Thad Allen: 'It's Logical to Assume the Oil Will Reach the Beaches.'" *Wonk Room*, May 1, 2010. http://wonkroom.thinkprogress.org/2010/05/01/thad-allen-beaches/.

Johnson, Paul. *A History of the American People*. New York: HarperCollins, 1997.

Johnson, Robert E. *Guardians of the Sea: A History of the U.S. Coast Guard, 1915 to the Present*. Annapolis, MD: Naval Institute Press, 1987.

Johnson, Thomas H., ed. *The Oxford Companion to American History*. New York: Oxford University Press, 1966.

Jones, Marlborro. "Let's Not Forget the Coast Guard Like President Obama Did When He Went to Afghanistan Recently." *USNavyJeep*, December 4, 2010. http:/usnavyjeep.blogspot.com/2010/12/lets-not-forget-coast-guardlike.html.

Kaplan, H.R., and James E. Hunt. *This Is the Coast Guard*. Cambridge, MD: Cornell Maritime Press, 1972.

Keil, Sally Van Wagenen. *Those Wonderful Women in Their Flying Machines: The Unknown Heroines of World War II*. New York: Rawson Wade, 1979.

Kemme, Steve. "Coast Guard Reservists Fight Oil." *Cincinnati Enquirer*, June 10, 2010. http://news.cincinnati.com//fdcp/?1276215724274.

Khalifa, Daisy R. "Unescorted Access." *Seapower*, February 2010, 38–41.

Kime, Patricia. "Bridge Work." *Seapower*, October 2009, 40–41.

_____. "Buckling Hulls: Damage Due to Extended Use Takes Navy Coastal Patrol Boats Out of Action." *Seapower*, November 2010, 40–41.

_____. "The Climate Challenge." *Seapower*, May 2010, 56–60.

_____. "Coasties to Join Navy SEAL Teams." *Seapower*, June 2010, 26–27.

_____. "MSSTs on the Block." *Seapower*, June 2010, 22–24.

Klobuchar, Richard. *Pearl Harbor: Awakening a Sleeping Giant*. Bloomington, IN: 1st Books Library, 2003.

Kneen, Sondra-Kay. "Coast Guard Commander Returns to Iraq." *Coast Guard News*, January 14, 2011. http://coastguardnews.com/coast-guard-commander-returns-to-iraq.

Knox, Robert. "Coast Guard Amending Rules for Pilgrim N-Plant." *Boston Globe*, October 11, 2009. http://www.boston.com/news/local/articles/2009/10/11/coast_guard.

"Kosovo (1999): Federal Republic of Yugoslavia-Kosovo War: Operation Allied Force." The Coast Guard at War: National Security and Military Preparedness, General Overviews. U.S. Department of Homeland Security. http://www.uscg.mil/history/h_militaryindex.asp (accessed November 20, 2010).

Kroll, Douglas C. *A Coastguardsmen's History of the U.S. Coast Guard*. Annapolis: Naval Institute Press, 2010.

Larzelere, Alex R. *The Coast Guard at War: Vietnam, 1965–1975*. Annapolis, MD: Naval Institute Press, 1997.

_____. *The Coast Guard in World War I*. Annapolis, MD: Naval Institute Press, 2003.

Latshaw, Candice Evans. "Assignment: Coast Guard Armed, Ticking Torpedo." *Daily Times*, December 11, 2010. http://www.delmaravanow.com/article/20101211/NEWS01/12110332.

Layton, Edwin T., Roger Pineau, and John Costello. *And I Was There: Pearl Harbor and Midway; Breaking the Secrets*. New York: William Morrow, 1985.

Leepson, Marc. *Webster's New World Dictionary of the Vietnam War*. New York: Macmillan, 1999.

LeFebvre, Brian. "The Forgotten Threat." Comments, *Proceedings*, December 2010, 6–7.

"Lt. Cmdr. Derek Smith." *Seapower*, June 2010, 56.

"Lt. Cmdr. Nicole Carter." *Seapower*, February 2010, 64.

"Lieutenant Jack Rittichier's Vietnam Rescue Missions, 1968." Coast Guard Oral History Program, *First Person Accounts of Coast Guard History*, 1–16. U.S. Coast Guard Historian's Office.

"LORAN Support Unit, Wildwood, New Jersey." U.S. Department of Homeland Security, *United States Coast Guard*, January 7, 2010. http://www.uscg.mil//hq/Isu/Isufact sheet.asp; and "LORAN Support Unit, Background Information: LORAN Termination." U.S. Department of Homeland Security, *United States Coast Guard*, January 8, 2010. http://www.uscg.mil/hq/Isu/.

Lucas, Fred. "Biological and Chemical Threats May Go Undetected at Nation's Seaports, Report Says." CNS News, November 11, 2009. http://cnsnews.com/news/article/56966.

Magee, Greg. "Operation Iraqi Freedom & the U.S. Coast Guard: Official History." U.S. Department of Homeland Security, U.S. Coast Guard. http//www.uscg.mil/history/articles/OIF_History.asp.

Marcario, John C. "Ahead of the Curve." *Seapower*, December 2010, 38–40.

_____. "Armed with Information: Pirate Attacks Spur Coast Guard Team to Ramp Up Data Dissemination About High Risk Waters, Trouble Spots." *Seapower*, February 2010, 26–28.

_____. "Balancing Act: Coast Guard Tightens Its Belt in 2011 Budget Request." *Seapower*, November 2010, 24–25.

_____. "Expanding MDA: Stubbs Leads Effort to Bring Whole-Government Approach to Maritime Domain Awareness." *Seapower*, February 2010, 30–33.

_____. "Finding the Funds." *Seapower*, November 2009, 42–45.

_____. "Port Technology R & D." *Seapower*, May 2010, 34, 36.

_____. "Sentinel Moves Forward." *Seapower*, December 2009, 48, 50.

_____. "Strings Attached." *Seapower*, November 2009, 22, 24.

_____. "Underwater Security: 9/11 Attacks Prompt Coast Guard Emphasis on Subsurface Threats." *Seapower*, March 2010, 24–25.

Marolda, Edward J. *By Sea, Air and Land: An Illustrated History of the U.S. Navy and the War in Southeast Asia*. Washington, DC: Naval Historical Center, 1994.

Martin, Timothy W. "Thousands Stranded on Disabled Cruise Liner." *Wall Street Journal*, November 10, 2010, A6.

Masson, John. "PSU-305 Returns Home." *Coast Guard Reservist Magazine*, May–June

2003, 16–17. http://www.uscg.mil/history/articles/OIF_USCGR_Article.asp (accessed January 19, 2010).

"Mayor of Mass. Port City Seeks Coast Guard Return." *Standard Time* (New Bedford), Associated Press, and *Boston Globe*, November 15, 2010. http://www.boston.com/news/local/massachusetts/articles/2010/15/mayor_of_mass_port_city_seeks_coast_guard_return/ (accessed November 15, 2010).

McFarland, Sheena. "Pilot of Crashed Copter No Stranger to Rugged Weather." *Salt Lake Tribune*, March 4, 2010, 1. http://www.sltrib.com/news/ci_14512849.

McLaughlin, Seth. "Senators Say U.S.–Canada Border Is Grossly Underprotected." *Washington Times*, February 7, 2011, 12.

McLay, James, and Adam Eggers. "Coast Guard Commandos." *Coast Guard*, no. 3 (2009): 10–11.

Medici, Andy. "Coast Guard HQ Rising on Future DHS Site in Southeast D.C." *Federal Times*, January 17, 2011. http://www.federaltimes.com/article/20110117/DEPARTMENT.

"Michelle Obama Christens National Security Cutter Stratton." Department of Homeland Security. United States Coast Guard, Acquisition Directorate. http://www.uscg.mil/acquisition/newsroom/updates/nsc072310.asp (accessed July 24, 2010).

Milburn, Ashley. "Maritime Drug Trafficking." *Navy News Online*. http://www.lookoutnewspaper.com/top-stories.php?id=405 (accessed July 31, 2011).

"Military Intelligence Specialists." CIA Film Library, National Archives Records Administration, Military History CD (ARC 1938 135, TF30), 1961.

Mimms, Sarah. "Coast Guard Hurries to Address Recent Rise in Mission-related Deaths." *Government Executive*, February 11, 2011. http://www.govexec.com/dailyfed/0211/0211 11sl.htm.

Monahan, Evelyn M., and Rosemary Neidel-Greenlee. *A Few Good Women: America's Military Women from World War I to the Wars in Iraq and Afghanistan.* New York: Knopf, 2010.

Mosher, James. "Coast Guard Chief Worries About 'Balance, Terrorism.'" *Norwich Bulletin*, January 07, 2011. http://www.norwichbulletin.com/newsnow/x389483785/Coast-Guard-chief-worries-about-balance-terrorism#axzz1RYt8Enpr.

_____. "Napolitano Pledges to Continue Coast Guard Capitalization Efforts." *Norwich Bulletin*, October 20, 2010. http://www.norwichbulletin.com/news/x2048880722/Napolitano.

Mugnier, Monique. "Race Against Time to Find U.S. Air Heroes." *Scotsman*, September 26, 2010. http://news.scotsman.com/news/Race-against-time-to-find.6550852.jp.

Murphy, Kim. "Arctic Shipping." *Los Angeles Times* and *San Francisco Chronicle*, October 18, 2009, A2. http://www.sfgate.com/cgi-bin/article.cgi?file=/c/a/2009/10/18 (accessed October 19, 2009).

"Nathan Bruckenthal." *Wikipedia.* http://en.wickipedia.org/wiki/Nathan-Brukenthal (accessed October 20, 2010).

"Naval Exercises to Occur Along the Washington Coast." *Seattle Times*, October 18, 2009. http://seattletimes.nwsource.com/html/localnews/2010089882_webcoastguardbrief 18.html.

"Navy Supports USCG in Fisheries Patrols." *Seapower*, April 2010, 8–10.

Neel, David R. "Analysis of a Helicopter Crash in the Bering Sea." *Proceedings*, April 2008, 76–77.

Negrin, Matt. "Obama Forgets About the Coast Guard." *Politico*, December 3, 2010. http://www.politico.com/politic044/perm/1210/is_that_what_i_heard_60e2e663-3a 68-4616-a7ee-2413fe2c3461.html.

Nemeth, Charles P. *Homeland Security: An Introduction to Principles and Practice.* Boca Raton, FL: CRC Press. 2010.

Novack, Edward W. "Return Marines to Their Naval Roots." *Proceedings*, May 2010, 44–45.

O'Brien, Michael T. *Guardians of the Eighth Sea: A History of the U.S. Coast Guard on the Great Lakes*. Washington, DC: Public Affairs Office and the Coast Guard Historian's Office, 1976.

O'Keefe, Ed. "Coast Guard Crews Got Early Look at Haiti Quake Devastation." *Washington Post*, January 18, 2010. http://www.washingtonpost.com/wp-dyn/content/arti cle/2010/01/17/AR2010011702319.html.

"One Rescued, One Missing After Navy Plane Crashed in Louisiana Lake." Fox News and the Associated Press, January 24, 2010. http://www.foxnews.com/story/0,2993,5837 76,00.html.

"Operation Iraqi Freedom." U.S. Department of Homeland Security. http://www.uscg. mil/History/articles/OIF_Units_Deployed.asp (accessed November 19, 2010).

Ostrom, Thomas P. Interview with Paul Inden, Petty Officer, USCG, World War II, August 21, 2009.

_____. Interviews with David Allen. Rochester, MN, April 1, 2010; September 15, 2010; et al.

_____. *The United States Coast Guard, 1790 to the Present*. Oakland, OR: Red Anvil/Elder-berry Press, 2006.

_____. *The United States Coast Guard in World War II: A History of Domestic and Overseas Actions*. Jefferson, NC: McFarland, 2009.

_____. *The United States Coast Guard on the Great Lakes*. Oakland, OR: Red Anvil/Elder-berry Press, 2007.

Parrish, Alton, ed. "Gulf Oil Spill: EPA and USCG Consider BP's Scientific Analysis of Alternative Dispersants Insufficient." *IDL*, May 24, 2010. http://beforeitsnews.com/ story/49/024/Gulf_Oil_Spill:_EPA_and_U.S._Coast_Guard_Consider_BP_s_Scien tific_Analysis_Of_Alternative_Dispersants_Insufficient.html.

Patch, John. "The Wrong Ship at the Wrong Time." *Proceedings*, January 2011, 16–19.

"Paul A. Yost, Jr." *Wikipedia*, February 25, 2010. http//en.wikipedia.org/wiki/Paul_A._ Yost_Jr.

"Paul A. Yost, Jr., 1986–1990." U.S. Department of Homeland Security, United States Coast Guard. February 26, 2010. http://www.uscg.mil/history/people/PAYostBio.asp.

Penn, Michael. "Medal of Honor Recipients Visit Juneau." *Juneau Empire*, January 5, 2011, and United States Coast Guard, U.S. Department of Homeland Security. http:// juneauempire.com/stories/010511/loc_765565221.shtml.

Phan, Suzanne. "Mid-Air Collision Report: No One at Fault, No One to Blame." News 10, KXTV, Sacramento, California, August 25, 2010. http://www.news10.net/news/ story.aspx?storyid=92429&catid=2.

Phillips, Donald T., and Adm. James M. Loy. *Character in Action: The U.S. Coast Guard on Leadership*. Annapolis, MD: Naval Institute Press, 2003.

Pugliese, David. "Force of Last Resort: Canada's Special Operations Forces Command Faces Challenges of Maritime Counter-Terrorism." *Seapower*, June 2010, 18–20.

Rabon, Susy. "Charleston Based Coast Guard Crew Rescues F/A-18D Pilots." *Military Community Examiner*, March 11, 2010, 1. http://www.examiner.com/military-com munity-in-national/charleston-based-coast-guard-crew-rescues-f-a-18d-pilots.

"Rear Adm. Burhoe Assumes Command of the Coast Guard Academy." *Coast Guard News*, January 5, 2007. http://coastguardnews.com/rear-adm-burhoe-assumes-command-of-the-coast-guard-academy/2007/01/05/.

"Rear Admiral Cari B. Thomas: Director of Response Policy, U.S. Coast Guard." U.S. Department of Homeland Security, United States Coast Guard, July 23, 2010. http://www.uscg.mil/flag/cg53.asp.

Rhem, Kathleen T. "Patrolling Guantanamo Bay." American Forces Press Service, February 21, 2005. http://usmilitary.about.com/od/coastguard/a/cubapatrol.htm.

Ridge, Tom, with Lary Bloom. *The Test of Our Times: America Under Siege ... and How We Can Be Safe Again.* New York: Thomas Dunne Books/St. Martin's, 2009.

"Rittichier Honored by U.S. Coast Guard Station Detroit." Kent State University Athletic Communications, June 14, 2010, 1. http://kentstate.prestosports.com/sports/fball/2009-10/releases/20100722enhxbp.

"Robert E. Kramek." *Wikipedia*, February 2010. http://en.wikipedia.org/wiki/Robert_E._Kramek.

"Robert J. Papp, Jr." *Wikipedia*, February 25, 2010. http://en.wikipedia.org/Robert_J_Papp_Jr.

Romerstein, Herbert, and Eric Breindel. *The Venona Secrets: Exposing Soviet Espionage and America's Traitors.* Washington, DC: Regnery, 2000.

Ryan, Jacqulyn. "As Arctic Melts, U.S. Ill-Positioned to Tap Resources." *Washington Post*, January 9, 2011. http://www.washingtonpost.com/wp-dyn/content/article/2011/01/09/AR2011010903400.html.

Sager, Michelle. "Coast Guard Unit Headed to Haiti to Assist Aid Effort." *Tampa Bay Tribune*, January 23, 2010. http://www2.tbo.com/content/2010/jan/23/coast-guard-unit-headed-haiti-assist-aid-effort/.

Scahill, Jeremy. *Blackwater: The Rise of the World's Most Powerful Mercenary Army.* New York: Nation Books/Nation Institute/Perseus Books Group, 2007/2008.

Schmitt, Ben, and Niraj Warikoo, and Robin Erb. "Radical Muslim Leader Killed in Raid." *Detroit Free Press*, Associated Press, and *USA Today*, October 29, 2009, 3A.

Scotti, Paul C. "Attack on the Point Welcome." *The Coast Guard*, Thomas Beard, editor in chief. Seattle, WA: Foundation for Coast Guard History, and Hugh Lauter Levin Associates, 2004, 93.

_____. *Coast Guard Action in Vietnam: Stories of Those Who Served.* Central Point, OR: Hellgate Press, 2000.

Scheina, Robert L. *U.S. Coast Guard Cutters and Craft, 1946–1990.* Annapolis, MD: Naval Institute Press, 1990.

Scully, Megan, et. al. "Waesche Hits Milestone." *Seapower*, November 2009, 10.

"Second Coast Guard Cutter Protecting Bangor Subs." *Kitsap Sun*, September 21, 2009. http://www.kitsapsun.com/news/2009/sep/21/second-coast-guard-cutter-protecting-bangor-subs/partner=RSS.

"Secretary Napolitano and U.S. Coast Guard Commandant Admiral Robert Papp to Honor Veterans at Wreath Laying Ceremony." U.S. Department of Homeland Security Media Advisory, United States Coast Guard. November 10, 2010. http://www.wadisasternews.com/go/doc/786/94863/.

Sheehan, Neil. *A Fiery Peace in a Cold War: Bernard Schriever and the Ultimate Weapon.* New York: Random House, 2009.

Simons, Suzanne. *Master of War: Blackwater USA's Erik Prince and the Business of War.* New York: HarperCollins, 2009.

Smith, Glynn. "Adm. Papp Thanks Auxiliary at National Conference." *Coast Guard Compass*, August 30, 2010. http://coastguard.dodlive.mil/index.php/2010/08/adm-papp-thanks-auxiliary-at-national-conference/.

Spagat, Elliot. "Navy, Coat Guard Trade Blame for Midair Crash." Associated Press, U.S. Coast Guard *Blue Water Journal*, August 25, 2010, 1. http://uscgbluewater.blogspot.com/2010/08/navy-coastguard-trade.

"State of the Coast Guard Address." Office of Coast Guard Auxiliary Mailing List." February 10, 2010. chdiraux-1@cgls.uscg.mil.

Stevens, Joe, and Mary Pat Flaherty. "More Tasks Put Coast Guard at Breaking Point." *Washington Times*, and reprinted in the *Duluth News Tribune*, August 14, 2010, A7.

Stolpe, Klas. "USCG Maritime Enforcement Officer Palmer Receives Enlisted Honor."

Juneau Empire (Juneau, Alaska), October 29, 2010. http://juneauempire.com/stories/102910/loc_727786639.shtml.

Stonehouse, Frederick. *Great Lakes Crime: Murder, Mayhem, Booze and Broads*. Gwinn Michigan: Avery Color Studios, 2002.

Storey, Jack. "A Drug Highway Could Exist," *Sault Evening News*, Marine Beat, June 1987. University of Wisconsin–Superior, Jim Dan Hill Library, Maritime Archives (Coast Guard Operations).

"Strategic Intelligence Studies." U.S. Coast Guard Academy, Department of Homeland Security. http://www.cga.edu/display.aspx?id=10239.

Strong, Jonathan. "Coast Guard Defends Grounding Oil-Sucking Barges in Gulf." *Daily Caller*, June 18, 2010, 2–3. http://dailycaller.com/2010/06/18/coast-guard-defends-grounding.

Sullivan, Eileen. "Coast Guard Pick Wants to Refine Homeland Mission." Associated Press, February 26, 2010, 2. http://www.google.com/hostednews/ap/article/ALeqM5h7mD.

Summers, Harry G. *The Vietnam War Almanac*. Novato, CA: Presidio Press, 1999.

"Superintendent's Welcome." Superintendent's Biography, United States Coast Guard Academy. http://www.uscga.edu/display1.aspx?id=335 (accessed October 24, 2010).

"The Terror This Time." *Wall Street Journal*, December 28, 2009, A16.

"Thad W. Allen." *Wikipedia*, February 15, 2010. http://en.wikipedia.org/wiki/Thad_W._Allen.

"Thomas Collins." *Wikipedia*, February 15, 2010. http://en.wikipedia.org/wiki/Thomas_H._Collins.

"Three in Coast Guard Helicopter Crash Back at NC Base." Associated Press, March 8, 2020, 1. http://www.google.com/hostednews/ap/article/ALegM5hDIC1.

Tibbets, George. "Coast Guard Sees Increasing Need for Icebreakers." Associated Press, March 11, 2010. http://www.cnsnews.com/news/article62635.

Tiron, Roxanna. "Easing Congestion." *Seapower*, February 2010, 42–44.

"Tom Ridge, Homeland Security Secretary 2003–2005." Department of Homeland Security. http://www.dhs.gov/xabout/history/editorial-0586.shtm.

Tripsas, Basil, Patrick Roth, and Renee Fye. "Coast Guard Operations During Operation Iraqi Freedom." Center for Naval Analysis, Alexandria, Virginia. D0010862.A2/Final: October 2004, 1–53.

Tucker, Spencer C. *The Encyclopedia of the Vietnam War: A Political, Social and Military History*. New York: Oxford University Press, 1998.

Tulloch, Eugene N. "The United States Coast Guard in Southeast Asia During the Vietnam Conflict." Washington, DC: United States Department of Homeland Security, United States Coast Guard (accessed October 14, 2009), 27.

"Two Stowaways Found on Boat Off New Bedford." WLNE TV 6, ABC News, New Bedford, Massachusetts, November 13, 2010. http://www.abc6.com/Global/story.asp?S=13497736&clienttyp.

U.S. Air Force. "Coast Guard Aviation in Vietnam: Combat Rescue and Recovery." May 8, 2010, 1–2. http://www.rotorheadsrus.us/documentary/388.html.

"United States Coast Guard Academy." *Wikipedia*, 1–2. http://en.wikipedia.org/wiki/United_States_Coast_Guard_Academy (accessed January 2, 2011). "U.S. Coast Guard Changes Leadership During Oil Spill." WAFF48News, Washington, DC, May 25, 2010. http://www.waff.com/Global/story.asp?S=12541444.

"U.S. Coast Guard Deployed to Gulf." WPBN TV News (Traverse City, MI), June 3, 2010. http://www.upnorthlive.com/news/story.aspx?id=465687.

"U.S. Coast Guard Helicopter Crash Kills Three." CNN News, July 7, 2010,1. http://www.cnn.com/2010/US/07/07/washington.helicopter.crash.

"U.S. Coast Guard Identifies MH-60 Helicopter Crew." *Oregonian*, July 8, 2010, 2. http://www.oregonlive.com/pacific-northwest-news/index.ssf/20.

"U.S. Coast Guard Nominee Would Reduce Terror Hunt." *USA Today*, February 25, 2010, 1. http://www.usatoday.com/news/washington/2010-02-25-coast-guard-nominee_N.htm.

"U.S. Coast Guard Yard." U.S. Department of Homeland Security, United States Coast Guard. http://www.uscg.mil/hq/cg4/yard/ (accessed December 11, 2011).

"United States Coast Guard Yard." *Wikipedia*, 1–2. http://en.wikipeida.org/wiki/United_States_Coast_Guard_Yard (accessed January 2, 2011).

"USCG Helicopter Crashes at Arcata." KCRA-TV News, Sacramento, California, April 29, 2010, 1. http://www.kcra.clm/news/23311168/detail.html.

"USCGC *Healey* (WAGB-20)." *Wikipedia*, June 17, 2010. http://en.wikipedia.org/wiki/USCGC_Healey_(WAGB-20).

"USCGC *Polar Sea* (WAGB-11)." *Wikipedia*, June 17, 2010. http://en.wikipedia.org/wik/USCG_Polar_Sea_(WAGB-11).

"USCGC Waesche (WMSL-751)." Department of Homeland Security, United States Coast Guard. http://www.uscg.mil/pacarea/CGCWaesche (accessed May 6, 2010).

Viotti, Paul R., Nicholas Bowen, and Michael A. Opheim. *Terrorism and Homeland Security: Thinking Strategically About Policy*. Boca Raton, FL: CRC Press, 2008.

Willoughby, Malcolm F. *The U.S. Coast Guard in World War II*. Annapolis, MD: Naval Institute Press, 1957/1989.

Wilson, Glenn. "USN/USCG Joint Interdiction Operations." Personal e-mail communication to the author, March 27, 2010.

Wittman, Amy L. "Editor's Note: Acting on USCG Authorization." *Seapower*, April 2010, 4.

The Wonk Room (blog), May 1, 2010. http://wonkroom.thinkprogress.org/20105/01/thad-allen-beaches/.

Wright, John W., ed. *New York Times 2010 Almanac*. New York: Times Books and Penguin, 2009.

Index

Numbers in **bold italics** indicate pages with illustrations

255